# BIG WHEELS ROLLING ON

*Verona — on the Highway
Drive safe on our road
and the Grand of Big-Rig's
it's my way
Paul B 21.02*

# BIG WHEELS ROLLING ON

Paul W. J. O'Brien

Copyright © 2021 by Paul W. J. O'Brien.

| | | |
|---|---|---|
| Library of Congress Control Number: | | 2021909939 |
| ISBN: | Hardcover | 978-1-6641-7289-0 |
| | Softcover | 978-1-6641-7288-3 |
| | eBook | 978-1-6641-7287-6 |

All rights reserved. No part of this book may be reproduced or transmitted in any form or by any means, electronic or mechanical, including photocopying, recording, or by any information storage and retrieval system, without permission in writing from the copyright owner.

The views expressed in this work are solely those of the author and do not necessarily reflect the views of the publisher, and the publisher hereby disclaims any responsibility for them.

Any people depicted in stock imagery provided by Getty Images are models, and such images are being used for illustrative purposes only.
Certain stock imagery © Getty Images.

Print information available on the last page.

Rev. date: 05/13/2021

**To order additional copies of this book, contact:**
Xlibris
844-714-8691
www.Xlibris.com
Orders@Xlibris.com
826504

To my wonderful wife Shirley
And my children,
Colleen, Connie, Charles, and Catherine

# CONTENTS

Prologue ..................................................................................... ix

1  Early Boyhood Years in a Small Town ........................................ 1
2  Young Boyhood Years in the Country ....................................... 31
3  Teenage Years Attending High School ...................................... 49
4  Humph! I'm Taking Yours ........................................................ 70
5  I Really Did That When Flying ............................................... 109
6  Working on the Railroad ........................................................ 139
7  A Blind Date Led to the Altar ................................................. 150
8  Crazy Memories of College Days ............................................ 179
9  Driving Intercity Bus for Greyhound ...................................... 203
10 Danger on the Petawawa River ............................................... 231
11 Fishing and Fighting a Forest Fire .......................................... 286
12 My First Job Driving Semi-trucks ........................................... 306
13 An Imminent Head-On Crash ................................................ 318
14 A Difficult Situation and Other Trucking Stories ................... 328
15 A Buffalo Stampede and More Trucking Stories ..................... 349
16 Pipeline Construction can be Dangerous ................................ 408

Postscript ............................................................................... 439

# PROLOGUE

THERE HE SAT as he had so often done, rocking gently back and forth in his old wooden rocking chair, his cane in his right hand, his left hand lying idle by his side. He stared into the distance. Was he staring into the future, or was he staring into the past? The creaking of the wooden runners on the wooden floor of the veranda was not heard by his ears.

She spoke to him. She was his wife of many years. He didn't hear her. He was lost in his dreams, or was it his memories? She didn't know. He never said. She looked down on his creased, lined face and saw tears flowing from his unblinking eyes. With a tissue she wiped them from his cheeks. He didn't acknowledge that kindly gesture but stared on and on.

His face had been clouded when she first saw him that morning. He was wrapped in an old blue checkered horse blanket to ward off the cold of the early morning dampness. It was now warm, yet the blanket remained. Quite suddenly there arose the sound of a distant whistle, a train whistle. He quickened, and a slight vestige of change appeared on his face. It wasn't a smile, but it was a visible recognition of something from his past. The train passed, and he resumed that unblinking stare, rocking gently back and forth, back and forth, back and forth.

She had begun to withdraw back into the house but stopped abruptly. She turned to look. She had heard the happy laughter of children. She noticed he also turned toward the joyful sounds of children running toward them. They were full of life, and it seemed as if their exuberance suddenly spilled over onto him. His countenance changed. His eyes followed them. A smile crossed his lips and remained. As they ran by, they waved to him. He waved back to them in return.

They were soon gone, out of sight. But were they gone from his mind? She thought not as she turned once more to look at his face. He had entered again into that stare. His dreams or his memories, she did not care, for his face shone with a happiness that appeared to make him glow. "I shall let him dream on," she silently whispered to herself. Turning, she slipped quietly back into the house.

# ONE

# EARLY BOYHOOD YEARS IN A SMALL TOWN

MY MOTHER AND father brought me into this world with love and tender care. I was born to Daniel Woodrow O'Brien and Rhoda Irene O'Brien who thoughtfully named me with two biblical names and also my father's name. I was named Paul Woodrow James O'Brien. The year and date of my birth was March 6, 1949. Born at that time into a Canadian family in the twentieth century qualified me as a baby boomer. I was and am part of that exceptional birth explosion that followed immediately after the Second World War. St. Thomas, Ontario, was the geographical location within Canada where I spent the first twenty-two years of my life.

### My Earliest Recollection Was a Dark and Scary Tunnel

My earliest recollection was at the age of two. I spent May, June, and July 1951 with my Uncle and Aunt Edgar and Iva O'Brien at their home. Edgar was my father's younger brother. I lived with them during that time because my mother was soon to birth my brother, David Edgar Charles O'Brien. David entered into this world the 30th of May.

Uncle Edgar and Aunt Iva pastored a small church in Orillia, Ontario. There was one interesting feature of their home that fascinated me, and this is the source of my earliest memories.

"Paul, you don't need to be afraid. This tunnel is not a scary place. It actually takes us underground from our home to the church. We don't have to go outside in order to go to church where you can attend Sunday school. I know it is a little dark, but Aunt Iva will hold your hand."

"But, Uncle Edgar, I don't know where I'm going because it's so dark."

"Trust your Aunt Iva, Paul, and hold her hand. She will keep you safe."

"Aunt Iva, I liked that tunnel. I not scared any longer because it is so bright here. I can see everything. Where are we?"

"Paul, we are in the basement of the church where your uncle is the pastor. Let's go up these stairs to the main floor. You will see a big room with lots of chairs. Uncle Edgar speaks to many people who come to this church to learn about Jesus Christ."

"Do you see now, Paul, where I stand to preach? The big wooden box is called a pulpit. I stand behind it when I talk to all the people who sit in those chairs down there."

For the next few months, I became very accustomed to walking through that dark tunnel. It did have some lights in it, but it always seemed so dark. But I was brave now, and I didn't have to hold my aunt's hand. I could walk through the tunnel all on my own.

"Paul, you need to put your pajamas on because it is time for you to go to bed."

"But, Aunt Iva, I want to go to church again. I don't want to go to bed. I like going to church with you. Why do I have to go to bed? I'll be a good boy."

"Paul, I know you would be a good boy, and I want you to be a good boy now and get ready for bed. I will sing a song to you to help you go to sleep."

"OK, Aunt Iva. I like it when you sing songs to me."

I was soon fast asleep, so my Aunt Iva quietly left me and turned out the light. She always put me to bed early every night, and Sunday night was no exception. When I was asleep, they would go through the tunnel to the church for the Sunday evening service.

*Rumble, rumble! Ka-boom, ka-boom!*

"What was that, Aunt Iva? Aunt Iva, where are you? I'm scared, Aunt Iva."

A strong electrical storm was passing over Orillia, and it made the windows in Paul's bedroom rattle. The noise from the storm and the windows rattling had scared him, and he made his way throughout the house looking for his uncle or aunt. They could not be found. Then he remembered the tunnel.

Going through the tunnel no longer made Paul afraid. He knew where he was going, and he remembered that Aunt Iva said she and Uncle Edgar would be in church.

There was a lot of spontaneous laughter as Paul, dressed in his pajamas, emerged on the platform behind Uncle Edgar. At first Uncle Edgar thought everyone was laughing at his sermon, but he soon realized they were laughing at something or someone behind him. It was Paul. He had entered the church sanctuary behind the platform and had climbed up on a chair behind his uncle. He sat there with a smug look of success and happiness.

Interrupting his sermon, Uncle Edgar spoke to Paul as he knelt beside him. "Paul, did the storm scare you? If you promise to be a good boy and sit quietly there, I will let you remain with us. Otherwise, Aunt Iva will have to take you back to your bedroom. Do you promise to be good?"

Paul nodded, and with a big smile on his face, he said, "Uncle Edgar, I promise to be good." And with that promise Uncle Edgar returned to the pulpit, and Paul snuggled into a comfortable position. Would you believe it? Paul had fallen fast asleep.

Uncle Edgar soon noticed Paul was asleep and used that to make a good point.

"Congregation, Paul can go ahead and sleep, but if any of you fall asleep, I will call you out from the pulpit. Then everyone else will chuckle at you."

Everyone laughed at Uncle Edgar's little joke, but no one dared to fall asleep that Sunday night in May of 1951.

## How Much Fun Can a Kid Have on a Summer Afternoon?

Near our home at five Ste. Anne's Place was a deep ravine. Everyone David and I played with never called it a ravine. We called it "the gully." My friends and I all thought it was the perfect place to play. Some days we pretended we were Tom Sawyer and Huck Finn, and other days we were something else—whatever we imagined ourselves to be. We not only had lots of fun in the gully, but also we got into lots of trouble. Of course, you know, young boys can dream up some crazy things to do, and when we did, well, trouble wasn't too far behind.

Being five years old, I just knew everything about everything. So this one day in the summer of 1954, I suggested to my brother David, who was three years old, and our buddy Don, who was five like me, that we go down the gully and have some fun. Fun for us was whatever happened at a given moment. Fun was never preplanned.

"Hey, David and Don. Why don't we go over to the creek out by the highway and go swimming?"

"Yeah, let's do it," exclaimed Don.

David nodded yes and blurted out, "Uh-huh. Let's do it."

You could call those three on that day "the three musketeers." They were on an adventure. Hiking along the bank of the Kettle Creek, they soon came to the place where there was some really cool clay banks running down to the water.

Paul's idea seemed to suit those other two musketeers because in no time they were stripped down to nothing.

"I found this pail over there, and I think if we pour water on the banks, we will make them slippery, and we can slide down them into the water."

"Let's do that!" Don shouted. "This will be lots of fun sliding down the bank into the water."

It didn't take too long before the three musketeers got that bank absolutely soaking wet, and they were happily sliding down it "bare bum." When those three boys were having fun, they didn't seem to notice that some other kids had come to the banks too.

"Hey, you guys, can we play with you on the clay banks?"

Paul looked up and saw three other boys looking at David, Don, and him, and so he answered for all three of them. "You sure can. You better take your clothes off first or your mothers will 'whump' you good when you get home if your clothes are full of mud."

Now there were six lads having fun on wet clay banks as they slid happily into Kettle Creek.

After they had played on the cliffs for a while, Don suggested they go hiking along the hills surrounding the gully.

Well, you can imagine, Paul, David, and Don had sizable amounts of mud stuffed up their bums, so it was into the water for the last time that day to wash the mud away. As Don said, "We sure don't want our moms to know we were skinny-dipping in the creek."

Paul replied, "For sure. My dad said he'd give David and me a good licking if he found out we were playing down the gully at the creek."

There were still lots of hours left to play before we had to go home for supper, so Dave suggested that they build a fort on one of the hiking paths.

"Hey, David, that was a great idea. Our fort looks really good," exclaimed Don who then said, "Let's give it a name. I like the name Fort Apache." So it was agreed by all the musketeers that this was the name of the fort.

But the day was still young. There was so much to do, and it was Paul's idea next that captivated all three of the musketeers.

"I just saw a whole bunch of cars over by that old church near your place, Don. I wonder what is happening. Let's go scout it out. We'll have to sneak over there because I think all those people are the enemy of the three musketeers."

"I'll lead," said Don. "I know that area the best. Stay low, Paul and David, and don't make any noise. We don't want to be discovered."

That was what those three musketeers tried to do—stay low and stay quiet. But it was David who led them right to the center of whatever was happening where there was a large crowd gathered around a big, deep hole in the ground.

David whispered to Paul as they squirmed on their bellies, "Paul, what is that big hole for, and look, they are putting a big box in the hole. Do you think they are burying treasure?"

"Aw, David. That big box is a coffin. There must be a dead man in it, and they are burying him in the ground."

"That's awful, Paul. That is really scary. Let's get out of here. Come on, Don. There is a dead man in that box."

The problem with the three musketeers was that they forgot to be quiet, and as they began to raise their voices, they got some very dirty looks from the adults gathered around that grave site. It was only a minute or two later when a couple of big men roughly grabbed the three musketeers and shoved them away from the grave site. One of those big men growled, "If you boys come back, I'm going to take you to your dad and make sure you get a good licking. Now get out of here."

That was all the encouragement the three musketeers needed and they hightailed it out of there on the run.

Now what do you think those tree ragamuffins would do next? What kind of trouble do you think they'd get into? Because trouble always seemed to follow them wherever they went.

Don came up with the next idea, and because it had started to rain, his idea was a good one. "Let's go to my house. We can play inside until the rain is gone. I've got lots of toys. Let's go."

By now the rain had started to come down quite heavily, so the boys ran quickly to Don's house. Banging through the door got the attention of Don's mom, who said, "You kids are wet. Why don't you go downstairs, Don, and take your friends with you, and you can play in the basement with some of your toys? In no time you will all be dry."

"Hey, Don," Paul asked. "What is that big box over there for? Is that where you put your dirty clothes?"

"Yes, our dirty clothes are dropped down that chute that is in the ceiling. Look at all the clothes that have already been dropped down the clothes chute."

"Wow, Don. That clothes chute is big enough for Dave to climb up into."

"No, Paul. Dave couldn't climb up the chute because it would be too slippery. But Dave could slide down the chute right into this big pile of clothes."

"Come on, David. Let's go to the second floor where my bedroom is because the entrance for the clothes chute is right beside my bedroom door. Are you coming too, Paul?"

"OK, boys, what are you three up to, and where are you going?"

"Mom, Paul and David and I are going to go to my bedroom and play for a while. Is that OK with you, Mom?"

"OK, Don, but don't make too much noise. Did you forget your sister Janet is feeling ill today, and I don't want you to disturb her?"

"OK, Mom. We'll be quiet," replied Don.

But could the three musketeers be quiet? Being quiet was absolutely strange to them. They would not be able to remain quiet for very long.

Arriving on the second floor, those three bad actors soon realized that it was truly a fact. David was small enough that he could climb into the clothes chute.

Don's idea was considered. "Look, Paul, if David will let us do this, we could drop him down the clothes chute, and he would end up on that huge pile of clothes. That'd be a fun trip, don't you think, eh, David?"

Both Paul and David agreed, and so being as quiet as they could, Don and Paul got David into the clothes chute feet first and let him go. Do you think he remained quiet as he dropped down that chute? Not a chance.

*"Yeow whoopy yaaaaa!"* David's screams of both fear and fun were loud, but not nearly as loud as the racket he made dropping two stories down the hollow metal clothes chute.

Don's sister starting yelling to her mother, "Mom, Don and his friends are making a lot of noise. I can't rest."

But more importantly, Don's mother instinctively knew those three boys were up to no good. It sounded like one of them had slid straight down the clothes chute.

"Don! Who did you drop down that clothes chute? You get down to the basement immediately and see if he is OK. You better hope he is because you're in deep trouble, young man."

Don and Paul raced to the basement to see how David was. Was he hurt? Was he dead? Now they were really scared.

"David, are you all right? Come on, David. Speak to us."

"Hahaha. I'm all right, Paul. That was a lot of fun, but it sure was dark until I landed in this pile of clothes. That part was scary, but landing in the clothes was fun. Let's do it again."

Don's mother had come down the stairs to the basement behind Don and Paul and was now standing behind them. She put on her angriest, upset voice and exclaimed, "Don, you are grounded for the rest of the day, and when your father gets home from work, I'm going to tell him what you did to your friend. You're getting a big licking for your misbehavior today.

"Paul and David, you two boys need to leave now and go home. The rain has stopped, and it's dry outside now, so be on your way."

But do you think that Paul and David did what Don's mother told them to do, to go home? Of course not. As soon as they were out of sight of Don's mother, they turned the other way and escaped back down to the gully.

"Come on, David. I'm not hungry yet, are you? I don't think it's time for supper, so let's have some more fun in the gully."

"Paul, I have to pee real badly."

"Yeah, David, I have to pee real bad too. Let's go over to that stone fence and climb up on it and see who can pee the farthest."

"Uh-huh. Let's go," David exclaimed with delight.

Wouldn't you know? Just right when Paul and David were in the midst of seeing who could pee the farthest while standing on the stone fence, a neighbor of their mom and dad happened by and loudly exclaimed, "Boys, you ought not to be doing that right out in the open. Shame on you both. I have a mind to tell your mother what you are doing."

Well, that startled both Paul and David, and they forgot about who could pee the farthest. They both jumped off the fence and ran the other way laughing as they ran.

There was a tall and very large pine tree just around the corner from where Paul and David lived, and it was David who spoke up. "Paul, I wonder how high we can climb up that tree over in the yard of that big white house?"

"Let's go, David. I think we can climb to the top."

Up the tree they went, David ahead of Paul and both of them scampering as fast as they could to the top.

"Climbing up this tree, David, is pretty easy. The branches are really big and strong, and it's sort of like climbing a ladder, isn't it?"

Neither of them had ever climbed as high as they did on that day.

"Is it ever windy up here, Paul? The tree is sure moving back and forth. Do you think the wind could blow us right out of the tree?"

"I don't know, David, but I'm kind of scared. We'd better climb down. But it sure is great up here. We can see all over the neighborhood."

Safely back on the ground, Paul and David set out for the gully. They'd gone swimming in Kettle Creek. They'd built a fort. They'd discovered what a funeral looked like, and they had climbed a very high pine tree. Oh yes, it was determined that Paul could pee the farthest, but who cared about that. David was the only one small enough who could drop down Don's clothes chute. Boy-oh-boy. They sure got into trouble for that.

"I'm getting hungry, Paul. Maybe we should go home now."

"Aw, come on, Dave. It can't be suppertime yet. Let's hike around on the trails in the gully."

"Oh, all right, but I'm getting hungry, and I want to go home soon, Paul."

"Oh, oh. It must be later than I thought. That's Dad hollering out for us. I think he's coming down the gully looking for us. I know we're in trouble now because he told me the other day if he caught us down the gully, he was going to give us a 'whale of good spanking.'"

"There you boys are. Paul, I told you and David not to come down this gully. You have been disobedient. You both march home on the double."

It just so happened that Mom's mother, Grandma Carter, was visiting with us, and she was sitting in the living room when Paul and David scampered in right in front of their very angry father.

"All right, you boys. Explain to me why you went down the gully when I very distinctly told you not to." David looked at Paul as if to say "You'd better tell Dad why we went down the gully."

"Paul, you're the oldest. You explain to me why you went down the gully against my orders."

"Aw, well, Dad, my mind went blank, just like your mind does sometimes."

"What do you mean your mind went blank just like mine does? I'll have you know, young man, my mind does not go blank. You've earned yourself a spanking, and I'm giving you David's as well because you led him down there. You have not acted in a responsible manner."

Well, I sure got a good licking that night, and to rub it in, Grandma Cartier laughed and shook like a bowl of jelly. I didn't think it was that funny.

## How Much Fun Can a Kid Have on a Winter Afternoon?

December 28, 1955, was the last Wednesday of the month, and it was also my father's day off. He was a barber in St. Thomas, and all the barbers agreed that they would take Wednesday off each week. So it was that my dad was home on this snowy Wednesday afternoon.

"Boys, you are making too much noise. Your father would like to have a little rest this afternoon, so I want you both to go down to the basement to play. Be sure to play quietly down there as well."

"OK, Mom. David and I can play with some of our Christmas gifts. Come on, David, take your favorite car, and I'll take my favorite truck. We can draw some roads on the basement floor with some chalk I found. Then we can drive around on them."

"Uh-huh, let's play cars and trucks, Paul."

It had been snowing all morning, and Mom had kept us in the house thinking that maybe we could go outside after the snowstorm had passed. It was still snowing, so down the basement we went.

"I'm getting tired of playing cars and trucks, Paul, what else can we do?"

"I was watching Mom do the laundry yesterday, David. She was using the new washing machine over there that Dad bought her for Christmas. It's pretty nifty, and it has a gear shift on the side of it. I think Mom shifted it so the thing in the middle would go back and forth."

"What's that thing in the middle do, Paul? It looks pretty big down there in that big tank."

"I don't know what it does, David. All it looks like it does is go back and forth."

"Hey, David, I think that would be fun to sit on it and go back and forth, don't you?"

"Uh-huh. That would be fun, Paul."

"Here, let me help you up so you can get into that tub, and I'll do what Mom did. I'll turn that switch on and move that big stick like she did, and you will have a fun ride, David."

"Wow-wee, Paul. This sure is fun going back and forth. I'm pretending I'm at the fair on the merry-go-round.

"But it does make a funny noise, Paul. It sounds like the dog next door when it growls at me when I poke a stick through the fence in the backyard."

Upstairs in the kitchen it was a different story. The lights in the ceiling were going bright and then dim. That alarmed Mom, so she awakened Dad who couldn't quite figure out why the lights were behaving like that.

"The boys are too quiet downstairs in the basement, but there is a growling noise coming from down there. I think it has something to do with the lights going bright and dim. I better get down there right away and see what those two are up to.

"Stop that immediately, Paul. Turn the washing machine off. David, get out of there right now. What are you two boys thinking? David is not supposed to be in the washing machine, and you, Paul, are not supposed to be turning it on. Neither of you know what you are doing. Your dad will be giving you a licking because you have both been bad boys."

"But, Mom, I didn't do anything bad. Paul put me into the washing machine and said it would be fun. I didn't want to go in the machine, but he made me do it, and it near broke my bones."

"Just for that, Paul, you will get David's licking as well as what you have coming to you."

"Boy-oh-boy, I'll tell you something now, David. My back side is really hot and stinging from that licking I got. Because you were a big suck, I got your licking too. Now I just want to go outside and sit in a snowbank and cool off my poor, aching bum."

"I heard what you said, Paul. That's the best thing you have said today. You and David put your winter coats on, you're going outside. You have caused enough trouble in the house for one day."

"Aw, Mom, I wasn't bad. It was Paul who was bad."

"That's over now, David. You two get outside and behave yourself."

"Now what are we going to do, Paul? Do you want to build a snowman?"

"No, not right now. Let's play hockey out on the street. Our hockey sticks are in the backyard. Let's get them."

"But, Paul, there is so much snow on the street. We will lose our hockey puck in no time."

"Nope. Not going to use a hockey puck today. I saw some older boys using the horse manure after it was frozen, and they used it instead of a hockey puck. That's what we're going to use."

It didn't seem very long before Paul and David had used up all the horse hockey pucks when David said, "Paul, there isn't any horse pucks left to slap around. But we sure did make a mess of the street. Pieces of horse pucks are everywhere."

"I guess those horse hockey pucks weren't very frozen, David. Oh well, I was getting tired of slapping them around anyhow. But I've got another idea."

"Let's go over to Don's house and see if he can come out to play."

"Hi, Don, come on out and play with David and me. We can go around the neighborhood and get all the Christmas trees that everyone has stuck out by the curb for the garbage man to pick up. We can drag them over to the gully, and then we can build a fort out of them. It will be a good fort, and we can hide out in it."

"OK, Paul, let's do it," yelled Don as he grabbed his winter coat hanging on a peg inside the back door of his house.

"I'm going outside with Paul and David, Mom. We're going to play in the snow."

"OK, Don. You boys have fun, but don't stay out too long and get cold. If you're getting cold, come in and play."

Don's mom was really nice, and David and I liked playing at Don's house in the basement. He had lots of toys, and there was a big room we could play in, but today we were going to build a big fort out of old Christmas trees.

"Wow, guys, we sure did get a lot of Christmas trees. How many of them did you count, Don?"

"I counted twenty trees, Paul. This is going to be one big fort. Maybe our moms will let us camp out in it overnight."

"That would be really great, Don. Maybe you and I could do that, but I bet my mom wouldn't let Dave camp out because he's so young."

"I'm not that young, Paul, I've been four since last May, so I'm old enough to camp out with you and Don."

The three of them argued with each other one minute and were buddies the next. That is how boys act. But they grew tired of building their fort and arguing with each other. It was Don who came up with a great idea, or at least he thought so.

"Hey, guys, I saw Ted, our neighbor, down the street do something really cool yesterday. He waited for the city bus to come down the street and stop at the bus stop. When he figured the bus driver wasn't looking, he went behind the bus and grabbed on to the bus's bumper. When the bus moved away and went down the street, Ted slid along on the snow behind the bus. He called that "bus skiing."

"That's really nifty, Don. Why don't we do that as well? That will be lots of fun," said Paul excitedly.

The three boys found a good hiding spot behind a big cedar hedge, and didn't have to wait too long before a big city bus showed up and stopped at the bus stop. No one got on or off the bus, so the bus quickly left, but the boys were quicker than the bus because all three of them quickly grabbed on to the rear bumper and away they went. They were bus skiing really well because there were lots of snow packed hard on the street.

"That was really fun, Paul. Let's do it again."

"OK, David. We'll just walk back up the street and hide again behind the big cedar hedge. When another bus comes to a stop at the bus stop, we'll grab the back bumper again."

That seemed to be a fun way to spend a couple of hours, bus skiing behind the city bus, but Paul, David, and Don soon got tired of it, and so it was Don who suggested they do something else.

"Why don't we go across the tracks and play in that old junkyard. There is an old bus there and a couple of really old cars and trucks. Maybe we can find some real treasure there, Paul."

"Yes, let's do it. Come on, David. Just don't tell Mom we crossed the train tracks, or she'll give us another licking today."

"Ho, ho, ho. Did you guys get a licking today?" Don asked in merriment.

"I didn't, Don, it was Paul who got the licking because he stuffed me in Mom's washing machine and turned it on."

"Shut-up, David. You're being a real suck all over again. Maybe you should go home if you're going to be a baby."

"Nope. I'm not going home. I'm going with you guys to the junkyard," David angrily yelled.

Paul, David, and their friend, Don, did indeed cross the tracks and in short order were in the junkyard.

"What did you guys find? I found a knife stuck in the back of the driver's seat of that old bus," Paul boasted happily. "I'm going to keep it, but I'll have to hide it from mom and dad, and if you tell that I found it, I'll beat you up, David. You'll be sorry."

"I won't tell, Paul, but you will have to let me play with it too."

"I'll show you how to throw a knife, David. That's how we can play with it." Turning to Don, Paul asked, "Did you find anything?"

"Nope, I didn't find anything, but I'm getting cold, so I'm going home. Are you guys going home too?" asked Don.

"We'll walk with you on your way home, Don, if we can go by that big boxcar sitting on the tracks in front of the co-op building. I want to look at it because someday I'm going to work on a railroad."

"OK, Paul. Let's go. But first I've got an idea. Let's go around by the door and knock on it. If someone answers when we knock, I'll ask if we can all have an apple to eat."

"That's a good idea, Don," said David. "I'm getting hungry, and I'd sure like an apple to eat."

The boys did indeed get an apple each from the kind man who answered the door. He recognized Don and said he'd get the apples from Don's dad's storage locker. He must have known that there were apples there.

As the boys, Paul, David, and Don, began to hike on home first to Don's place, David stopped by the big wheel of the boxcar and said, "Hey, Paul and Don. Why is this big piece of wood stuck between the track and the wheel? Do you think it keeps the train from moving?"

"I don't know, David," said Don. "Pull it out and let's see if the boxcar begins to move."

That was exactly what David did, and sure enough, the boxcar started to move. When David realized that the boxcar was going to go down the track, he got scared and started to run away.

"David, give me that piece of wood. I have to stop that boxcar from going down the track, or we'll be in deep trouble for sure," yelled Paul.

With the piece of wood in his hand, Paul ran beside the big boxcar wheel and tried to stick it under the wheel to stop the train.

"I stopped the train, David. Don't run away. Come back here and stay with Don and me."

"OK, Paul, but I want to go home. I'm cold now, and that big boxcar scared me."

That's about as much fun a kid could have on a winter day. Lucky for Paul, David, and Don, no adults saw them goofing around with the railroad's boxcar, or they'd have all got a real serious "whumping" and probably wouldn't have been able to sit down for a couple of days.

Paul and David were clumping up the stairs to the back door when Mom opened the door and called out to them. "Come to the kitchen, boys. I have some great news for you. I just got off the phone from talking with Mr. Tarry. He is your dad's friend. He would like to give you boys and Dad and I a ride in his sleigh. He has a big, strong horse that will pull the sleigh. Because we had so much snow today, the sleigh will slide behind the horse quite easily."

"Wow-wee, Mom," yelled David. "We'll get a sleigh ride. I can hardly wait."

"David, you and Paul put on some warm clothes and your snow suits and get ready because Mr. Tarry will be here very soon."

Paul, turning to his younger brother, excitedly said, "Look, David, here comes the horse and sleigh. Let's go outside now."

"Mom and Dad, the horse and sleigh are here," shouted David as he slammed the door behind him.

The sleigh had bells attached to the sides, and they jingled as the horse pulled the sleigh. That was enough for Paul to start an off-key rendition of "Jingle Bells." Soon everyone was helping Paul sing that Christmas carol. After all Christmas had just passed a few days past, so it was really still the Christmas season.

"Mom, this is lots of fun. I've never had a sleigh ride being pulled by a horse before," said Paul. "And do you know what else fun is? It's watching everyone walking on the sidewalk and waving at us as we go by. Do you think they know who we are?"

"Well, I'm sure they don't know who you are, Paul, but everyone in town knows Mr. Tarry. So they are waving to him," replied Mother.

Just about that time, David said, "Mom, I'm getting cold."

"David, you and Paul sit closer together, and I'll wrap you both up in this nice, big, warm blanket. Now you will be as snug as a bug in a rug."

What a beautiful way to end off a great year. Paul and David soon began to yawn as they snuggled under the warm blanket. The rest of the sleigh ride was forgotten as they fell asleep. They didn't even wake up when the sleigh ride was over, so their dad had to carry them into the house and upstairs to their bedroom.

## My First Long-Distance Train Ride

My mother used to live in Northern Ontario where she grew up when she was a girl. She had not been up to her childhood home to visit her mother since she married my dad. My brother David and I were going to go on a really long train ride all the way up to Haileybury, Ontario, with our mom. We would even get to sleep on the train one night.

"Paul, settle down and behave yourself. Why are you so wound up?"

"But, Mom, I'm going for a train ride. I just love train rides. This is going to be a lot of fun. Can David and I each take our favorite toy with us? I promise I'll be good."

"OK, Paul, you can take your favorite toy. What toy will you take?"

"Mom, you know my favorite toy is that little red truck. Hey, David, what is your favorite toy you are going to take?"

"My favorite toy is that blue car I like. Can I take it?"

"Of course, David. You can take your favorite blue car. OK, boys, Dad is ready to take us to the train station now."

We didn't have a car, but that didn't stop Dad from getting us safely to the train station, which was only about one mile away from our home at No. 5 Ste. Anne's Place in St. Thomas. He had a big wagon, which he put our luggage into, and then he sat David and me on top of the luggage. Mom walked beside the wagon while Dad pulled it. She kept her hand on us so we wouldn't fall off the wagon should it hit a bump.

"Hey, David, do you like wagon rides? I do. It's fun."

"Uh-huh. I like wagon rides too, and I like sitting real high on Mom's luggage."

Our wagon ride took us downtown all the way to the London and Port Stanley Railway Station. Dad called this railroad an "Inter-Urban Electric Railroad."

"Mom, when we get on this electric train, where are we going to go?"

"Paul, we are going to ride the L&PS train to London. Then we will get on a really big train that is pulled by a steam engine. I know you will just love your train ride because it has a loud whistle just like the trains with the loud whistles which go by near our home."

"When you and David look out your window on that train, you will see lots of passenger cars and a big steam engine. There will be lots of smoke coming from the steam engine. You will be able to see this as we go around curves."

The train ride on the L&PS was soon over, but that didn't matter to us. David was three, and me, I was five. We were so excited we were literally bouncing up and down even when we got to the Canadian National Railroad Station in London, Ontario.

Both David and Paul asked in unison, "Mom, how long do we have to wait for the big train to come and take us away?"

"Boys, the train will be here in just a few minutes. You will need to hold each other's hand while I carry a small suitcase on the train. The conductor will help us get on the train and show us where we will sit. So promise me you will both be good and obey the conductor if he tells you to do something."

"Wow-wee, is that ever a big train, David. Look how big the steam engine is, and does it ever make a lot of noise."

"Un-huh. It is real big, Paul, and scary too," said David as he held his mother's hand very tightly.

We were soon in a big passenger car, and we had two seats. David and I sat on one seat, and Mom sat on the other seat facing us. Mom put our little backpacks on the seat beside her, and she put her small suitcase on a rack over our heads.

We were soon going very fast. Everything was zipping past our window in a big blur. The passenger car swayed back and forth, and it was a little hard to stand up without wobbling around. It was fascinating to listen to the click-clack of the wheels on the track, and I think that was what lulled Mom to sleep.

"The conductor was a very nice man who came by our seats often to see how we were doing. He would always ask us if we were enjoying our train ride. Of course David and I always nodded yes. I spoke up once when he asked us that question and said, "Mr. Conductor, I like your big train. When I grow up, I want to run a big train like this, and I want to blow the whistle too."

Smiling, he said to me, "You would make a very good engineer. You could make the train go fast, and you could blow the whistle too."

When Mom woke up, I said, "Mom, Mr. Conductor said if I wanted, I could be an engineer and drive a big train like this, and I could blow the whistle too. So I want to be an engineer, Mom."

"Paul, you can be whatever you want to be. If you want to be a train engineer, I know you will be a very good train engineer."

By this time David had fallen asleep with his head on Mom's lap. I had the whole seat to myself, but I wasn't tired. All I wanted to do was dream about driving a big train as I looked out the window at the engine as it went around a curve. I could also look out the window toward the rear of the train and watch it too.

The Toronto Railway Station was very big. Mom told me, "Hold my hand, Paul, and hold David's hand with your other hand. I don't want you boys to wander away. I might not be able to find you, and you will get lost. We will have to wait two hours before we can get on the next train, which will take us to Grandma Cartier."

"Mom, why is this big train station called Union Station? What does that mean?"

"Paul, it is called Toronto Union Station because first of all it is located in downtown Toronto and also because there are four different railroads that come here and share this station with each other."

"What are the names of the four railroads, Mom?"

"Well, let's see. There is the Canadian National Railway. That's the name of the train that brought us to this station. Then there is the Canadian Pacific Railway, the Toronto Hamilton and Buffalo Railroad, and the Ontario Northland Railroad. We will get on the Ontario Northland when we leave here to go to Grandma Cartier's place."

"That wasn't a very long wait, Mom. Look, the lineup we've been waiting in is going through those doors. We're going to ride those stairs up to the train right, Mom?"

"That's right, Paul. Now hold your brother's hand tightly and watch your step as you get on those stairs. Those stairs are called an escalator."

"Wow-wee, Mom. Now we're sitting on the other side of the train car. We will be able to see the other side of this train. Will it be the same as the train we came here on?"

"Well, it is a passenger train, Paul. The car you're sitting in is called a coach. It is owned by a different railroad company, but that is about all that's different. There is another steam engine much like the one that brought us here to Toronto. I think this engine will take us all the way to where Grandma lives."

Paul and David soon became interested in their toys and began to play quietly on the seats they had been sitting on. And it wasn't too long before their mother had opened up a big bag she had been carrying and everyone had a nice supper of peanut butter and jam sandwiches.

It wasn't too long after supper that both Paul and David got sleepy, and soon their mother had covered them with a blanket the railroad had provided. They rested their heads on little pillows with the name of the railroad on them.

"Mom, is it morning all ready? Wow-wee. I slept all night, didn't I?"

"Yes, you and David both slept all night. I think the sound of the wheels going click-clack lulled you to sleep. Let's call it a railroad lullaby."

"Did you sleep really well too, Mom?"

"Yes, I did, Paul. I have a treat for you and David and me too. We are going to the dining car for breakfast. After we have had breakfast, we will come back here, and it will be soon after that when we will arrive at the railroad station where Grandma will be waiting for us."

Holding his mother's hand as they left the dining car, David happily said, "That was fun eating breakfast on the train, Mom. I liked the bowl of cereal that I had and the toast with marmalade too."

Too soon for Paul's liking, he and David and their mother arrived at the Haileybury Railway Station. "Oh, Mom, I wish we could ride the train all day today too."

"But, Paul, if we stayed on the train, we would not see Grandma, and we came here to see Grandma Carter. You will like where Grandma lives, and we will stay with her for a couple of weeks. You'll see, it will be a fun vacation for you and David both."

"And we'll ride the train back home too, right?"

"Of course, Paul. It will take us a whole day to go back home on the train, and you will be able to sleep on the train one night too."

Paul excitedly said, "I can hardly wait, Mom, for our next train ride. But I promise I'll have fun here too, and you said I'll be able to play with my cousins. I've never seen my cousins before. What are their names?"

"Your cousins' names are Rhoda and Ella. Rhoda is David's age, and Ella is one year younger than David."

"Look out the window, David. The train is stopping at a station, and there is still some snow on the ground. I hope there will be lots of snow where Grandma Carter lives. Maybe we can go tobogganing."

"Paul and David, you need to gather up your little backpacks and get ready to climb off the train. The conductor will help you as you climb down those steep steps."

"Mom, does Grandma Carter have a toboggan," asked Paul?

"I don't really know whether there is a toboggan at Grandma's house or not, Paul, but I'm sure we can come up with a fun way to slide on the snow."

Waiting for those three excited but weary travelers was Mom's older brother. He had arrived in a very old car, and now they were going to have to put their luggage in a small trunk. What luggage that didn't fit in that small trunk had to stay in the back seat with Paul and David.

"Boys, I want you to say hi to your Uncle Norman. This is his car, and we will ride it to go to Grandma's house."

Paul excitedly spoke up, asking, "Hi, Uncle Norman, does your car go real fast? My dad doesn't even have a car. What kind of car is this?"

"Whoa there, young man. That's too many questions all at once. This car doesn't go very fast because the roads are very bumpy at the end of the winter. Paul, this car is called a Buick. It was made in 1939, so it is very old now, but it still runs very well. It will get us safely to Grandma's house."

Both Paul and David were soon looking out the side windows from the back seat. Because they were so close to the windows, they were fogging them up with their breath. Paul, with a sense of smugness, said to his brother David when he was trying to clean the condensation off his window, "That is a natural thing that happens when the outside air is cold and the inside of the car is warm."

It seemed like a long ride from the railway station to Grandma's house, but of course Uncle Norman drove slowly because of the bumpy roads. When finally they arrived, Paul was excited to see a large two-story house all made from wood. There wasn't any paint on the wood, so it had a gray and black color. Uncle Norman said that the wood was well weathered from many years of being in the sun and the rain and the snow, but Paul didn't really understand Uncle Norman's explanation.

There were very soon lots of kisses and hugs going around. Grandma Carter had to give everyone lots of wet, smoochy kisses, which made both Paul and David wipe their faces off with the back of their hands more than once.

"Mom, who are those two girls? Are they are cousins?"

"Yes, David, they are your cousins Rhoda and Ella. Rhoda is the taller cousin and is your age, and Ella is your younger cousin. Why don't you and Paul say hi to your cousins and go play with them. You can play with them right here in the house because it is still a bit cold outside."

Paul and David made friends quickly and easily with Rhoda and Ella. They were soon running around the house and making lots of noise. Actually, they were making too much noise, and the adults were becoming frustrated because conversation was much more difficult with four noisy children nearby.

Aunt Mabel, who was Rhoda and Ella's mother, spoke up just when the noise reached a new high pitch. "Children, I want you all to put on your winter clothes and your boots because you are all going outside to play."

Once outside the four cousins began to have even more fun as they realized that their mothers weren't watching their every move. It was Paul who made the next suggestion.

"Hey, everybody, let's pretend we are explorers. Let's go behind the barn and explore there."

One and all they marched out toward the barn and soon disappeared from sight. David quickly exclaimed, "Hey, look, is that ever an old tractor. It has big back wheels and spokes, and it doesn't have any rubber tires. I wonder if we can make it run."

David and Ella climbed up on the tractor while Paul and Rhoda looked on. David yelled out, "Paul, there is a key in the tractor. Do you think it will run if I turn the key?"

"I don't know, David. Turn the key on and let's find out."

Ella was a little scared that the tractor might start up, so she quickly got off and ran toward the barn. David turned the key on, and the tractor made an awful noise—"*rrrrrr – rrrrrr*"—like it wanted to start. David continued to turn the key on, and the noise continued, but after a short time, it quit making any noise whatsoever. Jumping down from the tractor, David exclaimed, "That's no fun, Paul. I wanted to make the tractor go, but all it did was make that funny noise. Let's find something else to do."

As those four cousins traipsed beyond the barn out into the open fields, they came to a steep hill that went down to a frozen creek. It was Rhoda who said, "Why don't we find something to slide on and go sliding down this hill. That will be lots of fun."

Nothing was found as they ran around going from one side of the farm property to the other side. Finally arriving back at the farmhouse, Paul opened the back door and loudly called out, "Uncle Norman, do you have anything we can use to slide on? We want to slide down the hill behind the barn."

Uncle Norman came to the door scratching his head as he thought of an answer to Paul's question. Then he had a thought. "Let me put my coat on, kids, and let's go to the barn. I think I might find something that you can use to slide on."

"Well, well, would you look at that? Here are some large cardboard boxes that I think you could use to slide on. Let's go out to that hill and find out if they will work for you."

Paul, David, Rhoda, and Ella were very excited and ran to the hill while Uncle Norman carried two very large cardboard boxes with him. Setting the boxes down, he said, "Who would like to try out one of these boxes to see if they will slide down the hill?"

Paul and David yelled out together, "We will, Uncle Norman. Let us see if we can make the box slide down the hill."

Very quickly David climbed in the front of the box and Paul climbed into the back. It took a bit of work to get the box to slide, but once Uncle Norman gave it a good shove, off they went down the hill.

"Wow-wee, Paul, we are going really fast. Look at the snow flying up behind us. This is lots of fun." And it was fun until the box stopped rather abruptly as they got to the bottom of the hill.

Before they could get out of the box and start to drag it back up the hill, Rhoda and Ella slid right up beside them and stopped. They were as excited as Paul and David. Ella yelled out, "Let's go up the hill and do it again."

For the next half hour, those four cousins had a lot of fun sliding down the hill. Once Uncle Norman thought he'd try to slide down the hill as well, so he climbed into the box Rhoda and Ella were using. Boy-oh-boy, did Uncle Norman ever go fast. He nearly slid right into the frozen creek because he was going so fast. You could hear Uncle Norman laugh as he got out of the box. "Hahaha. That was fun. I sure went fast too. I think I'll try that again." Climbing to the top of the hill, he happily said to the four children, "I'll be back quick as a wink. I'm going to get another box just for me."

So it was that Uncle Norman and his two nephews and two nieces slid down that hill for a long time happily laughing and yelling with exciting exclamations of merriment.

It seemed all too soon that the daylight faded into early evening, and Uncle Norman sadly said, "I think we have had all the fun on this hill we are going to have today. The sun has gone down, and it's getting dark. Let's take our boxes back to the barn. We can use them again another day."

There was a lot of excited chatter that evening around the big family table in that large farm kitchen. Uncle Norman and all the cousins had rosy cheeks and bright eyes as they hungrily devoured hot chicken noodle soup and later some very delicious meat loaf that Grandma Carter had made while they were out sliding down the hill.

## My First Train Ride with David by Ourselves

I figured David and I were pretty grown-up because Mom and Dad were letting us go on the train all by ourselves. I was seven, and David was five. We were going to visit Aunt Grace in Toronto. Dad had to work, and Mom had to stay home with our youngest brother, Danny, who was now one year old.

"You can take us to the train station in London, Dad, because it's your day off, right?"

"That's right, Paul. We will leave in just a few minutes. I will make sure you get on the right train, and the conductor will keep an eye on you. You guys better be on your best behavior. If the conductor tells me later that you've been bad, I'll make sure you both get a good licking."

"I promise, Dad, we'll be good. Right, David?"

"Uh-huh. We'll be good, Dad."

You just knew that Paul and David were excited to be able to go on the train to Toronto all by themselves. They chatted nonstop in Dad's car all the way to London.

"OK, boys, tone the chatter down now. We're going to wait in this waiting room for your train to arrive. The ticket agent said it would be here in fifteen minutes. Are you boys OK, or should you both go to the bathroom?"

Paul and David nodded and spoke in unison, "I'm okay, Dad."

"Wow, Dad, that sure is a big steam engine. Look at all the wheels it has and those arms going back and forth. Pretty neat, eh?"

"The name of that type of engine, boys, is called a Pacific. The railroads give that name to it because of the number of wheels under it. There are other engines with different names because of the different number of wheels they have."

"Hello, Mr. Conductor. My two boys are going to ride your train to Toronto. Here are their tickets. Would you keep an eye on them and keep them on the coach until their aunt can arrive on the platform at Union Station? She knows they're coming, and she'll be there to pick them up. Her name is Ms. Grace O'Brien, and she'll show you some ID to confirm her name. Thank you, I really appreciate your assistance."

Paul and David's dad waved goodbye to them when they got to their seat, and they waved back to him from their window.

"Paul, this passenger car looks sort of like the one we rode on when we went to visit Grandma Cartier, doesn't it?"

"It sure does, David. Who knows, maybe it is the same passenger car."

Suddenly the train began to move and quickly left the station in London. It seemed only a few moments, and they were going very fast. David excitedly exclaimed, "Boy-oh-boy, are we ever going fast, eh, Paul? I think we'll get to Toronto very quickly if we always go this fast."

"I don't know how fast we're going, David, but here comes the conductor. I'll ask him if he knows how fast we're going."

"Hi, Mr. Conductor. My brother and I would like to know how fast the train is going. Is it going maybe one hundred miles per hour?"

"Hi, boys. I'm glad to see you are enjoying your train ride. But how fast is it going? Well, let me see. I know it's not going quite 100 mph as you might think, but it is still going fast. We are going 80 mph. So your guess wasn't too far off.

"Your dad told me you boys were going to see your Aunt Grace. Does she live in Toronto?"

Paul responded to the conductor's question with a knowledgeable nod of his head, "Yes, our dad told us she rents an apartment there. We're going to visit with her for a week. Dad figures we're pretty grown-up, so he is letting us have a vacation by ourselves—oh, well, with our Aunt Grace of course."

"That sounds very exciting. You will want to visit the Toronto Zoo if your aunt can take you there."

"She has a car, and how did you know we'd like to go to the zoo?"

"Well, it was just a good guess of course, but what young lads like you wouldn't want to go to the zoo? You would certainly see animals from all over the world there."

"My brother David wants to see the lions, and I want to see the elephants."

"Well, well, well. Boys, we're starting to slow down. I have to do some work now because we are going to make a station stop at a city called Brantford where we'll pick up some people who also want to go to Toronto. But I will come back later and chat some more with you."

Paul and David were having the time of their lives. They were so busy looking out the window that they didn't even think to play with their favorite toy that each of them had brought.

In no time the conductor was standing next to their seat again. "Well, boys, here we are coming into the Toronto Union Station. I want you two to remain here in your seats. When the train stops, you can hold on to your suitcases but remain here at this seat. Even if you see your aunt standing on the platform, still remain here until I come to get you. Do you both understand my request?"

Both Paul and David solemnly nodded, and Paul spoke up for both of them. "Yes, sir, we understand, and we'll wait here until you come back to get us."

"Hey, look, Paul, I see Aunt Grace. She is walking toward us. Do you think she might see me waving at her?"

"Sure, David. Wave at her. I know she will see you."

"She sees me Paul and is waving to me too. Now the conductor is talking to her, and they are both walking toward the doors, I think."

"Hello, Paul, and hello, David. The conductor let me come on the train so I'd be able to help you with your luggage. You both look like you had a fun trip. I'm glad to see you, and we're going to have a fun week together as well."

"Aunt Grace, the conductor said maybe you would take us to the zoo. Can we go to the zoo?"

"Why of course, David. We can go for a whole day and even have a picnic when we are there. You both will have so much fun at the zoo, and I've also got some more activities that we can do this week, and they are all lots of fun to do."

Would you believe that on the way to Aunt Grace's apartment we stopped at a store and Aunt Grace bought David and me each a box of Cracker Jack?

"Look, David and Aunt Grace. The little toy in my Cracker Jack box is a railroad passenger car. What did you get in your Cracker Jack box, David?"

"I got a train car just like you, Paul."

"Well, that's pretty good if I say so myself," responded Aunt Grace. "You both have little toy train cars that will help you remember your train ride when you came to visit me for a week."

We were both hungry when Aunt Grace brought us from the Toronto Union Station to her apartment. It was David who spoke up first. "Aunt Grace, Paul and I are hungry. We would like to eat something."

"Boys, would you like chicken noodle soup and a grilled cheese sandwich? When you have eaten your soup and sandwich, I have some apple pie and ice cream. Would you like that as well?"

Both Paul and David affirmed they would like that, by vigorously nodding their heads yes, and it was then Paul who asked, "Aunt Grace, can we go to the zoo tomorrow?"

"That was one of the things I thought we'd do, boys, so how would you like it if we went to the zoo tomorrow right after we've had our breakfast? We could take a picnic lunch and spend the whole day at the zoo. Would you both like to do that?"

It was agreed by both Paul and David that it would be fun to spend the whole day at the zoo. But it was Paul who piped up and asked, "Aunt Grace, what can we do for the rest of this day?"

"I have a great idea," said Aunt Grace. "I know you like train rides, but how would you like a train ride that goes underground?"

"But, Aunt Grace, why would a train go underground?" David asked.

"Well, boys, it's like this. In a big city like Toronto, a lot of people depend on buses, or streetcars, or subways to get around because the roads would be too congested if everyone used their cars. And not only that, but many people who live downtown don't even have cars, so they need the buses or streetcars or the subway."

David had a quizzical look on his face when he asked, "What does *congested* mean, Aunt Grace?"

"That word just means that there would be too many cars on the road and people would have a hard time getting around from place to place, David."

Lunch was eaten in a hurry by two excited boys who talked nonstop about riding around Toronto on a bus and a streetcar and even on the subway. So when their lunch was eaten, Aunt Grace took them outside and down to the corner where they got on a bus. When they arrived at their destination, both boys realized that they were back at the train station they had been at earlier in the day.

"Why are we back here?" asked Paul. "Are we going to ride another train?"

"No, Paul, we are going to ride a subway train. I think you will really like it too because I know you had so much fun riding the train to come and see me."

Aunt Grace did something special for Paul and David that day. They rode on the front car of the subway train, and they could look out the front window and see the long underground tube that the train was running through. They were so excited they could hardly contain themselves. It was great fun watching how fast they were going, especially when they came into a lighted underground station.

That was all they could talk about until they were ready for bed that evening. As they were climbing into bed, David excitedly asked, "Aunt Grace, when we go to the zoo tomorrow, will we ride a subway train again to get there?"

Aunt Grace answered David's question by saying, "We will ride a bus and an electric streetcar but not a subway train. And David, an electric streetcar runs on tracks just like a subway train does."

It wasn't until the boys had arrived at the zoo, that they realized it was a very large zoo. It had many different animals, most which neither Paul nor David knew what the many animals were called or where they came from.

It was Paul, who picked up a small stick lying on the pathway going around the big pen that housed the lions, and had been dragging that stick along the fence that separated the lions from the people, when an especially large lion approached the fence, and roared very loudly.

Paul jumped back in absolute fright and hid behind his aunt. David laughed at Paul, but Aunt Grace put her arm around Paul and said, "Paul, I don't think that any animal likes to be teased, and so that was why the lion roared at you. You had best drop that stick and stay a little distance away from the fence."

David spoke up with some excitement when they were all looking at the zebras. "Hey, Paul, I like the zebras the best. They look like horses, and I like the black and white colors they have. What is your favorite animal?"

Paul thought for a moment and then said, "My favorite animal is the monkey. I like how they can climb trees and can swing from branch to branch. They nearly look like little people too."

After spending several hours at the zoo, Aunt Grace noticed that both Paul and David were getting tired, so she suggested, "Boys, we've had a lot of fun today, but now you are tired, so let's go back to my apartment."

Paul and David enjoyed spending several days with Aunt Grace until it was time to return to their home, and wouldn't you know it, she went with them on the train back to St. Thomas because she said she wanted to visit with her brother and sister-in-law, which was the boys' dad and mom.

## TWO

# YOUNG BOYHOOD YEARS IN THE COUNTRY

A WHOLE NEW WORLD opened up for my brother David and me when the family moved to Centennial Ave. We were now in the country. The city was behind us. We had a lot of territory to discover.

"David, we can't play down the gully anymore because we've moved so far away from it, but don't be sad. We can discover a whole lot of new things."

"But, Paul, it's so lonely out here in the country. And besides, look at all the snow. What can we do in all that snow?"

"I was looking out my bedroom window this morning, David, and behind us in the fields are some really big snowdrifts. I haven't seen any snowdrifts this large in St. Thomas. Let's get dressed and take a couple of Dad's shovels and go build a fort in those snowdrifts."

It was Christmastime in December 1956. David was five, and I was seven. I would soon go to a new school called Centennial Avenue Public School, but David and I had a week to discover lots of things before I went back to school in grade 2.

"Wow, David, look how high these snowdrifts are. They're taller than me. I bet they are taller than Dad too. Let's dig some tunnels and make a fort inside this really big snowdrift here."

Well, that was exactly what we did. After an hour of shoveling snow and digging a tunnel into the drift, I asked David, "Would you like to crawl into our new tunnel and you can dig a big room there and I'll pull the snow out of the tunnel?"

"OK, Paul, let's do it." And so after another few minutes of digging snow and pulling snow out of the tunnel, both David and I had made a little fort.

"It's a lot warmer in here, Paul. I like it here. We can dig more forts and have a lot of fun, but we need to find some friends to have fun with us."

"Hey, David, Mom said this morning that there was a boy who lives across the street from us. His name is Brian. Mom said she was talking to his mom and Brian was there too."

"Let's go and see if Brian can come out and play with us, Paul."

That afternoon we knocked on Brian's door. His mom said he'd like to play with us too. That's how we got to know our new friend Brian.

"Brian, David and I have been digging out tunnels and forts in some really big snowdrifts behind our house. Do you have a shovel you can borrow from your dad? You can dig tunnels and make forts with us."

Thus began a new friendship with Brian. He was one year younger than me and one year older than David. From that time on the three of us were hardly ever separated from each other.

Far too soon the Christmas season passed, and I started at a new school in January, but Brian, David, and I continued all that winter to make snow forts.

It wouldn't be until I was ten years old before we had large snowdrifts again. This time there was a snowdrift in the backyard that caught my attention. It had become hard from a few days of warmer weather that then turned cold again.

"Mom, I'm going to make an igloo in the backyard. I can walk on top of the snow, and I want to dig some snow out of the drift and make an igloo. I got a book from the school library that shows me how to build an igloo."

I soon had a good-size hole dug out of the snowdrift. The book showed how to cut snow with something sharp. I had to make big bricks of hard snow and pile them up on each other until I could make the igloo high enough so I could crouch inside.

Later that day David came home from playing at Brian's place and he wanted to help me finish my igloo. "I can help you dig a tunnel to your igloo, Paul. You can make a roof over the tunnel just like you made over the igloo."

"OK, David, I'll finish working on the inside of the igloo making the snow bricks smoother. I'm going to ask Mom if I can sleep in my igloo tonight. I can use a couple of our sleeping bags and a rubber mat on the ground. The book says it will be warmer in the igloo than outside. I think it will be fun to sleep out here."

David said he didn't want to sleep in the igloo, but Mom said that I could sleep there if I wanted to. She would leave the back door unlocked if I got cold in the middle of the night and wanted to come into the house.

I not only slept in that igloo one night, but also I slept in it several times before spring came and melted it all. I kept a candle lit all night, so I always had some light, and I think the candle kept it a bit warmer inside the igloo as well.

**A Biking Adventure**

The summer of 1960 was a great time to be living at Centennial Ave. There wasn't very much traffic on our road, and everywhere you pedaled your bike the roads were not too busy. They were quiet country gravel roads.

"Mom, David and I want to pedal around on the gravel roads and discover new territory. Would you pack a lunch for both of us, and I can carry it in my backpack."

"OK, Paul, I'll do that for you, but you must promise to be careful. If a car is coming, you are to get off the road and wait until it passes. Remember where you have come from so you can return the same way and not get lost."

"Come on, David, let's go and discover new territory. Dad took us to a little park last month. I think it is not too far away. He said it was called Springwater Conservation Area, and the pond was called White's Pond. Let's go there."

"Do you remember how to get there, Paul? I don't want to get lost."

"Yes, I remember how to get there." Well, I didn't really remember exactly how to get there, but I wasn't going to tell David that.

It didn't take too long for David to figure out that I really didn't know where I was going, that I was lost. We pedaled our bikes for several miles until our legs hurt. It was much harder riding a bike on gravel. More than once our wheels would slip on larger stones and we'd nearly fall from our saddle.

"Paul, you said you knew how to get to the park we were at with Dad. I don't believe you. We've been pedaling for hours and hours, and I'm tired. Let's stop and take a break. Look, over there in that field are some horses. Let's climb on the fence and try and get them to come to us."

"You don't know how to ride a horse, David. The only horse I've seen you ride is that old rocking horse you had when we lived on Ste. Anne's Place. If you tried to get on one of those big horses, you'd fall off. More than likely you'd scare them all away when you tried to get on one. Anyhow, how do you figure you'd be able to get on one in the first place?"

With a lot of bluster in his voice, David stuck out his chin and bragged. "When I was at Gerald's farm, I rode some pigs bareback. They didn't like it and ran around like crazy, but I hung on. Well, I did slip off a few times, and once I had to run out of the way because the momma pig I was riding was going to run after me. I climbed up on a fence to get out of her way. So if I could ride a pig, I'll bet you I can ride a horse. If one of them comes over to this fence, I'll just climb off the fence and get right on his back."

In a challenging voice, I retorted back to David, "I'd like to see you try that one, David. Look, he's coming over toward us. Maybe he'll come up to you."

Well, that horse did come up to the fence. Maybe he thought David and I had some carrots for him. Actually, both of us had some in our lunches.

"David, I'll look in our lunches. I think I saw Mom put some carrots with our sandwiches. I'll give some to you, and you can feed them to the horse."

"Hey, that's a good idea, Paul. Hurry up. I want to give him some so he'll like me."

Real quick, I looked for the carrots in our lunches. "David," I said excitedly, "here are the carrots." Running back to the fence from where we'd left our bikes in the ditch by the side of the road, I gave them to him. Right away David gave them to the horse.

"He likes them, Paul. He's taking them out of my hand." David was really getting excited, and with a big grin on his face, he said, "He is going to be my friend for sure."

David was very nimble, and with one fluid movement, he had climbed over the fence and was sitting on the back of that big, beautiful black horse. "Look at me now, Paul." He bragged, "I'm going to ride him around the field." And he did just that while holding on to the horse's long mane. As he came by the fence, he yelled over to me, "Paul, this is a lot easier riding a horse than it is riding a pig."

I yelled back, "Sure, David. You are just walking the horse. Try to make him run and then we'll see how easy it is to stay on his back."

Was he too brave, or was he too stupid? I don't know, but when David kicked the horse in the sides with his boots, the horse didn't run. The horse reared up on his hind legs, and David landed on his butt in the grass. Laughing loudly, I hollered back to David, "Hey, cowboy, when you fall off a horse, you have a lot farther to fall than when you fall off a pig. I'll bet that your butt is hurting now."

His butt hurt for sure because he didn't run back to the fence. He limped back to the fence holding his backside with both hands.

David didn't say a thing to me but instead walked over to his bike and slowly picked it up. I joined him and asked, "Does it hurt badly? Maybe we should just walk our bikes for a little while until your butt quits hurting."

His response was a quiet whisper. "I'll be all right in a little while."

We did find White's Pond eventually, but as we walked our bikes, the day grew increasingly warm, and we got very hot. I had an idea as we came toward a creek that was flowing under a small bridge.

"David, I'm hot. Let's stop here at this creek and go swimming. That's a good way to cool off."

With a little more life in his voice by now, David quickly responded back to me, "OK, Paul, but we didn't bring our bathing suits." He liked the idea of going swimming, but he was also somewhat hesitant.

"I know that, David, but that doesn't have to stop us from going for a swim. Let's hide our bikes in these weeds. We can go down to the creek and walk along the bank until we're out of sight from the road. Then we can go skinny-dipping."

With no more convincing than that, David dropped his bike to the ground and turning to me said with a challenge in his voice, "OK, Paul, how come you are so slow?"

"Chill out, David," I challenged back. "I want to make sure my bike is well hidden in the weeds. I don't want it to get stolen and then have to walk all the way back home."

With our bikes now well hidden, we walked beside the creek and followed it for a while until we came to a couple of bends in the creek where we knew nobody would be able to see us from the gravel road.

Finally, I said with a great amount of satisfaction, "David, this is the spot where we can go swimming. Look, here is a good-sized pool, and the water isn't flowing very fast at all here. Let's leave our lunches on the ground and go swimming now. We can eat our lunches later."

The creek's water was cool to our hot bodies, and we enjoyed swimming around in that little pool. While splashing around, I joyfully said to David, "This is a great spot to camp out sometime. There are lots of grass here where we could pitch a tent, and we could spend a lot of time just swimming around in the pool or lying on the grass. We could pretend we were Tom Sawyer and Huck Finn."

"That's a great idea, Paul, but we don't have a tent. And Mom and Dad likely wouldn't let us camp out here anyhow." He shrugged his shoulders in a dejected fashion as he continued, "How would we get all our stuff over to this place anyhow? A tent would be too hard to carry on our bikes."

I had to agree with David. We would have a big problem convincing Mom and Dad that we could go camping on our own. But I didn't want to tell him that I'd already given up on that idea, so instead I tried to sound as sure of myself as I could, and so with an extra measure of bravado in my voice, I said, "You and me, David, we can figure this out together. We'll make it happen somehow."

We found out later that creek's name was Catfish Creek, but we didn't see any catfish. The fact is that neither David nor I knew what a catfish even looked like.

We enjoyed our little lunches Mom made us and then put our clothes on again and hiked back along the creek until we came to where we'd hidden our bikes. I guess we'd hidden them well because they were right where we'd left them.

By now we were feeling really good. David's butt didn't hurt anymore, and so we jumped back on our bikes and continued to follow the road wherever it might lead us. And wouldn't you know it, within a mile we were at White's Pond. That's what we called it, but its real name was Springwater Conservation Park.

"This is where we wanted to go, David, when we left the house this morning. We've finally made it here, and I'd sure like to go swimming again, but look at all the people on the grass at the edge of the pond. We sure can't go skinny-dipping. We'd get into trouble for sure if we did."

David spoke up first after we'd been sitting on the grass looking longingly at the pond and secretly wishing we'd now brought our bathing suits. "I'm getting bored, Paul, just looking at everyone swimming and we aren't."

"I am too, David, but I have an idea. Let's just go swimming anyhow. We can take our shirts off and our socks and boots off too, but we'll just leave our pants on. We'll be dry long before we get home."

David agreed that was a good idea, and we were suddenly having fun again splashing and swimming around in White's Pond.

They say all good things finally come to an end, and so it did that wonderful afternoon. David and I were back on the grass trying to dry out in the sun when I rolled over to face him and said, "This is going to take a long time for us to just lay here and let our pants dry out before we head back home. I think we'd better get going even before we're dry."

David's response was a simple "Yes, let's get going. Anyhow I'm getting hungry, and I don't want to be late for supper."

Quickly getting back on our bikes, we began to retrace our journey. Soon we were passing the creek where we'd skinny-dipped and then the horses where David had tried his luck at bareback riding. We paid no attention to the horses even though they were all standing by the fence watching us.

We were both getting tired when David verbalized his feelings. "Paul, how much longer is it before we get home? My legs are tired, and I feel like I've got lead in my boots."

"David, look up, will you? There's Centennial Ave just ahead. We'll be home in a couple of minutes."

## Skinny-Dipping in the Good Old Summertime

Skinny-dipping became a way of life for David and me. We had some ponds near our home, and we would often go swimming in those ponds. Behind Brian's house, maybe a half mile back in the fields, was a good-sized bush and a nice old pond on the other side of that bush. All three of us had been back to that pond a time or two last year, but so far this year we'd not been there or had even thought about going there.

It was Brian who came up with the suggestion that would get us motivated to revisit that pond. "Paul and David, why don't we go back to the pond that is behind my house beyond that bush back there. We've not been there for a long time." David and I were unanimous in our immediate response. "Let's do it, Brian."

Our hike didn't take too long as we walked through the field that farmer Small had planted with corn that would become feed for his pigs. It didn't take very long either to walk through the bush.

Arriving at the pond, I excitedly yelled out, "Hey, guys, it looks like someone was here before us and made a raft. We can pretend we are Tom Sawyer and Huck Finn. Let's get on the raft and float around the pond."

Both Brian and David agreed that would be fun, but Brian said, "Paul, I'd like to go swimming in this pond as well, but I didn't bring my bathing suit."

"Not to worry, Brian," I said. "David and I always go skinny-dipping. We're alone here, so why not skinny-dip here too, Brian."

There you go, three boys pretending they were on the mighty Mississippi River going downstream on their raft and skinny-dipping in the shallows. What more fun could three boys have?

"What more fun could three boys have?" you ask? Well, just let me tell you what more fun Brian, David, and me, Paul, had on one hot day in particular, the summertime of 1961.

"Hi, Brian, David and I are going to pedal our bikes a couple of miles down Centennial Ave to an old gravel pit. My dad said it looked like an older pit that wasn't used anymore, and it's on the corner of Centennial Ave and another road he called John Wise Line."

"That's a funny name for a road, Paul. I'll ask my mom if I can go with you."

Coming back to his door, Brian said his mom would allow him to go with us to that old pit, but she said we'd have to be very careful not to fall in.

Out of hearing from Brian's mom, I said to David and Brian, "We all took swimming lessons at the YMCA a couple of years ago. I don't think we'll have any problems swimming. Let's just stay close to shore and not go swimming out in the middle of the pond."

It was agreed that was what we'd do, so with lunches in our backpacks and after saying goodbye to our mothers, all three of us headed for the old gravel pit.

"Oh, nuts, it looks like some kids have beat us to the pit," I exclaimed, but in my next breath, I said, "But look, those three bikes are girls' bikes. We'll just sneak in real quiet like and spy on them. Maybe we can scare them and they'll leave."

David quickly responded. "OK, Paul, Brian and I will follow you."

"Shush!" I whispered hoarsely. "Look, guys, they must be skinny-dipping. Here are all their clothes. Let's have some fun and take their clothes and put them out by the road."

"No, Paul," David whispered back to me. "Let's take their clothes and put them on the other side of the road. Then we'll come back here and make a lot of noise and scare them."

"David, you're a crazy guy," Brian said.

But all three of us nevertheless sneaked back to the road with all the clothes that the girls left under a bush, and indeed hid them in the ditch on the opposite side of the road. We pretended to be just a little kind to them though, and left their shoes where they were under that bush because I'd whispered, "We should leave their shoes here so they don't get sore feet walking through this bush and the weeds to get across the road."

They didn't even know we had been there because we were so quiet. They were making enough noise amongst themselves that they wouldn't have heard us even if we weren't quiet.

"OK, guys, let's take our bikes and go back to the other side of the pit this time and make a lot of noise and pretend we're going to get into the pond."

"Why would we do that, Paul?" Brian asked in a whispered voice. "If our mothers ever heard about us skinny-dipping with some girls who were also swimming bare naked at this pit, we'd get one whale of a good licking and probably be grounded for life."

"No way, Brian. Those girls don't know us, and we don't know them. They must live around here somewhere, but I don't think I've ever seen their faces before. We're safe. Our moms will never find out. But I don't want to go swimming anyhow. I want to scare them out of the pond."

That's exactly what we did. We sneaked around to the far side of the pond, and then we made enough noise to scare the girls out of the water. But when they ran to get their clothes, they couldn't find them. It was funny watching those girls trying to hide behind a couple of small bushes and yell at us.

"You boys are mean. Tell us where you hid our clothes. Our moms will kill us if we go home without our clothes." They were becoming rather frantic, and one of them started to cry.

I think Brian had more compassion on those poor girls than either David or me. So after we'd had some more laughs at their expense, Brian yelled out to them, "Hey, you girls, you will find your clothes on the other side of the road in the ditch."

Well, if you're wondering if they ever did find their clothes, yes, they did. They were nearly hysterical crying and laughing at the same time. They called us a few names I expect they must have heard from their fathers. We three ragamuffins laughed until the tears rolled down our cheeks, but we didn't go swimming that day because we just knew that if we were skinny-dipping, they'd return and hide our clothes. That wasn't going to happen.

Sometime later, I thought I remembered who one of those three girls might be, but I never told David or Brian. I'd seen her at school sometimes, but she was in a different classroom, and I didn't know her name.

## Riding Bareback on Ole Paint

On the next concession south on Centennial Ave lived a friend. His dad had a small farm, which my father called a "hobby farm." Mike had a beautiful horse that he had named Ole Paint. I asked him once why he'd call his horse Ole Paint, and he said it was because of the three different colors on its hide.

On this particular day toward the middle of August 1962 as Brian, David, and I were just hanging around our yards, Mike rode up on his bike. "Hi, guys, what are you doing today?"

"Not doing anything, Mike," retorted Brian. "Do you want to hang around with us?"

"Sure, I'll hang around with you, but I've got a better idea. Why don't you all come down to my place and we can ride around on my horse Ole Paint."

Brian spoke up first and said, "Hey, that's a great idea, Mike. Give me a couple of minutes and I'll tell my mom where I'm going."

"Hey, Mike, I'll tell my mom as well where David and I will be," I exclaimed.

By this time, I had just graduated from grade 8. I was going to go to high school next fall. But I digress. This is a story about a horse called Ole Paint and a ride I'd never forget.

We all went with Mike down to his house about a half mile south of where we lived. We were leaning on the paddock fence when Ole Paint walked over to us. "My horse is as tame as a kitten. Look at him, he's as gentle as a puppy," whispered Mike as he gave his horse an apple to eat.

Brian was first to take a turn riding Mike's horse. David took his turn next. Then Mike said to me, "Paul, it's your turn. Have you ever ridden a horse before?"

"Well, I have but only a couple of times." Laughing, I said, "Riding a wooden horse on the merry-go-round at the London Fair doesn't count though, does it?"

"When I was a little kid, I was on a donkey once, but the man who owned it just walked it around in a circle at a carnival we had in St. Thomas."

"Well," Mike said, "you will like riding Ole Paint. You saw how nice he was when Brian and David rode him. Come on, climb up on the fence, and I'll bring him over to you."

When Ole Paint was beside me, I climbed over onto his back. "Here, take the reins," Mike said, and then he told me how to use them.

But unbeknown to me, because I guess I just wasn't paying any attention, was the fact that a very large mound of fresh horse manure was directly behind the horse. Before I could get Ole Paint to walk around the enclosed paddock, Mike picked up a switch and swatted Ole Paint on the rear.

Can you guess what happened next? Well, let me tell you. When Mike swatted Ole Paint, that horse reared up on its hind legs. That must have hurt because he let out a good snort. But I was sitting bareback on Ole Paint, and I slipped off the rear of that horse and promptly landed in that fresh pile of horse manure. Boy-oh-boy, did those other three boys laugh their heads off.

"Hey, you guys, that's not funny. Look at me. I'm covered in horse manure from head to foot." But that just made them laugh all the more. Now I had to go home, but I didn't want to ride my bike because I'd get manure all over the seat and probably all over the whole bike.

"Hey, Paul, we thought you knew how to ride a horse," yelled out my own brother, David.

Brian, David, and Mike were still laughing at me when I left that paddock and pushed my bike to the road. It was going to be a long, smelly walk home, and I wasn't happy at the least.

On the way out the gate from Mike's place, his younger sister ran up beside me and started to laugh as well.

"Serves you right, Paul. Do you remember last year when you went down to that old gravel pit another mile south of us? Well, I was there with my friends when Brian and David and you hid our clothes when we were skinny-dipping. That was really mean of you three guys to do that to us. We were having a lot of fun until you came along and spoiled our day. And it wasn't nice of you to laugh at us when we had to get out of that gravel pit, and we were all naked. And then on top of that, you hid our clothes in the ditch on the other side of the road. We had to run across the road and run around in the ditch until we found our clothes, and we were scared someone might come along and see us running around on the road or in the ditch naked as well."

"Yes, so what, Melody, but you have to admit, it was kind of funny. If it was the other way around and we three guys were skinny-dipping in that pit, you and your friends would have done the same thing to us or worse. You'd probably have taken our clothes completely away, and we would have had to go all the way back home naked.

"OK," I said. "So you were one of the girls there that day skinny-dipping. I wondered if it was you, but I wasn't really sure. I guess you got me back real good when you got Mike to do your dirty work."

Melody was having a good laugh at my expense and then said, "I'm going to call those other two girls up on the phone and tell them that today was payback time. I just wish they were here with me to see you land on your back in that fresh pile of horse manure."

But Melody continued to walk with me the half mile to my house. She teased me and laughed at me so much so that I began to laugh with her.

Still laughing, I said to her, "I figure we must still be friends, eh, Melody? At least I have my clothes on."

Arriving finally at my home, I didn't just go up the stairs and walk into the house. If my mother saw me do that, she'd kill me for sure.

Instead I got near the back door and yelled at the top of my lungs, "Mom, come out here. I need your help." Opening the back door and looking at me, she began to laugh hysterically. "What did you fall into, Paul? You really stink. I bet you've fallen into a big pile of horse manure."

"Yes, you're right, Mom, so hose me off with the garden hose, will you?"

"Go into the backyard, Paul, and wait for me. I'll get the garden hose and turn it on. I hope I can get all that manure off."

By now I'd forgotten about Melody. I guess I figured she'd just turn around and walk back to her home. But I was badly mistaken. She had hidden behind a bush by the garage and was a witness to all that happened next.

I stood there in the backyard, and by now I was shivering because the water was cold. Would you believe it, my mother didn't stop laughing the whole time she hosed me down from head to foot. And even at that, she couldn't get all the manure off me and certainly not any of the stink.

"Paul, get out of all your clothes. I mean everything. Don't you move because I'm going to hose you off again." With that comment she threw a bar of soap my way.

"Mom, no way. That water is cold and I'll be naked."

"Well, you have a choice, Paul. Either get naked and stand there while I hose you off some more, or maybe you'd like to take that soap and hike back to the pond behind Small's farm and wash yourself off."

"Great choice, Mom. Thanks a lot. Here I am naked as the day I was born and you're hosing me off in cold water and laughing yourself silly."

Mom wasn't the only one laughing herself silly. Do you remember I'd said Melody had hidden behind a bush by the garage? She was laughing herself silly as well, but I didn't know that until a few days later when she was riding her bike past my house. She saw me out in the yard and stopped.

Melody was laughing again when she came into my yard to talk with me.

"Hi, Paul. You sure were a sight for sore eyes when you fell in that pile and then had to go home and call out to your mother to hose you down. I didn't go home after I had walked with you to your house. I hid behind that bush beside your garage. I saw the whole thing. I saw you standing naked and getting hosed down with cold water. I nearly fainted, I was laughing so hard and trying to not make any noise."

"Oh, thanks, Melody. You were a real snoop, weren't you? I wondered why you would want to walk all the way back to my house when I was covered in horse manure. You must have figured I'd end up in the backyard getting hosed down."

"Yup, that is what I figured your mom would do. So here's the deal, Paul. If you talk about what you did when you and David and Brian hid my friends' and my clothes at the pit, then I'll tell everyone what I saw the other day when your mom hosed you down in your backyard. Oh, but I didn't tell you who the other two girls with me at that old gravel pit were. They were not only my friends, they were also my cousins."

"I guess you have a deal, Melody. You'll never hear another word from me. So does that mean that maybe we can be friends and not enemies?"

"Maybe, Paul, but you'd better be real nice to me from now on."

## Four Spots of Really Green Grass

I have another funny story that I'm sure you'll enjoy reading. It's a rather fishy story to say the least. It might be fishy, but it's not stinky like the story of me falling in a pile of fresh horse manure.

"David, we've got good fishing rods and some tackle, but we've never gone fishing. Dad's always too busy, or the weather just isn't nice enough to go fishing. Do you remember when we went to White's Pond and on the way we went skinny-dipping in that creek? Do you remember what the name of that creek was?"

"No, I don't remember that creek's name," David replied. "But I do remember swimming in it. I thought the water was pretty nice."

"The name of that creek is Catfish Creek, David. Why don't we take our fishing rods and pedal our bikes to that creek and go fishing. Maybe we'll even catch some catfish."

"What do catfish look like, Paul?"

"I saw a picture of a catfish in a book at the school library, David. It's ugly. It has a smooth body and is sort of green or blue. Its tail is forked, and it has whiskers around its mouth. I don't know if people eat them, but let's go fishing and see if we can catch some."

"Yes, if we can catch some, Paul, maybe Mom will cook them for us. Dad likes fish, and he's taken us to Port Stanley a few times so he could buy some Lake Erie perch from the fishermen when they come into port with their fishing tugs. Maybe catfish taste good like perch."

With lunches packed in our backpacks and fishing rods tied crossways on the handlebars, we said goodbye to Mom and pedaled our bikes to Catfish Creek.

It only took us about an hour to get there because by now we knew the way and we didn't get lost like the first time we went there. We were hot and tired from pedaling, but we figured if we went swimming we'd probably not do any fishing.

"Hey, Paul, this is a good place to hide our bikes in the tall weeds. Let's go down the creek like we did when we went swimming and fish from that pool of water in the creek."

"That's a good idea, David," I said. And in just a few short minutes we cast our fishing hooks into the water. We'd brought some worms we'd found in the garden so we put a worm on our hooks. I guess catfish like worms because, in no time at all, David caught the first catfish.

"This fish is ugly," David yelled. "It's as ugly as you said it was, Paul. I don't think I'd want to eat it."

"Hey, David, it's ugly, but you don't eat the head and that really awful-looking skin. Mom said if we caught some fish she would fillet them and fry them in the frying pan for us."

Before I could barely finish my sentence, I caught a catfish too. David, look at the fish I just caught and exclaimed. "It's a little bigger than the one I caught, and it's a whole lot uglier."

"I don't think I ever want to go swimming in this creek again, Paul. Do catfish bite?"

"They must have been in the creek when we were swimming, but because we didn't get bit by any fish, I guess they don't bite humans."

We hung around that pool for another hour, and wouldn't you know it, we each caught another catfish. These fish were just as ugly as the first two we caught, but I kept telling David, "I've heard that catfish are really tasty. I think Mom will enjoy frying them for us, and we even have enough so when Dad comes home he can have some too."

We put those four catfish into an old laundry bag I'd taken from the basement without telling Mom. When I'd hung that bag over the back of my bike seat, I said to my brother, "See, David, it's going to be easy getting these fish home. They're not in the way of my pedals, and it's not going to be too hard pedaling because they don't weigh that much."

Well, it was harder pedaling with the fish swinging back and forth in that old laundry bag, but I wasn't going to tell David that.

Banging on the back door, I yelled out, "Mom, come to the door. David and I caught four fish. You can cook them up for supper. I bet you Dad will like them."

When Mom poked her head out the door and looked into that laundry bag, she snorted. "Paul, those are the ugliest fish I've ever seen. How could they taste good if they look so ugly? I'm not going to cook them for supper. You two boys take them out to the garden and bury them in the farthest corner away from the house. Be gone with you and do it now."

"Aw, David, I thought Mom would like it that we caught four fish. I don't think they would taste bad, they just look ugly or maybe a bit scary too."

"Get a shovel from the garage, David. I've got an idea. Let's bury them in the backyard. I've heard Dad complain about his backyard grass dying because there hasn't been any rain for a long time. Maybe these dead fish will help the grass keep growing. It would be like putting fertilizer on the grass."

With that shovel, David and I dug four holes in the grass. "David, don't dig your hole too deep. Let's just make the holes shallow. That way I figure the grass will stay greener."

The job of digging four holes was soon completed. "It looks good, Paul. We've buried the four catfish and put the grass back on top of them. What should we do with the little bit of extra earth that is left over from the holes we dug?"

"Let's just throw that extra dirt in the garden, David. The grass looks nice and level again, and I can hardly tell where we dug those holes. Dad won't be able to tell where we dug the holes either. This will be really funny when the grass gets real green over the dead catfish. It will be greener than anywhere else in Dad's backyard."

By the time next spring had arrived, David and I had pretty much forgotten where we'd buried those four catfish until I noticed one day something interesting. Calling to David who was also outside in the backyard, I said, "Come here, David. Look at these four super-green spots in the backyard out here by the poplar trees."

"Wow," David exclaimed. "Those four patches are so different in color to the rest of the yard. And look how much longer the grass is at those spots than anywhere else in the yard, Paul. Those four catfish did it. They fertilized those four squares of grass. This is too funny."

Wouldn't you believe it? That night at the supper table Dad spoke up to Mom. "Rhoda, I cut the grass this afternoon, and there are four spots about one-foot square each in the yard out by the poplar trees, where the grass is incredibly green. It is really strange. I've never seen anything like it in the yard before."

David and I didn't look at each other because we knew if we did we'd end up laughing our heads off. Dad would ask us what was so funny, and we'd have to confess to what we'd done.

Later that night, I said to David, "We'd better keep our little secret about the dead catfish. Mom didn't know either why there were four especially green patches in the yard."

All that summer those four patches of grass remained incredibly green.

# THREE

# TEENAGE YEARS ATTENDING HIGH SCHOOL

## I Nearly Walked on Water

SPRING HAD COME early, and I felt stuck in high school. I was in grade 10 at Central Elgin Collegiate Institute on Chestnut Street in St. Thomas, Ontario, and I was daydreaming as usual.

"Paul O'Brien, answer the question please," came the voice of my teacher, Mr. Andrews, crashing in on my preoccupied state of mind. I'd been daydreaming again. How was I going to dodge the bullet on the teacher's question?

"Ah, Mr. Andrews, I've been pondering that question for a while, and I've been unable to fully formulate an answer to it" was my smart-aleck answer, which just seemed to flow off the top of my head.

I'd used that line on another teacher a few days earlier when he caught me sleeping with my head in my right hand. Fortunately, I was still holding my pen in my left hand as if ready to write an answer to any question that would be presented to me. But how many times could I use that excuse for daydreaming or outright sleeping?

I really think Mr. Andrews was catching on to my wayward attitude toward his class, so he didn't let my comment ride in this instance and instead responded with his own sharp comment aimed directly at me.

"OK, Paul, how about you give me a short synopsis on the subject you were daydreaming about. If I think it is a worthy answer, I will let it stand. If it doesn't stand the test of approval from me and the class, you are going to remain after school and address your attitude with me here in this room at 3:30 p.m. Your answer please."

"Very well, Mr. Andrews," I answered in my best deep and scholarly voice. "The fact is that I was daydreaming. I saw myself outside in the fresh air on my bicycle, my shirt open and flapping in the wind as I furiously pedaled toward the park, Pinafore Park to be exact. The expression on my face was pure joy. Forgetting about lunch, forgetting about this afternoon's classes, my intent was to seek only hedonistic pleasure."

"Mr. O'Brien, I must admit that your answer does indeed reflect an excellent response regarding the discipline of this class. Considering that this is an English class, I will accept your answer. Now, as to the response that the class will give, that will be the determining factor whether you remain after class or are free to pursue your own interests at 3:30 p.m."

"Class, is Paul free to pursue his own interests at 3:30 p.m., or is he consigned to remain here? Hands up if he is free. If no hands are raised, he stays after class.

"Paul, you and I will respect the class's response. Their answer to that question was unanimous. All hands were raised."

"You are free to pursue your own interests after school today. However, there is one caveat. You will present to the class an appropriate answer to the question presented to you today at the beginning of the next class. And you will also write a short essay describing the reality of your daydream. You will be graded on this essay as well."

Once the class was dismissed, I was able to catch up to my buddy, and grabbing him by the shoulder, I happily said with laughter in my voice, "Smitty, talk about good fortune smiling on me. I get to live out my daydream and write about it."

"Dude, I thought for a few minutes you were going down in smoke in Mr. Andrews's English class, but your mouth got you out of that jam. So what are you going to do?"

"I'm going to do exactly what my daydream was about. Do you want to have a part in my little adventure?"

"OK, Dude, you'd better tell me about this little adventure. I sure don't want to get into any trouble with Mr. Andrews."

"Come on, Smitty, have a little faith in me, eh? You and I are going to skip out of school at lunchtime, and we're going to check out our favorite swimming hole at Pinafore Park. We'll ride over there on our bikes, and we'll be back in time for the afternoon classes at 1:00 p.m."

"Dude, if you're going to use my name in your short essay, you'd better be careful. And you'd better let me read it before you present it to the class tomorrow too."

"OK, that's a deal, Smitty. Now let's get our bikes and get on over to the pond at Pinafore Park."

My daydream accomplished, we busted a kidney pedaling our bikes back to the high school at which point Smitty yelled out, "That was an absolute riot, Dude. And we made it back to school in time for the afternoon classes. So you'll let me read your essay tomorrow before English class?"

"I've got a spare this afternoon, Smitty, so I'm going to go down to the library, and I'll have my essay done before I go home. If you catch me before I bicycle home, I'll give you a copy of my short essay. I'll get it photocopied at the library when I'm done writing it."

"That's a deal, Dude. See you at 3:30 p.m."

**A Short Essay by Paul O'Brien**

The location was St. Thomas, Ontario. The setting was Pinafore Park Pond. The time of the year was specifically April 15, 1965, and it was Thursday midday. My buddy Smitty and I had skipped out of school at lunchtime just to check out our favorite swimming hole.

What a beautiful early spring day it was. There were no clouds in the sky. The rich, deep blue of the sky above me tapered to a light blue on the horizon. A gentle spring breeze stirred the long grass where I stood. The earthy fragrance of the soil as it awakened from a long winter sleep made me want to inhale deeply. In the background was Pinafore Park Pond. It was deep and bore the color of the richest dark blue of the sky that it reflected. This was my favorite swimming hole. I had been here countless times, but this year it was the earliest I'd ever been to the pond.

I remember the nature sounds so clearly. There must have been hundreds of young bullfrogs around the banks of the pond. They were all chirping their song in unison. The gentle sounds of nature always quieted my spirit. I drank in nature's orchestra deeply as I listened. It seemed like the few early-arriving songbirds wanted to harmonize with the frogs as well.

Trees devoid of foliage stood naked in the background. They still bore the marks of the frigid assaulting northern winds, but you could just detect their buds on the branches. There were no fences around the pond, and the terrain sloped gently down to the water's edge where early cattails were already poking their stalks out of the water.

Leaning casually on my bicycle, I had a big smile, and the happiness in my heart radiated on my face. My blue jeans were scuffed and somewhat tattered, and my shirttails were both in and out. The faded blue color of my shirt seemed to complement the light blue color of my eyes. I sported a brush cut, and what color you could see of my short hair appeared to be a dusty brown. A big grin on my face revealed the deep-seated happiness of my soul. My jeans jacket lay casually across the handlebars.

My willpower evaporated like early-morning mist on the pond. I couldn't resist the overpowering urge to jump in and experience the invigorating stimulation of cold water on bare skin. So I did exactly that. Wow! I will not soon forget the startling sensation of frigid water on warm skin. I literally came alive. I sucked in copious amounts of air and involuntarily held my breath.

There I was, quickly dropping my core temperature, and my buddy Smitty on the shore was nearly having a fit—he was laughing so hard. He was slapping his legs profusely as he doubled over in merriment. I only know of two people who ever walked on water, and one of them actually sank, but I assure you, I came out of that pond like I was running on water.

Ah! The joy of living out a daydream.

### The End

"Hi, Dude. Did you get your daydream essay done?"

"Yes, I sure did, Smitty, and here's a copy of it, which I promised to give to you. I've even had time to give a copy of it to Mr. Andrews. Boy-oh-boy, I sure hope I get a good grade on it."

"You probably will, Dude, but I'd be careful if I were you. Daydreaming in his class is going to get you into a lot of trouble if he catches you doing it again."

"I know you're right, Smitty. Hey, I'll see you tomorrow. I've got a three-mile bike ride before I'm home."

Catching up to my best buddy in the hall outside our homeroom, I jokingly greeted him. "Hi, Smitty, did you like my little essay from yesterday?"

"It was pretty good, Dude. But the real question is, will Mr. Andrews like it and give you a good mark?"

"Let's head off to English class, Smitty. I'll find out soon enough what kind of a grade I'll get."

"Good morning, Mr. O'Brien. Did you get a good sleep last night? I don't want to catch you sleeping in my class today, and no daydreaming either. Do you understand that?"

"Yes, sir. I think I have everything under control today."

"So far so good, Dude. I thought maybe Mr. Andrews might jump on you as soon as you walked through his classroom door."

"No way, Smitty. I could tell by looking into his eyes that I aced it.'"

The echo of the 9:00 a.m. bell hadn't quite disappeared before Mr. Andrews called the class to order.

"Good morning, class. Shall we put Mr. O'Brien on the hot seat? You'll remember I caught him spaced out yesterday in class, as he said 'daydreaming.'

"I've put his essay on the overhead. Take a moment and read it please. We will discuss it briefly after you've read it.

"You first, Mr. Smith. He put you in his essay. Were you in fact with him yesterday, and are you able to account for the accuracy of this essay?"

"Yes, sir, Mr. Andrews. I was with him. I'd say he described the events that transpired very accurately."

"Well, I did have my doubts that both of you actually went over to the Pinafore Park Pond, so after school was out, I drove over there myself.

"I have only one question for you, Mr. O'Brien. Are these your socks?"

You could have heard the class laugh even at the end of the hall outside the closed classroom door.

"Oh, yes, they are, Mr. Andrews. I forgot them yesterday after I'd had that short swim. I didn't remember that I'd forgotten to put them back on until I got home from school."

Well, the class also voted on my essay, and by their raised hands, they'd indicated I'd passed that test with flying colors.

## Oh the Embarrassment

There were some high school subjects that I really enjoyed, and shop was at the top of my list. Mr. Bower, the shop teacher, was a pretty cool guy. He let us have some fun while we were doing shop assignments right in class, if that fun wasn't overly disruptive.

I guess you could say the little prank pulled on me was good-natured, but this prank did cause me a lot of embarrassment, and it certainly was personally disruptive.

The rest of that Wednesday afternoon didn't move fast enough for me. Three-thirty was so absolutely slow in coming. Was the final bell never going to ring so I'd be free of these prison walls?

One of the most difficult things I'd ever had to do in high school was staring me in the face. How could I hide the telltale appearance that was so evident should anyone directly approach me or observe me?

At last the final bell rang. I escaped as quickly as I could. I didn't need my friends from shop class catching up to me to tease me or ridicule me even though what had happened to me was a prank.

I arrived at my car unscathed. It was then that I became aware that the issue that had been my source of embarrassment had pretty much disappeared. Whew. Thank goodness for that.

I needed to go somewhere and chill out, so on this particular hot fall day in October 1967 I headed for the Rendezvous Restaurant. I'd just plunked myself down in my favorite booth when a shadow crossed my table. Naturally I looked up to see who was standing beside me.

"Hey, oh, hi, Jo-Anne. I didn't see you here when I came in. Did I walk right by your table? My head must be in the clouds."

"No, Paul, you came in here before I did, but I was just about right behind you. For sure your head must have been in the clouds because I called after you and you just kept going. You didn't hear me, I guess."

"Oh, Jo-Anne, I'm really sorry. Hey, are you going to stay awhile? Come and sit at my booth and I'll buy you a Cherry Coke. Would you like some fries too? The waitress hasn't come to my booth, so I haven't ordered yet."

"Hey, that's swell, Paul. Yes, I'd like a Cherry Coke and some fries. What are you getting?"

"The same thing, Jo-Anne."

"I didn't see you in English class this afternoon, Paul. I knew you were at school today because you and I are in the same homeroom, and I saw you in the halls a couple of times as well. The last time I saw you was when you were heading for your shop class and I was heading for home economics. So what happened?"

"Well, as they say in the movies, 'here is my story and I'm sticking to it.' I did go to shop, Jo-Anne. Today all the guys were working on making a funnel out of tin. The project went like this. You had to cut a piece of tin out of a larger piece, and there was a pattern to be followed. Once it was cut, you had to run that piece through a set of rollers to bend it into a cone.

"I had already done that but was one of the last guys to get my time on the rollers, so there were others who had nearly finished their funnel while I was still working on mine."

"That sounds pretty neat, Paul. Sometimes I wish I could do shop with all you guys. But you know how it is, the guys do shop and the girls do home economics."

"Yes, I don't understand why the girls can't do shop, but I suppose if they could then the guys would have to do home economics too. I think that could get real messy."

"I don't know, Paul. I think I've heard that you like doing some cooking when you're at home. I think you'd probably do all right in home economics as well as any of the girls. And for that matter, I think any girl who wanted to do shop with the guys would be able to do as well as any of them could do."

"Yes, you're right, Jo-Anne, but today if you were doing shop with the guys, what happened to me might have just as easily happened to you. If it did, you'd be as embarrassed as I was."

"OK, OK, Paul, so what happened to you today in shop?"

"Well, as I'd said, I was still working on my funnel. I wasn't paying too much attention to the other guys because some of them had finished and were just hanging around back at the desks. They seemed to be having a bit of fun, and Mr. Bower was with them.

"Don had finished his funnel, and so had Gregg. They were going around to some of the other guys and sticking Don's funnel down the front of these guys' pants and seeing if when Gregg placed a penny on that guy's nose when he tilted his head back, if he could drop that penny in the funnel when he lowered his head."

"That seems simple enough, Paul. I suppose everyone was successful at hitting the funnel with the penny when he tilted his head down."

"That was pretty much the case, Jo-Anne. There was a couple of guys that missed the funnel, but nearly everyone was successful. I'd stopped to watch a couple of times, but I still had to finish my project, if I could before the end of class."

"Well, how does that become an embarrassment to you, Paul?"

"It went like this, Jo-Anne. Don came up to me and asked me to try to drop the penny in the funnel. I told him that would be a piece of cake and took the funnel from him and stuffed it down the front of my pants. Gregg gave me the penny to place on my nose when I'd tilted my head back, but before I could drop the penny in the funnel, someone else dumped a whole glass of cold water down the funnel."

"I'm sorry, Paul. Pardon me for smiling, I'm trying not to laugh, really I am."

"If it would have happened to anyone else, I'd have laughed as well, but I have to tell you that water was cold, and it spread all over the front of my pants and even ran down both of my pant legs too."

"I can just imagine what it looked like, Paul. Dare I say it? It must have looked like you peed your pants."

"Come on, Jo-Anne, wipe that big grin off your face, and yes, I looked a mess. Anyone who wasn't in shop class would naturally expect I'd had a big accident.

"There I was, Jo-Anne, looking like I'd peed myself, and how was I going to explain that some guys pulled a prank on me in shop? Do you think for a moment that anyone would believe me? Maybe you would, Jo-Anne, maybe you'd believe me, but not many would."

"You're right, Paul. That would be hard to believe it was just a prank and not an accident. So what did you do? English class was next, and you didn't show up. Mr. Andrews marked you absent. He even asked if anyone had seen you. Don had answered that you were in shop class, but he didn't know where you'd gone after that. A couple of guys sort of snickered, but nobody said anything about the water-down-the-funnel prank. I'll ask you again, Paul, what did you do, or where did you go?"

"I left shop and started to walk down the hall. Some girls had just walked by heading the same way, so I figured I'd walk right behind them. I knew they wouldn't look back at a single guy walking behind them, so I felt pretty safe. They didn't see my embarrassment, so all was good.

"I certainly wasn't going to show up in English class, no way. But I decided while walking behind the girls that I'd escape to the cafeteria and grab a seat at a table beside the windows. It would look like I had a spare, especially if I laid some books spread out in front of me and pretended to be doing an assignment or studying.

"A couple of people came and went while I was in the cafeteria. One person even said hi, but nobody really knew why I was there, and anyhow, they couldn't see my wet pants and legs because the table was my protection from prying eyes."

"Hey, that's crazy, Paul. Way to go. You dodged the bullet on that one, didn't you? And I guess while you were there you were also drying out, so to speak."

"Thankfully I was getting dry. When the final bell rang, I beat a hasty retreat to my car before anyone could check out my wet pants. It wasn't until I actually got to my car that I realized I had pretty much dried out."

"That is one crazy story, Paul. Although you missed English class, I can tell you what was assigned for homework. Here are the things Mr. Andrews wanted us to do for our next assignment. Good thing I have it in my backpack with me. You can copy it out. Here's a blank piece of paper for you."

"Thank you so much, Jo-Anne. I think I'll go back to the high school before I drive home and get the other books I need for the rest of my homework from the morning classes."

We chatted for a few more minutes before Jo-Anne looked at her watch and exclaimed, "Paul, I'm supposed to be at my dad's store in a couple of minutes. He wants me to work for a couple of hours today, and I'll be late if I don't leave right now. Sorry I have to run, but thanks for the Cherry Coke and fries."

With that brief explanation about her quick departure, Jo-Anne jumped up, blew me a kiss, and ran out the door.

"Aw, so much for wet pants and soggy shorts."

## Who Cut Your Hair, Paul?

One week before Canada's birthday in 1966, which was on a Friday, my friends Don, Bob, Dave (my brother), and Jo-Anne and Mary-Lynn (sisters) had gathered around a picnic table at Pinafore Park in St. Thomas to talk about what festivities we might be able to enter into because we knew this would be a celebration to remember.

"There is going to be a community parade next Friday, on July 1st," piped up Don. "It's going to go the length of Talbot Street starting at the east end from Timken's huge parking lot right through to Elgin Street on the west side of town."

Bob cut in at this point and said, "That's right, Don, and I heard it will then turn south on Elgin Street and proceed to Elm Street where it will again continue to Pinafore Park. There will be booths and displays set up here at the park, and there will also be a carnival set up in the huge ball diamond. Food booths will be located between the east pavilion and the swimming pools. And to top off these festivities will be a first-class fireworks display after nine at night."

Jo-Anne chimed in with the question that made us all stop and think. "We should all do something to celebrate in the parade. Do any of you have some suggestions?"

Dave had a great idea when he said, "Let's all dress up in something that would show that we honor and celebrate ninety-nine years. We could create some costumes that show some history of Canada's ninety-nine years as a nation."

"That's a great idea, Dave," said Mary-Lynn. "We could look at a few history books down at the library, and maybe we'd be able to design some costumes that reflect different periods in the past. For instance, maybe one of us could borrow a uniform of the Canadian Army for the First World War or the Second World War."

"I don't know about the First World War," said David, "but my father still has his uniform from the Second World War, and I know it would fit me."

This animated conversation continued until Jo-Anne asked me, "Paul, you've not said a word. Don't you have any ideas or suggestions?"

"I'm stuck on that because my dad and mom are going to have a float in the parade. They want to rent a flatbed truck and put up a big Amway display. Dad told me he wanted me to drive the truck. They'd ride on the float. What could I do to commemorate Canada's ninety-ninth birthday while driving a truck?"

Dave was fast on the draw with a smart answer to my question. "Paul, why don't you dress up like a Native Canadian Indian?"

"Sure, Dave, where would I get a full headdress for that costume?"

"No, forget about a feathered headdress. I could cut your hair and give you a Mohawk. Your hair is dark enough, but we could dye it blacker if it was needed, and I'd shave both sides and back of your head.

We could even put a band around your head and put a big old pigeon feather in the back of it."

"Uh-huh, Dave, and where are you going to get the clippers to cut my hair? Did you forget that Mom and Dad are away for a few days and won't be back until Thursday night, June 30th? How will I get into his barbershop and borrow some clippers? It will be too late by then to cut my hair."

"I know where you can get some clippers, Paul and Dave. We have some clippers at our home that we use to cut the hair on our poodle, Bridget."

"Hey, that's a great idea, Jo-Anne. Why don't we do that, Paul? I'll do the cutting, and you'll look really good sporting a Mohawk."

"I don't know about that, Dave. I'm not too interested in your suggestion."

Now Bob spoke up to challenge me. "Oh, come on, Paul. You have to be dressed up somehow even though you'll be driving the truck."

"Sure, Bob, and what about you? Both you and Don have become very quiet. Well, I have a suggestion for you two guys. Why don't you dress up like Voyageurs? Those guys helped to open up this country by canoe. One of you could even carry Bob's red canoe."

"Right on, Paul. Don and Bob would look great dressed as Voyageurs, and maybe they could even find some moccasins to wear with lumberjack shirts," suggested Jo-Anne.

It was soon decided that both Jo-Anne and Mary-Lynn would dress up in early 1900s period clothing. Long dresses and flowery hats would just be the style too.

"Hey, Paul, you haven't said you'd do the Mohawk. Why not?" asked Don.

"All you guys just get dressed up, but me, I have to get my head shaved. I don't like that idea too much."

"I have an idea, Paul," suggested Jo-Anne. "If each one of us chip in a dollar, would you get your head shaved by Dave? Where else are you going to make an easy five bucks?"

"How can I refuse five bucks? OK, I'll do it. So when is this going to happen? If you do it now, a week away from the parade, my hair will grow in quite a bit."

"I have a great suggestion," said Jo-Anne. "Let's have a party at my house on June 30th after our youth group meeting. Doesn't everyone remember that we will have our meeting one day early because Friday is July 1st? We could cut your hair at that time, and you'd be ready for the parade next day."

That's exactly how it happened. We all met again Thursday night. The party was great. Jo-Anne and Mary-Lynn fried up some hamburgers that we enjoyed with chips and dip and washed down with lots of sodas.

We had agreed beforehand that it would also be a dress rehearsal. Everyone changed into their costumes. Boy-oh-boy, did we ever look great. We had also acquired some Canadian flags, which we would wave as we walked in the parade.

Well, that is, everyone except me. I was going to drive my folks' Amway float.

"Your turn, Paul. Come over here and sit on this stool. Dave, here are the dog clippers. Do your magic on Paul's head. I've got the headband and a big feather I bought at a novelty shop in London. Paul can try it on after his buzz job."

"Not so fast, Jo-Anne. Where's my five bucks?"

"Hahaha. I knew you'd not agree to this haircut unless you had five bucks in your hand. Here you are, so sit down and shut up."

"You're heartless, Jo-Anne," I said. But I did sit down with that five bucks safely stuffed in my pants pocket.

I was presented with a mirror by Mary-Lynn who said, "You look absolutely handsome as a Mohawk, Paul. Here, check it out."

"I must admit, Mary-Lynn, I am one handsome dude."

"We know you're right, Paul, don't let it go to your head. You aren't that pretty," Bob said while sticking a finger in his mouth and making a sour face along with a disgusting gagging sound.

But it wasn't just smooth sailing for me when I arrived home later that Thursday evening. My father was still up, and when he saw my

Mohawk cut, he pretty near did a backward somersault. To say that he was a little ticked off would be an understatement.

"Paul, you're not going to drive my float tomorrow looking like that. You're going to have to wear a hat over your head."

"OK, Dad, I'll do that. I've got a nice red and white polka dot hat that will fit in with the celebrations," I said that just to get him off my back. I was tired and didn't want to argue about anything.

"Paul, are you going to chicken out and really wear an ugly hat after I gave you such a good Mohawk cut? I'm ashamed of you," said my brother as we were heading upstairs to our bedrooms.

"Shut up, Dave. I just said that to get Dad off my back. When I get in the truck and we've started to roll in the parade, I'll be looking the part that I've agreed to."

It was really crazy how that Canada Day Parade came together. The parade marshal put Bob, Don, Dave, Jo-Anne, and Mary-Lynn right in front of Dad's Amway float. Of course, I looked the part I was meant to be. I sported a beautiful dark Mohawk cut and a terrific red band with an awesome red feather in it.

Through the whole parade, we all got a lot of attention and a lot of waves too. Everyone looked great in their costumes and me in my band and feather. I think Dad and Mom thought everyone was waving and cheering for them. I wasn't going to tell them otherwise, but I knew it was because of us six chums. We were the reason for the loud cheers and boisterous waves from the bystanders.

But you know all good things have to come to an end, right? My dad shaved my head bald late that night. He said, "No son of mine is going to church on Sunday morning looking like that."

## Summer Vacation—Those Were the Days

A little background would be helpful here before I get into this story in a proper way. Growing up with my friends and my brothers we often gave each other nicknames and would go weeks, months, and often years never calling each other by our proper names but consistently by our nicknames.

For clarification purposes in the story I'm about to recount to you, my friend Bob's nickname was Horse Thief. David, my brother's nickname was Bing. And me, Paul, my nickname was Scallywag.

"Hey, Scallywag, did you know I'm turning seventeen the end of June, Thursday the 29th to be exact?"

"Well, no kidding Horse Thief, is that a fact? I suppose you want me to throw you a party, eh?"

"Well, sort of. What I was thinking was more like a weeklong party as in a camping trip. How about you, your brother Bing, and me, we head off to a provincial park somewhere and party-hardy?"

"OK, Horse Thief, sounds good so far. Fill me in with more details on this."

"We could rent an aluminum boat and motor and some life jackets. I'd get hold of my dad's big tent, and we all could contribute to the food we'd need for a week. My car wouldn't be big enough to carry a fourteen-foot aluminum boat on the roof, but my dad's car could. That Studebaker has enough room in the back for the outboard motor as well as all our gear."

"Hey, you old horse thief. That's way too much stuff to pack on your dad's station wagon. A better idea is to rent the boat with a trailer. You'd be able to keep the outboard motor with the boat, and the other stuff like the tent and food could go in the back of the Stude."

"Yes, your idea sounds good, Scallywag, and it makes sense, but I'm confident we can get the boat up on the roof strapped safely down on the rooftop carrier. I know the outboard motor will easily fit in the back, and anything extra that we can't put in the back we can put in that back seat. We could leave St. Thomas on Saturday the twenty-fourth and return on Saturday, July 1st."

"Well, that sounds good enough," I said with a bit of a frown on my face, "but why not stay in the park until July 3rd so we could celebrate Dominion Day there instead of driving back home? Are you forgetting that weekend will be a humdinger of a weekend, Horse Thief?"

"Oh, right. I forgot about that. We could pack a bunch of firecrackers and stuff, Scallywag. That would be a great place to celebrate my birthday and Canada's one hundredth birthday too."

"Sounds like a plan, Horse Thief."

The week preceding departure was busy. The boat and motor rental was secured and picked up Friday afternoon. The tent was packed and lots of food gathered up. Everything came together real nice-like.

We'd left St. Thomas when it was still dark, but by the time we were going by Milton on Highway 401, the sun had come up, and the day was already beginning to warm up nicely. Speaking to no one in particular, Horse Thief said with great enthusiasm, "Hey, guys, it sure is a beautiful day for a trip, eh? What more could we ask for?"

I answered back to the Horse Thief because I noticed Bing was sleeping in the back seat with his head up against some sleeping bags and other gear. "It sure is a grand day, and your dad's Stude looks pretty proud with that boat on its roof, eh? And we've made good time too because Toronto is just a few miles ahead of us. Going through there today should be a piece of cake."

"Should be a piece of cake, especially since we're going through at like 6:00 a.m. Good thing you're driving, Horse Thief, because I'm nice and comfortable back here in the back seat. Now would you and Scallywag like to tone it down so I can get back to sleep?"

"Aw, poor Bing. Why don't you just stick some Kleenex in your ears? Do you expect me and the horse thief to keep quiet because you didn't get any sleep last night? Whose fault was it that you were out on a date with what's-her-name until 2:00 a.m.?"

"Yeah, yeah, yeah! What's-her-name has a name in case you didn't know, Scallywag? Her name is . . . aw, forget it. Wake me up when we get there. Oh yes, and where did you say we are going, Horse Thief?"

"We're heading for Oastler Lake Provincial Park. It's on Highway 69 just south of Parry Sound about five miles. We should be there in a couple of hours, so go back to sleep, Bing. You're real grumpy when you don't get your beauty-sleep."

We drove on in silence for quite a while until I yelled out in alarm, "Look out, Horse Thief. That truck ahead of you is losing his cinder blocks."

"I've got nowhere to go," Horse Thief yelled back. "There's cars on both sides of me. Oh man. I hope none of those cinder blocks hit the oil pan or the fuel tank. I'd blow a tire if I couldn't miss one. This is crazy. They are all over the road."

The next few seconds sure were tense as Horse Thief tried valiantly to avoid the cinder blocks, many of them breaking up as they hit the asphalt in front of us and creating a hazard for cars and truck alike. Finally, I expelled my breath, and said somberly, "Good driving, Horse Thief. You missed the big pieces. Guess you got a few smaller ones though. They sure made a racket bouncing under the car. We'd better stop as soon as you can and check out the undercarriage on the Stude."

Letting the air out of his lungs with an expressive sigh of relief, Horse Thief said, "I can't believe we missed so many of those big pieces, Scallywag. They were bouncing everywhere. Here's a good spot to stop and check everything over."

"What's the commotion, you guys?" growled Bing from the back seat. "I'm trying to sleep back here. What'd you drive over, Horse Thief? Did you decide to take a shortcut and drive in the ditch or something?"

"Why don't you go back to sleep, Bing?" I said. "The Horse Thief was playing dodge 'em with a bunch of cinder blocks that fell off the back of a truck."

Looking under the car from the passenger side, I said with relief in my voice, "That's pretty amazing, Horse Thief. I haven't found any damage under my side of the car although you'd have thought there would be with all the noise of those broken cinder blocks bouncing around on the road. It was a good thing to stop and check though."

"I'm thanking God for providing safety in the midst of broken and bouncing cinder blocks, Scallywag. It wasn't my driving that got us through that mess of broken cement."

We all settled down soon after that emergency stop, and Horse Thief and I kept our voices low until Horse Thief sung out, "Here we are, guys. Let the fun begin. We made it to Oastler Lake Provincial Park. I'll go into the park office and register us, Scallywag. You'd better wake up Bing. We'll need him to help us get set up on a campsite. He'd sleep the whole day away if we let him."

"I've been awake ever since you drove us through that cement minefield, Horse Thief," muttered Bing.

It was a brief stop at the park office and Horse Thief was back in the car. As we approached our campsite, I commented with satisfaction, "Hey, Horse Thief and Bing, do we ever have a beautiful campsite. It's right at the edge of the lake on the back side of the park. Party time here we come."

"OK, Scallywag. First things first. Let's pitch my dad's tent and get our food straightened out so we can eat some grub. It's been a long time since breakfast when we stopped at the Fifth Wheel Truck Stop back there in Milton."

"Yes, Horse Thief. If we can get Bing to shake a leg, maybe he can rustle up some vitals, and then we can take the boat out on the lake."

"Now you're making sense, Scallywag. I'll get some grub rounded up. I've got first dibs on riding the surfboard behind the boat too," said Bing with a big grin on his face.

After we'd set up camp, we had a bite to eat, courtesy of Bing's astounding cooking skills. How could anyone screw up peanut butter and jam sandwiches?

We spent the rest of the day until nearly dusk playing out on the lake with the surfboard behind the boat.

Sitting around the campfire that evening after we grilled some hamburgers on an old portable Coleman cooking stove, all three of us began telling tall tales. That was a great way to end off our first day spent at the lake.

We weren't able to do any fishing because all three of us forgot to bring our fishing rods. But one thing was real popular, and that was the surfboard. Turns were taken riding it while the other two "bad actors" were in the boat. Bing was the lightest and seemed to be the fastest on the board. Horse Thief was pretty good on the surfboard too, but me, Scallywag, well, that's another story. That Johnson 25 Outboard just didn't seem to have enough power to keep me on the board. I was forever sinking deeply into the water. It was funny too because I was always yelling at the other two in the boat, "Go faster." They'd holler back, "We're going as hard and fast as we can."

The truth was that Horse Thief and Bing never really tried to make the aluminum boat go fast. They got a kick out of watching me sink in the water. They kept laughing and later said it was funny listening to me ball them out for not knowing how to operate a simple boat.

The days just seemed to literally fly by, and it came to the point where all good things had to come to an end, and so it was with that week of celebration. Horse Thief celebrated his seventeenth birthday on June 29.

But I set it up so Bing and I would have a good laugh at the horse thief. We knew it worked too when he came back from a short hike, and with a grumpy look on his face and a sour voice said, "Scallywag, what'd you do? Why did you tell everyone around us in the other campsites that it was my fifteenth birthday? Everyone was congratulating me on my fifteenth birthday. It made me feel like a real dolt. They kept saying to me that it was so nice that my older brother threw this weeklong party for me."

"Hahaha! That's real funny. I'm loving it. The old horse thief was fifteen this week."

"Shut-up, Bing. And you, Scallywag, wipe that grin off your face. I owe you for that zinger, and don't you ever forget it. I always repay my debts."

"Promises, promises, promises. You're boring us, Horse Thief. It's two against one, and Bing and I think you had it coming. Tomorrow we'll let you go back to being seventeen years old."

Saturday, July 1, 1967, came in as one big, beautiful, clear, and calm day. What a fantastic time to celebrate Canada's Dominion Day, and what a beautiful place in which to celebrate. Oastler Lake Provincial Park was the perfect setting to have a birthday party for Canada. Our nation was now one hundred years old.

"Hey, Scallywag and Bing. I was just over at the washrooms, and I saw a large notice on the bulletin board. Can you believe it? We can't light off any firecrackers or any fireworks tonight. This is Dominion Day. How else can we celebrate?"

"Guess we'll just have to settle for roasting chestnuts over the open fire."

"Hahaha. Horse Thief, that's the line you're supposed to use at Christmastime, not now. This is Party Central, and it's Dominion Day."

"Sure, sure, Scallywag. What'd you have in mind for celebrations? Popping corn over the open fire and sitting around roasting marshmallows?"

Horse Thief continued to mouth off. "I'll tell you something, Bing. If we follow up on Scallywag's idea of fun, we might as well go to bed before the sun goes down. Boring."

So it was that those three hombres did indeed sit around the campfire well into the night. But it would be anything but boring because Bing came up with an insane idea that half scared the pants off everyone within two hundred feet of that campfire.

The noise wad deafening. *Ker-wump! Bang! Puff-thump! Shufff-poo . . . Rum-paa . . . !*

"What the blazes did you just do, Bing? You're a nutcase. There's cream corn dripping off of a half-dozen pine trees. You near scared me and the old horse thief half out of our wits," I exclaimed while wiping some cream corn from off my red and white "puke-a-dot" hat.

"Hahaha. Would you look at Bing? He's got half a can of cream corn fixed on top of his head. And you, Scallywag, what a sight for sore eyes. You got cream corn all over the front of your pants. I'm not sure what kind of accident you've been in, but it looks real bad."

"Shut up, Horse Thief. Did you plan this all along and get Bing to do your dirty work? You knew we couldn't light off any firecrackers, so you planned on bringing those four cans of cream corn and got Bing to stick them in the fire when no one was looking. You've got a weird sense of humor. It's a wonder one or two of those cans didn't blow up and head off in a horizontal fashion and take out someone's tent."

"But you have to admit, Scallywag," Horse Thief said with a bit of swagger and pride in his voice, "the pine trees dripping cream corn do add a real vibrant sense of celebration to Canada's one hundredth birthday." Bing and I had a good laugh at that comment.

"If you say so, Horse Thief. But I still think that you and Bing are couple of real nutcases. Guess we got some work to do come morning, if we don't get kicked out of here before sunrise. What a mess your dad's tent is, Horse Thief, with cream corn dripping on it like rain from above."

So it was that Horse Thief, Scallywag, and Bing spent a rather memorable Dominion Day and Horse Thief's Birthday that June/July in 1967.

The pine trees by the lake at Oastler Lake Provincial Park still whisper to one another even to this day of the time when something sticky and yellow fell from heaven and bathed them in a wonderfully creamy yellow dew that the ravens seemed to just absolutely love.

# FOUR

## HUMPH! I'M TAKING YOURS

"Yeah! I DID it. I'm out of here. No more pencils, no more books, no more teacher's dirty looks."

I chanted loudly as I went down the steps of the high school for the final time. There wasn't anyone nearby that I could chant that old rhyme to, but that didn't matter. I liked it so much, that I did the chant again and again while running across the parking lot to my car.

I had just graduated from Central Elgin Collegiate High School. It was Friday, June 28, 1968. I felt free like a prisoner freed from prison. The pressure was gone. The weight of studying, writing exams, interacting with teachers, all of it—gone. Free as a bird. I felt like I could fly.

"I can follow my dreams."

There I was talking loudly to myself again while driving my car heading downtown to my favorite hangout, the Rendezvous Restaurant. "I hope Smitty is still there," I said loudly to myself.

My plan was to meet Smitty, and we'd celebrate my graduation together. Smitty had graduated earlier. He was a year older than me. I was jealous of him because he told me all the things he was doing. He had a great job driving a straight truck for a chemical company throughout the Greater Toronto area and was living in Brampton at the time as well. He bragged about making some really good money too. But over the phone a couple of days ago, he said he was coming back to St. Thomas to visit his folks for a week. He needed a little vacation.

Walking into the Rendezvous Restaurant, I saw him at the back sitting in my favorite booth. "Hey, Smitty. No more pencils, no more books, no more teachers' dirty looks." There, I'd said it again as I was sitting down opposite him.

"Well, well, well, Dude. You did it. Way to go, so how does it feel to be a free man?" That was like him, paying me a compliment while at the same time needling me low-key.

"Smitty, I'm going to do it. I'm going down to the airport, and I'm going to enroll in flight school. I'm going to get my pilot's license. Blue sky, here I come."

Within two months I had enrolled and begun the ground flight training school. Funny isn't it, I hated high school, but I absolutely knew I'd love flight training school.

If you knew me, you'd know that I liked anything transportation oriented. I had worked on the Canadian National Railroad two summers in a row when I was seventeen and eighteen, back in 1966 and 1967. It was hard work, but I loved it. I worked on an extra gang laying thirty miles of track from St. Thomas to the new Ford Motor Plant being built just north of Talbotville.

You might have expected I'd continue to work on the railroad now that I had graduated from high school, but that wasn't the case. I wanted to fly. I wanted a new adventure.

The St. Thomas Municipal Airport was less than three miles east of where I lived on Centennial Ave. In fact, the flight path for the east-west runway went directly over my parents' home, and many, many times over the years as a teenager, I had sat out on the porch and watched the airplanes fly over the house, often at an elevation of only five hundred feet.

"Hey, Dude, have you enrolled in the flight training school yet? Or were you just blowing smoke? How many times have I heard you say you wanted to fly? And here you are lying down on the grass at your parents' home and just looking up at the sky."

Smitty had a way of bugging me, so I slugged him in the arm as he lay down on the grass beside me. "It's going to happen," I said. "It's hard being patient, but I'll continue to suffer until I start ground school next weekend on Saturday, August 17.

"The ground school is held every weekend on Saturday. That's perfect for me because I'm driving for P. K. Hardware Wholesale during the week. In no time, Smitty, I'm going to be flying over your head, and you'll be looking up at me."

August 17 had finally come, and here I was, sitting in what had probably been the flight room back in the days of World War Two. After all, this airport had been built just prior to the Second World War. The hangar in which the flight room was located had a unique smell. Airplanes had a smell unlike any other type of transport. Cars and trucks have their smell. Airplanes have their smell too. I loved it—the smell, that is.

Various flight manuals, instruction books, a book on clouds and various weather formations and their significance, even a really keen book on navigation and map reading, were all part of the growing bundle of books sitting on the desk in front of me. This was a school I was really going to love.

"How did it go, Dude? How was your first day of ground flight training? Are you a pilot now? I don't think so because you don't have that pilot's swagger. You're still walking around like a truck driver of a little truck—only a three ton."

We'd met at the Rendezvous for a coffee later that first day of my flight training, and already Smitty was bugging me. That was OK. I bugged him just as much.

"OK, Smitty. Bug me just as much as you want." I was glad he'd moved back to St. Thomas. The fact was that we enjoyed bugging each other. "But there will be a day coming when you'll beg me for a ride, you and your girlfriend, and I'll only take her up in the air. You can shed big tears as you watch me steal your girlfriend away."

"That's low, even for you, Dude."

That's the way it was. Smitty bugged me. I bugged him back. We always did that, but we were the best of friends. We'd always been friends. We never fought each other, but we sure could pester each other. In a way it was fun because we were always trying to be one up on the other guy. I guess it was a competition thing. Who would be the best at jabbing the other?

Neither one of us really had bragging rights to that. He'd jab me, I'd jab him back, and on and on it would go. People would laugh at us, and that just motivated us to do it more and more. We didn't even need to have an audience. We just had a lot of fun jabbing each other anyhow.

My ambition was to acquire my private pilot license, and I excelled in the ground school course work. There wasn't any course or study I didn't enjoy. I literally thrived on those studies. I learned so much. I could study the clouds and tell you what kind of weather we were going to get. I learned how to read navigational maps and topographical maps. That was fun. I'd read the maps with the same joy and interest as I'd read a good novel, and in case you didn't know it, I loved to read. I'd spend hours and hours studying, so it wasn't any surprise to anyone who knew me when I passed ground school with near perfect marks.

In fact, I wrote my ground school exam in Toronto a little later that fall, October 9, at the newly built Toronto Dominion Centre. That was a high-rise building right downtown. The exam room was on the seventieth floor. When I looked out the window, I felt like I was already flying.

Back in St. Thomas later that day after writing the ground school exam, I found myself in the Rendezvous Restaurant sitting in my favorite booth nursing a coffee, the third one to be exact. While looking at a flying magazine and a brochure of used planes for sale, I heard a familiar voice calling my name.

"Hey, Scallywag. What are you doing sitting around on such a nice day?"

"Why, you ole horse thief, are you coming in here to bug me?"

Horse Thief was the nickname for Bob, and like Smitty, he was also my best friend. We first met each other at the early age of seven and eight. I was a year older than Bob. But I never called him Bob. I always called him Horse Thief, which was the nickname I'd given him many years earlier. He never called me Paul but Scallywag. Funny how nicknames stick to you. When I really wanted to draw attention to him, I'd call him an ole horse thief. That always made people look.

"I came in here, Scallywag, because I just knew you'd be here once you returned from Toronto. How'd your exam go?"

"Horse Thief, they gave me my marks before I left, and I did very well—got 98 percent. You're right. I came in here to celebrate. I'm glad to see you."

"What happens next, Scallywag? Can you begin flying lessons right away?"

"Not quite. I have to get a complete medical tomorrow. I'll need to pass a series of tests, such as a vision test and a test to see if I have any color blindness. I sure hope that everything goes well."

"Oh, OK. You'll start your flight training then this Saturday?"

"Yup. Can't wait to begin. The flight training school will start in the morning. It will go from nine until noon."

"What do you say, Scallywag, if you were to come over to my place then later, say Saturday afternoon? I'd like you to be my chase car driver. I'm going to take my dune buggy out for a shakedown cruise, and if I have any problems, you'll be there to help me get it running again or else tow me back to my place."

"Horse Thief, I thought you did a shakedown run last Saturday over at my place? You brought your wannabe dune buggy over, and we ripped up a half acre of my dad's alfalfa hayfield doing dirty donuts. My mom wasn't too impressed with the mud she tried to get out of my white jacket I was wearing."

Horse Thief's dune buggy was a broken-down, old Volkswagen Beetle. He'd fixed up the engine, so it ran again, and not too badly, I might add. Interestingly, he'd stripped that old VW of its body. It was down to nothing more than a chassis with two seats, center gear shift column, and its rear air-cooled 1,600 cc engine. With no fenders, you wore everything those four tires picked up.

"Better not bring it back to my house, Horse Thief. My mother will run you off the property with Dad's twelve-gauge. She's got it in for you now because you made that hayfield look like a wipeout."

"No, I won't do that, but what I had in mind was running it up some old country roads north of town. I've made a body for it out of one-fourth-inch plywood now, so no more mud or stone slinging."

"You like to take chances, don't you, Horse Thief? I'll bet you a dollar on a donut you can't put a license on that beast because it'll probably never pass muster. Hey, I'll sweeten the pot. I'll buy you a box of donuts if you get a license.

"Come-on, Scallywag. Don't you have any faith in me? Anyhow, my cousin Dave is coming up from Windsor, and he wants a ride, so are you going to be my chase car driver or not? You'd have to drive my dad's Studebaker."

"OK, Horse Thief, that sounds like fun. I get to see you utterly destroy your dune buggy, and on top of that I get to drive your dad's super-hot Stude. That'll be a win-win for me."

Early Saturday morning I was walking around Horse Thief's wannabe dune buggy. I have to tell you. It's so ugly—squared fenders, no doors, and a body made from one-fourth-inch plywood. At that point rear fenders were nonexistent. It didn't have a windshield, nor headlights and brake lights. It sort of resembled a Second World War German Gestapo staff car.

"Hey, you ole horse thief. Whatever you call it, you best call it ugly. It couldn't be uglier even if you painted it scaredy-cat yellow."

"Aw, come-on, Scallywag. Dave's not going to want to ride in it with you giving off all those negative vibes."

We soon set out for some quiet dirt roads north of town, where that ugly whatever was, would be driven on its shakedown run. Horse Thief and his cousin Dave were approximately one-tenth of a mile ahead of me. I held back a bit because I didn't like breathing all the dust they were kicking up. What I saw about to happen totally scared me.

"Horse Thief, you're going to get hit by that farm truck coming at you from your right. He's on that crossroad right in front of you."

I was yelling to the wind. Of course they couldn't hear me. What I saw next I will forever remember. That farm truck hit them broadside square on. Plywood went everywhere. The dune buggy seemed to go a couple of feet in the air, and both Horse Thief and Dave cleared their seats. I could see a couple of feet of daylight between their butts and the top of the seats.

On top of that the dune buggy stayed upright, and did a 180-degree turn ending up between two trees up against a fence. Before I could stop, both bad actors were out of the dune buggy and standing there looking dumbfounded.

I had to feel bad for the farmer. He was shaking and sputtering.

"You fellows all right? What are you doing driving around in that thing? You shouldn't be on the road with that. You want to get yourselves killed? I see you don't even have a license on that bucket of scrap wood. I ought to call the cops."

Nobody called the cops. Nobody saw what happened except the farmer and me. But I did verbalize something that I saw was lacking on the farm truck. "Hey, mister, you don't have a current license plate on your truck either. Maybe you ought to get that off the road, or I'll call the cops on you."

Horse Thief wanted to get out of there, so did the farmer, but I had the last word. "If you guys hang around too long, sure as shooting, someone will come along and call the cops on all of you."

I towed that wannabe dune buggy back to Horse Thief's house. Pulling into the driveway, we all saw his dad at the same time, and I spoke up, "You guys are in deep trouble now. Your dad looks like he's on the warpath. I'm history, I'm out of here."

**I'm Ready to Fly**

I received a phone call from the doctor's nurse about noon that day. "Mr. O'Brien, you have passed the medical that you had here yesterday with flying colors. Why don't you stop by the doctor's office, and I'll give you a copy of it? You will need to give that medical to your flight instructor."

That sounded like a play on words. Did you get it? I could fly, and my colors were good. Color blindness ran in the family, but I dodged the bullet on that one. I was good to go, and I didn't waste any time getting down to the airport, and setting up an appointment for my first real flying lesson.

One of the instructors at the airport could see my happiness when I walked into the flight room. "Paul, it looks like you come bearing good news." Incidentally, everyone at the airport called me by my first name. "Are we going to get you started on your flight training?"

"You bet. I'd like to start as soon as possible. Here's my ground school exam that I wrote in Toronto. I have also received my medical. I passed that too."

"Bert, come here. Paul, I want you to meet Bert. He will be your flight instructor. You two guys ought to get to know a little about each other right away."

Bert was a great guy. I liked him immediately. He was a real transportation nut just like me. He not only flew planes and was a flight instructor, but he also drove highway coach for a local bus company.

While talking to each other, Bert said, "Paul, I want to get you going on your training right away. Look, I have an open hour at five o'clock today. Will that work for you?"

"You can take that to the bank, Bert. It sure will work for me."

I started flight training school Saturday, October 12, 1968, and I was visibly excited. In fact, I could hardly contain myself. It showed because Bert made a comment.

"Paul, I can see you are going to really enjoy your flight lessons. But before we take to the air, I need to show you how we do our preflight inspections and also our post flight inspections. Every time you fly, you need to do thorough inspections. Your safety and your life may depend on your ability to make an accurate analysis of impending problems or issues before they happen."

The gravity of the situation was not lost on me. I would follow to the letter everything I had been taught. "I will be a very captive audience of one, Bert."

Preflight inspection ended, and we entered the plane. It was a Piper Tri-Pacer. Here are some important stats concerning the Tri-Pacer.

The Piper Pacer and the Piper Tri-Pacer were identical in many respects. They were a civil utility aircraft made by the Piper Aircraft Company shortly after the Second World War. They each had a cabin, which seated four, typically one pilot and three passengers.

The Piper Pacer was a tail dragger while the Tri-Pacer had conventional landing gear. It had a nose wheel. The power for the

Tri-Pacer was a 160-horsepower Lycoming Engine. It could cruise at 134 mph and a top speed of 141 mph. It had a ceiling of 16,500 feet and a range of 536 miles. Takeoff distance was 1,480 feet in order to clear a fifty-foot obstacle. When landing, the distance over a fifty-foot obstacle was 1,280 feet.

The Tri-Pacer I was trained in was based out of the St. Thomas Municipal Airport located on the south side of Highway 3 approximately four miles east of St. Thomas. The plane was owned by Hicks and Lawrence, a local company based out of Tillsonburg, Ontario. They also managed the St. Thomas Airport, and specialized in crop-dusting, charter service, and flight training.

I recall that the Tri-Pacer had the rear seats removed. Only a student pilot and the instructor would occupy the aircraft.

Bert oriented me to the layout of the cockpit and then abruptly said, "OK, Paul, let's get airborne. Your first flight won't be very long, but you will nevertheless get a good feel for this aircraft. This will be the plane that you will do all your training in, so I really want you to get familiar with it quickly."

Bert did the takeoff and the landing all the while explaining in great detail everything he did.

"All right, Paul, now I want you to put your hands on the yoke, and put your feet on the rudder pedals. I'll keep my hands and feet on the controls as well, and I'll guide you through each movement I ask you to make."

The first flight lesson went quickly, and we were soon heading back to the airport. Bert eased us down on the tarmac. I watched very closely everything he did. I vowed I would copy everything Bert did perfectly and very soon as well.

Flight training progressed rapidly. I hung around the airport practically every day that fall. If I wasn't up in the air with Bert, I was in the flight room listening to the other pilots. I was learning things from them just by being there.

The fall of 1968 was wonderfully long and warm. Lots of sun and minimal clouds blessed my flight training. I tried to spend as much time in the air with Bert as I could afford. That worked out to about three hours a week.

At the sixth hour of flight training with Bert, we were flying near the old, abandoned Second World War pilot training base in Fingal, Ontario. At an elevation of five thousand feet Bert informed me that we were going to learn today how to get out of a stall with the aircraft.

"OK, Paul, this is how a stall if it should happen must be corrected." And he proceeded to cut the engine to an idle and pull the aircraft up into a climbing attitude. In short order the aircraft began to mush. It was beginning to lose height and controllability. At that point, Bert pushed the yoke forward. The nose dropped, and he pointed the aircraft into a forty-five-degree descent. Applying power, he very quickly brought the plane up to normal flying speed and pulled back on the yoke in order to conclude our descent and to maintain altitude.

"OK, Paul, do exactly what I did. You are going to learn how to recover from a stall. This is very important as there may be a situation in your future where you experience a stall, and you must be able to correctly move through that stall and safely correct your flying altitude."

Bert talked me through the procedure a couple of times then informed me, "I'm going to keep my mouth shut. Let's see you do a proper stall recovery safely."

Looking at his wristwatch, Bert said, "You are doing it correctly, Paul. Let's do the stall recovery three more times and then return us to the airport. We'll be able to make it back within the hour."

Every new event that I learned from Bert just increased my desire to fly, and be as professional in that experience as I could be. It showed because he said to me a couple of hours later, about the eighth hour, "I'm going to show you how to stall the plane, enter into a spin, and safely recover. This should never happen that you would end up in a spin, but it would be to your advantage to know what to do because if you don't know what to do, you will crash.

"To get the aircraft to spin, several things need to first take place. I'll show you how it works. Bert then proceeded to explain where the "PARE" acronym comes into play.

There were four steps to take. Step one was to cut the power to idle. The second step was to set the Ailerons to Neutral. The third step was to move the rudder opposite the spin, and the fourth step was to move the elevator forward.

The aircraft was doing exactly what Bert said it would do. All of a sudden the nose was pointing directly at the ground, and we started to rotate. Bert now said, "It is vital that you do not exceed three complete rotations of the craft. If you do, you will again lose control and will not be able to pull out. You will crash."

He was serious, and while explaining the events and the order in which they would happen, he was doing the procedures at the same time. At this point in the completion of the third rotation, Bert applied full power. Pulling back on the yoke, the plane began to decrease its descent, and within a moment we had leveled off, and were flying at a safe altitude.

"Look, Paul, I know you are hot to learn as much as you can. I am not supposed to instruct you on how to spin an aircraft, but I felt it was something you would appreciate learning. This is between you and me. I don't ever want to hear that you have told another soul of this learning experience. The powers that be will come down heavy on us both."

Bert never let me practice the stall and spin again. We never even talked about it. But I didn't forget how it was accomplished. In my mind I rehearsed the procedure continuously.

Another procedure Bert taught me was to sideslip the aircraft. This activity would drop the plane very quickly. It was especially useful when a landing was attempting, and the plane's elevation was abnormally high. Instead of tracking true as you approached the tarmac, you caused the plane to sideslip. This would make the plane look like it was flying sideways. The craft would begin to rapidly descend while still flying with full control. The sideslip was very effective for a short landing strip and looked very impressive to onlookers on the ground. I fed on that because I was a bit of a show-off.

"Hey, Dude, I thought you'd be in the Rendezvous Restaurant today, especially since it is one of those low, overcast, rainy days. I know you're just a fair-weather flyer. I'd call you a scaredy-cat, but I'm afraid you might beat me up. Oh yes—you scare me."

"Smitty, are you trying to jazz me? I can fly in the rain as well as the sunshine. I've done it, so there. I've run out of cash, so I have to wait until my next paycheck. That will be this Friday. My twelfth-hour flying dual is Saturday, and I think Bert, my instructor, is going to let me go solo."

"So are you going to sit down and have a coffee with me, Smitty, or are you just going to stand there running at the mouth?"

"I'll sit down if you're buying, Dude."

"Oh, sit down. I can afford to buy you a coffee. You can buy your own donut.

"What have you learned so far, Dude? Can you actually fly the plane, or are you just paying those big bucks to go for a ride?"

"It would take me a couple of hours to tell you the things I've learned and I already am doing when I fly. Of course the instructor is still with me, but he thinks I'm ready to fly solo, so this Saturday will be the day. Smitty, why don't you come down to the airport and hang out while I'm there. You can watch me do a solo flight."

"I just might do that, Dude. If you make it and land without smacking up the plane, I'll buy you a hamburger and fries at the Food and Foam Drive-in."

"If I do that, Smitty, you'll also buy me a large root beer."

"OK, Dude, as long as we go there in your car. I'll not be able to afford all that grub and gas for my car too."

"Sure, Smitty, once a tightwad, always a tightwad, eh?"

**First Time Flying Solo**

Saturday couldn't come fast enough. I was excited. "I'm going to fly solo today," I announced to my mother as I sat at the breakfast table.

Moms are like that I suppose. They worry about their children. "You be careful, Paul, and come back in one piece." I think she always thought I'd do something risky and get into a predicament that could maybe injure me or another person.

Preflight inspection was done under the scrutinizing gaze of Bert who finally said, "OK, Paul, let's do a circuit and see how it goes. You're ready to fly solo, just remember everything you have been taught. Think it all out and do it."

Preflight was done, and the runway was cleared for takeoff. I applied full power as we headed into a light westerly breeze. We lifted off in just over 1,200 feet. At an elevation of one thousand feet, pretty much right over my home, we banked to the left and headed south for approximately two miles.

Speaking to me again, Bert said, "Look, Paul, you know the drill. Continue the circuit and head east. Maintain one thousand feet and keep the airport in sight. Turn left again, maintaining your elevation at a point directly over the eastern border of the golf course. Turn left for your inbound final leg when you get over the point where the railroad and the creek meet. You know the drill. You've done it many times.

"When you land, turn off at the taxi and head for the hangar. I'm getting off, and you're going to do a circuit. I'll be outside the hangar watching the whole show."

Was I nervous? Yes, sort of. Was I excited? Very much so. I took the most easterly taxiway to runway 270, stopped shy of the runway, and let an inbound airplane land. When the runway was clear and no other aircraft was on final, I turned onto the runway and pushed the throttle to the maximum power setting. That Tri-Pacer jumped into the air in no time.

I talked to myself audibly through the whole circuit. I knew I could do this, but I was nervous too. I repeated the circuit just as I had done with Bert not more than twenty minutes ago. It's funny, but I even looked to my right side where the flight instructor would sit, to make sure I was flying solo, and Bert wasn't there.

Coming inbound on final, I got really nervous. I was coming in too fast and too high. I hadn't cut back on the power enough. I was going to overshoot the runway. That would look bad at the least, and at the worst, I might not land with enough length of runway left to do a safe stopping procedure whereby I'd run off the end into the swamp. That wasn't going to happen.

While still thirty feet above the runway and already past the eastern threshold by a good five hundred feet, I applied full power and took that Tri-Pacer back up into the wild blue yonder. I didn't care if they were laughing at me over at the hangar.

I'd do another circuit, and this time I'd paste that Tri-Pacer on the tarmac and do it right smartly, right on the runway number. No overshooting this time.

I brought that aircraft in on the second circuit, and it was a picture-perfect landing. I'd accomplished the goal both Bert and I had set. I soloed on my twelfth hour.

As I taxied up to the fuel pumps by the hangar, not only Bert, but some mechanics in the hangar and a few other private pilots came out to meet me. Oh yes, and Smitty too. He'd come down to the airport while I was doing a circuit with Bert before I went solo.

Climbing out of the plane, everyone came over to greet me and shake my hand or slap me on the back. "Congratulations, Paul" were shouted out by many. It sure made me feel good. I had flown solo and done it well. No one mentioned the first attempted landing. Well, no one except Smitty.

"Hey, Dude, did you get scared or something? Why did you go around for a second circuit?"

I didn't tell him I'd overshot the runway. "Smitty, I was greedy. I wanted to do it again, so I did." I'm not sure he bought that excuse, but he never pushed me on it either.

After I'd filled in my logbook and chatted with a few fellows for five or ten minutes, Smitty dragged me aside. "You still want that hamburger, fries, and shake? Or was it a root beer?"

"Yes, I do. I worked up a real appetite up there, Smitty, and I'm famished. We'll leave your car at your place and go out to the Food and Foam in my car."

"Why is it that food always tastes so much better when you're buying, Smitty?"

"Yeah, I know the answer to that question, Dude, but I'm not going to give you the pleasure of me answering it."

I changed my mind when we arrived at the Food and Foam. When the young lady came to the window to take our orders, I said, "Hi, Sharon, I'd like a foot-long hot dog with everything on it, a large order of fries, and I'm going to order a large chocolate milkshake."

"You might as well duplicate that order, Sharon, but instead of a chocolate shake, I'll have a strawberry shake. Oh, and give me the bill please."

"Wow, Smitty, you're a real gentleman. You spoke so nicely to the carhop. Kind of glad you did too. She lives across the road from me. She graduated when I did, and she attended Central Elgin as well. We used to ride the same school bus every day."

Smitty and I were never without lots of conversation. It didn't matter what the subject was, we'd talk about it like we knew everything there was to know about it. Of course that was rarely the case, but that didn't stop us from waxing eloquent.

My flying lessons continued over the next few months, but I reduced the hours as we approached Christmas. I needed to reserve most of my paycheck for the added expenses that gift purchases for the Christmas season bought. However, during that time, roughly mid-October to the end of November 1968, I put in another twelve hours. Approximately six of those hours I was told to fly solo and practice "touch and goes" at least twice each hour.

The other six hours I flew with Bert, my instructor. Toward the end of November, Bert said, "Paul, the next time you come in for an hour, instead of one hour, you should plan on taking three to four hours. I want to fly cross-country with you. You need to learn a few skills that are important as you fly into other airports. You don't have to use the radio for communication with the hangar here because we are an uncontrolled airstrip, however, the airports I'll have you fly into have air traffic control. That will be a good time to brush up on your two-way radio skills and landing in new and different airports.

"I will give you the destinations for the two airstrips we'll land at as well as two alternative airstrips should we run into any issues. Therefore, I want you to study about these four airports. Learn everything you can about them. You'll be using the radio, so you will need to learn their call identifications.

"The other thing I want you to practice is map-reading skills. While you will be flying VFR (visual flight rules), you should familiarize yourself with the lay of the land, so to speak.

"The last thing, Paul, you should prepare for is in the event that we can't fly out on November 30th, we could try again on December 1st, the next day. The third option would be the following Saturday, December 7th. Are you good with all that, Paul?"

"I think those plans, Bert, will work out okay for me. Regardless of which date we do the cross-country I'll be ready for it. There is one thing that will happen once the cross country flight has been concluded. I will not be flying again until the middle of January.

"Three to four hours are going to cost me more than a few bucks, Bert, and Christmas is just a month away after that cross-country. I'll need to reserve some serious coin for the usual Christmas gifts and parties and all that stuff. I'll have spent all my cash reserves right down to nothing. I'll have to save some substantial money to continue with my flight training."

"I totally understand, Paul. I don't see any problem with those plans. You shouldn't worry about taking a month off. You are developing some good skills, and you have an excellent touch on the controls. You're not going to lose any of those skills if you have to take some time off."

"Thanks, Bert, for that vote of confidence. I might just come over to the flight room and the hangar once in a while even if I don't go up. It's a great place to hang out and talk with other pilots if it's not a trouble to anyone."

"That's not a problem either, Paul. In fact, it's a good idea. Just showing up once in a while and talking shop with the other pilots who are here when you arrive is good for you. You can always learn something from them. The other thing I might suggest is that you hang out a bit in the hangar. If the mechanics don't seem to be too busy, you can also learn a thing or two from them. And if you have any questions, I know they are more than willing to give you good answers. So even if you don't fly, you are welcome here. You are still in a win-win situation."

November 30 came and went. The same was true for December 1. It looked like a winter wonderland, and boy did it ever snow. The storm started about midnight Friday, November 29, and it didn't let up until midday on Monday, December 2. In that period of time, we got dumped on with more than eighteen inches of snow.

St. Thomas is approximately ten miles north of Lake Erie. When there is a strong southerly wind sweeping across the lake from Cleveland, Ohio, early in the winter, a large accumulation of snow is to be expected. A cold wind over a warm body of water, and there is snow and more snow. Basically, the St. Thomas Airport was shut down for flying from Friday right through to early Tuesday morning, December 3.

**Waiting for Good Weather**

"Hey, Smitty, what're you doing today? Do you want to go to London? I'm thinking of going so I can do a little Christmas shopping at the Wellington Mall. I couldn't do my cross-country today on account of the bad weather. But it's not so bad we can't drive to London."

"Sounds like a plan, Dude. I sort of thought you'd be grounded today and likely tomorrow too, with all the snow that's coming down. It doesn't look like it's going to let up anytime soon. We'd better go in your car though. My VW Beetle doesn't like all this snow, and I've not bought any snow tires either."

"You're kind of slow on the draw, Smitty, when it comes to buying snow tires. Maybe you'd be better buying the snow tires than going to London with me?"

"Tell you what, Dude, I'll drop my Beetle off at the Firestone Dealer. You can pick me up there."

"That's a good suggestion, Smitty. Oh, by the way, Horse Thief is coming as well. I was talking to him an hour ago, and he's bored out of his gourd sitting around and just looking out the window at the snow."

"Great, Dude. The more the merrier I say."

Sometimes it's hard to tell the sane ones from the crazies, and in this case when my friends, Smitty and Horse Thief, get together with me, I think we are all a bunch of crazies. Let me tell you a story that drives home that point. I'll set the stage. We were on our way back to St. Thomas after spending Saturday afternoon at Wellington Mall in London, and Horse Thief was his usual crazy self. He was on the back seat of my car and reading out loud to Smitty and me from the comic section of the *London Free Press*.

All of a sudden Horse Thief piped up in an excited voice, "Did you guys know that Fearless Fosdick was just in the same comic strip as Dick Tracy? He was Dick Tracy's sidekick. Not only that, but they were trying to solve a worldwide pandemic called the Artic Trench Mouth, which was caused by penguins being reestablished in the Canadian Artic from Antarctica.

"Dick Tracy and Fearless Fosdick had a cool way of communicating with each other through a wireless phone embedded in their wristwatches. No one else on this planet has any technology that advanced."

"Sure, sure, Horse Thief. You're just spinning another of your tall tales and fabulous fables," barked out Smitty. "No one has ever heard of such a phone, and there isn't anything like it that has even been invented. With an imagination like yours, why don't you invent a two-way wristwatch? And don't tell me you have already done it because the dude and I know you aren't that smart. About the best you can do is put some ten pound test fishing line between two empty soup cans and call it a two-way telephone."

With that backhanded comment Smitty could contain his laughter no longer and fell into a two-minute fit of uncontrolled noise.

"Horse Thief, you are a true nutcase," I blurted out in merriment. "What do you say guys if we stop at the California Restaurant just ahead at the next intersection and go in for a coffee?"

Finally controlling himself, Smitty chortled out, "I'm with you on that, Dude. You coming in too, Horse Thief, or are you going to sit there and reinvent the comics so that Fearless Fosdick not only works with Dick Tracy but is also the Batman's sidekick, otherwise known as Robin?"

"Aw, come-on, guys, you know I read the comics funny that way when I practice being cross-eyed at the same time. Yeah, I'm coming in too."

So the stage being set, the three of us walked into the California Restaurant together and no sooner did we find a booth and sit down than the ole horse thief began talking to his wristwatch, and real loud too, I might add.

"I hear you loud and clear, Dick. Where can we catch up with you? Sounds bad. No, I'm with Bite and Bark. Yes, I know. Bite and Bark are on call today. Did you want us to get right over there? No, just having a coffee is all. Be right on it, Dick."

"You got to be kidding, Horse Thief. Talk quieter," I whispered. "Half the restaurant is looking at you."

Horse Thief loudly responded to my whispered caution, "Chill out. I'm serious here. I was talking to Dick."

All of a sudden Smitty with a twinkle in his eye stuck his wristwatch right into his left ear and nodded a few times while muttering under his breath. Then putting his wristwatch to his mouth, he emphatically exclaimed, "No way, not on my watch. I'm on my way."

I could hardly contain myself and keep my composure. I began to laugh, not too loudly at first though, and then I figured I might as well join those two crazies and get in on the act.

"Hold it, guys, keep the noise down. My watch is vibrating. I'm getting a message." With that I put my watch to my ear to listen for a moment. Placing my watch to my mouth, I could be heard saying, "Yes, I hear you loud and clear. No, I can't speak any louder. I'm in a public place."

I pursed my lips and nodded several times while mumbling into my watch, "Dick, I thought you were just funning the ole horse thief. No, we are on our way. We'll be there right away. Over and out."

This nonsense carried on right after the waitress had taken our orders. By now, all three of us were in a competition to see who could be the craziest. We had an audience, and we were playing to them. The other patrons in the restaurant were laughing, probably for the most part at us. But we were oblivious to that and carried on, now more so with serious and stern looks on our faces.

When you put Smitty, Horse Thief, and me together, stuff like that is bound to happen. That Saturday we played to an audience of twelve to fifteen other folks who truly seemed to enjoy our antics. And would you believe it? As some of the patrons of that restaurant left, after paying for their meals, they stopped by our booth and laid down a few dollar bills. One of them said, "You guys are crazy funny. Why don't you get a shtick going and make yourself some real bucks?" I think some of them probably read the same comic strip we had read.

**My First Cross-Country Flight**

What a beautiful day. Saturday, December 7 was a day that pilots referred to as a CAVU day. That meant Clear and Visibility Unlimited. This was the day I had waited for, and it would be my first cross-country flight.

The cross-country flight with Bert was booked for a 9:00 a.m. departure. I would normally be at the airport one hour before any flight training, but I was so excited this day that I arrived at 7:30 a.m. It wasn't long before everyone in the hangar and in the flight room knew I was taking a cross-country training flight with Bert.

Right on the money at 9:00 a.m. Bert said to me, "OK, Paul, all your preflight paper work is in order. You have submitted your flight plan to the proper authorities, and you have a green light on everything. Let's get your preflight inspection done and get airborne."

The beauty of the crisp winter morning on the ground was breathtaking, but in the air at five thousand feet elevation it was absolutely majestic. With calm air we made good time flying eastward to Hamilton, Ontario.

At approximately fifteen minutes out from Hamilton, Bert said, "It would be a good time to identify yourself to Hamilton air traffic control. Let them know your intentions and your flight particulars."

We were given a clear shot to proceed to the selected runway, and the landing was uneventful. Under Bert's watchful eye, I followed the landing protocol to the letter.

"Locate your parking allocation according to the ground map of this airport and we'll go inside to the flight room, sign their books, and get them to sign your logbook. We'll take a short break there, Paul, then carry on with the next leg of your cross-country."

There were no hiccups during the next leg of my cross-country flight northward to the Waterloo, Ontario, airport. We had been cleared to fly at seven thousand feet on this portion, and again the air was calm and the flight was smooth.

"Paul, we'll go inside, get all your paperwork up to date, then what do you think would be our best plan before we are airborne again?"

"We should fuel up, Bert. We have enough as it is to reach St. Thomas, but our reserve would not be sufficient if we had to bypass St. Thomas for another destination."

Bert was happy with my observation and replied, "Good call, Paul."

We were cleared for takeoff from Waterloo and were to proceed southwesterly at an elevation of six thousand feet.

"We are experiencing a considerable head wind now, Bert, and I notice our ground speed has been substantially altered because of it. This final leg of my cross-country will be a half hour longer than originally planned. I can see where refueling was a wise choice."

About forty minutes into our flight on this last leg of my cross-country, Bert said, "I'm going to pull a quickie on you, Paul," and with that he cut the power. The engine continued to run, but our airspeed dropped immediately, and we began to lose altitude. "Pick a spot where we can do an emergency landing."

Well, that was a surprise to me as there had not been any previous talk or reference to doing an emergency landing. But a pilot has to be ready for anything, and Bert was good with surprises.

Looking over the terrain, I quickly spotted a location that seemed favorable for an emergency landing and verbally indicated it as such. "Look to the port side, Bert. Approximately two miles at a forty-five-degree position to our present location is a field that parallels our heading. It's located between two good-sized bushes. Can you affirm the location I'm referring to?"

"Affirmative, Paul. Proceed with your emergency plan."

I wasn't too impressed with any location to speak of considering the amount of snow covering at that time, but once the plan is made and the location identified, it is best to proceed. As we came closer, I verbalized my previous silent observations.

"Bert, this appears to be the best selection for an emergency landing. The depth of the snow in St. Thomas is about one foot six inches, and considering our location relative to St. Thomas, I expect the snow base here to be about the same. The snow will pull us into an immediate nosedive, and our runout will be mere yards. Prepare for a very sudden and immediate stop once we touch down."

With that warning Bert immediately responded. "OK, Paul, you have made an accurate assessment." He remained fixed in his determination that I continue with my emergency plan. At about one hundred feet above the terrain below, he reached over to the throttle and pushed it to full power. "Well done. Climb back up to our cruising altitude, and continue toward our base."

"I must admit, Bert, I wasn't looking forward to touchdown because I knew the snow would pull us into a nosedive. The wheels would catch the snow and dig in quickly. My only hope was to lose as much airspeed as possible and basically stall out at about ten feet of altitude. Our ground speed would be below fifty knots, and possibly damage would be minimal."

Bert responded with a serious tone of voice, "I follow your line of reasoning, Paul. I think that your observations are quite accurate taking into consideration the present ground condition."

We proceeded to our final destination and quickly regained altitude to six thousand feet. I mulled that scenario over for a few more minutes and quietly smiled to myself. Bert was happy with my quick action and emergency landing selection. I figured he'd give me good marks for that.

Once back on the ground at St. Thomas, we immediately pulled up to the fuel pumps to refuel the Tri-Pacer. Before I could begin refueling, Bert called out over his shoulder as he walked toward the flight room's door, "Paul, do your post flight inspection before you refuel, and after you have fueled, go into the hangar and get a couple of guys to help you pull the Tri-Pacer into the hangar."

You can believe me when I tell you I had a big smile on my face as I walked into the flight room a bit later. It was obvious I had passed my cross-country with Bert because three or four other pilots that were just hanging around were ready to congratulate me with thumps on the back and handshakes.

**Christmas Holiday Celebrations**

A month would pass before I would return to the airport. Christmas 1968 was just seventeen days away, and there would be lots of family and friends like Smitty, Horse Thief, and my brother David to celebrate the festive season with. I was one happy camper, as they say.

My girlfriend, Joyce, was in training to be a registered nurse at the School of Nursing located at the St. Thomas General Hospital. I had been dating Joyce for about a year, and we were looking forward to Christmas as she would be getting about three weeks off before classes resumed in January 1969. Home for Joyce was Mount Bridges, Ontario, and was located west of London about fifteen miles.

Calling Joyce on the telephone and with some excitement in my voice, I said, "Hello, Joyce. I'm back from my cross-country flight. It was a good one, and everything went well. If you are free later today, I'd love to take you out for dinner. I'm thinking of Johnson's Steak House on Talbot Street that is near my father's barbershop."

With evident anticipation in her voice, Joyce responded, "I'd love that, Paul. What time would you come by to pick me up? Do you want me to dress up?"

"Joyce, why don't you wear a nice, warm sweater? It's been cold all day, and that cream-colored sweater you like will be perfect to keep you warm. I've got a cool Christmas sweater I've had for a couple of years, and I'll wear it. We'll both look very Christmassy. We can go tenpin bowling after we've eaten if you like."

I didn't horse around with Joyce like I did with my buddies, Smitty and Horse Thief. After all, girls were different. They didn't want to be treated like a guy. I knew that, so I was on my best behavior.

Arriving at Johnson's Steak House, I knew Joyce would wait until I opened her door. So I hurried around to the right side of the car, and opening her door, I offered her my hand to assist her as she exited the car.

"My, oh my, Paul, you are such a gentleman." And with that Joyce put her arm through my arm, and we walked a few steps to the entrance to the Steak House. I smiled warmly to Joyce, and we continued to walk arm in arm to the table as the maître d' escorted us. I just knew there would be some warm and tender moments we'd share as we enjoyed our dinner.

"I'm waiting to hear how your cross-country flight was, Paul," Joyce said with anticipation in her voice. "You need to tell me all about it."

That was all the encouragement I needed. Beginning with my preflight inspection and takeoff from St. Thomas, I filled Joyce in on all the highlights of my cross-country flight experience. Of course, I dramatized the sudden emergency landing procedure I was thrust into by Bert, the instructor.

"Bert surprised me with something we'd not discussed before leaving St. Thomas to do my cross-country. He pulled the plane's throttle back to idle and announced we were going to do an emergency landing. We were just fifteen minutes from of St. Thomas on the final leg of my cross-country, and now all of a sudden I was looking for a place to land. Mind you, it would be in at least one foot six inches of snow, and that wouldn't be easy to accomplish."

I continued to relate to Joyce all that I thought, all that I said, and all that happened in that brief period. I knew I really impressed her by the look in her eyes and the big, proud smile on her lips. Secretly, inside me I knew this was the start of an awesome night out with Joyce. She indicated with subtle body language that she was proud of me and I would be rewarded with lots of hot, wet kisses. Oh boy, oh boy. Lucky me.

"Paul, that was the best steak I ever had, and I'm looking forward to whatever else you planned for us tonight," Joyce excitedly whispered.

"I'm glad you enjoyed your steak, Joyce, and I thought it was exceedingly good as well. So if you are comfortable with my thoughts on what I'd like to do with you tonight, I was thinking it would be fun to take you tenpin bowling."

"That would be fun, Paul, let's do it."

It didn't take long to get to the bowling alley. In short order, we had our bowling shoes, the game record sheet, and were sitting on the bench in front of our lane putting on our shoes.

Of course, being the absolute gentleman that I was, I bent down on my knees and tied Joyce's shoelaces for her. I knew that impressed her because she cooed softly, "Thank you, Paul, you are so kind to tie my shoes for me."

We had a lot of fun bowling. Joyce was very good and bowled like a real pro. I must admit, I was mesmerized just watching her body movements as she wiggled her derriere and bent over to roll the ball down the alley.

Being as competitive as I am, it was somewhat difficult to let Joyce win one of the two games we played. But I knew it would pay off later.

"Paul, did you throw your last game just to let me win? Now tell me the truth. Let me look into your eyes as you answer me."

"Oh, Joyce, you won fair and square. You are such a good bowler. It was all I could do to scrap up a win in the first game we played."

"Paul, you are just lying to me, I know it because I can see it in your eyes. But you are such a sweet liar, I'm going to reward you for letting me win anyhow." And with that Joyce bent over my shoulder and gave me a long, hot kiss on the side of my cheek.

While still lingering on my cheek, she whispered into my ear, "Now, sweet Paul, what do you have in mind? The evening is still young."

"Hum. My thoughts are leading me toward taking you down to Port Stanley. There is a place close to the beach where we can sit in the car and still see the lake quite well. Joyce, the moon will be up over the horizon by the time we arrive there, and I can't think of a better place to snuggle with you."

"Oh, Paul, you are so romantic." Joyce spoke those words softly with warm lips brushing lightly against my ear.

The moon was indeed beautiful and shining so clearly upon the face of the quiet, cold water of Lake Erie. But why am I telling you that? I don't think Joyce or I really gave much attention to the moon.

"You are really heating me up, Joyce. Would you look at all the condensation on the car windows? You sure do have some kind of power over me," I said in a somewhat husky voice.

"Maybe, Paul, but don't you think you are doing the same to me? It is getting quite late though, and we do want to go to church tomorrow morning, don't we?"

"Whew. Joyce, I know you are right. If you will only give me one more long, hot, wet kiss, I'll take you back to the student nurses' residence."

"You are so greedy, Paul. Shame on you. But I'll give you one more of those kisses after you have brought me to the doors of my residence. In the meantime, this kiss will suffice." And with that Joyce stuck her tongue in my ear and blew hot air gently at the same time.

Friday night, December 20 I took Joyce to her parents' home in Mount Bridges. I hesitated to just drop her off at her doorstep, and Joyce could sense my hesitation, so she asked me straight up, "Paul, you have something on your mind, don't you? I can read it in your eyes, and I know what you want too."

"Oh, come on, Joyce, you're not that good. You don't know what I was thinking, do you?"

"Of course I know what you were thinking and what you want as well. The fact is that I was thinking the same thing, and I want the same thing you want. And my parents aren't home right now, so come on in and make yourself comfortable on the couch. I'd like to slip into something a bit more comfortable than these winter duds I'm wearing, but it won't be a minute or two and I'll join you."

It was quite funny actually. Joyce and I both thought her parents wouldn't be home from their Christmas shopping for a couple of hours, but they arrived before we could even get the living room windows steamy.

I visited with Joyce and her parents for maybe another hour then thought it best to return to St. Thomas. As I was parting and wishing everyone a merry Christmas, Joyce took me aside for a moment and gave me one of her special kisses. I won't describe it other than to say it was a long, hot, and wet kiss, and I didn't even have to stand under some mistletoe. Oh, that girl could just about turn me inside out.

Joyce would stay on her Christmas break at her parents' home until she had to return for her next semester of studies, which began on Monday, January 6, 1969. I would go to Mount Bridges early on January 4 and bring Joyce back to St. Thomas to the student nurses' residence.

Christmas Eve had arrived. It was a good time to spend with family and friends. I think some of the best times during the Christmas Season are spent at church. I enjoyed singing Christmas carols, and it was always a blessed time to read the "Christmas Story."

During the Christmas Eve celebration, Smitty came up to me and said, "Dude, it's been awhile since we last got together and hung out. I'm thinking we ought to get some guys and girls together and go tobogganing, what do you say, maybe Saturday night? We have such a good base of snow, if we go down to the Union Golf Course, we'll have a riot, eh?"

"I like your idea, Smitty. Let's get Jim and Jo-Anne and Marilyn, Horse Thief and Esther, Dave and Joyce, Murray, you and Pam of course, and I'll get hold of Joyce and see if she would like to come as well. Who are we missing? Oh yes, Lyle and Louise and her sister, I forget her name though."

"Well, you have missed Cheryl and her sister Patty, Cliff and Bruce and Edith and her sister. What about Horse Thief's sisters Sandie and Beverly? I think that about covers it."

"I'll tell you what, Dude, I will call the YMCA and see if we can book a party room for Saturday night say eight to midnight?"

"Do it, Smitty, book the room, and I'll get Horse Thief to help me call everyone. Of course I'll call Joyce first and get her early Saturday morning if she is able to come.

"Maybe the three of us," I continued, "Horse Thief, you, and me, can get some party food from Jo-Anne's dad's IGA store."

I called Joyce on the telephone later in the afternoon Christmas Day and asked her if she was free for next Saturday and maybe Sunday as well.

"Merry Christmas, Joyce. Did you have a good Christmas with your folks and your sister?"

Of course Joyce would have a wonderful time with her family. They were lovely people. You could always feel their love for each other when you visited them in their home.

"Merry Christmas, Paul. I did indeed have a lovely Christmas with family. How was your Christmas?"

"Joyce, my folks had a typical Christmas arranged for all of us. We opened gifts late Christmas Eve after we read the 'Christmas Story' from the Gospel of Luke. My grandmother played several Christmas carols on the piano, and we all gathered around to sing."

Getting back to the reason I'd called Joyce, I said, "Joyce, many of the young people from my church are planning to have a toboggan party Saturday evening. We'll toboggan on the slopes at the Union Golf Course then later come back to St. Thomas and all meet at the YMCA in their party room. There will be lots of food and fun, and we'll have different table games we can play.

"I'd like to take you if your Saturday is free? Would you be able to come? I'd come up to Mount Bridges earlier in the afternoon. Joyce, would you also consider remaining overnight at my folks' place? They have a guest bedroom. I'd take you back to Mount Bridges after church Sunday afternoon."

"I'd really love to go to the toboggan party with you, Paul. Staying overnight at your folks' place is OK too. I'd stay at the student nurses' residence, but they shut everything down for the holiday."

## Nighttime Tobogganing

Joyce and I had a real blast Saturday night out on the slopes of the golf course. The snow was crisp and cold, making a good base for tobogganing. Because I was sitting behind Joyce on the toboggan most of the time, I mentioned to her, "We've gone quite fast down this steep slope. Are you getting cold with the wind blowing directly in your face?" To which she laughingly responded, "Yes, I am getting cold, Paul. I think you've been staying warm because you are not only behind me, but also you are hugging me for warm." To which I responded with a hearty laugh, "You see right through me, Joyce."

When the toboggan stopped and we began to climb up the slope, with a strong tug on my hand, Joyce firmly stated, "Paul, from now on you get to ride the front of the toboggan and I get to stay behind you and keep warm."

"How can I argue with that, Joyce?" I said that with false defeat in my voice. "I know it will do me no good if I try to debate you, so I acquiesce to your wishes. Just one request, you must hold me tight."

Joyce retorted mockingly, "Are you afraid of falling off, Paul? I don't believe for a moment you have any such fear. I perceive that you just want some hugging. You're more interested in me giving you some hugs than you are about sliding down the hills and being concerned about my safety."

I repeated myself by saying, "You see right through me, Joyce. But I must admit that I am looking forward to more hugs and maybe a few kisses too after we've had enough of these slopes for the night."

It wasn't too much longer when both Joyce and I admitted we were cold enough to want some warmth. "Joyce, I believe I have felt you shivering, and I will admit that I am feeling somewhat colder now as well. I think it is best if we head for my car and get into some heat. And while we are getting warm again, I will drive us back to St. Thomas, and we can join the party at the YMCA."

By the time we arrived at the YMCA, we had warmed up and were hungry. The food had been set out before Joyce and I arrived, and it was plentiful. We were soon satisfied and joined in with everyone else playing table games.

As Joyce and I were looking at some table games that were not being played, she lightly said, "Paul, I want to play a game of checkers with you. But I must warn you, I'm very good at checkers. I'm the champion checker player in my home back in Mount Bridges. Are you up to the challenge?"

I immediately responded, "Joyce, you're on. I accept your challenge."

We played two games of checkers, and Joyce won the first game. I won the second game. "We are tied at one each, Paul." Joyce said. "Let's play one more game to see which of us will be the champion."

We were evenly matched, but I knew that Joyce had a competitive spirit, and so I let her win. I didn't tell her that, but what I did say was, "Joyce, you are the winner. You are the champion. I will be your slave. What would you have me do?"

Joyce immediately got back to me after I commented that I'd be her slave and pretending to have authority said, "It's about 10:30 p.m. Paul. I would like it if you'd take me down to Port Stanley. It would be nice to park in our favorite spot and look at the water. I'm not sure there will be a moon tonight though."

Whispering in her ear, I said, "Sometimes it's nicer when there isn't a moon. We won't be distracted by its brilliance. It will be darker, and well, ah, you get the picture?"

Well, of course she got the picture. Joyce loved having hugs and kisses, and so did I. But I didn't want my car turning into a pumpkin, so I had her back to my parents' home safe and sound just two minutes before the bewitching hour of midnight.

"Sunday morning sure seemed to come early, Joyce. Did you get enough sleep? It's next to impossible sleeping in because everyone is running around the house trying to get breakfast and get to church on time."

With a twinkle in her eye and a sultry look on her face, Joyce alluringly whispered, "Well . . . I could have slept a little longer, but . . . we were sort of busy last night . . . and we were quite late getting back to your home . . . right? It's all your fault, Paul."

I just shook my head and laughingly said, "I'm not even going to attempt to defend myself against those accusations. I know when I'm busted. Anyhow, how could I argue with a lovely young lady who totally captivates me? You have me in your spell, Joyce."

True to my word, after the Sunday morning worship service and a wonderful meal at my parents' home, I willingly took Joyce back to her home in Mount Bridges.

Joyce and I had arranged that I would return to Mount Bridges January 4, 1969, in order to bring her back to the student nurses' residence at the St. Thomas General Hospital where she was in her second year of studies.

Driving back from Mount Bridges, Joyce chatted about resuming her studies. She enjoyed her studies and often told me some of the things she was learning and experiencing hands on.

"Why don't you come in when we get to the nurses' residence, Paul? We can visit with each other in the common room. That's the only place you are allowed to be, but I expect it will be quiet there today."

"Sounds like a great plan, Joyce. But can we sit close to each other, or is there some sort of rule that says twelve inches must separate us?"

**Back to Flight Training**

As they say in the movies, "Life must go on." January, February, and March seemed to pass in rapid succession as I spent several hours each month practicing my newfound skills in flying the humble little Tri-Pacer.

"Hey, Scallywag, how come you seem to be ignoring us, like we're your best friends, eh? What's the story? Where've you been hanging out since Christmas? Oh, I know, you've been hanging out with Joyce, eh? What's she got that we don't have? Don't answer. I already know what you'd say, and I don't want to hear it."

"Come on, Horse Thief, you know I've been spending every hour and every dollar I can afford to scrape together for my flight instruction down at the airport. What are you trying to do, make me feel guilty about something?"

Horse Thief continued to taunt me with more sarcastic chatter. "Well, if you feel guilty, it's because you know you've been ignoring us and you feel bad about it. And it shows all over your face."

"Right you are, Horse Thief, and I'm going to feel guilty ignoring you? Hahaha. I don't think so. But since you asked as if you didn't already know, I'm working hard on getting my pilot's license, and every spare hour I can scratch up I'm in the air."

"OK, OK, I know, I know. I was just bugging you. Don't take it so personal. So where are you in your flying course?"

"Glad you asked, Horse Thief, because I wasn't going to tell you otherwise. I'm just about ready to do my solo cross-country flight. I'm planning on doing it the middle of the month, Saturday, April the 19th. Of course, that all depends on the weather, but the long-range forecast is calling for perfect flying conditions."

"Hey, Scallywag, April 19th is only a week away. After you've done your solo cross-country, I'll get a few guys rounded up, and we can celebrate."

"That sounds great, Horse Thief, but why not wait another week or so after my solo cross-country. I'm anticipating that I'll be able to do my flight exam on April 26th. I've had to book that date in advance because a flight examiner must come down to the St. Thomas airport from Toronto."

"Wow, sounds like you've just about got it all wrapped up, Scallywag. I'm thinking you'd likely have your private pilot's license then sometime early May."

"Horse Thief, you amaze me. Your deductions are right on. Maybe I'd better start calling you Sherlock Holmes instead of an ole horse thief, eh?"

"You know it's a fact, Scallywag, that I amaze everyone I converse with. I'm glad you have finally recognized that. Maybe you're not as dumb as I thought you were?"

Conversations like that were normal when I got together with my buddies. It was always good-natured jabbing or verbally poking at one another. We never seemed to tire of it, and of course we knew that if we did it in a public setting we were sure to get lots of attention and more than a few laughs. Horse Thief, Smitty, and I were all extroverts, and we could spar with each other for hours on end.

Saturday, April 19 and I was up out of bed, showered and shaved, and already had my breakfast by 7:00 a.m. The early morning was absolutely beautiful. There were buds on all the trees, and I just knew it would be a CAVU day.

Dad was always up early because he started work at his barbershop before eight in the morning. When he saw me coming down the stairs and heading for the kitchen, he asked me, "Paul, you're up bright and early. What is the occasion for such early morning activity on a Saturday?"

"Good morning, Dad. Today I do my solo cross-country flight. I'm excited about doing it, and I didn't want to sleep in. I hope to be airborne by 9:00 a.m."

Dad replied with a very affirming statement. "Well, well. That day has finally come. Be sure to make us proud. Do it well and do it safely, Paul."

The airport was bustling with activity, and I happily added to the controlled confusion as I hurried to prepare my flight plan. I had decided to repeat my earlier cross-country flight with Bert, my instructor.

"Good morning, Paul. Isn't today the day for your solo cross-country flight?"

"It is indeed, Grant." Grant was the Hicks and Lawrence manager of the St. Thomas Municipal Airport. "I'm going to do a three-leg flight, first to Hamilton then Waterloo and finally back to here. Here is my flight plan. I believe you will find everything in order."

Looking over my flight plan carefully for a couple of moments, Grant acknowledged positively. "Paul, everything in your flight plan is good. You are ready to proceed with your preflight inspection. Of course you'll be taking our beautiful little blue and white Tri-Pacer. It has been refueled."

"Thanks, Grant." With that brief exchange I proceeded to do my preflight inspection and upon its completion was soon waiting patiently for two inbound aircraft to land before I would be cleared for takeoff.

It was a beautiful early spring day for flying, and I was soon at an elevation of four thousand feet above sea level. The ground below was a patchwork of brown and green. Crops were not necessarily in the ground or were very early in their growth stages, but it was beautiful to see green leaves coming out on many trees. Yet attention must be given 100 percent to flying. I was not a tourist this morning.

The Tri-Pacer handled well in the calm, cool morning air, and it seemed that in a very brief time I was being cleared to land at the Hamilton Airport. I knew the drill. After I'd been cleared to park near the flight control center, I proceeded to get my logbook signed. I enjoyed a quick coffee offered to me and was soon airborne again. This time I would repeat the second leg of my cross-country flight and fly at three thousand feet as I headed for Waterloo.

This part of my cross-country flight was uneventful as well, and I was soon airborne again and leaving Waterloo behind me as I headed home to the St. Thomas Municipal Airport. My anticipated arrival time would be 12:00 p.m. This leg of my journey would be at an elevation of 1,500 feet.

You could nearly say that my cross-country flight was boring. There were no strong winds to contend with. There were no thermals to buffet me around. Dare I say, I was being lulled into a complacent state?

"What is that in the sky directly in front of me?" I actually yelled out loud to no one, but I was now on heightened alert. Several black dots appeared just to the right of my flight path. It wasn't bugs on the windshield.

"Geese," I yelled out. How I missed hitting them, I do not know. In just a split second I had flown right past them. A couple of those Canadian Geese were just mere yards from my right wing.

Had I hit even just one of those geese, my flight would have come to an abrupt descent and crash. God had spared my life from certain death. Of that I was certain.

I felt elated as I landed and taxied up to the fuel pumps at the St. Thomas Airport. One of the mechanics working that day had just come out of the hangar, so he approached me. "Hey, Paul, where have you been today? I heard you were doing a solo cross-country."

"Hi, Ron. I did a cross-country to Hamilton, Waterloo, and back here."

"Good deal, Paul. I'll fuel up for you and park the Tri-Pacer next to the hangar doors."

Can you believe it? I had a welcoming committee waiting for me when I went into the flight control center.

"For he's a jolly good fellow, for he's a jolly good fellow, for he's a jolly good fellow that nobody can deny." Here were my buddies, Smitty and Horse Thief, and my brother Dave singing quite loudly and totally off-key as they celebrated my safe return from my solo cross-country flight.

Several other private pilots who were just hanging around toasted me with their coffee cups. Some even slapped me on the back or shook my hand. It was my moment, and I lived it up. Nobody had a bigger smile on his face than me.

I knew we would soon celebrate somewhere in a restaurant, and my choice would be honored. Of course I chose the Rendezvous Restaurant on Talbot Street in St. Thomas. It had been a few months since I was last there. We would take a booth at the back of the restaurant and party hard. But first I had to debrief with my instructor, Bert, and the manager, Grant.

"I was on the last leg of my cross-country flying at 1,500 feet above sea level just south of Highway 401 with Ingersoll off to my right maybe two miles to the north when I suddenly flew through a flock of Canadian Geese. I narrowly missed two geese off my right wing."

Grant just stood there shaking his head, but it was Bert spoke up. "Paul, you are very fortunate. You most certainly would have crashed had you hit one of those geese."

"I know that for sure, Bert. I believe God spared my life."

Nodding affirmatively, Grant said, "God was your pilot today, Paul. You were just His copilot."

My buddies threw me a nice, noisy celebration party at the Rendezvous. It was noisy until I related my near-crash scenario with the geese at 1,500 feet. They all knew that I would have met certain death had I crashed on account of hitting a flock of geese. It was Horse Thief who spoke first.

"Scallywag, we need to all right now thank God for your flight that it was safe, that you didn't hit any of those geese." And with that, Horse Thief led out a quiet but audible prayer of thanks to the Lord.

It would be just one week later and I'd take to the air again. This time it would be my flight exam. If I passed, I would be a true certified private pilot. That week seemed to pass so slowly, yet all of a sudden it seemed that Saturday had arrived, and I awoke with a start.

## Humph! I'm Taking Your Watch

Another CAVU day. It was cool, clear, and visibility was unlimited. April 26, 1969, was made just for me. I was confident in my ability to pass my flight exam. At nine o'clock it would all come together. I would take off with a certified Ontario government flight examiner.

I must tell you about one incident regarding my flight exam. You see, I didn't have a watch with me that morning. No excuse whatsoever. My watch remained on my dresser exactly where I had placed it the night before. I had forgotten to pick it up that morning and had gone about my day preparing for my final flight exam oblivious of the fact I wasn't fully prepared. I had allowed my anticipations for the day get in my way. My excitement clouded my forward thinking. I knew how to do a preflight aircraft inspection, yet I had neglected to do an inspection of myself.

After being introduced to the government flight examiner whom I will call Mr. White, he mentioned to me, "Mr. O'Brien, we can't proceed with the flight examination because you don't have a watch. You do not have an appropriate timepiece that you will need in order to perform various exercises which I will put you through."

The flight examiner was a bit of a crusty old chap, and he was ready to fail me before I started because I didn't have my watch with me. Here I was in a bit of a situation so to speak, and speak out was what I did. Without any premeditation, I blurted out, "HUMPH! I'm taking yours." With that I thrust out my hand to take his watch from him. He was so surprised he didn't even hesitate and immediately gave me his wristwatch.

My final flight exam was going well. I was picture-perfect on my preflight examination of the aircraft, that Tri-Pacer I had spent so many hours with in flight training as a student pilot. My takeoff once I had been cleared was stellar. Of course that beautiful day with calm air was in my favor as well.

Every scenario Mr. White, the flight examiner, presented to me I executed with skill and precision—no mistakes, no hesitation. Reclaiming proper flight control after a stall situation went smoothly. Of course I didn't tell him I knew how to spin the plane out of a stall situation. Had I done that he'd probably have failed me right on the spot and told me to take my hands and feet off the controls, that he would fly us back to the airport.

"OK, Mr. O'Brien, I want you to take me through every step necessary for an emergency landing." With that comment he immediately pulled the throttle back to idle and turned the engine off. "I want you to verbally explain every action you take and explain why you are taking that action."

I spoke confidently to Mr. White. "OK. We are at four thousand feet elevation, and the terrain below is fairly flat according to my topographical map. There are plenty of wooded areas and also plenty of cleared areas. The cleared areas appear to be either barren or with crops growing, which in this area would undoubtedly be winter wheat.

"Our elevation is dropping at approximately 750 feet per minute, and I have trimmed the aircraft for landing. I have selected that cleared field at approximately twenty degrees to our port side. I am initiating a shallow bank to port now in order to keep this field in my vision. I will continue to then circle this field as I lose altitude. All the while I will have clear vision of this field through the windshield and through my portside door window. We are now approaching an elevation of one thousand feet, and I will continue to parallel this field to my left until I have completely passed it.

"We are now at 750 feet in elevation, and I am making a left shallow bank to descend at right angles to the field. We are continuing to descend now going through five hundred feet, and I am now enacting a left bank to align the aircraft with the field I have chosen.

"We are coming toward this field a bit high, so I am engaging three quarter flaps. With the execution of three-quarter flaps we will descend more quickly.

"Now at an elevation of 250 feet, we are on a flight path that will bring us safely over those power lines, which are running at right angles to the selected field.

"We are now at an elevation of one hundred feet and will safely pass over those power lines. I anticipate touchdown approximately one quarter of the field length past the power lines.

"We have just passed over the power lines at an elevation of sixty feet. Touchdown is anticipated momentarily. The terrain below appears level with a base of winter wheat well established. The ground surface will be sufficiently hard enough for a smooth touchdown as we've not had significant rainfall recently."

I think he was more nervous than I was because when I brought that Tri-Pacer in with a dead stick to about twenty feet above the ripening winter wheat, he turned the engine on and shoved the throttle to full open.

"OK, Mr. O'Brien. That was well executed. Proceed to climb back to an elevation of two thousand feet and select the proper heading to return us to the St. Thomas airport."

I had performed that emergency landing scenario about eight miles to the north of Tillsonburg. I was familiar with this area as I had practiced takeoffs and landings on the grass strip in Tillsonburg many times.

I continued to explain every action I took as we returned to St. Thomas. Contacting the airport I was told, "You are cleared to land on runway 270. Wind is variable at five to ten knots out of the west-southwest."

Back in the flight room after a perfect textbook landing, I was curtly congratulated by Mr. White who I think was mocking me a little bit with these words, "Humph! Give me back my watch." Those were his final words to me as he turned on his heel and walked out of the flight center.

With lots of noise and whooping it up, there to greet me and congratulate me were Smitty, Horse Thief, and David. "You did, Dude," yelled Smitty. "You passed. Way to go."

"Hey, thanks, Smitty. Next weekend what do you say I take you, Horse Thief, and David up for a flight? But first I'll need to get checked out in Hicks and Lawrence's Cessna 172. Then I can take you guys up, so I'll get that done early next week. Later next weekend all four of us can go for an hour flight."

Smitty spoke up for all three of them. His voice betrayed his excitement. "That sounds like a great plan, Dude, and by the way, congratulations as well. Now that you're a private pilot, does that mean you get to wear one of those captain's hats we see the airline pilots wearing?"

"Yes, that's right, Smitty. I'm still going to wear my ball cap. But maybe you'd better salute me from now on, eh?"

Before Smitty could respond to my sarcastic response that he salute me, Horse Thief cut in and made an unmistakable loud noise with his open mouth, "*Baaaa*," while at the same time sticking his finger into that gaping hole.

All that verbal jostling aside, my three buddies were proud of my accomplishment. I had earned my Canadian private pilot's license on April 26, 1969.

## FIVE

# I REALLY DID THAT WHEN FLYING

**A Flat Tire on the Super Cub**

"SCALLYWAG, IT'S GOOD to see you again. We haven't had too many opportunities to get together since you moved to Winnipeg. I'm glad you are able to take a week off and catch up with me here at Manhattan Beach Camp."

"Hey, you old horse thief, I didn't want to miss the opportunity to spend some time with you, especially since you've come all the way from Toronto with your family. Southern Manitoba is a nice place to spend a weeklong vacation, eh?"

Scallywag was a nickname Bob stuck on me when we were teens back in St. Thomas, Ontario. Not to be outdone, Horse Thief was the nickname I pinned on Bob.

"I haven't heard much from you, Scallywag, about flying, so it's true then, you've let your license lapse?"

"Well, I really couldn't afford to continue to fly after I married Shirley and we started our family. Renting a plane at more than one hundred dollars per hour got really pricey if I wanted to spend a couple of hours in the air every week. Even at one hour a week that came in at more than four hundred dollars per month. It was fun while I did it, but with four kids and Shirley staying home to raise them while I was trucking long-distance, I just couldn't justify that expense hitting the monthly family budget.

"But I still have great memories of those days when I flew. I'll never forget some of the things that I did or that happened to me. That's the nice thing about memories. They never grow old. With your memories you are transported back in time to the place where the event happened, and it's as if that event happened just yesterday or last week."

"OK, Scallywag, so let's hear a couple of those events. Bring them back to life. If it's true that you can remember them like they were yesterday, then put me in the picture, or better yet, put me in the airplane with you."

"You know, you ole horse thief, that will be easy to do. You need to imagine that you are in the copilot's seat, which is on the right side of the cockpit. Are you ready for takeoff?"

"I sure am ready, so put the throttle to the firewall, Scallywag. Let's take off for the wild blue yonder." Immediately I thrust Horse Thief and me back in time.

"Hey, Scallywag, I thought we'd be flying in that big plane over there. It looks like it would be pretty fast. What kind of plane is it?"

"You've got good taste there, Horse Thief. That plane is a Cessna 172. I've been checked out in it, but I decided not to take you up in that plane, but rather I'm going to take you flying in this pretty little yellow number."

"Well, it is kind of cute, Scallywag, but it looks really small too. Oh, and how cool is that. It has another seat, but it is behind the driver's seat. I mean it's behind the pilot's seat. What kind of plane is it?"

"That little number is a Piper Super Cub. The seating is in tandem, and you can actually fly the plane from the back seat as well. You'll be sitting in the back seat, but I'll do the flying."

"That's OK with me, Scallywag. I'll just be the tourist and look out the windows. This is my first time I've ever been in a small plane. So where are we going to fly to? Would you take a request for a destination that is close to my heart?"

"Well, it all depends, Horse Thief. If you want to fly all the way to Toronto or Windsor, then I'd have to say no way because I'd have to rent the Super Cub for at least five or six hours. Way too expensive on my budget. OK, so give me a practical destination."

"How about flying to Rodney where my grandma lives. You know where that is because you've been there with me lots of times."

"Horse Thief, that's a great plan. We can do that, and it would be fun to see your grandma's place from the air. Tell you what, why don't you run back to the hangar while I do a preflight inspection and call Grandma Csikos and tell her we'll fly over her farm in about one-half hour. She could come into the backyard and wave at you."

Running toward the hanger, Horse Thief yelled back over his shoulder. "Scallywag, I'll tell my grandmother to stand in the garden near the barn."

A few moments after takeoff, Horse Thief excitedly exclaimed, "Wow, was the liftoff ever fast in this little plane, Scallywag. It's climbing pretty fast as well. How high are we going to fly?"

"Here's the deal, Horse Thief. Over open country we can fly at an elevation as low as five hundred feet. Over a city or town or residential area we can only fly as low as one thousand feet. We are now flying at one thousand feet above St. Thomas, but I'll drop back down to five hundred feet as we pass by Fingal."

"Hey, Horse Thief, I'm going to do something I didn't tell you about beforehand. Watch this. The side window opens up. We can fly with it up, and it won't affect the flying at all. What do you think of that?"

"Scallywag, it's just as good as riding in a convertible. I'm surprised there isn't more wind buffeting us with it open. It will be great for taking pictures, and I thought I'd do just that, so I have my camera with me."

"Look down there to the left, Horse Thief. That is the old Fingal Airport. Looks pretty barren, don't you think? The highway crews have put up construction barriers here and there on all the runways, so it's not safe to land anymore. I spent many hours nearby or over this abandoned airport when I was learning how to fly because at that time the barriers weren't installed on the runways.

"Horse Thief, can you recognize and name the small villages as we fly past them or near them? Right now we are flying over Iona Station. What's just up ahead on our left?"

"OK, we are coming up on Dutton to our left, Scallywag. I recognize it because of its close proximity to Highway 401. That means that West Lorne will be showing up in a couple of minutes as well."

"You've got it, Horse Thief. And just past West Lorne will be Rodney. At Rodney we'll turn south and fly over Highway 3 and continue west to where your grandma's farm is near New Glasgow.

"I'm dropping down to five hundred feet, Horse Thief. Would you look at what is right in front of us? Here comes your grandma's farm. I'm going to circle around it a couple of times. Don't tell anyone, but I'll drop down to about two hundred feet, and you can put your arm and hand out and wave at your grandma. She's already in the garden near the barn. Here goes."

"Hi, Grandma Csikos." The old horse thief was beside himself yelling at the top of his lungs, and waving his right arm frantically out the open window to Grandma Csikos. And we were so close to her she could see him waving, and she waved back. Well, it was a touching moment to be sure.

After doing several circles around Grandma Csikos's farm, we headed down to Lake Erie, which was pretty much right there anyhow.

"Horse Thief, I'll fly us back toward St. Thomas, and we'll fly at just five hundred feet altitude as we follow along Lake Erie's shoreline. We'll have to go to one thousand feet over Port Stanley, but we'll drop back down to five hundred feet until we get to Port Bruce. Once we are back up to one thousand feet over Port Bruce we will then head back to the airport. That ought to just about round out an hour's worth of flying."

"I'm loving it, Scallywag. This is a real thrill and what a beautiful day to do it in. Too bad we couldn't just keep flying for hours and hours looking all over the place at the landscape below us. It sure is beautiful up here. Makes me feel like a bird, floating free on the wind."

Once past Port Bruce I turned to the northwest in order to fly back to St. Thomas. The day had been stellar. The views were awesome, and the winds were calm. Looking at the crops brought a smile to my face as I nodded, affirming my thoughts. There would be a good harvest this fall. What Horse Thief said about wanting to fly forever I also felt. The freedom of flight was hard to explain, but it sure wasn't hard to enjoy.

"OK, Horse Thief, the airport is coming up in a couple of minutes. I'll bring the plane down to an altitude of five hundred feet. We've got a clean shot right in, and we'll land on runway 270."

"Scallywag, can we leave this side window open when we land?"

"I don't see why not, Horse Thief. It's been a good flight with it open. You can't do that with the Piper Tri-Pacer or the Cessna 172. Seat belts tight please. Here we go. We're coming in. I'm going to plant this Super Cub right on the numbers."

The Piper Super Cub was a sweet little plane to fly. It just wanted to fly as if it owned the skies. A gentle breeze out of the west hit us head-on. This would be a numbers perfect landing.

"Touchdown in thirty seconds, Horse Thief." No sooner did we touch down as I planned right on the numbers than everything immediately went crazy.

"Hang on, Horse Thief. I can't control the plane. Something's wrong. We're heading into the cornfield."

We had barely touched this little tail dragger down when we began to make a very abrupt right turn.

"What's happening, Scallywag?" the Horse Thief was yelling. "Your left wing just barely missed touching the runway as we made that hard right turn into the cornfield."

I was doing everything I could to regain control of the Super Cub. But all I could do was cut the power and hang on. This tail dragger had a mind of its own, and we chewed up about fifty feet of cornstalks.

I cut the power and shut the Super Cub down. I was totally confused, and not only that, this was a frightening experience. It is a wonder the plane didn't flip over on its side or at least rip the left-wing tip all to shreds.

The boys in the hangar were watching us land, and when they saw us lose control and head abruptly into the cornfield, it seemed like only mere seconds and several mechanics were at our side.

As he was running from his truck toward me, one of the mechanics yelled out, "O'Brien, what were you doing flying this poor bird into standing cornstalks?"

"Guys, save your expressions of sympathy and look at the right wheel. Would you care to notice that the right tire is dead flat? It is no wonder we took a high-speed detour."

"When you did your preflight inspection, did you notice anything out of the ordinary with this tire?"

"No, guys. It rang as hard as the left tire when I gave it a couple of good thumps. So I'm asking you why it is flat now."

"We'll have to tow her back to the hangar and do an inspection. Stick around for an hour or so and maybe we'll have an answer for you, O'Brien."

The old horse thief and I chilled out in the pilot's flight room drinking a couple of Cokes while we waited for the verdict on the Super Cub.

"OK, O'Brien, you're off the hook. You didn't do anything wrong on landing. We had just changed the tire and tube on the Super Cub yesterday, but we noticed when we took the tire off the rim, the tube had been pinched. When you had taken off you were the first to fly the

Cub since that repair. The motion of the wheel caused the tube to lose air so that when you landed the tire was already flat. You were unable keep the plane landing straight and true because of the flat tire. You know something, O'Brien, it's a good thing the Super Cub can land at such a slow speed. Otherwise, there would have been damage to the left wing. But it was an easy fix. We have a new tube and tire on her, and she's ready for her next flight."

"Thanks for that encouraging news. I was going to blame my buddy for jamming his right foot into the right rudder pedal."

"Well, thanks a lot, Scallywag. Here I was scared half out of my wits because you didn't seem to know how to land and you were ready to blame me for the mishap."

"Aw, come on, Horse Thief, you know I'd never really hold you accountable for the plane's fault. That's not to say I wouldn't hold you accountable if it was my fault though. Hahaha. I mean, if I could pass the buck off on you, then for sure I'd do it."

"Friends like you, Scallywag, and who would need any enemies."

"Come on, Horse Thief, let's get down to the Rendezvous and have us a Cherry Coke each and some fries."

Back in the present time, in real time, my story over, Horse Thief and I had a few more good laughs, and then we sat a spell just quietly lost in our own thoughts.

Then Horse Thief asked me this question. "OK now, Scallywag. I want to know how much of that story was true. I never flew with you in that Super Cub. The fact is I don't recollect ever flying with you at all. Nevertheless, I will say that you painted a pretty convincing story. It kind of makes me wish I had been with you when that flat tire caused you to go pick corn."

"Horse Thief, there was some fiction in that story, but you should be able to discern where there was also truth. What is your response? Where do you perceive the truth to be?"

Scratching his chin for a moment and looking at me with slight merriment in his eyes, Horse Thief laughed as he answered me. "That's a no-brainer, Scallywag. The flat tire on that Piper Super Cub was the real truth."

"You have correctly discerned where the truth lay in that story, Horse Thief. You have won that Kewpie doll hanging on the hook over there." My response left us both laughing.

"So you liked that story, eh, Horse Thief? I'll have to tell you another story soon, say maybe tonight after the evening camp service. I'll mull it over for a while and see what I can come up with."

**Tangling with a Business Jet**

"Hey, Scallywag, Karen and I would like you and Shirley to come over to our motor home after the evening service? We can get a campfire going, and what do you say we roast some marshmallows? Can you think of anything else we might cook over the campfire?"

"You bet, Horse Thief. Shirley and I would like to spend some quality time with you and Karen around a campfire. How 'bout we not only cook the marshmallows. I think it might be possible to cook up lots of popcorn as well, loaded in butter and salt. We have some at our place, so I'll bring lots of it over."

"Now you're talking, Paul," interjected Shirley in an excited voice. "And for drinks I'll get Karen to make some lemonade, and I'll make some iced tea."

Manhattan Beach was the name of a church camp located on the north shore of Rock Lake near the village of Ninette, Manitoba. Bob and Karen and their four children had come to Manhattan Beach Camp the second week of August 1985 as Bob was the morning speaker.

Since Shirley and I and our four children had moved to Winnipeg, Manitoba, back in 1980, we had not seen Bob and Karen very often. They lived in Mississauga, Ontario, and the distance was too great to have more frequent short visits. It meant that we or they would have to commit to a vacation where some quality time could be spent with each other. This was such an occasion.

Later as we all sat around the campfire, I spoke up, thereby ending a short spell of quietness as each of us were lost in our own thoughts. "The popcorn was a nice touch adding to the fun of roasting marshmallows, wouldn't you say, Bob?"

"It was, Paul. Thanks for suggesting it earlier and bringing lots of popping corn over with you. Say, how about you tell us one of your adventures while flying?"

"OK, Bob. I think I have a good story that will hold your interest for a little while. Would you like for me to interject you into this story, Horse Thief?"

Without waiting for him to answer, I continued, "Ladies and gentlemen, we are now stepping back in time. Make sure your seat belts are tightly fastened, and hold on tight. Here we go!"

"Good morning, you ole horse thief. So you decided to get out of bed and answer your phone. I was just about ready to hang up and get in my car and come over there and dump a pail of cold water on you. Look at your calendar. Today is Saturday, August $2^{nd}$. Do I need to tell you the year as well? If you're wondering, it's 1969. What a beautiful day for flying, and it's about time I took you up for a ride around the countryside.

"What are you up to? Have you got anything planned for today, or are you interested in going for an hour long flight with me? I'm not thinking of any destination in particular, just around the local countryside, maybe down to Port Stanley and Port Bruce and then over to Long Point Provincial Park for a flyby."

"That sounds like a plan, Scallywag. I'd be happy to chip in for the cost of the fuel too. I know you have to pay for the fuel on top of the rental of the plane. By the way, what plane are you thinking of renting today? Probably the Cessna 172, right?"

"Nope. You called that one wrong, Horse Thief. The Cessna 172 is a nice craft to fly around in. It's very comfortable and stable too. I like flying it, but it's away all day on a charter, so I'm taking the trusty blue and white Piper Tri-Pacer. Come to my home around 2:00 p.m. I'm having a late lunch. Then we can head down to the airport at 3:00 p.m. I've lined up the rental for 3:30 p.m."

Just as I was hanging up the telephone, the doorbell chime sounded. Since I was alone at the house, I hurried to the door, and opening it I called out happily, "Well, I'll be, look who just showed up on my doorstep. Smitty, what's happening with you today? I thought you had a trip to Windsor with a load of Ford Auto Parts."

"The load got canceled or rather put back a couple of days. Seems Ford in Windsor still has too much stock of the part I'd be taking to them, so they put back delivery until Monday. I'm happy about that because I now have the day off. What are you doing, Dude?"

"Smitty, Horse Thief and I were going to go flying today. Hey, do you want to come? The more the merrier I say, and if we all chip in a buck or two, it'll be easier on my pocketbook."

"Dude, I'd be happy to chip in some dough. What are you going up in?"

"I'm renting the Tri-Pacer, Smitty. I'll call the hangar and get them to stick a third seat in the back. There are usually only the two front seats in this plane, but it was made to handle four people, so a third person is still good."

"Here comes Horse Thief now. I'm just making a few sandwiches right now, so I'll make a few more. Stay for my late lunch because I've got the plane rented for 3:00 p.m."

Without even knocking, the horse thief entered through the kitchen door to which I gave a snide remark. "I see you didn't want to be late for lunch, eh? So sorry I couldn't get to the door in time to open it for you. Guess I didn't hear you knock. Smitty just showed up, so he's going up with us. This ought to be a great day. We'll have lots of fun for sure.

"Let's get going, Horse Thief. You too, Smitty. You guys will make the plane too heavy for liftoff if you keep eating like that. Looks like neither of you had any breakfast, eh? We need to be at the airport soon because I need to do a preflight inspection, and that takes a good twenty minutes."

The preflight completed, I hollered out, "OK, guys, thanks for hanging around while I did the preflight inspection. Jump in the plane. Smitty, grab the back seat, and, Horse Thief, take the right-side front seat and keep your feet on the floor, not on those two pedals in front of you."

"Yes, right, Scallywag. Are you trying to draw attention to the last time I went up with you and you took us into a cornfield?"

"I'd never blame you, Horse Thief, for what happened."

Laughing loudly, Smitty cut in on the conversation. "I don't know, Dude, whether I'd trust Horse Thief in the front seat. He's a wild driver in his Chevy, and I'd think he'd be wild in the plane just as much."

"It's called a leap of faith, Smitty," I said as I tried to show some faith in the horse thief. "But maybe you and I should cross our fingers to be sure."

"We're cleared for takeoff, guys. We'll taxi out to runway 270, and we don't have to wait shy of the runway. We're cleared for immediate takeoff. The wind is from the west at ten knots gusting to fifteen knots, so we'll be taking off directly into the wind. We'll have an easy takeoff because the wind will help us in liftoff."

"I just love it, Dude, watching the earth disappear beneath us. We're climbing pretty well too, I'd say."

"Yes, Smitty, our rate of climb is a modest five hundred feet per minute. We could do better, but this is a comfortable rate of climb."

"Scallywag, if it was just you in the plane and you wanted to get the maximum rate of climb say on a perfect day like today, what do you think you'd be able to achieve?"

"Horse Thief, it might be possible with half tanks of fuel and just me in the cockpit on a day like today to get upward of one thousand feet per minute.

"Bear in mind that it takes more work to gain elevation than it does to lose elevation. I can drop this little lady quite fast if need be. I can sideslip her, and it will literally drop out of the sky. For instance, if I'm too high coming in for a landing and I don't want to overshoot the runway, I can make the plane fly sideways somewhat, and when I do, it will really drop fast. At the last minute I can then straighten her out and touch down right on the approach numbers. I'll maybe show you how it's done today."

"As long as you don't plant us in that cornfield like you did with the Super Cub."

"Aw, come on, Horse Thief. Have faith in me, eh?"

"What's your flight plan, Dude? I know you said earlier you'd fly over Port Stanley. Then where to after that?"

"Smitty, what do you say we fly a few miles south over the open water of Lake Erie? I'd climb to an elevation of five thousand feet and it might just be possible to see Cleveland, Ohio, at that elevation.

"Then I'd return to the north shore and bring us down to five-hundred-feet elevation. You can look out of your side window and check out all the people sunbathing on the beach.

"Next, I'll do a one-eighty and head back east, and when no one is looking, I'll take us down to a hundred feet as we go by Hawks Cliffs. That ought to be a good vantage point in which to observe the cliffs. I'll then take us back up to one thousand feet, and we'll continue east toward Port Bruce."

"What are you pointing at, Horse Thief? Speak up, lad, cat got your tongue?"

"Scallywag, check out those sailboats ahead of us further out in the lake maybe a couple of miles. Do you think maybe we can fly over them and wiggle-waggle our wings for them?"

"Horse Thief, that sounds like fun." Smitty was quick to affirm Horse Thief's request and shouted to me in the same breath, "Would you look at that, Dude? There must be at least a dozen people waving at us on those six sailboats. Give them another wiggle-waggle."

That slight detour didn't cost us much if anything in time, and we were soon coming up on the next destination. "Here comes Port Bruce, guys. We'll circle around the town a couple of times before we head further eastward toward Long Point Provincial Park."

Leaving Port Bruce behind, I motioned with my hand pointing out through the windshield and saying loudly, "Hey, guys, I just thought of it. We'll be flying over the Sand Hills. We've just left Port Bruce. Let's drop back down over the lake to about five-hundred-feet elevation as we fly past them. It's been years since I've been there."

Continuing my conversation now directed at Horse Thief, I questioned him, "Do you remember the time, Horse Thief, when you and my brother Dave and I camped out there for a couple of days? Your dad's tent suited us really well. It was big enough for us all to spread out and it was well positioned under some tall poplar trees. It was downright comfortable."

"I'd forgot about that, Scallywag. Yes, we did have fun, and I remember now there was another tent close by with something like a half dozen girls."

"You exaggerate, Horse Thief. There were only four girls in that tent. They were Mennonite girls as I recall."

"Come on, Dude, cut the idle chatter and tell me where we are right now."

"Smitty, Port Burwell is coming up just ahead on our right side. You should be able to see it right now."

"Yes, I see it now," responded Smitty. "I've never much gone down to Port Burwell over the years. Either of you two been there much?"

"No," I responded. "I've not been there much at all, maybe just once in my car in the past couple of years. How about you, Horse Thief? Have you ever been to Port Burwell?"

"I've not really wanted to, I guess. Don't think I've ever been there. I sure don't recognize it from the air."

"When we have such a good beach at Port Stanley and it's only a few miles to get there, why would we ever want to go anywhere else, except maybe going to Grand Bend over there on Lake Huron?"

"I agree with you, Horse Thief, so say goodbye to Port Burwell and let's head over to Long Point Provincial Park. I'll fly around it, right out to the tip and keep it on the right side of the plane so you two bad actors can keep it in your sights as we circle around it."

"I've got to say, Dude, I'm enjoying this flight even from the back seat. It's always so cool to see places you know and then look at them from the air. They look the same, but at the same time they look vastly different as well."

"Right on, Smitty. I think the three of us ought to go camping at Long Point. I've only been there once, and that was just to see it when I was out for a drive a couple of years ago."

"Well, there you go, guys. This is Long Point Provincial Park. From the air it looks rather boring. It's flat as a pancake, and there isn't a lot of trees for shade. I do expect it would get some nice breezes off of Lake Erie though. But really, after having looked it all over, I think I'll change my mind about camping there. I'd rather go up to Grand Bend."

"I guess we don't have enough time to fly over to Grand Bend and Port Franks to look that provincial park over, eh, Dude?"

"No way. Smitty, I've only rented the plane for one hour, so we're heading back to the St. Thomas airport now. We should be there with a couple of minutes to spare. I've also noticed the wind has changed from the west to the southwest, so we'll be landing on runway 210, and it is 2,607 feet in length. We will fly over Belmont on our final approach.

"Well, Horse Thief, did you enjoy yourself? We should be landing in five minutes. That was Belmont we just flew over."

"Scallywag, I have to tell you, I think I've enjoyed this flight as much as that one we took over my grandma's farm. But I can't tell which plane I like better. The Super Cub is different from the Tri-Pacer, but they both have their good points, don't they?"

"You're right, Horse Thief."

All of a sudden Smitty cried out in a startled voice, "Dude! There is a jet coming in behind us."

Smitty sounded alarmed, but I just figured he was pulling my leg, so turning slightly and speaking somewhat harshly, I said firmly, "No way, Smitty. The airport doesn't have runways long enough for jets. The three runways are only two thousand feet and a bit of change each."

His alarm now was even more pressing and loud. "DUDE! I'm not kidding you. Look behind you. PLEASE! There is a jet coming in behind you."

"OK, I'll wiggle a bit right and left. Can you see a jet, Horse Thief?"

Now Horse Thief entered an escalated state of excitement, or was it fear when he yelled, "Scallywag. Smitty wasn't kidding. There is a jet coming in behind you, and it's getting very close."

I held fast, and in a firm voice stated unequivocally, "I'm committed to land, and I'm first in. He cannot land on top of me, but will have to overshoot and return to a safe height, and attempt a second landing. Keep your eyes on him, Smitty, and I will continue forward. When I land, as soon as I'm able I'll pull over to the side, and run us onto the grass. There has never been a jet land here, ever. What the blazes is a jet coming in here for anyhow?"

With a new element of fear now in his voice, Smitty quickly questioned me, "Dude, what if it's an emergency landing that he has to do? He wouldn't be able to do a bypass and come back."

"I hadn't thought of that, Smitty," I said with a level of uncertainty. But then in a positive voice, I called out, "Hang on, guys. Touchdown is in ten seconds."

Adrenaline pumping through my veins, I hollered, "OK, we're down and brakes are full on. I'm taking it to the right onto the grass as hard as I can without flipping us over. Hang on!"

Still in a heightened state of alertness, I yelled at Horse Thief, "Where is he behind us? Can you see him, Horse Thief?"

With relief now audible in his voice, Horse Thief's response subdued that intense moment. "Scallywag, he's right over the numbers. Now he's going past us."

Still in a heightened state of excitement but now with a sense of relief in my voice, I exclaimed, "Wow! Guys, no fooling. That is a Business Jet. I recognize it as a De Havilland DH125. I can't believe he just landed and did it safely, bringing it to stop without going off the end of the taramac. Amazing!"

"Dude, I'm thinking we just got out of his way with only a few seconds to spare. Like who is crazier here? You or him?"

"Well, I can tell you one thing, Smitty and Horse Thief, I'm going to get up to the hangar as quick as I can and find out why he landed here."

Horse Thief, Smitty, and Scallywag (also known as Dude) got into the flight control room as quickly as possible. The DH125 Business Jet was already parked in front of the hangar, and there were six guys standing on the tarmac and chatting with Grant who managed the uncontrolled municipal airport.

Grant entered the flight room a few minutes later with a big grin on his face and bellowed. "So, O'Brien, had a bit of a scare, did you? I noticed you like running on the grass. The tarmac too hard for you?"

"Yes, Grant, I took the grass as soon as I could safely do so without flipping over. Care to tell me why Mr. Hotshot Jet Jockey wanted to fly up my exhaust?"

"Those guys were on a test flight out of Montreal and chose our airport to attempt a short landing and takeoff. The pilot said that the DH125 could easily land on a two thousand five hundred foot runway, and he did it with a couple of feet to spare."

"He also said he was sort of sorry, but not too much, about scaring you on your final. He thought it a bit funny watching you take the Tri-Pacer into the grass. He said he would have overshot the runway if you'd carried out your landing like you owned the runway."

"Maybe I ought to go out there and tell Mr. Hotshot Jet Jockey to . . ."

"Chill out, Dude. You got us back safely, and he landed safely and did it within the length of the runway, so all is good."

"Yes, you're right, Smitty. But I'm going out there anyhow and chat with him for a minute."

Back in the pilot's waiting room, Horse Thief quickly asked, "OK, Scallywag. Clue us in on your conversation with Mr. Hotshot Jet Jockey, as you call him."

"He was a nice guy, Horse Thief. He told me just what Grant had said a few minutes ago. And check this out. He gave me twenty bucks and told me to get a coffee and donut on him for the three of us. So I guess he's all right after all."

"Hahaha, that's funny, Scallywag. Mr. Hotshot Jet Jockey sucked a few minutes ago because he scared you out of your wits, and now he's Mr. Nice Guy because he gives you twenty bucks so you can buy us all a coffee and donut."

"Right on, Horse Thief," piped up Smitty. "The dude always gets happy if you feed him."

"Aw, shut-up, you bad actors. Come on. Let's get going. I've got twenty dollars to burn."

"Ladies and gentlemen, we are now passing through a time warp and will leave 1969 behind and enter back into 1987. Make sure your seat belts are fastened tightly and your protective glasses are on as there will be some intense bursts of light as we reenter the atmosphere of 1987. Thank you for flying with Memories Take Flight Incorporated."

With the memory flight now over, Bob remarked excitedly, "OK, Paul. You had my full attention with that story. I really did feel like I was in the plane with you. So it's true, there really was a jet that landed at the St. Thomas Airport?"

"Yes, there sure was, Bob. It even made news in the *St. Thomas Times Journal* the next night's edition. I really did clip out the article about that DH125 DE Havilland Business Jet landing at the airport. Fact is, I still have that article to this day. I've preserved it for posterity's sake, I guess."

"And it was Smitty who was with you too? Bet he was a bit freaked out, eh?"

"It was kind of funny after it had all happened. Smitty was going crazy really. He thought that jet was going to fly right into us, and he was in a real state of panic."

"He had a good laugh later, but at that moment he wasn't laughing. He kind of said he'd not be in a hurry to fly with me again. So I told him I'd let him hold the yoke the next time we went up. He changed his mind and thought that'd be OK and promptly forgot he was ripped."

"So, Paul, do you and Shirley have any more room for some more popcorn and roasted marshmallows?"

"Aw, come on, Bob. You know we've had enough, but I think Shirley and I might have room for a little bit more."

## I Turned Her Face Green

"Paul, we've come to the last night of our time here at Manhattan Beach Camp. Would you and Shirley like to come over to our motor home one more time for a visit around the campfire? I thought it would be nice to roast some corn and some potatoes wrapped in aluminum foil in the fire while I get you to help me BBQ some hamburgers."

"Yes, sure, Bob, as long as it isn't cream corn. You know I'll never turn down an invitation to a BBQ with roasted potatoes and corn. I always think of a time or two when we did that as teenagers with the St. Thomas Church Youth Group."

"Those were good times, Paul. Do you think you could weave another tall tale about flying? Karen and I really enjoyed your last couple of stories."

Sitting around the campfire later that night, Bob finally said with some anticipation and excitement, "OK, Paul. You've had time to think about another flying story, so let's hear it."

"I've given it some thought, Bob. I've struggled with this one because it's hard to select just one story when my memories are jam-packed with many stories. But I have indeed selected one, and I'd like to now draw your attention, Bob and Karen and Shirley, to those days when you were courting Karen and I was courting Shirley.

"Ladies and gentlemen, welcome aboard Memories Take Flight Incorporated. Kindly prepare yourself for this final journey into the past. As always, Memories Take Flight Incorporated requests that you take this flight seriously and follow instructions completely.

"As this flight will take us briefly into earth's stratosphere, please place your now-suspended oxygen masks over your nose and mouth. Your protective glasses must be placed before your eyes and your seat belt securely fastened."

"We will be leaving August 1987 and returning to 1970. Please note that we will be arriving at the Wayside Inn located in Talbotville at the junction of Highway 3 and Highway 4 approximately three miles west of the city of St. Thomas."

"Yes, sir. Do you have a question?"

"Hello. My name is Bob, and I was wondering how long this memory flight will take? Will there be a meal served on this flight?"

"Actually, Bob, this flight will be so fast there won't be time to eat a meal or even think about eating a meal. However, I will tell you that you will enjoy a wonderful Good Friday noontime meal in just a short time once we arrive at our destination of Talbotville, Ontario."

"One more question, kind sir. I don't want to prolong our departure, but what date and time are we travelling back to in time?"

Before the steward on that flight could answer Bob's question, there was a sudden burst of intense light and a sensation of settling down upon the ground.

"Welcome to Talbotville, Ontario. The date is March 27, 1970, and the exact time is 12:30 p.m. Ladies and gentlemen, do you recognize this location? You are standing in the foyer of the Wayside Inn located at the junction of Highway 3 and 4 approximately three miles west of St. Thomas."

Returning from a brief conversation that I had with the gentleman at the entrance to this beautiful restaurant, I said quietly to my old buddy, "Horse Thief, the maître d' just informed me we will have a short waiting time before we can be escorted to a table for four. I hope the wait isn't too long because the noise I'm hearing is the growling of my stomach."

"What's new about that, Scallywag? Your stomach is always growling. I wonder if the Wayside Inn cooks skunk? I've heard you often say that you are so hungry you could eat the tail end out of a skunk."

Karen looked disgusted and spoke up quickly, "Bob, you should be ashamed of yourself talking like that to Paul. After all, isn't he your best buddy?"

"Aw, Karen, he can take the ribbing I give him. Does he look ticked off? Look at him. He isn't even paying attention to me. He's so engrossed in your sister Shirley. It's like we aren't even here with them."

Horse Thief and I were always trading jabs at each other. Life would be too boring if we couldn't have fun doing that. But I heard what he said to me, and I assured myself I'd get him back for that poke at me before the day was over.

Interrupting my quiet conversation with Shirley, Horse Thief stuck a finger in my ribs and said rather loudly, "Scallywag, what are you and Shirley thinking of doing later today?"

"As a matter of fact, Horse Thief, Shirley and I were discussing our plans to go flying a little later. I have a Cessna 172 booked for an hour flight at 3:00 p.m. I know I am a bit short on notice, but would you and Karen like to enjoy an afternoon flight with Shirley and me? Incidentally, you'd be required to chip in half the cost. I'd give it to you for free, but with that jab about eating the tail end out of a skunk it'll now cost you big time."

"Scallywag, you cut a hard deal, but I still think it's a bargain." Karen nodded her affirmation that she'd enjoy a flight with Shirley and me as well while Horse Thief continued to ramble on in a long discourse of no consequence.

Having now enjoyed a delightful meal at the Wayside Inn, I spoke directly to Horse Thief about how we could modify our plans for the afternoon flight. "Let's drop your car off at my folks' home, Horse Thief, and the four of us will continue on to the airport in my car. I think Shirley won't mind if you sit up front with me in the Cessna. Karen and Shirley will be comfortable in the rear seats."

Now the four of us travelling together in my car soon arrived at the airport, to which Horse Thief commented, "Scallywag, you wanted to be here by 2:30 p.m., and would you look at that, we're right on time."

"Horse Thief, I have a few things I must accomplish in a preflight inspection, so would you, Karen, and Shirley, remain here in the flight center while I'm doing that? I'll come in and get you as soon as I'm ready to get you all on board."

In a short time, all four of us were walking on the tarmac when Horse Thief exclaimed, "She's a pretty good-looking plane, Scallywag. The Cessna 172 looks somewhat bigger than the Tri-Pacer we were up in with Smitty when the biz-jet just about flew right up our tailpipe."

"I don't think we'll ever forget that flight, will we, Horse Thief? There were more than a few tense moments at the time that got our adrenal glands working overtime."

We were soon cleared to take off on runway 270. There was a good steady wind out of the west, and it would give us an excellent liftoff.

We were passing through one-thousand-feet altitude before anyone spoke aloud; then Horse Thief broke the silence. "So far, Scallywag, you haven't told us where you are going to take us? Are you open to requests?"

"Well, I do have a plan Horse Thief. I was just going to let it play out without really tipping my hand ahead of time. But since you asked, I've determined that we'd fly a triangle first over to Grand Bend Provincial Park then down to Rondeau Provincial Park, then finally back to St. Thomas. I told my plan to Grant, the airport manager, just before we took off, so I'd better stick to my plan."

Horse Thief ginned widely as he spoke, "As they say in the movies, Scallywag, 'sounds like a plan.' It's a beautiful day, so I think we'll all enjoy this flight."

As I continued to describe in some detail my planned adventure, I said, "I will set our altitude for three thousand feet. We'll get a good picture of the land although we'll be too high to see smaller details. So that being the case I'll reduce altitude to one thousand feet when we fly over the two different provincial parks. Everybody good with those plans?"

I really didn't expect any negative response from Shirley or Karen, although I wondered if the Horse Thief would rather fly lower. I knew how much he appreciated flying really low over his grandmother's farm down near Rodney.

I was correct on that hunch when he looked at me with a bit of a pout on his face and said, "Aw, Scallywag, I'd like to get real low once or twice. I mean I don't want you to get into any kind of trouble, but it is fun to come in low sometimes just to see lots of detail."

"OK, Horse Thief," I responded. "I'll keep that in mind at some point in this flight, and I'll try to oblige you."

Continuing my conversation with Horse Thief, I remarked, "You know, it's been a long time since I was last in Grand Bend. I believe I was a teenager around the age of sixteen or seventeen, back in the mid-sixties. How about you? When were you last up to Grand Bend?"

"The truth is, Scallywag, I've not been to Grand Bend ever, if my memory serves me correctly. I've heard that the Grand Bend Beach is really a super-nice beach though. Maybe someday, I'll get there, but no promises on that."

Turning my head slightly to the right, I asked over my right shoulder, "How about you ladies in the back seats? Are you enjoying the flight? We're coming up on Grand Bend. Have either one of you ever been there?"

Shirley responded to my question, "Paul, I think I remember our father taking us as a family up to Grand Bend when I was about twelve. Do you remember that, Karen?"

"I do remember that, Shirley. You're right, that would have been when I was eleven. Wow, that's going back some years now, isn't it?"

We continued to enjoy conversation between the four of us until I cut in and said, "Here we go, I'm going to drop us down to one thousand feet as we fly over Grand Bend."

"Can you circle around the Bend a couple of times, Scallywag? I'd like to take some pictures."

"OK, Horse Thief. I can do that for you. That shouldn't take too long."

As I'd mentioned to Horse Thief, I couldn't take too long flying around Grand Bend because we still had much ground to cover, so to speak. Bringing the Cessna 172 back up to three thousand feet, we then set a course for Rondeau Provincial Park.

Another period of silence overtook us as each in turn became engrossed in looking out the windows at the terrain below. I broke that silence when I commented to Horse Thief, "I remember reading a book about the Second World War that was fought in the air over Great Britain. The Huns, that was the German pilots, would use the sun to their advantage. They would spot their target on the ground and come out of the sun. It was hard for those on the ground to spot them even though they could hear them. To look into the sun would blind them quickly."

"That does make sense, Scallywag. So how would that look if we were to dive down on something right now? The sun is past its highest point in the sky."

Speaking quietly to Horse Thief lest Shirley and Karen overhear our plans, I said, "Look down there directly to our left about forty-five degrees. There is a car travelling on a gravel road. He's heading in a westerly direction. Do you see the plume of dust he's kicking up behind him?"

"Yes, I see him, Scallywag."

"OK, Horse Thief. Keep it quiet, but I'm going to dive on him. I have to lose over two thousand feet. I'll bring us down to five hundred feet rather quickly. Here we go."

I didn't slack off much on the power but I did dive steeply. It was just a brief moment, and there was a commotion coming from the back seat.

Karen spoke up in an alarmed voice and asked, "Paul, what's wrong? Why are we losing altitude so quickly? Is something happening?"

"It's OK, Karen. I'm just showing the horse thief something."

"I think you'd better be careful, Paul. It looks like Shirley isn't enjoying this flight. Her face is going several shades of green."

Because we were diving quickly, I pulled up rather abruptly as well once we got to five hundred feet. I guess that made everyone's stomach kind of do a backflip.

With an audible groan, Shirley cautioned me, or shall I say, she implored me, "Paul, you are making me feel sick. Please don't fly like that."

With contriteness in my voice, I apologized, "I'm sorry, Shirley. I'll behave. I wanted to show the horse thief something, but I'll take my time and get back up to the three-thousand-foot altitude where it will be smoother for you."

The horse thief gave me the look and whispered, "You're screwed if you try any other tricks. Shirley will come down hard on you later."

I nodded, affirming his comment, but said nothing.

"Here we are at Rondeau, everyone. For Shirley's sake, I'll stay at this same altitude, and we'll just fly around Rondeau once before we head back to St. Thomas."

"Horse Thief," I whispered, "I'll behave myself on account of Shirley's tender stomach. I really do love her, and I want her to be my wife someday, so I've made the choice to be gentle on her even though I'd planned another little episode before we arrived back at St. Thomas. It wouldn't be fair to tell you what I'd planned to do if I don't follow through on those plans now, would it? You'll just have to guess."

I must say I was somewhat chagrinned. There were no more shenanigans on our return flight to St. Thomas.

Once again the four of us, Horse Thief and Karen and Shirley and I, Scallywag, stepped into the most beautiful spacecraft. Memories Take Flight Incorporated certainly had a wonderful-looking flying machine. It was cylindrical about twenty feet in length and had round portal windows on both sides. The now-familiar voice of the flight steward greeted us, and we prepared for takeoff without even waiting for instructions. We knew the drill.

With a burst of intense light and a distinct pulsing of the craft, we were immediately back in 1987.

"Paul, I must tell you," Bob blurted out. "You had me feeling like I was with you in that Cessna 172. I know we weren't there because on that particular Good Friday, March 27, 1970, Karen and I were visiting my grandma at her farm near Rodney.

"So who was actually with you and Shirley when you went flying? Did you go up on Good Friday, or was that a different day when you took Shirley flying? And did you fly in the Cessna 172 or the Tri-Pacer?"

"Bob, Shirley and I did indeed go flying that day. Smitty (Don) and his fiancée, Pam, went with us. The Cessna 172 was the plane of choice that day, and Smitty did sit in the right-side front seat while Shirley sat behind me and Pam sat behind Smitty. Shirley did indeed go several shades of green, and I got scolded by Pam because of it. That's my story, Horse Thief. Both the truth and the fiction."

"Pass the popcorn please. I've worked up an appetite, and my throat is dry from weaving that tale, so I'll have another glass of ice tea as well if you please?"

## Liking Airplanes to Flying Airplanes

"I've really enjoyed your stories, Paul, over the past few nights as we've had some good times around a campfire with Bob and Karen. There were a couple of stories that I'd forgotten about, I guess because many years had passed since the time when they had happened. But I've got a question for you, my dear. What was the event or situation or thing that happened that brought you to that place where you wanted to fly?"

"That's quite a question, Shirley. I'm not sure I can answer that in just a few brief moments. If we can set aside a special time say tomorrow before we leave Manhattan Beach Camp, I'll try to answer your question."

"I agree with you, Paul. Tonight wouldn't be the time as it is now quite late. We've the kids alone for a couple of hours, and I know they're OK by themselves, but it is late, and I'm getting sleepy just walking back to our cabin with you."

Saturday came in just absolutely wonderful. Using flying jargon, it was a CAVU day. It had been some years since I used that acronym.

"Shirley, let's go down to the beach with the kids. They've told me they want one last swim before we pack up and head back to Winnipeg and home. While they are enjoying this beautiful sunny day, we can sit on a bench under a shady tree, and I'll answer your question from last night."

"First of all, Paul, you used a word I don't remember hearing before, or if I did hear it, I don't remember what it means. What is a CAVU day?"

"CAVU means 'clear and visibility unlimited,' my dear. Today is truly a CAVU day. Atmospheric pressure is high, and there is next to no humidity. There are no clouds in the sky, and winds are gentle. Today would be a delightful day for a cross-country flight in a small private plane or even in a large commercial jet."

"I'll try to remember that term, Paul. Now tell me all about your interest in flying. What happened that made you want to do that?"

"It wasn't until my family moved to Centennial Ave just outside the city limits of St. Thomas that I became interested in airplanes. Up until that time my only interest had been growing up and working on a railroad.

"The flight path for airplanes flying out of St. Thomas Municipal Airport when they used runway 270 was directly over the family home. And by the same token, the flight path for inbound airplanes when they were flying into the airport was runway 90.

"If there was a westerly wind on takeoff, the runway used would be number 270, and if there was an easterly wind when landing, the runway used would be number 90. Number 270 and number 90 were the same runway. The number 270 was painted at the eastern end of the runway, and number 90 was painted at the western end of the same runway.

"OK, so back to your question. I would often take a blanket and lay down on the grass and look up into the sky. I loved to study the clouds and often imagined faces or animals or different things portrayed in the clouds. And of course, I had a great view of all the airplanes as they flew over my house."

"I guess you could be described as a daydreamer, eh, Paul?"

"Oh yes, I have often been accused of being a daydreamer, Shirley. I could see me flying those planes. I just knew it must be exhilarating. Sure, I was just a kid back then, but I just knew I wanted to fly. It had to be wonderful to be free like a bird, soaring above the earth."

"I've heard you say many times over our married years that a dream you often have had centers around flying, but if I correctly recall, you always said you could just jump into the air and fly if you wanted to. You didn't need an airplane. You just wished to fly, and you were flying."

"That is such an amazing dream, sweetheart. I might dream it sometimes two or three times a year. It is never the same dream, but it always has the same dynamics. I can fly whenever I want to, so I just jump into the air and soar over the trees. I can soar over tall buildings and fly over the open countryside."

"Shirley, I never had to flap my arms as if they were wings. I never had to lay on my stomach and hold my arms out. I could do that in my dreams, and I could also lay on my back and still fly. Most often I would just remain in a standing position and then just soar into the air effortlessly. No physical work was needed."

"Didn't you once tell me, Paul, that you had a dream about flying over water?"

"I will never forget that particular dream. I was flying over a beautiful river. The water was an exquisite transparent blue, and it was deep. There was a waterfall up ahead, but before I saw myself flying over it, all of a sudden I decided to fly into the river. Yes, I mean into the river. I flew under the surface of that deep blue transparent river.

"Shirley, I remember realizing that I could still breathe when I was submerged in the water. I didn't have to paddle like a dog or kick my feet as if I had swim fins on. I just moved effortlessly through the water still in a vertical position and without holding my breath.

"Then I flew up out of that river and was immediately over a very beautiful waterfall. It was so amazing, however, it was at that point that my dream ended. My memory of that dream is as vivid today as it was when I had that dream. I'm not even sure I can tell you when I had that dream other than it was a long time ago."

"That is truly an amazing dream, Paul. The way you described it made it seem so real too."

"I guess daydreams and even night dreams can play a vital role in personal ambitions, wants, and desires, can't they, Paul?"

"I certainly believe they can, Shirley. As I got older, now into younger teen years, I joined a travel club when I entered high school in grade 9 at Central Elgin Collegiate. The main focus of that club in the year I joined was to raise enough money amongst all the members so that we could charter a large passenger airplane and take a flight."

"That's an amazing goal, Paul. Did the club realize their ambitions by raising enough money to live out that goal?"

"We sure did, Shirley. In the spring of 1963, the club chartered a bus to take us to Malton, Ontario, where Toronto's international airport was located. The community of Malton would later be absorbed into Mississauga, and the airport was renamed Pearson International Airport."

"The travel club had raised enough finances so that a Trans-Canada Airlines Viscount airplane with four turboprop engines was chartered for a half-hour flight around Toronto and surrounding countryside."

"I sat in the first row of seats on the left side of the aircraft beside the window. To say I was excited would be an understatement. I bought that bill of goods immediately. Liftoff was sensational. I saw the ground disappear beneath me and the horizon take on a completely different focus. I could see forever, I thought. I was so excited I could barely contain myself. At the age of fourteen I now had a new goal. I was going to learn how to fly an airplane."

"Really, Paul, just like that?"

"Not actually, Shirley. My folks had observed my interest in aircraft, and I distinctly remember either getting a model airplane for my birthday or else buying a plastic model airplane kit that needed to be painted and assembled. Over the course of a few early teen years, I must have assembled several airplanes, so I had already developed a great interest in flying long before I flew in that beautiful turboprop Viscount the spring of 1964.

"My interest in learning how to fly was further tweaked when I was in grade 10. I had the wonderful privilege of flying to Ottawa from the London airport. But let me set the stage first, Shirley. I will give you some background that will help you to be able to more clearly see how my love for flying was developing."

"Was this another daydream that came to life?"

"No, actually, I would have never thought to dream this big, but here's how it all happened. It was mandatory that all grade 9 students enter the Armed Forces Cadet program that my high school subscribed to. In fact, Shirley, this was a time in Southern Ontario when most collegiate secondary schools had a cadet program. It could be Air Force Cadets, Sea Cadets, or Army Cadets.

"I liked Army Cadets immediately. I was given a private's uniform that I had to wear at least once a week when we went through various drills. I was proud to wear that uniform because very simply, I was proud of my father. He wore the Canadian Army uniform during the Second World War when he fought on three fronts, two in Europe and one in North Africa.

"Very quickly I became enamored with the rifle range. It was open every day during the lunch hour, and I soon revealed to the teachers my great interest in all things relating to the army, the militia, or the exacting discipline expected in the drills."

"When I returned to school for grade 10, I was given the grave responsibility of being the captain of the Rifle Range. My math teacher, Mr. Norm Lancaster, was the faculty head of the Rifle Range. I taught many students how to properly handle the various weapons at our disposal, and I only had to answer to Mr. Lancaster."

"That's amazing, Paul. You had a lot of responsibility. How old were you when this responsibility was given to you?"

"Shirley, I was fifteen years old. Incidentally, I held that position as captain of the Rifle Range right through until I graduated in 1968. But back to my story."

"Yes, please continue, Paul. Tell me how it was that flying to Ottawa had anything to do with Army Cadets."

"That year, Shirley, each collegiate secondary school in Southwestern Ontario that had an Army Cadet Program was entitled to select five students to represent that school's program. There would be approximately two hundred of us plus an adult instructor representing each school who would fly from the London, Ontario, airport on a Canadian Air Force Hercules Transport aircraft to Ottawa. We would march in a parade, do various drills, eat in the forces mess hall, and visit the aviation museum as well as the Parliament Buildings."

"That's pretty heady stuff for a fifteen-year-old, isn't it, Paul?"

"I should say it was indeed pretty heady stuff. I was as proud as a peacock to represent my school. My only regret was that the day seemed to pass too quickly."

"I remember you told me something about that day quite a few years ago, when I asked you where you got that beautiful book you keep in your library, which shows all the Canadian Military aircrafts, the air force, the army, and the navy, from the earliest days up to the present day that the book was published."

"That's right, Shirley. Do you remember that I said I purchased that book while I visited the aviation museum that eventful day in Ottawa?"

"I remember it now, Paul. That book is a great trophy to have and to keep from that day you spent in Ottawa as a captain in your collegiate cadet program."

"There is one more thing which really inspired me to strive toward learning how to fly an airplane. Each one of the cadets on that Hercules aircraft that day had the privilege of spending five minutes on the flight deck. I stood behind the captain and watched him maneuver that craft. I looked out of the cockpit windows and was amazed at the visual distance I could see when we were flying at 25,000 feet above sea level."

"Wow, Paul, it's no wonder you were stimulated to learn how to fly."

"I will always remember those days before I met you when I learned how to fly. Even to this day, I often think of them. I have no regrets that I don't fly now because of course family responsibilities are much more important than hopping around the country in a private plane."

"Paul, that's a great life story. I'm proud of you because of your love of transportation. Just think of it, Paul, you have worked on two different railroads. You have driven for some different intercity bus lines, and you have driven many thousands of miles for various trucking companies."

# SIX

# WORKING ON THE RAILROAD

"HI, GRANDPA, CAN you tell Shantel, Cheyne, and me some of your railroad stories? Mom has told us you used to work on the railroad when you were in high school and later when you graduated from high school."

"That's the truth, Austin, and in fact I worked on two different railroads all before I reached the age of twenty-one. I've got lots of stories, but I think I have time to tell you a few of them. Maybe after supper if we have time and you are interested I can tell you a few more. There may be some that your mom and dad have not heard yet."

Speaking for all three grandchildren, Shantel said, "Grandpa, I remember our train ride with you and Grandma when we went up to Churchill, Manitoba, and back. We had a lot of fun on that train ride, and I thought that Churchill was a really different kind of town compared to all the towns around here. What year was that, Grandpa, when we went up there to Churchill?"

"Let me see, Shantel, I believe it was in the spring time of 2012. If I'm not mistaken, you three kids were on your spring break from school. Do you remember that, before we began our train ride, the engineer let all of us go up into the diesel and see what it was like up there?"

"I sure do remember that, Grandpa," responded Cheyne quickly. "It was so neat up there, and I thought it would be exciting to be an engineer on a big train like that one. I was ten at that time."

"Did you know that was the second time I had a train ride to Churchill and back? Grandma bought me that train ride back in October of 1983 because she thought I had been working too hard driving semi-trucks, and she wanted to give me a little rest. Of course she knew I just loved train rides too. But I didn't stay in Churchill overnight like we did when you three and grandma and I went up in 2012. I arrived in the morning just like we did on your train ride, but I left that night to return to Winnipeg. That train ride was about six days long. The train ride we all had in 2012 was about six days long as well."

"Grandpa, when was the first time you had a train ride that you can remember?"

"Oh boy, Shantel, my mother told me I had train rides when I was just a baby, but the first time that I remember was when I was about three or maybe four years old. My home was in St. Thomas, and my parents didn't have a car. Port Stanley, was maybe ten miles away, and there was a small train that was referred to as an Electric Inter-Urban. It ran from St. Thomas to Port Stanley where there was a really nice beach right on Lake Erie. We could go to the beach and swim then have a picnic on some cliffs overlooking the beach. A little incline railway car took us up the cliff to the picnic grounds. That was pretty cool.

"I was always fascinated with trains from that time onward. The fact is I'm still fascinated by trains, and I love to have a train ride whenever I can.

"Where I lived in St. Thomas, there were six different railroads that came into that small city, but my favorite was the New York Central. It was an American railroad, and its trains ran through Southern Ontario from Windsor to Niagara Falls. Those were big, beautiful passenger trains that would start in Chicago, Illinois, and go by my place all the way to New York City, New York.

"My friend, Don, and I would ride our bikes to the big station, and watch those beautiful trains go by. They always stopped, and the diesels would get fueled up because it was the midway point between Chicago and New York City. Oh boy, did Don and I ever want to ride those trains. We wanted to ride all the way to New York City for New Year's Eve so we could watch all the celebrations that took place. But we never did. I guess life got in the way sometimes."

"Grandpa, you said you worked on two different railroads. How old were you when you started?"

"Well, Austin, I had turned seventeen in 1966, and I got a summer job working for the Canadian National Railroad on an extra gang near where I lived. We were making about thirty miles of track into a new Ford plant. We had to make a large yard for all the boxcars and about six or seven miles of track from a Canadian National main line into that yard."

"What did you do, Grandpa?"

"Cheyne, I shoveled ballast up to ten hours a day. That was hard work. I had a couple of scary moment when I was doing that. The ballast was limestone rock crushed to a certain size, and sometimes if it had rained, this ballast wouldn't flow out the bottom of the hopper cars very well. We had to go into the cars and shovel the ballast down to the open chutes at the bottom of the cars. Once I slid accidently down to the chute because the ballast dust was very slippery. Just before I would have gone through the chute and been dumped on the tracks where the hopper's wheels would have killed me, I turned my shovel sideways and stopped myself from going through the chute.

"The other time that I nearly had an accident where I could have been killed was when I tried to go from one hopper car to the next by climbing out at the end and reaching over to the next car to climb into it. The ballast train lurched, and I lost my footing, and I would have fallen to the tracks and got run over, but I was able to hold on to each car with my hands, and when I could plant my foot on something solid again, I climbed into the next car. I never did that again. I always got down off the one car and ran beside the train to the next car and then climbed up into it.

"All that happened the first year I worked with CNR on the extra gang. When I turned eighteen, during summer holidays from school, I went back and worked with the extra gang again still doing the same thing I had done the year before. This time I worked safely and didn't take any chances."

"Was that all you did, Grandpa, shovel ballast?" asked Shantel.

"No, Shantel, I also helped to move the rails into place on the railroad ties, and I hammered the big spikes into the tie plates which held the rails in place. It was all hard work, but I was strong and healthy, and I worked ten hours a day five days a week."

"You said you worked on the railroad after you graduated from high school, didn't you, Grandpa?"

"Well, not quite, Cheyne. I said I worked on two different railroads before I had turned twenty-one years of age. But I did get my first full-time job after I had graduated from high school, and it was with the Chesapeake and Ohio Railroad. This was an American railroad that went through Southern Ontario as well, and the head office in Ontario was at St. Thomas. I hired on as a relief operator in the summer of 1968. As I recall, they didn't have a lot of work for me, so I didn't stay too long. However, I did enjoy travelling to several different stations to go to work. The job of relief operator was easy enough. I would type out bills of lading for new loads that originated in the community or at the station where I worked. I would check all the freight cars once every day by keeping a record of what siding track they were on, and I would give train orders to the engineer in the diesel cab and also give orders to the conductor in the caboose.

"I wanted to work full time on a railroad, so after I left the Chesapeake and Ohio Railroad, I went over to the Canadian National Railroad in London in 1969, and hired on as a relief operator. That meant I would be going to stations all over Southwestern Ontario, and relieving other operators who were sick or on vacation or even for their days off. I was always busy, and I enjoyed seeing a lot of different stations."

"Did you have any scary moments when you worked for the CNR, Grandpa?"

"As a matter of fact, I did have one scary moment, Cheyne. I was working in Glencoe, Ontario, and it was winter time. I had to stand on the platform and hoop the train orders up to the engineer as he passed by in the diesel. The platform was slippery with some ice on it, and as the engine passed by, it began to suck me into its side. I just about got sucked under the engine and was only a few inches away from it but was able to stop myself before that happened."

"Oh, Grandpa, that must have been very scary."

"It certainly was, Shantel. But I will tell you a couple of true stories that were told to me by the railroad's safety department. These stories were meant to teach me that working around trains can be very dangerous. People can lose their lives if they don't pay attention to what they must do.

"I was working in St. Catherine, Ontario, and I had just hooped the train orders to the engineer. I was standing near the train as it passed by. I was maybe three feet away from it as it went past at about 40 mph. I noticed a boxcar coming toward me, and something was flapping out of its open door. It was a large metal strap that must have at one time secured a load. I jumped back in time as it passed. If it had hit me, I could have been hurt. I mentioned this incident to a safety instructor a little while later when I was doing a safety course, and he told me this little story.

"In another part of Canada, the same thing had happened to another operator. A metal strap had come free from the load it was meant to secure and was flapping off to the side of the open lumber car. The operator didn't see it coming, and like me he was standing near the train because he would have to hoop the train orders to the conductor as well. What happened next was awful. The strap cut into him so deeply that it killed him instantly."

"Grandpa," Cheyne moaned loudly, "that could have happened to you."

"It certainly could have had I not been watching the train as it went by, Cheyne."

"Grandpa, you said two stories. What is the other story? Is it scary like the first story?"

"Shantel, it is a tragic story. I have never forgotten this story because it had such an impact upon me. We must always do our work safely and to the best of our ability. If we lose our ability to do our work safely, we or others will pay a terrible price for our mistakes. This sad story shows what happened when a conductor on a passenger train neglected to perform his task with integrity and understanding."

"That sounds really bad, Grandpa."

"Two people lost their lives because of it, Cheyne."

"This is what happened. This passenger train was travelling through the western part of Northern Ontario. A young mother and her infant were travelling on that train to their home somewhere in the north. The conductor was aware that they needed to be let off at a particular place, which as I recollect was just a clearing in the surrounding forested area. Her family would meet her at the train that she and her child were travelling on.

"It was the middle of the night when the train stopped. The conductor did not check his schedule to make sure that the train was stopping in the correct place. All he did was open the passenger coach door and let the mother and her child off in a dark, in a cold snowstorm.

"The train began to move again and continued for the next one-half hour whereupon it stopped again. The conductor radioed up to the head engine to ask the engineer why they had stopped. The engineer told him that he, the conductor, had requested this stop so that two people could get off.

"The conductor immediately knew he had made a grave mistake and ordered the engineer to back the train up. He had to locate the mother and her child that he had let off in the dark in a cold snowstorm.

"When the train stopped, by then one hour later, where the conductor had let the mother and her child off, they found to their horror that the mother and child were still beside the railroad tracks, but they were dead. They had frozen to death.

"It was said that the conductor's hair turned snow-white in those dark hours of that night, the night he let two people off his train. That mother and child died because that conductor did not do his work with integrity. He did not safely and consciously do his job to the best of his ability."

"Oh, Grandpa, I want to cry. That is such a sad story. Was that story really true?"

"Shantel, I was told by a safety supervisor that story was absolutely true."

"I don't want to hear any more sad stories, Grandpa. Just tell me happy stories or funny stories, OK?"

"Shantel, I promise to only tell you happy and funny railroad stories from now on. So I have a funny little story to tell you. I was working at the passenger station in Kitchener, Ontario, doing what I most often did, and that was writing train orders for the engineer and the conductor of each train that passed through Kitchener. Of course I had to hoop those orders up to them like I always did at all the other stations I worked at.

"But this story isn't about working in the station or hooping orders to the engineer or the conductor. It's a short story about me sleeping in my van one night near the station in Kitchener. Sometime after midnight I was awakened by the van shaking violently. It took me a moment to try and figure out why I was being shaken so violently. Then it came to me. Someone was trying to break into my van and was trying to shake the right-side door open.

"Can you guess what I did? Well, I stuck my face right into the window and yelled at the top of my lungs. I sure did scare that fellow. He ran away as fast as he could. I had a good laugh over that one.

"But I have been looking at the time because your mom caught my attention when she pointed to the clock on the wall. Do you guys know what that means?"

"Yes, we do," responded Austin. Cheyne and Shantel nodded in unison. All three of them had little pouts on their faces.

"But, Mom," begged Austin, "it's Friday night, and we don't have to go to school tomorrow, so can Grandpa tell us a couple more railroad stories? I promise we'll go to bed right after."

"All right, children," their mom said. "But no problems from any of you when Grandpa has finished those stories. The fact is I enjoy listening to his stories too. Some I've heard before and some I haven't."

"Did you know, children, I purchased that van, which was a 1962 Ford Econoline Van, in 1969 when I went to work on the Canadian National Railroad as a relief operator? It was a cargo van, so it didn't have any window on either side, just two windows in the back barn doors. I insulated and paneled the interior. I made some shelves and a bed and a place for a space heater. The van was wired for electricity so I could cook food on a hot plate and heat it in the wintertime from the space heater."

"I bet that was real cozy, eh, Grandpa?"

"Yes, it was, Cheyne, but I still was able to pack into that van everything I needed to sustain myself for up to two weeks. Of course I did purchase food items during those times, but I had clothes, boots, coats, you know, everything that you'd need to wear considering the season.

"In the summertime of 1970, I was working in St. Catherine, Ontario. I worked the afternoon shift, so every morning bright and early I'd drive my van from the railway station where I parked overnight out to Lake Ontario. I'd lay around in the sun or swim in the lake. Sometimes I'd go to a park near Niagara Falls where I had a favorite picnic table. I'd sit there while I wrote your grandma love letters. I wrote her at least one long love letter each week."

"I enjoyed working the afternoon shift which was from 4:00 p.m. until midnight at St. Catherines. I even had weekends off, but it was too far for me to drive to Chatham every weekend in order to visit with your Aunt Shirley. I continued to work there for a whole month. Then I was dispatched to a place nearby called Welland Junction.

"Welland Junction was located near Welland, Ontario. This was a very interesting place to work, because this junction was shared with three railroads. These three railroads were the Canadian National Railroad, the Toronto, Hamilton, and Buffalo Railroad, and the Norfolk and Western Railroad. Of course I hooped orders to all the engineers and conductors of the trains of these three railroads. That made me very busy even when I worked the midnight shift.

"But my favorite part about working at Welland Junction was that I made a friend in the control house of the large lift bridge nearby, that went over the Welland Canal. This canal brought large lake and ocean freighters from Lake Ontario to Lake Erie, or the other way as well. I'd sit in his control house on top of this large lift bridge, and I'd ride the lift bridge up to its full height above the canal when a large ship needed to pass underneath. It was incredibly interesting to see these large freighters from above as they passed beneath me.

"My first job after I'd graduated from High School was working for the Chesapeake and Ohio Railroad. This American railroad went through Southern Ontario from Sarnia, Ontario, to Fort Erie, Ontario. It wasn't too long after I started working for the C&O, that I was dispatched to work in Wallaceburg, Ontario. This was where I worked on a swing bridge over the Sydenham River. When there were trains coming, I'd line the bridge up so the trains could cross over the river, and when there were no trains, I'd line the bridge up so the boats could pass. The boats on the Sydenham River were only pleasure craft, not like the boats that passed through the Welland Canal.

"Often, when I was not at work because my shift was the midnight shift, I'd get a lawn chair and sit on the swing bridge when it was lined up so the pleasure craft could continue to navigate the river either going upstream or downstream. I'd lean over the edge of the bridge and wave to the people on those cabin cruisers. Sometimes they would be drinking some beer, and they'd thrown a cold one up to me. Of course I caught it and waved a thanks to them. But I'd never drink it and only save it for any other operator who was working at the time. He'd take it home with him after his shift. I must have caught at least half a dozen cold beers over the time that I worked there."

With big eyes, Austin exclaimed, "Boy-oh-boy, Grandpa, you sure did work in lots of different places. That must have been exciting."

"It was indeed exciting, Austin. I'll tell you kids just one more story, and then it's off to bed for the bunch of you.

"When I worked for the Canadian National in Sarnia, Ontario, I often went to Point Edward. That place was like a borough of Sarnia. There was a nice little beach there right on Lake Huron. I spent lots of time swimming or lying on the beach when I wasn't working, but one day something very scary happened."

"Grandpa, you said you wouldn't tell any more scary stories," said Cheyne.

"Yes, I did say that, Cheyne, but I think this is a story you all need to hear.

"A strong thunderstorm had come up over the lake. When I heard the rumbling of the thunder and looked into the sky, I realized that this storm was coming toward me. I did the smart thing and went to my van. I just sat inside while the storm passed over me. But there was a teenage boy and girl who remained on the beach and continued to play in the sand even though the storm had come upon them. What happened next sure did scare them, and me as well.

"While I was watching them, a bolt of lightning hit the sand right in the middle of the distance between my van and these two people. When the lightning hit the sand, it kicked up a lot of sand, and of course the boom was exceedingly loud and instantaneous.

"The way I figured it out after was that my truck was attracting the lightning bolt and those two people were attracting it as well. So the lightning bolt hit the sand exactly halfway between them and me.

"Did it ever scare them? They took off on a dead run heading for their car. Hey, it scared me too, but I was protected because I was in my van."

"How were you protected, Grandpa?" asked Shantel.

"This is how you are protected when you are in a car and a lightning bolt hits your vehicle, Shantel. Because your car is sitting on rubber tires, you are grounded out. But if you are on the sand like those two people, you are not grounded out, and if that lightning bolt were to hit you, you would likely be severely injured or even killed."

"This is how it works now, kids. That was two more stories that I told you, and we all promised your mom that you would head for bed once I told you those stories, so you know what that means—off to bed with you."

"Thanks, Dad. I know you have lots of stories, and since you and Mom are still visiting with us for a few more days, maybe you might tell them a few more of your stories. I know for sure they will want to hear about your Cream Puff Caper story even though they have heard it several times."

"You enjoyed hearing that story, didn't you, when you were a child?"

"I still enjoy hearing that story, Dad, about you and Uncle Don."

"It has always been a thrill telling the Cream Puff Caper, Connie, but I think I'll change directions tomorrow, if the children want to hear a story. Shantel came up to me just before she ran off to bed and whispered in my ear that she really wanted to hear the story of how I met Grandma."

"I saw Shantel whispering in your ear, Dad, and just thought she was wishing you a good night. But listen, I was noticing the weather forecast for tomorrow, and we are expecting a rainy day, so I'll probably keep the children inside. I think you will have a ready audience when you tell them the story of you and Mom. I'd like to hear that story as well."

# SEVEN

# A BLIND DATE LED TO THE ALTAR

## A Three-Day Blind Date

CHRISTMAS 1969 HAD come and gone. It had been good to be home for a few days away from the business of the railroad. But I had a sense of being lonely. It was great to be with my mother and father and my three brothers; however, in a conversation with David and his girlfriend, Joyce, I verbalized my feelings.

Joyce was keen to pick up on this and asked me a direct question. "Paul, you don't seem to be your usual self. I think we are all missing your humor and laughter. How come you're so melancholy?"

With an audible sigh and a pursing of my lips, I began to recount this woeful tale. "Aw, look, Joyce. I guess I'm just lonely because I haven't had a date with a woman in at least six months."

"But who's fault is that, Paul?" queried Joyce. "Dates don't just happen or pop out of nowhere. You have to contribute something to get something. It's obvious to David and me that you've been giving all your attention to your work."

"Yes, you are correct, Joyce. I guess I have to take ownership of the funk I'm in. Enough of my moaning and groaning. I'm going to clean up my act."

Her next question to me became obvious that I really didn't have any plan whatsoever. "OK, Paul, so you're going to ask a woman for a date. When, where, and who are you going to ask?"

Shaking my head and shrugging my shoulders, I blurted out, "Joyce, I don't know who to ask. Do you have any suggestions?"

Looking at me for a moment or two before responding to my question, Joyce began to nod, and a big smile emerged on her face. "Actually, Paul, I do believe I know a girl who I might be able to set you up with in a blind date."

"No kidding, really, Joyce? Could you do that? Who is she? Do I know her?"

"Whoa, slow down, Paul." Joyce had a grin on her face, but she put her right hand up to indicate I should stop. "I'm not going to tell you who she is or even where she lives because it wouldn't really be a blind date if I gave you the Coles Notes about her. Leave it to me, Paul. Trust me. I will talk to this girl today, and if she is willing to meet you on a blind date, then I'll set up the date for this Friday evening."

"Joyce, this Friday is January $2^{nd}$. It's Sunday, December $28^{th}$. Wouldn't that be more than enough time to set up a blind date? Why not set me up for a date with this young lady earlier, maybe for this coming Wednesday?"

"Usually, Paul, most people work during the week and have the weekend off. Leave it with me. No more questions. I promise I'll get back to you on this in a couple of days. Let's have some patience on your part, OK?"

With those parting comments, Joyce grabbed David's hand and standing up said, "Come on, Dave, let's get out of here before Paul beats me to death with questions about this girl that I have in mind for his blind date."

Now I remembered what it was like being put into a holding pattern. That happened a couple of times when I'd be flying and would want to land at a particular airport. I was put in a holding pattern and had to wait my turn. It was like flying around in circles and going nowhere.

But Wednesday evening I received a phone call that created an immense amount of anticipation and excitement.

"Hello."

"Hi, Paul, this is Joyce. Are you still interested in having a blind date, or are you reverting back to your old ways?"

"Joyce, don't tease me. Do you have some good news for me? Were you able to set up a blind date for me for this Friday evening?"

Laughing for a few seconds, Joyce finally recomposed herself and said, "Paul, I have set you up for a three-day blind date starting Friday evening, and it will also include all day Saturday and most of Sunday. Are you able to handle a three-day blind date?"

"Wow, Joyce. That's crazy. Of course I'm able to handle a three-day blind date . . . I think.

"So tell me all about her, Joyce. I want facts and figures. Where does she live, and what does she do? And most importantly, what is her name? Do I know her? Have I ever met her before? Come on, Joyce, what does she look like?"

"Paul, slow down. I will only give you a couple of pieces of information about her. First of all, she doesn't live in St. Thomas. She lives in Chatham. She is your age. I think you are a couple of months older than she is, but I'm not even going to tell you her birth date.

"She will come to my place around suppertime on Friday, and Dave and I will bring her to our church youth group's Friday gathering at eight in the evening. Of course we will arrive a bit earlier than eight so that I can introduce her to you. That's all I'm going to tell you. Oh, one other thing. She dresses very nicely, so you'd better be looking your best too."

"Joyce, what did you tell her about me? I hope it was all good."

"Come on, Paul, I'd never tell her about all your bad habits. Trust me. I did tell her a few things like what color your hair was, how tall I thought you were, and if you had nice teeth and a good smile. Maybe I lied about that—just kidding. I told her you had blue eyes and worked in the Canadian National Railroad. Of course I told her you had a private pilot's license. I think that was all I told her—well, that's all I'm going to tell you that I told her. The rest will have to remain a mystery to you."

"I know you told her about me, Joyce, why don't you tell me about her?"

"Real simple, Paul. If it remains a mystery to you, then that will heighten your anticipation and desire to meet her."

"I'm not going to tell you I think you are cruel for not telling me more about this mysterious lady, Joyce, but you are cruel and you know it."

"Suck it up, buttercup" was all Joyce said to me as she laughingly hung up on our phone conversation.

My impatience waiting had no bearing whatsoever on my ability to speed things up. I couldn't hasten one moment of one day to make time move quicker. But as I stood inside the main doors of the designated location where I would meet my blind date, she appeared in the company of my brother and his girlfriend, Joyce.

Oh my, this young lady was beautiful. She wore low pumps and a light blue dress. Her hair was a luxurious auburn, and her complexion was clear and smooth. Her eyes were a mysterious color of brown, deeply penetrating yet delightfully mischievous.

*Please, Joyce, introduce me to this lovely young woman.* My thoughts were broken by Joyce's laughter.

"Paul, Paul, I'd like to introduce Shirley Tomen to you. Shirley, this gentleman is Paul O'Brien."

Did I perceive my heart skipping a few beats? My heart continued to beat rhythmically, but I had to inwardly remind myself to breathe. I extended my right hand to shake Shirley's hand in a cordial fashion and with a strong, resonating baritone voice said, "Shirley, I'm so pleased to meet you," to which she replied, "And I, Paul, am delighted to meet you too."

Her sultry voice made me think of gentle waters flowing over smooth stones. I was absolutely captivated by her presence.

The youth gathering where we would meet was about to begin, so I offered Shirley my left arm, which she willingly took by placing her right arm through mine and resting her hand lightly on my forearm. Just that innocent gesture of arm in arm sent goose bumps down my back.

The youth meeting came to an end but not before I stole countless sideways glances at this beautiful girl sitting close to my left shoulder with her hands clasped together and placed demurely on her lap.

My brother David and I had planned earlier to take Joyce and my blind date Shirley to Johnson's Steak House on Talbot Street in St. Thomas. It was just a few miles away from where the four of us had been at this youth gathering.

Once we were shown to our table and menus were handed to us, we entered into a delightful conversation. I wanted to know more about Shirley.

She responded, "Chatham is my hometown. I moved out of the family home a couple of years ago, and I'm living at a widow's home where I pay for room and board. Nearby is the church where I worship. My vocation is secretarial, and I am employed at Libby's, a local food industry."

Upon being asked a little bit about myself, I gladly replied, "I am a relief operator for the Canadian National Railroad in Southern Ontario. I travel extensively between railway stations within this district. I have a 1962 Ford Econoline Van, which I have converted. If I'm not spending a day or two at my parents' home here in St. Thomas, I am living in my van."

Our waitress appeared at our table and wished to take our orders. David suggested Joyce order first. When it came to Shirley, she hesitated shyly and said, "Could I pass for the moment. I'm not quite ready to order."

Our waitress obliged, and I gave my order. "I'd like to order steak, baked potato, and a salad please."

David and Joyce had ordered identical plates, but when the waitress turned back to Shirley for her order, Shirley quietly said, "I would just like to order a baked potato please."

We continued to enjoy our conversations, but in my mind I was thinking Shirley had a shy side too.

The food was excellent, and the conversation was enjoyable. I think I was becoming mesmerized by Shirley's deep brown eyes, her melodious voice, and her light touch on my arm when she touched me periodically in our conversation.

Far too quickly for my liking the evening of January 2, 1970, had come to an end. Because the four of us were riding in David's car, we proceeded to Joyce's home. Shirley would remain with Joyce overnight and also through to Sunday afternoon.

Now I think it was my turn to be shy. How dearly I would have loved to give Shirley a good night kiss, but with David and Joyce nearby, I turned down the opportunity.

Holding Shirley's hand, I asked, "Would you accompany me tomorrow morning? I'd like to take you tobogganing. There are some gentle slopes nearby which should give us some enjoyable opportunities for downhill sliding."

Her response was in a quiet yet sexy voice, which suggested that Shirley would be a fun-loving girl who'd enjoy just about anything. "I'd like to go tobogganing with you, Paul."

Those words echoed over and over in my head. I was completely captivated, and I wanted to pursue her, to know her better, and of course be open and transparent with her as well.

We parted company that evening with a promise to continue our weekend date experience. "I'd say I was a happy camper," I said when Dave asked me how it went.

**Tobogganing That Went South**

Saturday morning was absolutely beautiful. The sun shone brightly from a clear blue sky upon the glistening snow. Everywhere you looked it was like you observed complete fields of diamonds. But I digress. I was on a mission.

Picking up the house phone, I called Joyce's home. When Joyce answered, I identified myself. "I know who you are, Paul. I recognize your voice. With whom would you like to speak?" she asked in a teasing voice.

Before I could chide Joyce, knowing full well she was playing me, she continued, "Oh, for a moment I thought you wanted to talk to me, but I'm getting poked in the ribs by Shirley."

Joyce could be too funny sometimes. This was one of those times as she tried to mimic Ed McMahon with a rather humorous rendition of "Here's Johnny" while substituting Johnny with Shirley. This time my heart skipped a beat as I heard her melodious voice.

"Hello, Paul, this is Shirley."

What was happening to me? I had to hold my breath. Her voice totally captivated me. "Good morning, Shirley." The usual introductory comments were exchanged, such as "Did you sleep well?" but as soon as was politely possible, I asked, "Shirley, would you like to accompany me on a little tobogganing adventure?"

Her immediate and elated reply was, "I would enjoy that, Paul."

And then this idle thought went through my head. If she enjoyed that, how much more would I enjoy that? I was envisioning us sitting on a toboggan, my arms around her holding her tightly as we glided down a slope.

My plan was soon fulfilled. We had arrived at the first toboggan run, and Shirley and I stood on the crest of a nice, long slope. I wanted to give Shirley a good first ride down the hill so suggested, "Shirley, sit in front of me. I will hold you tight. I won't let you fall off. You'll be safe, I promise. This will be lots of fun."

Down the hill we sped. The snow was smooth and crisp because there had been a slight thaw yesterday and then a cold night last night. But it was nearly impossible to steer the toboggan.

"Oh no. Hang on, Shirley. I can't seem to steer this thing." I was digging my left heel into the snow to try to steer to the left. I had to because there was a large tree looming before me. All I succeeded in doing was turning the toboggan sideways. The inevitable happened. We hit the tree on our right side with a hard crunch.

"Oh no, Shirley, you have a bloody nose." I pulled out a clean handkerchief from my pocket to try to stem the flow of blood. All I could think of was that I was done in. Shirley won't want to continue our blind date.

I think Shirley read the forlorn look on my face accurately and said soothingly, "Paul, I'm okay. I know you tried to avoid that tree and that you wanted me to have an enjoyable time."

Of course I apologized profusely. "Shirley, I'm so sorry." I must have repeated that sentence several times until Shirley took my hand

and looked earnestly into my eyes and said, "Paul, it's OK. See I'm not bleeding now. It was just a small bang to my nose. No harm done. But let's go back to Joyce's home, for I see a few small drops of blood on my parka. I think there is a way to remove those stains."

## The Blind Date—Back on the Rails

I think we both soon forgot about the tobogganing fiasco, especially when I asked, "Shirley, would you like to go bowling with me tonight? I could ask a few other couples to join us, and then after bowling, we'd all gather at my parents' home for some snacks."

Shirley affirmed my request with a captivating smile, and in a melodious voice said, "Paul, it would be my pleasure to be your date this evening. Please do take me bowling. I would enjoy that immensely."

Arriving at Joyce's home to pick Shirley up for our date Saturday evening, I was totally captivated by her beauty. Her gentle smile, somewhat shy, but at the same time very alluring, drew my attention to her full red lips. I had to check myself. I was beginning to stare. I didn't want to embarrass her so I shyly averted my gaze. It was then that I noticed how luxurious her auburn hair was. Dare I say it? I was being swept off my feet. I wanted to sweep Shirley off her feet, but instead I was captured. My heart felt it would burst. I was sure she could see the blush on my face.

Three other couples joined Shirley and me, and our games went without a hitch. Everyone had a wonderful time. I was especially happy that Shirley really seemed to enjoy herself, and she made friends so easily.

The bowling was great fun, and the food later was fulfilling especially since we could wash it all down with my mother's famous hot chocolate topped with mounds of whipped cream.

I had borrowed my father's car, so later that Saturday night, Shirley and I sat for a long time in Joyce's parents' driveway and talked and talked. We both wanted to get to know each other more fully. But at one point I just put my arm around her shoulders, and drew her close to me, and without any hesitation kissed her on the lips. It was a good, long kiss too.

Forget about talking, we'd found a new interest and took to it with passion. Finally, in a husky voice, I said, "Shirley, I really must let you go. But I'm looking forward to tomorrow."

To which she responded, "Thank you for a lovely day and evening, Paul. I'm looking forward to tomorrow as well. Will you pick me up and take me to church with you?"

"I'd be delighted to have you accompany me to church, Shirley." And with that—oh yes, and one more kiss—I bid this lovely lady a good night.

Sunday, January the third was another stellar day. I don't remember what the weather was like. Was it sunny or cloudy, mild or cold? I didn't care. What was beautiful about that day was that Shirley was on my arm as we walked into church. My, oh my, did she look beautiful.

I had to comment on her beauty, and with soft words I said, "Shirley, you look absolutely beautiful. Your green parka complements your brown eyes and gorgeous auburn hair. I am so honored to have your company."

Shirley gave my arm a special squeeze and smiled demurely while looking into my eyes for a long moment. She said nothing, but I knew she had said it all just with that look and that squeeze.

I was amazed how quickly Shirley and I became comfortable in the company of each other. Sunday afternoon after we'd enjoyed a wonderful roast beef dinner with Yorkshire pudding that was topped off with warm apple pie and vanilla ice cream, we retreated to a quiet spot on the couch. Sitting close together and holding hands, we began to learn more about each other. I began to share details about my life, and Shirley shared many details about her life. We had so much in common that I believe those few hours sharing with each other solidified an immediate warm and caring friendship.

Late that afternoon, Shirley finally said in a quiet, sultry voice, "Paul, I must return to Chatham. I truly wish I could remain longer, there is so much more I want to know about you. But I would like to arrive before the evening becomes late as I need to prepare for work tomorrow."

Responding to Shirley as I helped her into her pretty green parka, my husky voice a mixture of happiness and emotion, I quietly whispered close to her ear, "I have enjoyed these past couple of days getting to know you. And I would like to get to know you even more."

It was at that point I was able to look into her soft brown eyes, and without saying another word, I bent in close and kissed her lightly on the cheek. Shirley, with a cute little smile, puckered her lips slightly and gave me a tender kiss.

We parted waving to each other as she drove away.

The rest of my Sunday evening was spent quietly reflecting on the blind date weekend I had just experienced as I prepared to drive back to Preston, Ontario (later known as Cambridge). I was working as the railway station's relief operator and needed to be on the job by seven in the morning.

**In Pursuit of Shirley**

Every spare moment I had during my work in Preston, I thought only of Shirley. I relived the past weekend in my mind many times. It was the following Wednesday evening when I was shopping in a Simpson Sears store in Kitchener for a pair of brogues that I could no longer be quiet. Going into the central concourse of the mall, I found a pay phone and quickly dialed her phone number. My heart quickened when she picked up on the third ring.

"Hello, Shirley, this is Paul," I blurted out. "Shirley, would I be too forward if I asked you if I could come down to Chatham this coming weekend? I would like to spend more time with you. There is so much more I want to know about you."

Shirley's response was quick and affirming. "Hi, Paul, I would like very much for you to come to Chatham this weekend to visit me. When could I expect you to arrive?

We had a short, delightfully animated conversation, and our plans were established. I would spend the weekend with Shirley at her parents' home. Thus began a relationship that grew and developed into a mutual care for each other.

That second weekend in January was when I knew I wanted to continue to date Shirley. We spent some time with her parents and her younger siblings. There were many similarities between her family and mine, and I rapidly became comfortable in her home setting.

"Paul, I would like to go for a walk with you this afternoon. It is a mild day, and the walkways in Tecumseh Park on the Thames River, downtown Chatham should be clear." It was Saturday January the tenth when Shirley took me aside after a very good meal her mother had prepared to ask me to accompany her.

Tecumseh Park was indeed a pleasant little park. The Thames River was not frozen, and a few confused Canadian geese swam freely. While on the walkway adjacent to the river, I took Shirley's right arm and placed it through my left arm so that I might hold her hand with my right hand. I wanted her to be secure should there be any slippery patches.

"My Paul, you are such a gentleman," Shirley cooed. "Let's not be in any kind of a rush. I enjoy being close to you."

"And you, Shirley, are truly a lady," I purred back to her. "A slow walk with a pretty girl on my arm, I assure you I am in no rush to end this stroll."

Later that evening, Shirley and I had complete privacy as we sat snuggling close together on the couch watching the late movie. I don't remember what the movie was about, but I sure do remember that I enjoyed holding Shirley's hand. All right, you guessed it, we shared a few tender kisses as well.

Sunday passed in flurry of activity but started with a wonderful breakfast made by Shirley and her mother. When we had settled into a pew at her church later that morning for the worship service, I couldn't help but notice that several friends of Shirley's sneaking a peek at us from time to time.

Later as we enjoyed a few quiet moments after Sunday's dinner of roast chicken with all the trimmings, I whispered into her ear, "Why is it that when one is having such a good time the clock seems to run twice as fast? Shirley, I must soon depart and return to Preston. This will be the last week I'm working there.

"The following week I'm transferred to the Canadian National Railroad station in Glencoe where I'll be working the afternoon shift from 4:00 p.m. until midnight. However, I won't have any days off on the weekends. I'm not sure how that will work out for me to see you during the week, but I would like to keep in touch with you."

"I understand, Paul, and I do wish for you to keep in touch with me. You can phone me any evening, and we can talk. Are you able to make calls from the station when you are working?"

"There may be a few moments from time to time where I'll have that opportunity, Shirley, but I can't promise. One thing I can promise is that I'll phone you when I have my days off, and I'm told those two days are Tuesday and Wednesday each week."

We parted soon after that somber conversation. With a final kiss and a wave from the window of my van, I returned to Preston, and Shirley returned to her room at the boarding house.

The days seemed to go by so slowly. It was frustrating. I wanted to return to Chatham and see Shirley, but it was not to be. The relief operator position I held down at Glencoe was extremely busy. This station was on the main line between Windsor and Toronto, and it seemed trains, both passenger and freight passed by my operator's window in quick succession.

February came, and still there was no opportunity to see Shirley. I had just returned to Glencoe for my next five days of afternoons. I had visited my parents back in St. Thomas but had not been able to visit with Shirley in Chatham.

When I was back at my parents' home, I'd complained to my mother that I'd not seen Shirley since the eleventh of January. My mother lightly responded with a smile and a shrug of her shoulders, "Paul, don't you know how to write a letter?"

"Bingo! That's what I'll do, Mom. I'll write letters. I don't want Shirley to forget me."

That night, February 5, after my shift, I sat in my van/camper and wrote a six-page letter. The three sentences I really wanted Shirley to read were simply structured. "Shirley, I have missed you, and wish I could be with you to tell you this, but I can't wait for that opportunity. I want you to know that I've fallen in love with you. You are very special to me."

I poured my heart out in that letter to Shirley that night and prayed she would not just read it but tell me that she loved me too. I felt vulnerable having done it, but oh, how I wanted to hear those words come from her sweet lips.

My work as a relief operator kept me from seeing Shirley every weekend, but it didn't keep me from writing love letters to her. I did this gladly and with each letter told her more about myself. I didn't neglect to tell her that I loved her, but writing several *X* and *O* at the close of the letter was a poor substitute for real kisses and hugs.

Might you ask, did Shirley write me letters in return? Yes, indeed. In her letters she also told me more about herself. I found her letters so intriguing that I would read them several times before receiving another letter from her.

I longed to read those words, *I love you,* from Shirley's pen, and I was rewarded with that term of endearment in her second letter to me. I shivered in excitement as I read and reread those sweet words. She said she loved me. I could have danced all night. I was full to overflowing with happiness and joy in my heart.

I spent nearly a month working in Glencoe at the CNR station and then was sent to St. Thomas to work as relief operator at the freight yard shared jointly be the Canadian National Railroad and Norfolk and Western, an American railroad. Now I could see Shirley again. I would have weekends off, and so I immediately phoned her the evening I received that wonderful news from the railroad.

"Hello, Shirley. I have some great news. Starting February 17th I'll be working back in St. Thomas for a few weeks. But the best part of that news is that I'll have weekends off. I would like to take you to Toronto on February 21st and we could visit Castle Loma. I was there when I was fourteen. It is a magnificent castle. It looks very similar to the castles one would see if he were to visit the British Isles. It has all the features both inside and out that you expect to see. It even has tunnels and secret hallways."

"I've heard about that castle, Paul, and it is really a castle, isn't it? I would love to go with you. Should I come down to St. Thomas Friday evening?"

"Yes, please come Friday evening. You can stay at my parents' home as they have a spare bedroom. I'll stay in the basement where I've made a place for myself when I'm home for a day or two. I've also purchased two tickets for seats in the first row right down on the ice to see the Ice Capades at the London Gardens for the Saturday late show. We'll be back in time from Toronto to see it."

Shirley and I had a wonderful time visiting Castle Loma, and watching the Ice Capades later that day. We constantly held hands or locked our arms together as we walked about. When we sat together, we whispered to each other, and when the lights were darkened during the show on ice, we'd try to be discreet, but often kissed each other. Oh the joy of being in love. However, the day wasn't complete until I took her to Port Stanley late that evening, or should I say, early Sunday morning. It was too cold to walk on the beach late that night, but the heater in my vehicle certainly kept us warm as we chatted and kissed each other.

Shirley and I continued to see each other as often as we could. We would alternate weekends visiting each other's home when it was possible, and we always sent love letters back and forth to each other at least once a week.

**Passion Got in The Way**

When Shirley arrived in St. Thomas Friday evening, May 15, I excitedly told her something I'm sure she never forgot. "Shirley, tomorrow, I have reserved a Piper Tri-Pacer for an hour's flight in the afternoon. We could fly around the local area, but I'd really like to fly as far as Chatham, so you could see your city from the air."

"Oh my, that sounds like fun, Paul. I can hardly wait," Shirley excitedly responded. "I sure hope the weather will be good for tomorrow."

"The weather won't be too bad, Shirley. I expect from the weather reports we will have high-altitude cloud cover over Southern Ontario and the possibility for some sun as well. Basically, it will be a warm and humid day."

Awakening early Saturday morning, I realized that the weatherman's forecast was accurate. It was indeed the beginning or a warm and humid day. Yet, I had no concern for the weather. Once at a reasonable altitude, we wouldn't experience the heat the same as would be experienced on the ground.

I wanted to practice my culinary skills on Shirley so decided I'd prepare breakfast for her, and bring it to her while she was still in her bed. The effect of that gesture was what I wanted and anticipated.

With a delightful gasp, Shirley happily said, "Paul, how sweet of you to make my breakfast for me, and bring it to me. That was so sweet of you.

"But Paul," speaking hesitantly, she continued, "have you eaten? It wouldn't be nice or polite for me to eat in front of you."

"Shirley, while I was making your breakfast, I did indeed eat mine. Please enjoy yours while it is still hot."

Shirley very kindly invited me to stay with her as she ate, and said she would enjoy my company as we visited with each other.

During our conversation Shirley asked, "Paul, how will your plans for our day together unfold? Is the weather today suitable for flying?"

"We will have reasonably good weather conditions, albeit a little warm and humid, Shirley, but nothing extreme is forecast. Our flight should be delightful, and I promise I'll not do anything to upset your stomach."

Later in the morning, Shirley asked, "Paul, would it be OK if we went to Pinafore Park and walked through the beautiful flower gardens? I'm sure the flowers will be in full bloom by now and the fragrance will be refreshing."

"That's a wonderful idea Shirley. And later, say around noon-time, why don't we enjoy a little picnic while we are there. What I will do is purchase a couple of picnic lunches from Kentucky Fried Chicken before we arrive at the park."

While walking arm in arm through the many flower gardens of Pinafore Park, I mentioned to Shirley more of my plans for the day.

"I want to be at the airport by 2:30 p.m. You will be able to wait inside the hangar where there is a waiting room attached to the flight center. I need to do a preflight inspection, which should take approximately twenty minutes. We can then board the Tri-Pacer, and I'll continue a preflight inspection of the instruments. Then we'll taxi out to the active runway and prepare for takeoff. Basically, I've rented the plane for an hour, and we'll need to be back to the airport by 4:00 p.m. at the latest."

After a lull in our conversation while enjoying our picnic lunches, Shirley spoke up with a question, "Paul, do you have to tell the people in the airport where you want to fly to, and what your destination would be?"

"That's a great question, Shirley. Yes, I would give them that information. I will tell them I'd like to take us for a flight down to Chatham so can could see what your hometown looks like from the air."

We ate our picnic lunches slowly as we sat side by side on the picnic table. How could I be in a hurry to do anything else when Shirley sat close beside me? Her presence made my heart beat faster, and her melodious voice drew me under her spell.

Looking at her wristwatch, Shirley commented on the time and said, "It's about 2:00 p.m., Paul. Do you think we should soon leave Pinafore Park?"

With a big smile on my face and in a cheery voice, I said, "We're right on time, Shirley. If we leave now, we'll be at the airport in twenty or twenty-five minutes, and everything will work out just perfect."

Once the preflight inspections was done, and we had begun to taxi out to the active runway, Shirley turned to me and asked, "Paul, what is that orange thing on that pole which is on top of the hanger?"

I responded with a smile and said, "Shirley, it is called a wind sock. When there is a wind it will fill up with air and indicate the direction that the wind is blowing. It's more like there is nothing other than a gentle breeze today. Right now there seems to be no breeze whatsoever."

Because the wind blowing out of the east was so gentle, and there was no airborne traffic in the vicinity, I made a rather hasty decision to take off from runway 270. I really should have taken off from runway 90.

Once I made that decision and began to follow through with it, I very quickly realized I had not been connecting all the dots, as is so often said. It was a warm, humid day. There would not be the same lift under the wings that there would be if it was less humid and cooler in temperature. Furthermore, though the winds were light, I should have taken off facing the wind. This would have meant that runway 90 would have been the correct choice. The formidable result was that the Tri-Pacer didn't want to rotate and lift off. Very quickly I used up the complete length of runway 270 and only struggled to get airborne mere feet from the end.

I said nothing to Shirley at the time but determined to inform her of my error later. If she realized the serious issue I had created, she said nothing. For that I was grateful. I vowed to myself right then and there that I would not let passion get in the way of clear thinking ever again.

I put on my happy face and with a cheery voice said, "Shirley, I will fly at an elevation of three thousand feet above sea level. We are now flying westward toward Chatham. The air isn't very calm nor would it be at a lower elevation. That is why it seems to be a very bumpy flight."

Chatham became visible, and I dropped to one thousand feet so that Shirley could pick out landmarks more easily. As I flew around the city in a counterclockwise circle, she excitedly was able to point out her parents' home on Gregory Drive.

With a happy and excited voice, she asked, "Paul, would you fly around my folks' home again? Maybe they just might hear us flying around and come out to look." Sadly, no one came out of the house to look into the air at us flying around above them.

Again climbing to an elevation of three thousand feet, I looked at my watch and suggested we head back toward St. Thomas.

"Shirley, as we return to St. Thomas, I will fly a more southeasterly route closer to the north shore of Lake Erie. We are experiencing many updrafts from hot air rising from those freshly plowed fields right below us. I'll fly closer to the lake for a while. It might be smoother."

I didn't make an error in my decision to land on runway 90. The easterly breeze had picked up to a not so gentle wind. As we were descending on final, I spoke to Shirley saying, "Look just slightly to your right, we will fly just about directly over my parents' home at an elevation of five hundred feet."

Back on the ground, I took Shirley aside and hesitantly said in a quiet voice, "I need to tell you something that I regret doing."

I briefly described my error in judgement when we were beginning our flight, and I concluded my explanation by somberly stating, "I'm so sorry Shirley. Please forgive me putting our lives at some risk."

Of course Shirley forgave me, and gave me a squeeze, and a kiss to affirm it. But quickly said, "I think you had better treat us to something nice and cold to drink, like maybe a Cherry Coke at the Rendezvous Restaurant."

## Courtship, Our Mutual Desire

A short time had passed from that weekend when I was able to ask, "Shirley, could you come to St. Thomas even if it is just for a couple of hours on a weekday evening after you are done work? I want to talk to you about something that is pressing on my heart."

"Of course, Paul, I'll come down to see you tomorrow evening if that is good for you. I'll leave right after work, and I should be there by six or six-thirty."

"That will work perfectly for me, Shirley. I need to be in St. Catherines the next morning for seven. I'm starting a relief operator placement at the C.N. station and will be there for a couple of weeks."

Wednesday evening came, and I became concerned when Shirley hadn't arrived by six-thirty. I was at my parents' home and spoke to my mother, "I hope nothing has happened that would cause her to not be able to come. She hadn't called me to postpone our meeting."

My mother was looking out the kitchen window at that moment, and happily said, "Paul, you need not worry. Shirley has just arrived."

I opened the door and went out to greet her. "Shirley, I'm so happy to see you. I'm glad you were able to come. Let's go into the house and find a quiet corner so we can have an important conversation."

Shirley's eyes grew big when she heard the words "important conversation," and speaking softly, she said, "Paul, is something wrong?"

"No, Shirley, nothing is wrong. On the contrary, everything is right." And sitting down on a couch, I held Shirley's hand and said in a quiet voice, "Shirley, I have grown to love you more and more, but what I want to ask you tonight is something very important to me, and to you I hope as well."

Shirley's eyes grew wide as she whispered back to me, "Paul, please tell me everything."

"I have grown to love you, Shirley, more and more. But I realize that I have come to a crossroads in our relationship. I know in my heart that I want to continue to see you and be with you, but I also know that I'm at a point where I could walk away from our relationship. I don't want to do that.

"What I'm saying is that I want to date you exclusively from now on with a focus and goal of matrimony in the future. It is called courtship. I want to court you, and allow my love for you to grow more and more. I'm not asking you to marry me, but what I am asking you to do is to allow me to court you."

"Oh, Paul, I do so dearly want you to court me. I am willing to let my love for you grow more and more each day as well. I am willing to completely devote myself to this courtship."

We talked of many things that evening, mostly about what courtship would mean to each other. But I knew I could not keep Shirley long into the evening because she still had to drive back to Chatham, and I had to drive to St. Catherines that evening as well.

As we were parting, I held Shirley close to me. I wrapped both arms around her, and whispering close to her ear, I said those simple words that meant so much, "Shirley, I love you."

"I love you too, Paul." Her words were tender and sounded like beautiful music to my ears, and with another hug and kiss, we parted company.

Shirley and I saw each other as the opportunity afforded me. In June of 1970 I was able to visit Shirley more often because I was working the midnight shift as relief operator at the CNR Sarnia freight yard. It was just an hour's drive to Chatham.

On the evening of June 13, 1970, while sitting on a couch kissing Shirley at her landlady's home, I stopped for a moment, and looking into her eyes, I simply said, "Shirley, will you marry me?"

Without hesitation, her instant reply was, "Yes, Paul, I will marry you."

## Engaged to Be Married

I don't think I ever knew what the feeling of being high meant until I asked Shirley to marry me. I was totally consumed with happiness, so much so that when I saw my best friends Smitty and Horse Thief a few days later at the Rendezvous Restaurant, their first comments were that I appeared different.

"I guess it shows guys. I can't hide it. I'm walking on cloud nine."

"OK, Dude. Spill the beans. What has happened to you anyhow?" Smitty had a genuine look of astonishment on his face as he asked me that question. And before I could answer him, Horse Thief with a big smile on his face said, "Smitty, I know what the dude is all excited about. I heard through the grapevine that he got engaged to Shirley last Saturday the thirteenth."

"I'm astonished, Dude. You got engaged. Way to go." With a big grin on his face, Smitty continued, "When are you going to get married? Oh, and I'd better be your best man."

Raising both hands in the air, I pleaded with my buddies, "Look, guys, Shirley and I haven't set a date yet. There are many things that must be done before that can happen. Hey, I haven't even given her a diamond yet."

"What, Dude? You asked her to marry you and you haven't even given her an engagement ring? What kind of backward-facing clown are you? How do you ask a girl to marry you when you don't even have a ring? Where have you been living—on the back side of the dessert? Don't you know anything?"

Finally, Horse Thief got his two cents' worth in. "Scallywag, I bet you didn't even ask her father ahead of time if you could have Shirley's hand in marriage, did you? And how do you ask a woman to marry you if you don't get down on one knee in front of her and hold out a pretty little box covered in some kind of soft velvet with a diamond engagement ring inside?"

I kind of sputtered out an answer with somewhat of an astonished look on my face.

"Aw, guys. First of all, I didn't get down on my knees. I was cuddling and kissing Shirley on the couch in her landlady's home around midnight. We were necking up a storm when I suddenly stopped and just blurted out, 'Shirley, will you marry me?' She sat up and didn't even hesitate but said she would marry me. So we went back to kissing again. Oh, I did say to her that I'd get her an engagement ring as quick as I could."

I continued with my rant, "And why should I ask her father for her hand in marriage. She doesn't live at home. I wouldn't be taking her from her father's home. Shirley has been living on her own since she graduated from high school. As far as I was concerned, her father wasn't really in the picture.

"And back to you, Smitty, why should you be my best man when you called me a backward-facing clown?"

Smitty and Horse Thief started laughing and didn't stop for at least two or three minutes. Long before they stopped laughing, everyone in the restaurant was looking at us and probably wondering what in the blazes was so funny.

Finally, Horse Thief caught my attention when he asked me this question. "Scallywag, why don't you buy Shirley an engagement ring as soon as you are able and get down to Chatham and give it to her. She is probably holding her breath waiting for it to be placed on her left hand."

"Aw, guys, I was down to see Shirley yesterday the eighteenth after I completed my last shift at Sarnia freight yards. I gave her a really nice ruby birthstone ring for her birthday, which is coming up soon on July eighth. I'm likely not going to be able to see her again for a week or so because I'm starting a swing shift at Welland Junction."

Horse Thief spoke up with a degree of concern in his voice. "Scallywag, it you don't give an engagement ring very soon, Shirley might begin to think that you were living just in the moment when you asked her to marry you. The longer she waits, it could be that the less she will believe you. The diamond rings proves your commitment. No ring, no commitment."

"I see your point, Horse Thief. I'll work this out as quick as I'm able, but I'll remind her every day when I phone her that I love her, and I really do want to marry her. I won't let her forget me."

A short time passed before I was able to get back home to St. Thomas. Then I made a quick trip to London and bought my dear Shirley a beautiful diamond solitaire. That night I phoned Horse Thief and told him I finally bought the diamond engagement ring.

"That's great, Scallywag. When are you going to give it to Shirley?"

"Horse Thief, I have tomorrow off, but I haven't talked to Shirley. It may be that I won't be able to see her for another week, until I have two more days off."

"Listen, Scallywag, I'm going to Chatham tomorrow after work to see Karen. Why don't you come with me? We can ride down in my 1935 Oldsmobile."

"I like that idea, Horse Thief. I'll tell Shirley I'm coming down to Chatham to see her and I'd like her to dress up in her long pink and white dress. Then I'll take her to Tecumseh Park, and I'll get down on one knee and ask her again to marry me."

"I'll ask Karen to wear her long dress as well, Scallywag. With you and Shirley in the rumble seat and Karen and I up front in the '35 Olds, we'll be strutting our stuff."

Horse Thief and I arrived in good time at the sisters' parents' home. The weather was spectacular, and both Horse Thief and I were excited. Right after the evening meal, the four of us would do a little driving around town and then head for Tecumseh Park.

While at the dinner table, something caught Horse Thief's attention. Out of the corner of his eye, he observed the twin boys, Jimmy and Danny, playing with a small blue velvet-covered box. He knew instinctively that was Shirley's engage-ment diamond ring. Scallywag had left it in the '35 Olds' glove compartment for safekeeping. Without drawing attention to himself, Horse Thief caught up with the twins and took them aside where neither Shirley nor I could observe what was about to transpire. He safely retrieved the ring and the blue velvet box and quietly placed them in his own pocket. It seems the twins had been snooping around in that old car and taken the little blue velvet box without really comprehending its significance.

Drawing me aside after the evening meal, Horse Thief withdrew the little blue velvet box from the safety of his pocket and informed me of the reason he was in possession of it. Needless to say, I was very thankful for Horse Thief's keen eyes and quick thinking.

Karen and Shirley arrived presently. They sure did look lovely dressed in their beautiful long dresses. This would be a very special evening for sure.

As Shirley and I were walking a little later arm in arm through Tecumseh Park down by the Thames River, we stopped at a pretty little bench in a section called the Sunken Gardens. When Shirley was comfortably seated, I rose and bent down on one knee in front of her.

Tears were welling up in her eyes as I presented an open blue velvet box that contained a delightfully vibrant diamond solitaire engagement ring. In an emotional voice, I quietly asked, "Shirley, my love, will you give me your hand in marriage?"

Her response was filled with emotion and excitement. Shirley presented her extended left hand to me whereupon I nervously placed that beautiful ring. Momentarily looking at the diamond on her slender finger, she jumped to her feet and embraced me with a strong hug and many kisses.

Her words flowed easily and quickly into my ear. "Paul, I love you so much, and I want to be your bride. Yes, I will marry you."

We stood locked in a tender embrace for I don't know how long until we were interrupted by happy voices beside us. It was my buddy Horse Thief and his girlfriend Karen. It seemed they both spoke at the same time.

"Paul and Shirley, we are so happy for you both."

## A Thirteen-Month Engagement

When we were able to set some time aside to make plans, Shirley and I began to look at the dynamics of a long engagement.

I had early in that year determined that I would attend Bible college for a year. Thus, we didn't foresee that a wedding would be manageable because September was just a month away. We both came from large families, and we didn't want to restrict our loved ones from our future happy celebration.

But I did see a viable option that I hoped Shirley would embrace when I presented to her. "My dear, would you wait for me to complete one year of college, and next summer we could tie the knot in holy matrimony?"

I knew that Shirley would rather we marry much sooner than thirteen months in our future, but she was brave even though tears were in her eyes when she quietly said, "Paul, I will wait for you. I love you so much. I will remain true to you in our engagement no matter how long it is going to be."

I was able to see Shirley several times during that long engagement while I was in college in Peterborough, Ontario. Once a month many miles would quickly pass beneath my van as I drove to Chatham. Oh, how I longed to be in her warm embrace smothered in her kisses and held close in her hugs, and I was amply rewarded upon arrival.

Christmas 1970 was a delightful time as we continued to get to know each other more. I had two weeks off from my college studies, and Shirley booked the same amount of time off from her work at Libby's.

Arriving at Shirley's parents' home December 19, I was barely able to get out of my van before this beautiful lady was at my door laughing and crying both at the same time.

"Paul, I have been looking out my window for your arrival since I arose from my bed this morning. I'm so happy to see you."

I know she tried to say more, but I muffled her words while I passionately kissed her warm and tender lips. Neither of us said a word as we walked arm in arm toward the house.

To be polite, I spent the first couple of hours visiting with Shirley's parents and family after I'd arrived in Chatham. But it was with my lover that I wanted to spend time with, so as soon as it was possible, I took Shirley aside and quietly whispered, "Sweetheart, let's you and me leave the house and go out. Maybe we could do a little shopping, but what I really want to do is go for a walk with you at Tecumseh Park. I have a particular fondness for that park."

Shirley demurely smiled as she quietly whispered in my ear, "I have a great fondness for that park as well. That is where you gave me this beautiful diamond engagement ring." And lightly sticking her tongue in my ear, she breathlessly whispered, "I love you."

We spent many quiet hours together that Christmas. We walked in the snow, and we drove around the local countryside as we marveled at the beauty of the snow covering the trees and all of nature. But of special note was the short trip we made to Wallaceburg.

I wanted Shirley to meet my former pastors when I was a young boy in St. Thomas. Reverend George Johnstone and his wife Olive were my pastors until I was fifteen years old. They were now pastoring the Pentecostal Church in Wallaceburg, and had been for a couple of years.

We had a delightful visit with the Johnstones. It was good to hear how their pastorates went after they left St. Thomas. They pastored in Hamilton for several years before they came to Wallaceburg. They would soon retire and relocate to the Johnstone family compound near Nanaimo, British Columbia, on Vancouver Island.

Christmas Eve had always been a special time, and this year it was truly a delight. Earlier that morning shortly after breakfast with Shirley's family, she took me aside and spoke with excitement and anticipation.

"Paul, I want you and me to go to the Christmas Eve service at my church. You haven't been to many church services with me, and I want to show you off."

I had to laugh, and when I regained enough composure to reply, I simply said, "Shirley, I'd be delighted to accompany you tonight, and might I add, I'll be showing you off too."

I was completely captivated by Shirley's radiance when she walked with me into the church that Christmas Eve. She was absolutely beautiful, and I spoke quietly to her as we entered the sanctuary. "You, my dear, are entirely radiant in your beauty. I am so honored to escort you."

It was difficult to find a place where we could be alone in Shirley's parents' home with such a large family, so on more than one occasion, either of us would mention to the other that we should go for a walk. Most often we would stroll through Tecumseh Park or up and down the main drag arm in arm while whispering our love to each other.

I must tell you of one situation that was both funny and intimidating. Early one morning there was a knock on the bedroom door to which I responded, "Who is it?" I recognized the sweet voice outside my door belonged to my dear Shirley. "Paul, may I come in?" I was still in bed under the sheets, but I responded, "Yes, Shirley, come in." But it wasn't just Shirley who came in. It was Shirley and her sisters Karen and Esther and her mother.

I was pleased to see them, but I was somewhat nervous, for you see, they all sat on the bed and began to talk with me. So what, that's not a big deal, is it? Well, it's like this. I always slept without wearing any PJs. I was worried they might try to get me up out of bed and in doing so would rip the covers off me. Whew. I managed to dodge that bullet, and I held on to those sheets real tight, just in case.

While sitting alone with Shirley on the couch after breakfast, I solemnly said, "Why, oh why, Shirley does it seem that good times pass so quickly?" We had enjoyed spending time at her parents' home for the Christmas holidays, and now New Year's had come and gone as well. "Here it is January 2, 1971, and it is the first anniversary of our blind date weekend. My dear, I have only today and tomorrow left to enjoy your company. I need to return to Peterborough Monday the fourth, and you must return to your work at Libby's."

Placing her pouting mouth close to my ear and with warm breath caressing my ear and neck, Shirley whispered, "I have had such a wonderful time this Christmas and New Year. I will desperately miss you when you leave, and while away from my arms, I will long for you. I'll only be satisfied and fulfilled once you return to me."

I returned to college in Peterborough, and Shirley returned to her room at her landlady's home in Chatham. We would continue to write love letters back and forth to each other weekly. Her love letters became the highlight of my week, and my love letters to her were also the highlight of her week.

Our love continued to grow, and we affirmed with each other in those love letters that the long wait until August 28, 1971, would be worth it. Our anticipation for that day knew no bounds. Although it truly was a long engagement, we discovered that our love continued to grow deeper and richer as we honored our commitment to each other.

Toward the end of April 1971, and just before I would see Shirley, she excitedly told me over the phone the developments of our future wedding day. "Paul, I have selected the color of the bridesmaid's dresses. They will be your favorite color of green. I have been fitted, and I will get my wedding dress in May. I won't tell you anything else about my wedding dress, but I know you will love it when you see it on me when I walk down that church aisle on my father's arm."

"Shirley, you must tell me all of your plans when I see you at Massey Hall in downtown Toronto on April 23$^{rd}$. That will be where the graduation ceremonies take place for the graduating class."

My parents brought Shirley to Toronto, and I drove us back to St. Thomas after the graduation exercises. We didn't talk too much as we drove westward toward our future and destiny. We just enjoyed the physical closeness that we experienced sitting beside each other.

Our wedding plans continued to move forward, and our love grew deeper and deeper as we shared what time we could manage to get together. I had begun working for a local trucking company in St. Thomas, and Shirley continued to work at Libby's in Chatham.

The first of August we rented an apartment. Shirley moved to St. Thomas and got work at Singer Controls, a local industry. She stayed at my parents' home, and I moved into our new apartment.

My two best buddies were married to their sweethearts during that summer of 1971. Smitty was married in June to Pam, who had been his fiancée for a couple of years. My other buddy, Horse Thief, was married to his fiancée, Karen, Shirley's younger sister, in July.

Shirley and I were married August 28, 1971, and began our lives together in St. Thomas. I would join her a month later at Singer Controls. We worked there until we moved to Windsor in 1973, when I hired on with Greyhound Bus Lines.

PAUL W. J. O'BRIEN

# EIGHT

# CRAZY MEMORIES OF COLLEGE DAYS

### My Old Friend Pays Me a Visit

"PAUL, WILL YOU answer the phone please? I'm working on your favorite homemade meat pie meal, and my hands are covered in the spicy ingredients I'm preparing to mix with the Hamburger."

"OK, Shirley, I've got it."

"Hello, Paul speaking."

"Good morning, Paul, this is Josh speaking."

"Josh, what an absolutely delightful surprise to hear your voice. Where are you?"

"I'm in Cobourg visiting family and friends. Mary Ann and I are spending a couple of weeks here before we return home the end of July. We were hoping you and Shirley would be home because we'd love to get together with you."

"Wow, Josh, I can't think of a better time to get together than today. Shirley and I would love to see you and Mary Ann. Listen, Shirley is putting one of my favorite meals together. I've put you on speaker phone, and Shirley is affirming that we'd be delighted if you and Mary Ann would come to our place for dinner. Would 5:00 p.m. be good for you?"

"It sure would, Paul. This is exciting. Mary Ann hasn't seen Shirley since we visited you when you were living in Otterburne, Manitoba. That was quite some time ago as I recall. Wasn't it in the fall of 1988?"

"Josh, that has to be over thirty years ago. A lot of water has gone under the bridge, as they say, since that time."

Shirley and I had the perfect setting in which to entertain guests. Our backyard had just been renovated. The deck as well as the pergola had a fresh coat of paint. The grass had been treated for weeds and was well fertilized. Even the patio looked fresh and inviting where two outdoor swings with seating for two each faced each other.

The privacy wall also had a fresh coat of gray paint, and the cross cut out of the plywood insert was a silent witness of our commitment to Jesus Christ, the one who through his death on the cross and his resurrection on the third day had purchased our salvation and given us eternal life with Him.

I had gotten to know Josh when both of us had enrolled in Eastern Pentecostal Bible College in Peterborough, Ontario, in 1970. Josh had arrived from South Africa, and I'd arrived from St. Thomas, Ontario. We had soon become good friends. In fact, we even shared a flight together in a Piper Cherokee, but I'm getting ahead of myself.

"That was a wonderful dinner, Shirley. Thank you both for inviting us over. It has been so long since we have had any fellowship with you and Paul."

"It really has been too long, Mary Ann. But why don't we each take our coffee and go out to the patio? We have two delightful swings, and we must sit for a while and reminisce."

As was so often the case, when I got together with friends from days gone by, I waxed eloquent with my stories. Sometimes it was hard to believe those stories actually happened as I described them, but they were always entertaining for sure.

"All right, Paul, I know you are going to tell the story about me flying with you in that small plane. I've heard that story from your lips a few times, and I think you exaggerate more and more every time you tell it, but I imagine Mary Ann would like to hear it, so give us the unedited version."

"Hahaha, Josh. What's the unedited version anyhow? Do you mean the version where I can use some literary license to expand on the facts?"

"Expanding on the facts, Paul? Don't you mean stretching the truth or spinning a yarn?"

"Say what you will, Josh, but as they say in the movies, it's my story and I'm sticking to it."

"Ladies, it was a Saturday afternoon on campus. We'd enjoyed a delightful meal of beans and wieners. Beats me what else was on the menu at lunch that day, and as you will soon discover, no one could really tell what was eaten even though we had evidence of that meal lying on the floor in the baggage compartment of that Cherokee."

"Aw, come on, Paul. Be nice. Do you have to verbally illuminate all the details of that flight?"

"Sure do, Josh."

"Mid-October had been a beautiful month with the leaves turning color. I had been planning to rent a plane at the Peterborough Airport for that day, and I wanted to have the other three seats filled with able bodies. After all, it costs money to rent a Piper Cherokee, and I was a student on a limited budget."

"Well, I know I was one of those able bodies, as you say, Paul, but I've forgotten who the other two guys were. Do you remember?"

"Sure do, Josh. Besides yourself there was Ivan and Peter. Do you remember that Ivan also had his pilot's license? He sat in the right front seat. You sat behind me, and Peter sat behind Ivan as I recall.

"After takeoff, we'd decided to fly up to the Haliburton area. I remember asking Peter and you, Josh, if you'd ever been up in a small plane before, or for that matter if you'd ever flown before. You assured me you had been on jets many times flying from South Africa to North America. Peter had also mentioned he'd flown as well on large aircraft where he'd grown up in California.

"That was good enough for Ivan and me. We looked at each other with an unspoken slight nod of our heads and a couple of smirks on are faces. We were going to give Peter and you a really good flight for your money.

"Do you remember, Josh, that we put that plane through its paces? We stalled it and let it fall out of the sky. We actually spun it through three full rotations before we brought it out of that spin. We took a couple of steep nosedives and brought it out of the dives, pulling hard back on the yoke to bring it back to a steep climb before we leveled it out, sparing ourselves another stall. We wanted you to experience some good G forces.

"I think Ivan and I were having so much fun we weren't aware of your physical discomfort, Josh. And for that matter, I think we were enjoying the paces we were putting that Cherokee through even though it was causing you discomfort.

"As I recall, we were somewhere over Fenelon Falls or Bobcaygeon when you hollered out from the back seat that you were going to be sick. You yelled out, 'Doesn't this plane have a barf bag somewhere?'

"I responded back saying, 'No way, Josh. There aren't any barf bags on this plane. If you're going to be sick, turn around in your seat and barf in the luggage compartment. Don't even think of barfing on Ivan or me or even on the floor in front of you.'

"I remember still more of that conversation. It went pretty much like this.

"'Josh, I thought you said you had been on lots of flights. Way to go. You're really going to stink up this plane.'

"'I know he doesn't hear me yelling back at him, Ivan, because he's too busy hanging over the back of his seat and retching his guts out. And boy does that ever stink.'

"'Yuck, sure does, Paul. Just about makes me want to puke in my boots too because it stinks so badly.'

"Now Ivan asked, 'How about you, Peter, you going to barf your biscuits too?'

"'No way, Ivan, but if I do have to barf my biscuits, give me one of Paul's boots to barf in. He set us up for a barfing good afternoon.'

"With absolutely no sympathy in my voice whatsoever, I hollered back to Josh, 'You going to be OK?'

"'No way, Paul. That had been a good meal I just heaved in the baggage compartment.'

"'Oh well, Josh. Look at the bright side.' I was laughing while I spoke. 'We can put this plane through a whole lot more, and now you'll enjoy it.'

"Josh simply growled back to me, 'I'll enjoy it when you take me back to the airport, you muttonhead.'

"'What do you think, Ivan? Should we cut this flight short or carry on with our plans?'

"'Paul, I think we'd better head back to the Peterborough Airport. The stink in here is ripe, and my eyes are beginning to water from it.'

"'I know you're right, Ivan. I didn't think anything could stink as bad as that. Josh has proved me wrong.'

"'Hey, Josh, your puke stinks worse than the stink bombs I like to set off on campus.'

"'I'm not talking to you, you muttonhead. Take me back to the college.'

"It wasn't too long before we landed at the Peterborough Airport. The fact is that we were in a hurry to land because the ripe smell was getting to all of us. When I informed the airport of our dilemma, they gave us an immediate clearance to land.

"Do you remember, Josh, what happened after we'd landed?"

"Not sure I do, Paul, but I know you'll tell us anyhow."

"It went something like this, Josh."

"'Josh, you'll have to clean up the rotten mess you made back there in the baggage compartment. No one else is going to clean that mess up. You really can't expect the hangar crew to do that.'

"'OK, Paul, so how am I going to clean it up then?'

"'Simple, Josh. I'll get a couple of buckets, one with water and cleaner and the other to put the dirty rags in that you're going to mop up with.'"

"I remember that now, Paul. That was disgusting. I'd forgotten that part. When I bent in to start cleaning up my mess, I barfed my biscuits all over again on top of what I'd already heaved up."

"Yes, that was quite an afternoon, Josh. You went and wrecked a perfectly good meal of beans and wieners. So my question to you, have you enjoyed beans and wieners since that day?"

Shaking her head negatively, with a quirky smile, Shirley said, "I've heard that story more than a few times, Mary Ann. I really think Paul gets a bang out of telling it, but I'm not sure it is quite the same story each time."

Looking at Shirley, Mary Ann laughingly commented, "But it was a funny story, and I'm sure Paul has a few more stories he'd tell if we asked him. So how about it, Paul, would you care to tell us some more college stories?"

"That's easy to do, Mary Ann. I have a couple or more I could tell. I have to ask myself sometimes when I reflect back on those days, was I there to study or just goof off?"

**The Water-Bomber Caper**

"Here's a story you might remember, Josh. I don't recall that you were involved in it, but after I've told it, you can fill me in on any blanks if you were a part of this dastardly deed that at least a half dozen of us guys did on Saturday, April 17, 1971, before we wrote our final exams and prepared for the graduation of the 1971 class of the Banner Men."

"Just to preface this story, Josh, the two individuals, other than myself, that I distinctly remember being involved in this caper, which I will call the Water Bomber Caper, were Jake who you might remember was the assistant photographer for the Torch, and Dan who was the vice president of our student government.

"Let me tell this story as if you were a silent witness following me and observing all that happened.

"I was sitting at my desk studying for my finals when Dan came to my dorm room door and began banging on it like the men's wing was on fire. He sure got my attention, and when I opened the door, I yelled at him with some frustration because of the noise he'd created. 'Hey, hey, hey, Dan, what's up? Why are you banging on my dorm room door like this residence is on fire?'

"Dan was breathless in his response answering my question, but said something like this. 'Listen. There is at least a half dozen girls on the second-floor balcony. You know where it is on the girls' wing. I just got a note from a female informant that these girls are lying around up there getting a suntan while in their bikinis. I suppose they might be trying to study for finals, but I doubt it.'"

"I responded to Dan's comment while shrugging my shoulders and said something like this. 'OK, Dan, so how does that involve me?'

"His response brought me to immediate attention when he said, 'Come to my room on the second floor of the men's wing. There is a trapdoor onto the roof from my room, and when we get up on it, we can go over to the flat roof on the third floor of the girls' wing. I've got a half dozen fire pails of ice-cold water that a couple of guys and I have filled up, and we need you to help us carry one of the pails over to the edge of the flat roof where we will be able to see the girls on the second-floor balcony. We're going to dump the water on them. This ought to be crazy.'

"'Fun times here I come. I'm with you,' I muttered while I slipped on my shoes.

"In a matter of a couple of minutes, Josh and Mary Ann, I had joined Dan and Jake. There were four other guys with us. Jake was tagging along in order to take pictures. Six pails of ice-cold water and six guys to do this dastardly deed. If the female informant was correct in her count of female bodies lying around on that balcony, there would be one pail for each them.

"Guys, when we get to the edge of the roof and we're above the girls, wait until Jake gives the count of three. Then we'll dump the pails in unison," whispered Dan as we sneaked across the flat roof.

"Can you folk imagine the degree of excitement and even suspense as we gathered at the edge of that flat roof and peered over the retaining wall to observe six girls all lying on their bellies getting a sunburn. At least four of them had removed their bikini tops. It was true, they did have their study notes before them, and it would appear that they were trying to study."

With a look of astonishment, Josh asked, "Paul, did you guys really dump cold water on those poor, unsuspecting girls? Do you even remember who they were?"

"Seriously, Josh. All we saw were six girls lying on their stomachs. We didn't see their faces. No one could have told you who the six girls were.

"Back to the story, guys. Jake counted to three, and in unison each of us dumped a pail of ice-cold water on the girl we had predetermined would receive that pail of water."

With a degree of alarm in her voice, Shirley asked, "What happened next?"

"Hold on, Shirley, here's what happened next. There was high-pitched screaming like I'd never heard before. It nearly sounded frightful it was so loud. I think we expected to hear some screaming but nothing like that. I don't think a jet engine on takeoff could make more noise.

"To say that notebooks and study notes went one way and bikini tops went another way is a bit of an understatement. In retrospect, I can't imagine the shock of that much ice-cold water hitting hot, bare flesh.

"Get this, Jake was standing there leaning over the retaining wall on the roof and snapping pictures as fast as he could make his index finger preform its task.

"We didn't hang around to laugh at the girls in their anger and confusion but lit off across the roof on a dead run. Because the girls were all lying on their stomachs, none of them were able to identify us. However, one person did see us.

"When the girls screamed, it drew the attention of the gardener who was down on the lawn in front of the library raking the dead leaves that had lain there all winter. I remember clearly what he yelled out. 'There they are six, no seven. They're running across the roof.' Fortunately for us he was unable to identify us by name, and because we were three stories above him and running fast, he couldn't with any clarity see our faces."

Both Mary Ann and Shirley responded in unison. "You guys were nasty. That wasn't nice at all. And you probably wrecked their study notes and books also."

"Seriously, ladies, we were not too concerned about their study notes or books. We weren't even concerned about them losing their bikini tops in their fright. What really concerned us was not getting caught.

"We figured that if we got caught, every one of us would be expelled from the college. And right before final exams, that would have been catastrophic. Can you imagine losing your whole year because of that stunt?"

"You guys should have been caught, Paul. That was absolutely dreadful what you did to those six girls. It's too bad there was no way they could retaliate."

"Oh, come on, Shirley. Yes, I know, but at the same time I'm glad we got away with it because it makes for a better story if nothing else.

"Anyhow, here's the rest of the story as Paul Harvey would have said."

"You mean the story isn't over yet? So what happened next?"

"Oh boy, Josh, let me just tell you what happened next. All of us dropped through the emergency trapdoor exit in the roof above Dan's bed, and hit the floor running as we made a quick exit from his dorm room. I remembered there was a fire escape ladder just down the hall from Dan's room, so I went down that as quickly as I could. That ladder dumped me out in the inner courtyard between the two wings of the boys' dorms. My room faced that inner courtyard, and fortunately I'd left the window open when I took off on this adventure.

"I ran through that courtyard on a dead run and piled through that open window, landing on my desk and my study notes.

"I'd no sooner got into my chair when the dean of men burst through my door without even asking for entry. He was breathing hard from running down the hall. You might remember, Josh, that his apartment was at the end of that hall where my room was located.

"I was also breathing hard having come down the fire escape ladder and piling through the window landing on my desk. I had just straightened my notes after having scattered them around in my haste to appear normal. I must have expected the dean to check on my presence before checking on anyone else.

"I spoke first when the dean threw open my door. 'Can I help you, Dean?' was all I said. The dean of men didn't say anything. He just stared at me for a couple of seconds and then took off on the run heading for the central common area, I guess.

"Funny how the dean chose my room first to check. But of course I know why he did. He'd been trying to catch all year because he'd heard through the grapevine that I was probably behind most of the shenanigans that had taken place over the course of the year.

"I'd sure come close to getting expelled one week before graduation day.

"Oh, a postscript to this little story was that Jake came and told all of us bad actors he wouldn't allow us to see the pictures he took of the water-bombing caper. They were not rated for Bible college eyes. He had destroyed the negatives forthwith."

## Nighttime Fire Scare

"Josh, how often do you think I somehow was involved in a college prank, or was often at the center of an outrageous stunt?"

"Knowing you now as I do, Paul, I'd say that you were most likely the prankster who instigated it."

"You hit the nail on the head, Josh. I was at the center of nearly every prank, and the first one was soon after I'd entered college.

"Josh and Mary Ann, I'd gotten to know Dan a few days early during the college initiation week for the freshman class. I could see almost immediately that he would enjoy getting into mischief.

"So I approached him when he was alone. The conversation and the ensuing prank went something like this. Pretend once again you're like a shadow to Dan and me.

"'Hi, Dan. I'm Paul. That was a funny little trick you pulled on those two freshmen guys the other day during freshman initiation week. I can see that you like a good laugh. I'll tell you what, Dan, I've got a little idea that you might be interested in. It'd involve stealth and cunning. Are you up to having a little fun?'

"'Hi, Paul. You're a freshman too, aren't you? What do you have in mind? It would have to be really good because I don't want to stick my neck out for something that would be a dud.'

"'Dan, I was working on the railroad before I came to college. It was there that I managed to acquire through a five-fingered bargain several railroad fuses. These fuses come in two colors—red and orange. They mean different things when lit on the railroad, but that doesn't matter here.'

"'OK, Paul, let's hear your plan.'

"'This is how I can see it working, Dan. Early this coming Saturday morning around two when basically everyone is in bed and asleep, you and I will show up on the west lawn outside the dean of women's apartment windows. We'll light four fuses off, two red and two orange, two under each window. We'll beat it out of there on a dead run and hide out somewhere north of the main campus.'

"'Sounds pretty good so far, Paul. What do you expect lighting these fuses off will accomplish?'

"'Here's my idea on that. The light that they give off is pretty intense. It will cast a lot of red-yellow light into the apartment and will quickly awaken the dean. Her first thought would be that the west wing of the girls' dorm is on fire, and she will immediately pull the fire alarm. That will bring all the female students out of the college on the run. It ought to be very interesting watching them in their PJs and baby dolls.'

"Let me interject my story here, Josh and Mary Ann, and Shirley. The fire alarms at the college would sound throughout the dorms and other buildings, but they would not trigger an alarm at a local fire hall. Were there a true fire, a call would have to be made through the emergency phone number 911.

"OK, I'll get back to my story and pick it up where Dan and I are having this conversation about this ensuing prank. Dan's comment to me went something like this.

"'I like you, Paul. You have a deviant mind. But I have a couple of questions for you. First, how are we going to sneak out of the men's dorm without being caught? And second, how are we going to get into the college without raising any suspicion after we've pulled off this prank?'

"'Good questions, Dan. First, we're not going to sneak out of the men's dorm. We'll leave the library after it closes for the night, and go to my vehicle located in the north parking lot. We'll hide out there in the back of the van until after midnight. We'll then sneak through the campus avoiding as much nighttime illumination as possible.'

"'When we get outside of the dean's apartment, we'll quickly light the fuses, stick them in the ground, and beat a hasty retreat.'

"'Secondly, when all the students are out on the grounds, and I expect the men will empty their dorms just as quickly, you and I will casually melt in with the men and just watch and see how both deans handle the situation. My expectation is that the dean of women will quickly recognize the joke we pulled on the girls and send everyone back inside to bed. You and I will just be two of the guys doing what we are told. We'll go back to bed.'

"'Paul, you're a real nutcase. I like it. When do you want to pull this stunt?'

"'Tomorrow is Friday, Dan, so there won't be any classes on Saturday. Everyone will be more at ease because the weekend will be upon them. We'll hear a lot of chatter about it on Saturday, but we'll have to play dumb, and ask stupid questions like everyone else. It will blow over in a couple of days. The deans will want to know who did the dastardly deed, but with precise execution of our plans, we'll be another couple of dudes who laughed about the incident but won't know anything more about it than the other guys.'

"'So, Dan, are you with me on this little caper? It will have to be just us. It won't be like the more the merrier. Too many guys, and the potential will be greater getting caught. There will also be too much risk in keeping it quiet. Someone would be sure to spill the beans.'

"'Yes, that is likely what would happen, Paul. OK, so it's just you and me. This is going to be good, real good.'

"Early Saturday morning came quickly, and Dan and I executed our plans. We pulled it off without any hitches. Absolutely no one suspected that we had been the instigators of this nefarious caper.

"Hey, Josh, just a sidebar on this little stunt. Dan and I both heard from several different guys that they really enjoyed the prank played on the girls. The fact is, pretty much all the guys at the college vocalized the same sediments."

## Stink Bombs and Swimming

"Paul," Mary Ann asked in a quizzical voice, "did you ever really study, or were you just involved in one prank after another?"

"Mary Ann, there were a lot of students who were serious about their studies. I know I should have been serious as well, but the truth was simply that I did the least that needed to be done in order to pass each course. I'm not saying that the professors were boring, they were interesting enough, it was just that I had found a few guys who were much like me. We were into parties, pranks, and shenanigans. In retrospect, looking back on that time, I acted very immaturely. Hahaha, I wonder if I've ever really grown up."

As I spoke about myself not ever really growing up, I looked sideways toward Shirley. She was violently nodding, affirming that I was still anything but a mature adult.

Turning toward our guests, I asked, "Josh, do you remember there were times when the smell of rotten eggs was overpowering? Well, let me tell you another couple of times I pulled a few pranks on my own without Dan's help."

Josh, shaking his head, just muttered, "Paul, this is how I see it. Once a muttonhead, always a mutton head."

While laughing at Josh's terminology to describe my character, I nodded and said, "You are the only one who has ever called me a muttonhead, so I guess this muttonhead might just as well get back to the story.

"There was a store located in downtown Peterborough which sold pranks, gags, and tricks amongst other things such as costumes and masks. I found this store captivated my waking hours on more than one occasion. I would wander the aisles and look for items to use in pranks. One such prank was to use stink bombs.

"These stink bombs were little glass vials full of an awful-smelling substance, somewhere between a cross of rotten eggs and skunk scent. They were easily broken by crushing them. It could be dangerous to break them with your hands, but putting them in places where they would eventually be pinched or walked on was safe enough.

"Josh, Mary Ann, and Shirley, this is how these series of pranks played out.

"I caught up to Dan one day in the halls and told him that I was going downtown to the gag store. I asked him if he wanted to go along, and without any hesitation, he said he'd tag along. Oh, and another thing I told him was that I'd first thought I'd go to the YMCA and enjoy running on the track for a while then jumping in the pool for a swim.

"Dan said he liked my idea about going to the YMCA first and asked me to wait for a few minutes while he got some gym gear from his room. 'I'll be back down in the common center in a jiffy.'

"My response was 'Dan, I'll be out at my van. Just meet me there in the parking lot.'

"When Dan jumped in my van, I told him I needed to shore up on some stink bombs.

"Dan chortled and made this comment. 'So it's you, eh, who has been lighting off those smelly little things?'

"'Keep it a secret, Dan,' I replied as we headed for the Y.

"I asked him what he thought he might do while we were there, and he said he'd run a couple of miles on the indoor track and then spend a half hour in the pool.

"I'm thinking of doing some weight lifting, and then I want to spend a half hour in the pool doing some laps and diving as well," I said.

"About an hour later, both Dan and I had finished what we'd set out to do and had taken a shower and were dressing in the men's change room.

"Dan commented on my idea of diving was different than what he thought diving was all about. 'I figured you would spend time on the diving board but noticed that all you did was skin-diving. I noticed that you were staying down a long time as well. Have you been practicing that for some time?'

"'Here's my little secret, Dan. Keep it under your hat,' I snickered.

"'Mums the word, Paul,' he said as he pulled his forefinger and thumb across his lips.

"'Dan, I've been practicing not just holding my breath but holding it after I've exhaled. When you let the breath out of your lungs, you will sink like a stone. I sink down by the drain and stay there watching everyone swim above me. After a minute or better, I push up to the surface and get a good lung full of air then exhale and sink to the bottom again for another minute or better.'"

By now Josh, Mary Ann, and Shirley were laughing uncontrollably at my story, but it was Shirley who spoke up. "I don't know about you, Paul. Are you some kind of weirdo?" She continued laughing as she asked me that redundant question.

I was laughing too when I answered her. "That's funny, Shirley. Those were just about the exact words coming out of Dan's mouth."

"This was my answer to Dan. 'Let's be real here. Do you get tired of looking at the girls? I know what your answer is because I saw you looking at the pretty little blonde when you were in the pool.'

"Raising both arms and hands in the air, Dan muttered, 'You got me there, so what's next? Are we heading over to the gag store now?'

"'Yes, we've just got enough time to get there and buy a few gags and then get back to the campus in time for supper.'

"On our way back to the campus, Dan asked me how many stink bombs I'd purchased.

"'Let's put it this way, Dan, I bought enough to keep me happy letting those things off from now until graduation.'

"I didn't know of anyone else who had stink bombs at the college, Josh, so it's fair to say that I was the culprit every time there was a foul smell lingering somewhere on campus. Sometimes Dan would see me from a distance and just shake his head when a stink bomb had gone off."

Shaking his head, Josh muttered again, "Once a muttonhead always a muttonhead."

"I remember a couple of occasions when the smell was particularly offensive. Of course I was to blame, but Dan never squealed on me. He was a true compatriot in crime you might say.

"But one day after the stink bomb's pungent smell had lingered for awhile, Dan asked me how I'd set it up to happen. The smell had emanated from the hallway leading to the tuck shop. I had stuffed a stink bomb into the two-way hinge on the tuck shop door and left the door shut. I did it when no one was around.

"A half hour later when tuck was open after the morning chapel service, Josh and Mary Ann, whoever was first into the tuck shop had to open the door, and when they did, it crushed the stink bomb and *budda-bing, budda-boom*, let the stink time begin.

"Dan caught up to me while I was still close by the tuck shop and shook his head as he gave me both a question and a comment.

"'You are real crazy, you know that? Give me one of those stink bombs, Paul. I've got an idea for setting it off.'

"It was just a day or two later, and another foul smell poured forth from the dean of men's office. I wasn't involved in the placement of that stink bomb. It had to be Dan with the stink bomb I'd given him. Boy-oh-boy, did it ever smell up the hallways.

"I was across the hall when it went off. Evidently Dan had done something similar to what I'd done with the tuck shop door. He later told me he'd put a stink bomb in the hinge on the dean's door. That had to be a trick doing it without getting caught. That door wasn't a two-way door.

"But I had a good laugh nevertheless watching the dean of men come out of his office coughing and wiping his eyes. There are just some things that give an upstart like me great merriment.

"Josh, Mary Ann, and Shirley, can you guess what happened next?" I was laughing while asking that question because I just knew that they would automatically think that when the dean came out of his office and saw me that he'd head right over to where I was standing, leaning against a wall adjacent to the tuck shop.

"That question is a no-brainer," responded Josh with merriment in his voice. "The dean knew you were a bad dude and was going to pin it on you."

"For sure, Josh, for sure. And that is what he did. He was in front of my face in a second and glaring at me growled out his question.

"'Paul, are you the one who has put a stink bomb in my office?'

"'No way, Dean. I've been standing here talking to my roommate Larry while we have been enjoying an ice cream cone each. I'm as surprised as you are at what has just happened in your office.'

"'Paul, I think you are behind some of these shenanigans that are happening on campus,' the dean snarled. 'I'm putting you on notice. If you are caught doing something nefarious, you will pay a heavy price for it, is that understood?'

"'Understood clearly, Dean, I said with a slight upturn of my lips. Sorry, I can't help you, but I didn't see anyone foul up your office.'"

"No kidding, Paul, the dean had it out for you. What did you do to get him so ticked?" Josh asked.

"Yes, he did have it out for me, Josh, but I was not the culprit in that instance. I suppose he figured I was his archenemy because it seemed I was always nearby when something happened. I'd say that was just coincidence, but I don't think Dean Earl saw it that way.

"While I was still there in the hallway talking to Larry, who should approach but Dan."

"'Hey, Dan, I was just about to leave. I've had an ice cream cone with Larry. You sticking around for a bit? I'll get a coffee for you and me if you are.'

"'Paul, that's mighty nice of you to buy me a coffee. You going to hang around for a bit too, Larry?'

"'Can't, Dan, I've got a study engagement with Judy. I'm heading over to the library right now. See you later guys.'

"'You missed all the commotion, Dan. Seems someone lit off a stink bomb in the dean's office. I was here when it happened, but it beats me how it came to be. Anyhow, the dean comes storming out of his office and sees me standing here with Larry. Immediately he's blaming me. It was a good thing Larry was here to vouch for me. The dean wanted to hang me up by the thumbs.'

"Laughing before he could speak, Dan chortled out, 'Too funny, Paul.'

"'Yes, I thought so too, Dan. I'm going to head over to the library. I've got a spare right now, and I need to do some work on my Romans paper for Professor Ratz. What are you up to?'

"'Seems like the safest place to be right now is in the library, Paul. There is just too much excitement happing in these hallowed halls. Hahaha.'

"Hey, Josh, did I mention a little earlier in this story that I bought so many stink bombs that I'd have enough to last right through to graduation? Well, it's true if you didn't expect me to light one off every day or two. The idea there was to let the excitement die down for a week or two then release another one of those little gems.

"And so it was that it came to be the night before Christmas break, and there was lots of excitement throughout the whole campus. I just happened to be in the common room chatting about nothing in particular, with a couple of guys and girls. But it is true, I did have a stink bomb in my pocket. My intent was to flick it into the girls' elevator, so when the opportunity presented itself and I was basically unobserved, I did just that. I flicked that lonely old stink bomb into the girl's elevator as I walked by."

Begging me with a tone of hopelessness, Shirley groaned out her plea. "Paul. Not another stinky story, please."

"Shirley, it is a true story, honest. I beat a hasty retreat because just then coming down the hall was the dean of women and three other girls. I didn't know what mission they were on, but I wasn't about to ask. I was going to melt into the woodwork, so to speak."

"It would be hard seeing you melt into anything, Paul, except maybe a big lemon pie."

"You're too funny, Shirley. By the way, do we have enough lemon pie for the four of us?"

Shirley just stuck out her tongue at me but said nothing.

"Back to my story, folks."

"It was later that night as I was hanging around the tuck shop and one of the girls I was friendly with came along and bought a coffee for herself. I was standing alone, so she approached me and asked if I was going to get a coffee and stick around for a while?"

"Being the charmer that I was, my answer was that yes I would buy a coffee and I'd be delighted to have an enjoyable chat with her.

"Do you remember Marlene, Josh?"

"Yes, I remember Marlene, Paul. So it was Marlene you had a coffee with?"

"Yes, it was Marlene, and she started our conversation with a question.

"'Did you hear what happened tonight over in the girls' dorm?'

"Not wanting to give myself away, I responded with a question. 'What happened over in the girls' dorm, Marlene?'

"'Seems someone, nobody knows who, slipped a stink bomb into the girls' elevator. The dean of women and three seniors were going to take the elevator to the third floor. I guess the stink bomb was on the floor and one of the girls or maybe the dean stepped on it. They had to suffer all the way to the third floor. When they left the elevator, they were choking and crying big crocodile tears.'

"'I happened to be nearby on the third floor when they got off the elevator. What a sight for sore eyes, and they really stunk too. I sort of felt sorry for them, but at the same time, it was kind of funny watching them stumble about while wiping their eyes and gasping for breath.'

"'Oh wow, Marlene,' I responded with a bit of a twinkle in my eyes. 'Those poor girls and the dean. She's getting on in years. That must have been hard on her, to say the least.'

"'I didn't stick around to witness anything else. The whole third floor stunk like crazy in a matter of a couple of minutes. It's a wonder someone didn't pull the fire alarm or something.'

"'That would have really been something else if the fire alarm had been set off,' I said to Marlene.

"I wanted to change the subject quickly so immediately asked her what she was going to be doing for Christmas.

"With bright eyes and a big smile, Marlene told me she was just going to spend time with her folks at home in Quebec City. 'How about you? What are you going to do for Christmas, Paul?'

"'I'm going to spend most of the Christmas holidays with my fiancée, Shirley, at her home in Chatham, Ontario. But I will also take Shirley to St. Thomas with me so she can visit with my folks as well.'

"After a few more minutes of conversation, I wished her a merry Christmas, and with a wave she replied, 'Merry Christmas and Happy New Year.'"

## Black-Balling a Fellow

"January was a cold month in Peterborough. Well, it was a cold month everywhere in Southeastern Ontario. The idea was to stay warm where ever you were going. There's ice on the pond and snow on the hills. Maybe it's fun skiing down a slope or skating on a frozen pond, but it is immensely fun getting some poor bloke dressed up in a woman's dress and forcing him to walk anywhere outside. But that is what Dan, and a couple other guys, and I did.

"Let me take you back in time, Josh, Mary Ann, and Shirley to the event that I am speaking about which happened on campus, on a cold winter night early in January 1971.

"'What's up, Dan? Looks like you've been up to some mischief, eh?'

"'You're so discerning, Paul. Fact is a couple of guys and myself want to black-ball Daryl. He got engaged over the Christmas holidays, and we want to pretend we're his friends, and it's a cause to celebrate his engagement, but in reality, we're going to strip him down and make him wear a woman's dress. Then we'll drop him off in the cemetery, and he'll have to walk back to the college in the cold and snow all the while dressed like a woman.'

"'Wow, Dan. That's nasty, and I like it. So where do I fit in with these plans?'

"'Paul, you have the van. We can get a half-dozen guys in there, so there is enough room to shanghai Daryl and feed him a line that we want to take him out for a coffee and donut. When we have him in the van, then we pull the dress stunt on him.'

"'So when does this plan come together, Dan?'

"'Right now, Paul. Are you with us?'

"'I'll be right on it, Dan. I just need to get my ignition keys and license. I'll meet you guys at the north parking lot in ten minutes.'

"It was no trouble getting Daryl to go along with our plans. He was truly impressed that we'd like to buy him a coffee and donut to celebrate his engagement. Poor fellow didn't know what was about to happen.

"'Daryl, we've changed our minds. Instead of going to the coffee shop near the campus, we're going to go to the restaurant across from the Holiday Inn. That OK with you?'

"'Hey, Dan. I'm fine with that,' responded Daryl.

"But I didn't turn into the plaza where the restaurant we spoke of was situated. Instead I turned the opposite way and entered the cemetery.

"'Hold on, guys. What's going on? You said we were going for a coffee and a donut. We can't get those things here in the graveyard,' sputtered Daryl.

"'Guys, pin Daryl down. I have to pull his pants off,' shouted Dan.

"Well, of course there was a struggle. Daryl wasn't an easy pushover. He did put up a valiant fight, but with four other guys holding him down, it wasn't too long before he began to take on a rather scary likeness to a big lady in a tight dress."

"'You guys are nuts. I'll get you all back for this,' was about all Daryl could sputter out of his mouth before the back door to the van was opened and he was unceremoniously dumped out in a snowbank.

"'Drive, Paul. Let's get out of here. Let's head up to the coffee shop near the campus. We can sit there by the window and watch for Doug to walk by.'

"'Good idea, Dan,' a couple of guys in the back of the van chortled out in unison.

"But this story took an unforeseen turn of events. Unknown to us, Daryl had managed to keep his money in his winter parka and not in his pants pockets. When the five of us returned to the college, we were very surprised to see Daryl waiting for us inside the doors to the men's dorm.

"Dan spoke up first. 'Daryl, how'd you get here so fast? We figured it would be at least one hour before we saw you walk by the coffee shop. We didn't see you, but we didn't expect you back so soon either.'

"'Guess I've got the last laugh on you guys. I had stashed my money in my parka, so I just walked up to the street, and at the Holiday Inn I got a taxi to take me back here. I've been here for an hour already.'

"Well, so much for the best-laid plans of mice or men, everybody. But just a footnote here. Earlier in the fall season before Christmas, those same bad actors had tried to pull that stunt on me. You see, I was already engaged to my dear Shirley here. I leveled with them forthwith.

"In no uncertain terms, I said, 'Don't try that on me. I let you use my van sometimes to do this tomfoolery, and if you guys cross paths with me, the van will be permanently out of any future plans.'

"I can only guess that Dan told them not to bite the hand that feeds them."

"I must say, Paul, you sure did get into a lot of stuff, and it's a wonder you never got caught, or did you ever get caught?"

"No, Mary Ann, I evaded the campus cops and lived to tell the tale. But looking back in retrospect, I guess I'd say my grades suffered somewhat because of my propensity for goofing off."

"Paul, you should have studied harder and applied yourself more to your studies. After all, it was me who was helping you with your finances all through those two semesters."

"I know you're right, Shirley. I've always been something of a party animal though, haven't I?"

"I've got time to listen to another story or two, Paul, if you haven't run out of air yet."

"I've always got another story, Josh. I'm blowing my own horn here, but those who know me know I never run out of air, and I never run out of stories either. I'll restrain myself to maybe one more short story.

"It was near the end of the winter semester, maybe a week or so before finals. I was in Romans class. Professor Ratz was getting a little boring, or at least I felt he was. Remember, Josh, how we could sit anywhere we wanted in his class?

"On this particular day I had the last seat in the back row. I was the farthest from the door, which was to the left of where I was sitting. I was closest to the bank of windows and was more interested in what was happening outside than what was not happening inside.

"I was talking to myself, well, not out loud in case you ask. How I was wishing to be outside in the fresh air. Then this cockeyed plan formulated in my mind. I was going to sneak out of class, but how could I do that?"

"Oh yes, I remember that class now, Paul. I was sitting in the back row closest to the door. Something caught my eye to my right. There you were on the floor on all fours with your notebook under your arm and trying to crawl toward the door and to freedom."

"Yes, I remember you sitting there, Josh. You and four other guys were chucking the boots to me as I crawled by your desks. I took more than a few shots to the ribs that day."

"You got away with that stunt too, Paul. Ratz never saw you leave and never missed you sitting at your desk. He'd taken the attendance at the beginning of the class, and then he got into the lesson. It was brave and stupid at the same time for you to do that, and I wonder what would have happened if he'd caught you?"

"It was a good thing, Josh, that the door was open. I guess Ratz wanted fresh air from the open windows to flow through the room, so the door being open would allow decent airflow. Maybe he even thought if the fresh air blew through the classroom, we who were in the back row might stay awake."

"Do you remember what you did when you escaped to the hallway, Paul?"

"Not sure I remember. What did I do?"

"You stood there in the hallway and made faces at all of us in the back row. It was hard not to laugh. Maybe we should have laughed out loud. Ratz would have thought he accidently cracked a joke that he wasn't aware of."

"Well, I got away with that little stunt, and hey, I did pass my finals in Romans, so I guess that little adventure was worth it, Josh."

## Not Another Stink Bomb!

"Oh, here's another quick story. It was just a day before the senior class graduation in Toronto at Massy Hall. Do you remember, Josh, Mrs. Smith had the college students in the chapel to practice the songs we were to sing at graduation?"

"Can't say I remember anything special about that, Paul, but knowing you, there must have been something going down."

"Hahaha, Josh. I had one final stink bomb in my pocket. Mrs. Smith had told us guys to get out of the chapel and wait outside for a short while. She needed to have the girls concentrate on a part of one selection where they were struggling to get it right."

"Yes, now I get it. You planted the stink bomb in the girls' section."

"I sure did, Josh. I flicked it on the floor as all of us guys were making our exit. We had to hang around outside the main doors to the chapel, but it wasn't very long before all the girls and Mrs. Smith came quickly out of the chapel coughing and rubbing their eyes."

"Paul, you were bad. I kind of wish you had got caught."

"Oh, come on, Shirley. You know me. I'm made out of Teflon. Nothing sticks to me."

"Shirley, you were at that graduation. Do you remember there was a confrontation that I had with another first-year student, just as we were about to leave after the graduation program was done?"

"No, I don't recall anything like that. What happened?"

"Robert, a first-year student, came up to me, and he was ticked off. He said, 'How is it that you were engaged and still dated some girls, but I've not had one date?'

"My answer was to the point. 'The girls saw me as safe because I was engaged. You, on the other hand, were on the prowl, so they saw you as not safe.' Maybe I should have told him he needed to change his socks daily, not once a week."

# NINE

# DRIVING INTERCITY BUS FOR GREYHOUND

## The Cream Puff Caper

THERE WAS SO much in life that Smitty and I enjoyed. We grew up together. Our parents were friends with each other. Smitty and I attended the same youth group, and we even dated the same girls, albeit at different times.

We were partners in a business venture, and we worked together in the same company on several different occasions. This story is about one of those occasions when we worked together on Eastern Canadian Greyhound Bus Lines.

Smitty hired on with Greyhound in 1972, and I hired on in 1973. On this occasion which I have often referred to with great affection as the Cream Puff Caper, we were protecting several runs on a beautiful summer day in August 1974.

Let me give you a few details or descriptions that will help you understand some of the terminology that bus drivers use.

Protecting a run meant that a bus driver would stand by as a scheduled run was loading. In this case, it would be Windsor, Ontario, but often a driver would protect a scheduled run in Toronto or London as well. The scheduled run would have an assigned driver, but if there were more people desiring to ride the bus than there was room on the scheduled bus, then another driver would bring his bus to the loading platform, and the remaining passengers would get on his bus. His bus would then be considered the second section on that particular scheduled run.

Smitty and I had protected two runs this fateful August afternoon, and there was one more scheduled run to protect, but that wouldn't happen for another two hours. I'll pick up this story then at that point.

"Smitty, we've got another two hours to kill here in the driver's room before we need to protect the evening scheduled run to Toronto. I'm beginning to get stir-crazy just sitting around here. How about you? What do you say we give our dispatcher Herb a call and see if he'll release us for an hour or so? I'd like to go to the Country Style Donuts over there on Walker Road South. You and I need a serious coffee break."

"I like the way you think, Dude. I'm with you. I'll give Herb a call and tell him our plans. He won't have any problem with that I'd think."

"Promise to bring him back a coffee and donut, Smitty, and he'll give us his blessings."

"Right on, Dude."

"Hello, Herb. O'Brien and I would like to go over to the Country Style Donuts on Walker and get a coffee and donut. Are we good for an hour or so? Herb, what do you like in your coffee, and what kind of donut can we bring back to you?"

"Don, you and Paul enjoy yourself. I would like a double-double and a chocolate-glazed donut. Hey, and thanks a lot, guys."

"OK, Dude. Herb is good with our plans, and he wants a double-double and a chocolate-glazed donut. I'll by his coffee and donut, and let's use your car to go there and come back."

"Sounds like a plan, Smitty."

The Country Style Donuts was just a couple of miles away from the Greyhound Bus Barns where Smitty and I were spending the afternoon protecting the scheduled runs. We'd be there in less than ten minutes. We could spend an hour at the coffee shop and still have sufficient time to protect the last run that day.

"Smitty, let's sit at the counter. We can tease Brenda if she's working today."

"Dude, what you really mean is that you want to flirt with the waitress."

"You're so discerning, Smitty. Fact is you do the same thing, flirting with the waitress every time we go there. It's become a regular exercise, and you know what I think, Brenda likes the attention."

"You must admit, Dude, we've perfected our little shtick, and it seems to go over pretty good every time we do it, me being Mr. Bad and you being Mr. Good."

"Yup, that is one of life's little pleasures, Smitty. We are two of a kind because we both enjoy getting lots of laughs."

"Hey, Dude. Brenda is waitressing at the counter today, and there are two empty stools. When we get her laughing, it is so contagious, everybody begins to laugh even though they might not know what she is laughing about."

"Right on, Smitty, so you start with a bit of a whinny voice and complain about your day. You know the drill, get her to stop and listen to you, and then unload your gripes and complaints. Do a little badmouth about your plain donut while you're at it. When you have her attention, I'll butt in and smooth things out. I'll soften her up with some gentle, sweet talk."

"Come on, Dude, why don't you ever let me do some gentle, sweet talk?"

"You know the answer to that, Smitty. You've tried a few times, and you always fall flat on your face. Let me do what I excel at, and you do Mr. Grumpy."

"Well, hello, boys. Have you come to pester me, or are you going to be nice today?"

"Oh, come on, Brenda. You know us. We're always nice and respectful."

"That's not exactly the truth, Paul. You are always nice, but Don, well, he's pretty much grumpy all the time."

"Really, Brenda, I'm not grumpy all the time. I just call a spade a spade. I don't beat around the bush like the dude here. I always shoot straight from the hip so to speak. And speaking about shooting straight from the hip, Brenda, this coffee is old and cold, and the donut is stale."

"Smitty, learn your manners. Don't talk to Brenda like that. She served your coffee from the same pot as she served mine, and you know that the donuts here are always fresh. They sell so many donuts they don't stay on the shelf long enough to get stale.

"Brenda, I'm so sorry. Smitty's gitch must be on too tight. He's been whining and complaining all afternoon.

"I'll speak up for everyone here this afternoon, Brenda. This is the best place to get hot coffee and fresh donuts anywhere in Windsor, and you've always been the sweetest waitress in ten counties."

"Oh, Paul, you're the sweetest. I should take you home to Momma."

"Brenda, don't ever think like that. The dude here burps and farts all the time, and when he's home, he never runs around with his clothes on. He's always only in his underwear and that isn't a pretty sight."

"I don't believe you, Don. I think Paul is the kindest and nicest guy who comes in here. And furthermore, he always leaves me a nice tip."

"Brenda, I think you've been fooled by the dude's false charm. If you knew him the way I know him, you'd think otherwise. He's one bad actor."

"Dear Brenda, I apologize for Smitty's bad attitude. He's just having one of those days. It's just too bad that one of those days is just about every day."

That's how it went. Smitty would shoot down Brenda or me—he didn't care. And if that wasn't enough, he'd complain about the coffee or the donuts. He'd pretty much complain about anything and everything. It could be about the weather—it was too hot or too cold, or it was too dry or too wet. But the funny thing was that he always did it in a way that got other people laughing.

Then of course I'd counter his negativity with lots of positive thought. I would speak kindly to Brenda, and smooth over everything he said. We were good at being Mr. Bad Guy and Mr. Good Guy. The time always went by fast when we did our shtick.

The truth was that Brenda knew what we were up to, and so that made it all the more humorous. And could Brenda laugh. When she laughed, then everyone laughed.

All too soon our short stay at the counter came to an end. Smitty always made up to Brenda with sweet words. I know she liked that. You could see her eyes just glow, and she always took his hand and forgave him.

As Smitty and I were getting ready to leave, Brenda patted my arm and softly said, "Paul, you are my favorite customer, and well, Smitty and you both are my favorite customers."

With a bewitching and somewhat indignant look, Brenda said, "Smitty, you know you're about the world's worst liar. Paul's even told me that you love my coffee and donuts, and I've also heard that you really do adore me."

"Aw, Brenda. You see right through me. Oh, and I've been looking at those cream puffs behind the counter. I want one of those to go."

"Sure, Smitty, would you like this chocolate one with all that yummy beautiful cream stuffed up high in the middle?"

"You know that's the one he wants, Brenda. Look at his hungry eyes, and isn't it funny that he can't stop licking his lips when he looks at the cream puff behind the counter."

"Would you like one too, Paul?"

"No, thanks, Brenda. I know they're really yummy, but I'd better not. I'm going to take my wife out for dinner tonight if I don't need to be the second section on the run to Toronto in about an hour or so."

You need to understand that this wasn't the end of the story. Because it is called "The Cream Puff Caper," there has to be an ending that involves the cream puff.

"Smitty, are you going to give me a bite of that beautiful cream puff?"

"So sorry, Dude. This one's for me. You can watch me eat it and weep.

"You're hardhearted", Smitty," I said as I opened the door to exit. When I had stepped across the threshold, I gave the door a cuff with my right hand. I put some strength into that backhanded cuff, and the door came back at Smitty right smartly.

I wish you could have seen what Brenda and the customers saw. In that instant that I cuffed the door back at Smitty, he was putting his right foot over the threshold to step down, and at the same time he was holding his cream puff up to his mouth in order to take his first big bite.

I won't lie. It wasn't nice, and I don't know what motivated me to do that, to cuff the door back at Smitty. But sometimes you just do what you do without thinking or without remorse.

The door not only crunched Smitty's foot, but it simultaneously hit his hand, the one holding the cream puff up to his mouth. For you see, he was ready to take a big bite of that beautiful cream puff.

Well, this is what happened next. Smitty let out a loud yell. The door crunched his foot, and it hurt. The door also hit his hand, thereby shoving the cream puff, just about all of it, into his mouth. Actually, there was so much cream puff that didn't make it into his mouth that much of it was spread on his face from ear to ear and even stuffed up his nose.

Poor Smitty, he didn't get to enjoy his cream puff, but I must say, everyone in the coffee shop enjoyed what happened next.

Sputtering and yelling with cream puff still in his nose and up to his ears, Smitty ran after me. "I'm going to kill you, Dude, I'm going to kill you."

It's hard to run fast when you just want to bow over and laugh you head off and slap your legs in merriment. But run I did as I yelled, "Smitty, you look like a sight for sore eyes. Why don't you eat that cream puff instead of wearing it?"

I jumped in my car, started it, put it in gear, locked the doors, and started driving around the parking lot. All the while Smitty was running behind me just a few steps behind my car frantically waving his arms and yelling "I'm going to kill you, Dude, I'm going to kill you."

Can you believe this? Every time I drove by the front of the coffee shop, Brenda and all the customers were standing at the window and laughing. I must have driven around that parking lot three or four times before Smitty stopped running, and just stood there panting. Of course the cream puff was still all over his face, and up his nose and in his ears.

Finally, I unlocked the door, and Smitty climbed in. Still panting and looking like a sight for sore eyes, his famous words to me were "I'm going to kill you, Dude. I'll owe you for life because of what you did to me today. I'll owe you for life."

"Really! I'm not scared of you, Smitty." I smirked. We were always pulling stunts on each other. "My only regret is that I don't have a camera to take your picture so I can remind you forever how ridiculous you look today."

Back at the terminal, I said to dispatch, "Oh, by the way, Herb, Smitty forgot to buy your coffee and donut." But when I explained to him how it was that Smitty forgot, he said, "That's all right, Paul. I can't stop laughing when I think how Smitty must have looked dressed in his Greyhound uniform with cream puff from ear to ear, in his nose, and stuffed in his mouth."

Smitty just stood there and finally said, "Herb, you're my witness. I will owe the dude forever. I will never be able to repay him for what he did today. He'd better grow eyes in the back of his head."

Many times later even after Smitty would pull a stunt on me, he would say, "Dude, just don't forget. I will always owe you for life."

## A Front Tire Blowout on the Bus

"Hey, Dude. I've got the weekend off. How about you? Are you off for this weekend too?"

"Actually, Smitty, I'm off for the weekend but still going to be driving bus."

"What's that, Dude? Are you giving me some kind of riddle and you expect me to solve it? Are you playing word games with me?"

"Why not, Smitty. I'd like to see you figure it out. I'm off for the weekend, and I'm driving bus for the weekend. There's the riddle, solve it if you can."

"I don't know about that riddle, Dude, but what I do know is that your head is one big bunged-up riddle."

"Solve the riddle, Smitty, and I'll buy you a coffee today at Country Style Donuts. Don't solve the riddle and you buy my coffee."

"Dude, I've already solved that poor excuse of a riddle long before you bet me a coffee. What I was waiting for was to see what you'd bet me because whatever it was I'd win, and you'd lose. So get ready to buy my extra-large coffee."

"You haven't told me what the riddle is, Smitty. Solve it or weep."

"Here's the riddle, you lug nut. I won't be driving a bus for Greyhound this weekend, but I'll be driving a bus for Calvary Community Church. Now it's your turn to weep because you're taking me to Country Style Donuts right now, and I'm getting an extra-large coffee. And hey, if you're not a cheapskate, you can throw in a cream puff as well. Don't forget, Dude, you owe me one."

That's how the day started for me on Friday, September 26, 1975. I thought I'd get a free coffee out of Smitty. He looked so sleepy-eyed and out of it when he banged on my door real early that Friday morning. Now I realize he was just putting on a show. And it's true. His little caper had me fooled.

"OK, Smitty, since I'm buying your coffee and a donut, we're going in your car, not mine. Oh, by the way, you're dreaming if you think I'll buy you one of those really expensive cream puffs."

"Listen to yourself, Dude, you're whining. You hate being a sore loser, don't you?"

"You're right, Smitty. I do hate being a sore loser so be careful, or I just might buy you a cream puff and plaster it all over your face. I'm still laughing over that little caper last year where you and the door made intimate friends with each other."

That's the way it was with Smitty and me. We were the best of buddies, and there wasn't anything we wouldn't do for each other. Like they say in the movies, we had each other's six.

Smitty headed for our favorite Country Style Donut shop because our favorite waitress would be working the day shift there. Brenda was always amused by our antics. We could tease her to no end, and we could rail on each other. Inevitably other patrons would enter into our merriment, the coffee would flow, and the cash register would ring up more sales of coffee, donuts, and cookies.

"Well, look who the cat dragged in. If it isn't Smitty and Dude." Brenda laughingly mocked us while she pointed us out to no one in particular.

I really don't need to recount Smitty and my nonsense and levities. If you knew us, you'd know there was never a dull moment when we were in the house.

"Dude, on a serious note for a moment or two, explain to me this trip you're doing later today with your church bus."

"Smitty, Calvary Community Church has organized a busload of folk who want to attend a Tim Lahaye conference in Hamilton, this weekend. I booked the weekend off from Greyhound so I could have the pleasure of driving the church bus. Shirley will be able to come with me as she conscripted her sister Esther into babysitting our daughter."

"I have to tell you Dude, it sounds like you'll have a good time. When does the conference start tonight, and when do you figure you will have to leave Windsor?"

"The Friday evening conference starts at 7:00 p.m. I figure four hours from Windsor to Hamilton with one stop on route for a short break. I have to bear in mind that the church bus doesn't have a washroom. The other fact worth mentioning is that we've all booked rooms at the same hotel, and I'm sure everyone would like to freshen up before the conference begins. So to answer the second question, we'll leave the church parking lot at 2:00 p.m."

"You'll probably be back sometime Sunday evening I presume?" That question from Smitty was directed toward me with both eyebrows raised.

"I anticipate our arrival back into Windsor Sunday evening at approximately nine o'clock, Smitty."

"Dude, I wish I was going too, but c'est la vie. Just one thing, give me a phone call later Sunday evening. I'd like to know how your weekend went."

On the way to the cash register, Smitty loudly reminded me with a boastful voice you could hear to the other end of the donut shop, "Dude, don't forget you lost the bet. You're paying for my coffee and donut." And in the same breath, he motioned to Brenda to come closer and with these words said, "Throw in a chocolate cream puff, Brenda. The dude owes me one, and he said he'd come good for it today."

Brenda looked at me with a smile that was more of a smirk and headed for the show case. I knew I'd lost at that point. But not to let it go unnoticed by others, she emphatically directed her next comment to me with a pointed forefinger. "Dude, you behave yourself today and be a gentleman. You'd better hold the door open for Smitty too."

Needless to say, Smitty was strutting his stuff as he walked out the door of Country Style Donuts. And Brenda? Well, with both hands placed on her hips, she gave me the look. Everyone knows what the look is. We've all had it from our mother at one time or the other, or maybe like in my case, many times.

Shrugging my shoulders and holding up both hands in an "I surrender" fashion, I called back to Brenda as I was preparing to leave the donut shop, "I have nothing to say. I'm a humbled man." Her laughter was ringing in my ears as I crossed over the threshold of the doorway.

The bus trip to Hamilton had come and gone. It was Sunday evening, and the people had been let off in the church parking lot. Shirley and I had barely arrived home when the phone rang.

Looking at the phone I said to her, it is probably Smitty calling me because he wants to know how the trip went.

Upon hanging up, I mentioned to Shirley, "That wasn't Smitty that called, it was Greyhound dispatch. I have a trip set up for tomorrow. I'll be doing the midday scheduled run as the regular driver, Detroit to Toronto."

Then the phone rang again just a moment later. This time it was Smitty.

"Hi, Smitty. Perfect timing. I just got home, and Herb called. Now you."

"Hi, Dude, I wanted to know how your weekend in Hamilton went. I'm doing the morning's scheduled run Detroit to Buffalo, so fill me in quickly. I'd better get some rest as five in the morning will come quickly."

"Hey, Smitty, it's late, so I can catch up with you in a few days and tell you about my Hamilton trip with the church bus when I see you."

"Dude, I stayed up to hear about your trip. I'd heard a rumor that you'd had a serious problem on your trip as you were heading for Hamilton. I know Karl, one of the fellows on that trip, and he chatted with me this morning. So spill the beans, Dude, or do I have to drive over to your place at this late hour and pound it out of you?"

"OK, OK, Smitty. Don't work yourself up into a frenzy.

"I was heading east on the 401 highway just a few miles west of the Dutton Service Center. I'd just gone by the West Lorne exit, so you know approximately where I was when my left front wheel lost the retaining ring. Remember, the wheels on that bus are the older style. They are a two-piece assembly. Incidentally, you need an inner tube with the tire on those two piece wheels. One the tire has been placed on the wheel, the retaining ring is then pounded onto the wheel where it naturally is locked into place."

"Got it, Dude. I know the drill.

"I was running the speed limit, Smitty, doing at least 70 mph while in the right-hand lane. All of a sudden, *bang*. Before I had time to react, the bus cleared the left lane beside me, and as I started to respond to this sudden lane change, already my left front wheel was on the gravel at the edge of the median ditch."

Smitty exclaimed in a loud voice, "That is what I would call an immediate and swift lane change, Dude."

"I'm so thankful there was no other vehicle, car or truck, in the left lane beside me when I did that sudden lane change, Smitty. You'd have read about it in the Saturday morning *Windsor Star*."

"That old church bus doesn't have power steering, Smitty, and it was all I could do to keep it from heading right into the medium. I had to stand up and pull on the steering wheel with both hands placed on the right side. Even at that I could barely keep the bus on the road."

"Dude, that sounds rather scary to say the least. And how was it you were able to release your seat belt at the same time?"

"Real simple answer for that, Smitty. I didn't have my seat belt on. It was a good thing too because I could only get enough strength to keep the bus on the road by standing up. Don't forget that old bus had arm strong steering. I guess power steering must have only been an option when it was built."

Questioning me with concern in his voice, Smitty said, "It had to get better regarding your control of the bus as you applied brakes, didn't it, Dude?"

"Yes, you'd think so, Smitty, and I did start to apply brakes, but the strangest thing happened. That old bus went into a front-end speed wobble. Something similar to a speed wobble on a motorcycle. The front end of that bus started slamming right and then left. As I endeavored to slow the bus down more and more it slammed harder and harder in that side to side uncontrollable state."

"I know about speed wobbles on motorcycles, Dude, but I'd never expected it could happen to a bus," exclaimed Smitty.

"It had to be attributed to the fact that I was running at high speed with only one front tire holding me on the pavement. That flattened rim was doing nothing to help me regain control but was rather contributing to the bus's uncontrollability."

"How did you regain control then, Dude?"

"Believe it or not, Smitty, I had to speed up instead of slow down. I remained standing and holding onto the right side of the steering wheel. All the while, I planted my right foot on the accelerator, and it wasn't until I had accelerated the bus to eighty miles per hour where I was able to then slowly and safely reduce speed. I had run that bus past the speed wobble and kept it going in the right direction.

"Smitty, when I'd reduced my speed under 40 miles per hour, I was then able to sit down. It took me better than two miles from the moment of blowout to where I made a safe stop on the right shoulder."

"Hey, Dude, Karl told me it seemed like everybody held their breath for those two long miles, and then when you were stopped, they all audibly exhaled at the same time."

"I don't remember anything like that, Smitty, but I can well imagine they did hold their breath. Shirley was sitting right behind me, and she told me she involuntarily held her breath."

"It was interesting to note that there were no vehicles that passed me when I was going through all those speed wobble contortions, but when I stopped, there had to be at least four cars that pulled over behind me. It must have scared them as well seeing that old bus going into convulsions like it was."

"How'd you get it fixed and still make your time to Hamilton?"

"One of the car drivers asked if he could help. I actually got one of the guys on the bus to ride with him to the Dutton Service Center where he got a local wrecker to come to me and replace the left steering wheel. To say the least, I was happy to supply a good spare wheel.

"We were up and running in a relatively short time, and after a quick pit stop at the Dutton Service Center I put the hammer down and we continued to Hamilton. I'd only lost about one-half hour, so we easily made the conference on time. The only thing I was unable to do was stop first at the hotel so everyone could freshen up. Needless to say, I had no complaints from anyone. Rather, they all wanted to shake my hand and thank me profusely."

"Did the bus give you any problems on the way back to Windsor, Dude?"

"No problems, Smitty. The good folk on that bus were so happy to arrive safely in Hamilton and then back in Windsor they lifted a good tip for me."

"Hey, that's great, Dude, so now you can buy me a steak dinner."

"Where did you get that crazy idea, Smitty? The only two people getting a steak dinner is Shirley and me. Eat your heart out, and hey, get to bed. You're bugging me now."

## Drunk Passengers Pose Problems

What do bus drivers like to do just about as much as drive? They like to get together and tell their stories. I was no exception. If I could find an audience of one or two others, it wasn't long before the stories came. It was a great way to spend a few hours while on duty and waiting for a dispatch.

Dennis and I had trained on Greyhound together back in the spring of 1973. While we both worked out of the Windsor garage, we didn't often see each other, so it was a particular delight to happen to be waiting with him for assignments on a beautiful autumn day in October of 1976.

Denis had come over to Greyhound after he'd been a policeman in London, Ontario, for several years. He had recounted a couple of stories about his run-ins with drunks during that time.

"Dennis, there seems to be an issue with drunks here at Greyhound as well. I have had three situations with drunks just in the past year alone. Two of these three drunks were quite challenging, and with one drunk there was just a funny conclusion to his trip."

"Let's hear your stories, Paul. Two bad drunks and one good drunk, I'm intrigued."

"Well, it went like this, Dennis. I had been doing the midnight scheduled run out of Toronto to Detroit for a couple of months when this particular night as I was in the midst of taking on my passengers, this big, tall fellow tries to hand me his ticket. He wants to go to Brantford. This night run doesn't go to Brantford, so I told him when the next bus would leave so he could get to his destination. I could smell alcohol on his breath, so I kept a close eye on him.

"He immediately became belligerent, and obviously he knew while I didn't stop in Brantford, I did run through Brantford on Highway 403. He demanded I take him and then let him off on the side of 403 somewhere near the Highway 24 exit.

"I realized that I was going nowhere with this fellow as he'd continued to try and get on the bus. He was starting to get into my face, so I was getting cautious because when I had refused him entry to the bus for the third time he clenched his right fist. I saw this and ducked just as he took a big windmill swing at my head. I wasted no time getting out of his way as I ran around the front of the bus and locked the entry door. I had already shut the door barring his entry when I perceived a problem developing.

"It was a quiet night down at the Toronto Bus Terminal on Bay Street, and the Gray Coach Dispatch observed everything from their windows at the far end of the terminal. When that drunk took a swing at me, which thankfully I saw coming and was able to duck out of the way, they immediately called for the city police who amazingly arrived almost immediately."

"That was observant of you, Paul, to see a punch coming and get out of the way before he was able to connect."

"Right on, Dennis. The last thing I needed was to tangle with this fellow. Incidentally, there must have been at least fifteen to twenty people waiting to board my bus, and when they saw that drunk take a swing at me without exception, they all dispersed in several different directions.

"I beat a hasty retreat around the other side of my bus while Craig, the baggage man, grabbed the baggage cart and faced down the drunk with the cart between them. I figured Craig would try to break that drunk's legs if he should try and get our baggage man to open the door to the coach.

"The drunk was still trying to pull the locked door open when two police constables arrived. They immediately tried to restrain that drunk, and he responded by taking a swing at one of them. What I saw when that fist connected with the head of the cop closest to him made me realize there would be some serious stuff going down in a moment or two.

"The two cops did, however, quickly restrain that drunk, and with the back door of the cruiser already open, they sent him flying from several feet back through the open door and sprawling onto the back seat. With that he was locked in and no way out.

"I asked the police if they needed a statement from me, and they said no. I then suggested they take that drunk and find a quiet alley and give him back what he gave them before they turned him in to sober up. The cop while still rubbing his sore jaw just shook his head and with a snarl on his lips growled that would be their plan. They would beat the tar out of him."

"I'd have done the same as those two cops, Paul. When a drunk made my night beat tough, I settled the score quickly just like they probably did.

"So let's hear the story about the happy drunk, Paul."

"Sure, Dennis. I was doing the afternoon scheduled run from Toronto to Detroit as the regular driver, and Ron was the second section on this particular day. We'd both arrived in London. This was the only stop on that run before we arrived in Windsor and then Detroit. Ron came up to me and stated that he had a fellow on his bus who'd been drinking ever since he'd left Toronto. He was a quiet fellow and wasn't giving any other passengers a hard time but was nonetheless making those closest to him very nervous. Now that we were parked at the terminal, the drunk had gotten off the bus and was probably in the restaurant.

"I suggested to Ron that we see if that fellow had any booze remaining on the bus. We went to where he'd been sitting, and sure enough there was a half-empty bottle of Vodka, a couple of empty cans of ginger ale and two cans of ginger ale not yet consumed. Let's dump his Vodka down the toilet and fill the bottle to the same amount with water. Ron agreed that would be a great idea.

"When I met up with Ron again in Windsor at the bus station, we had a good laugh. That Vodka drinker was drinking himself sober mixing ginger ale with water."

"That's too funny, Paul. Let's hear your third story. You said this guy was also a problem."

"He was a problem, Dennis. I'd arrived in Hamilton working the local scheduled run from London to Toronto on this particular evening. I knew this guy had been drinking on the bus because another passenger had come to the front of the bus as we were arriving in Hamilton and informed me.

"He had remained on the bus as others had left the coach at the bus station. When I had a moment before we departed for Toronto, I walked to the back and suggested that he leave the bus as I wasn't able to transport him any further in his inebriated condition. He became belligerent and told me where to go and how quickly I needed to get there. I didn't argue with him. I still had at least fifteen to twenty passengers destined for Toronto.

"I could tell from that drunk's insulting remarks made toward me that many of the passengers nearest to him became visibly unnerved."

"Come on, Paul, you didn't take him to Toronto, did you?"

"No way, Dennis, however I did return to the front of the bus, and putting the bus into gear, I drove immediately to the Hamilton Police Station, which was just a couple of blocks from the bus terminal. I stopped directly in front of the police station and ran inside where I caught up with the policeman at the front desk. I informed him of the situation I was facing, and two big cops quickly accompanied me into the bus. When they got hold of that drunk, they walked him or rather they carried him while his feet barely touched the floor. He was ejected through the door unto the pavement below where he sprawled facedown.

"Before I could shut the door or put the bus into gear and release the brakes, all the passengers on the bus who had seen how that insolent drunk was ejected from the bus gave those two big cops a loud and resounding cheer."

"Hey, that was a great story, Paul. I'd have done the same thing. I'd have thrown that drunken sod so hard off the bus he'd have been doing forward somersaults before he came to rest on his face. Then I'd have done exactly what those two Hamilton cops did. I'd have thrown him in a cell where he'd spend the rest of the night getting sober."

"I don't get it, Dennis. Don't these clowns know that if they've been drinking they are not welcome to ride the bus?"

"Have you ever had to kick anyone off the bus for other reasons, Paul?"

"A couple of times, Dennis. Back a couple of months ago something had happened to the regular driver for the midday scheduled run from Toronto to Detroit. It was a through coach destined for Chicago. This run had originated in Montreal, but for some reason the Voyageur driver was really late into Toronto. I was still in my room at the Lord Simcoe Hotel when I got a call from dispatch to pick up a coach at the Gray Coach Bus barns and get it up to the bus terminal on Bay Street ASAP. By the time I got there that run was now one hour late."

"Not a great way to start your day, Paul."

"No kidding, Dennis. There was a lot of very unhappy folk waiting for me. I listened patiently to their complaining, but once on board and on route, I informed them over the PA system that I had permission to make the time up by running as an express from Toronto to London instead of the local that the schedule called for on this segment of the Montreal to Chicago run. Evidently another driver had been assigned to run the local section between Toronto and London and had left somewhat earlier from that bus station on Bay Street."

"That should have worked out well enough, Paul, but you still had a problem?"

"I sure did, Dennis. I still had to go into the Sunnyside bus stop as there was one passenger waiting for this run. When I arrived, I was confronted with one very angry lady who would not sit down even after I'd explained that she would still make her connection in Detroit for Chicago. She refused to shut up and stood in front of the white line on the floor, which indicated no passengers should be there when the coach was in motion. I informed her she must sit down as it was a safety risk for her to stand where she was right beside me. To no avail. She just ran at the mouth on and on.

"I hadn't passed the Seaway Inn yet, so I kicked her off the bus in front of the Inn and told her she could find another way to get to Chicago. Oh yes, and I returned her ticket to her which I had not cancelled."

"Hey, I remember that event, Paul. I was in London when you arrived on that run. I was heading for Toronto, but my run didn't leave for a few moments until after your arrival. I remember Bill, the terminal manager, confronted you right on the platform as you let your passengers off for a short break in the restaurant."

"Yes, and was Bill ever angry with me. I think he was ready to fire me for kicking a sweet little old lady off the bus. When I informed him of the dynamics which led to her quick exit from my bus, because it was a safety matter of course, he sided with me and said he'd have done the same thing."

"I think you've perfected the knack of dodging the bullet Paul." Dennis laughed as he jumped up to answer the ringing phone on the driver's room wall.

"Well, it looks like neither of us will get any second sections today, Paul. Herb told me to tell you that we can both call it a day and head for home. But before you go, tell me that other story of kicking someone off the bus for something other than being drunk."

"Dennis, if I tell you all my stories today, I'll not have any for the next time we're sitting around waiting for some work."

"Sure, sure. I know you're right, Paul. I doubt you'd run out of stories anytime soon."

"OK, Dennis, I'll make this a short one because I'm starting to think about what might be waiting for me at my house when I get home in time for supper."

"Come on, Paul, don't let a good meal get in the way of a good story. Don't go cutting corners. I want the straight bill of goods and not some *Readers' Digest* version."

"OK, Dennis, that's what I'll give you, the unedited version. I had an express run Windsor to Toronto on this particularly bright and sunny day. I'd picked up passengers in London and had a full bus. A second section was close behind me. I had a MC5, and this bus had the little vent windows on the driver's side window.

I always like to keep that little window open, and on this particular day as I was eastbound on Highway 401 around the Ingersoll area, I could smell that someone on the bus was smoking marijuana. I informed that individual over the public address system to butt out—no smoking on the bus. I hated that smell as well. It always reminded me of burning green grass.

"I could see that a guy and a girl riding at the back of the bus on the long bench seat beside the washroom were not honoring my request to stop smoking. Not to worry, I just pulled off at the Highway 2 exit to return to Woodstock. It's just a quarter of a mile to the Ontario Provincial Police Precinct for that area.

"*Buda-bing, buda-boom.* A big Ontario Provincial Police officer escorted this guy and his girlfriend off my bus."

"I thought you said that you'd give me the unedited version, Paul. If that was the unedited version, what would the *Coles Notes* version be like?"

"Hey, Dennis, did you want me to tell you that the guy smoking a joint came to the front of the bus and threatened me or told me where to go? Or maybe he just flipped me the finger from the back of the bus? Or that maybe he just kicked up a big stink at the back of the bus and had all the other passengers upset and concerned about what that clown and his girlfriend might do next?"

"Yes, something like that, Paul. So what's the real story here?"

"Hahaha. Dennis if I told you it was two out of the three options I gave you, which two of the three would you think it was?"

"Smart, real smart. So you want me to tell you what your story was, eh?"

"You're on, Dennis. Finish my story for me if you think you can. I'll even sweeten the pot for you on a dare. If you get it right, I'll buy you a coffee, and if you get it wrong, you'll buy me a coffee."

"Oh, for a moment, I thought you were going to play a little gambling game with me, Paul. Like I'm going to fall for that ruse. No matter which of the three I say was the real story, you'd want that coffee bad enough that you'd tell me I was wrong."

"Dennis, you have to have faith in me. I'm a man of my word. Make your selection. If you are correct and since we are both heading east and on the same road toward our homes, we can stop at the Country Style Donut shop on Tecumseh Ave once we leave here and I'll buy you a coffee or, you'll buy me a coffee."

Shaking his head with a big smirk on his face, Dennis said, "OK, Paul. Here's my best guess as to the real story. Once you told him to butt out the joint he was smoking, he flipped you the finger. Then he really kicked up a big stink at the back of the coach, and had all the other passengers upset and concerned about what would transpire next. That's my ending to your story, and I'm sticking to it."

"Very good, Dennis. You win the Kewpie doll, or should I say, you get the free coffee on me. Come on, let's get out of here before Herb in dispatch thinks we've moved in and set up living quarters here."

## Rocks and Wrong-Way Drivers

I began driving for Eastern Canadian Greyhound Lines May 1973. I was placed on the spare board, which meant I would be placed by dispatch anywhere they needed me. Shirley and I had moved from St. Thomas, to Windsor, in June of that year, and quickly established ourselves. I settled comfortably in my new occupation and role as an intercity bus driver. But within three months that comfort level I had enjoyed came to a furious and abrupt end.

"Shirley, I just got a phone call from Herb in dispatch. He informed me that I'd better prepare myself for some strenuous work conditions starting today."

"Paul, what is so important about today, Saturday, August 25$^{th}$, that Herb would tell you that your work conditions will change so dramatically?"

"Both Canadian National Railroad, and Canadian Pacific Railroad have gone on strike. Consequently, their passenger services have ceased immediately. All intercity bus services, and that includes Greyhound will be required to accommodate a huge influx of people who would normally travel by train between these points in Southwest Ontario, which include Detroit/Windsor and Toronto, Detroit/Windsor, and Niagara Falls/Buffalo and Toronto/Niagara Falls/Buffalo."

"I will pack a larger travel case with extra clothing, Shirley. I won't necessarily be home each day, but could be gone for few days at a time."

It wasn't more than an hour had passed when Herb called me again. After a brief conversation, I hung up and called out to Shirley. "I'm called in for the midday scheduled run today from Windsor to Toronto. I will protect that run as a spare driver for the second section. Herb told me that in all probability, each run will have several sections. He also informed me, Shirley, that when I arrive in Toronto, I should expect that I will be turned back to either London or Windsor the same day."

It was like Herb said it would be, basically crazy to the n*th* degree. I drove seven days a week. I had never experienced work conditions to be so hectic. Fatigue became normal, but still I pressed on.

Arriving home in Windsor late one evening in September, Shirley noticed how tired I looked and commented, "Paul, you look like something the cat dragged in."

"I not only look like it I'm sure, but I feel like it too, Shirley. It has been a very challenging Sunday."

"What happened, Paul?"

"I left Windsor on the early morning run Detroit/Windsor to Toronto as the regular driver. It was so busy that I loaded my coach exclusively for Toronto. I wouldn't have to go into London but would give my passengers a twenty-minute break at the Ingersoll Service Center on Highway 401.

"We were so busy that Greyhound had to lease a couple of buses from Chatham Coach Lines to service the third and fourth sections. Even though my run was a local run, my second section was also deemed an express. He would run directly to London and then on to Toronto. The other two buses, which were from Chatham Coach Lines, had our Greyhound drivers on them, and they would do all the local work.

"It was about forty-five to fifty minutes later after the break at the Ingersoll Service Center that I entered an ongoing highway construction site near Cambridge, Ontario. The speed had been reduced to 25 miles per hour for both the eastbound and the westbound traffic. I was travelling east and approaching a cross-over for the westbound traffic. My side had obviously been reduced to one lane, which was the lane I was in, and just as I was abreast of the cross-over, an auto-carrier tried to negotiate it with excessive speed.

"He was beginning to drift into my lane, and as he realized that, he jerked his steering wheel harder to the right. That caused his low-slung trailer, which was fully loaded with at least six cars, to bottom out on his left side. Basically, Shirley, the frame of that trailer was dragging on the asphalt and gravel mixture, and whipping up some large stones and rocks."

"Yikes, Paul. You must have been pelted with those rocks and stones."

"I was, Shirley, and one incredibly large rock hit my windshield right at my chest level. That rock was travelling so fast it actually broke completely through the windshield. If it were not for a clear membrane between the outer glass and the inner glass, that rock would have likely hit me and busted a few ribs. As it was, I was completely covered in shards of glass."

"But you said the rock broke through the windshield, yet you weren't hit by the rock. How did that work?"

"The hole it left in the clear membrane would have been about the diameter of a dime. The rock ultimately fell away from the windshield. I had to stop as soon as I was able to do so safely, in order to assess if any passengers were cut by flying shards of glass. Fortunately, most of the glass impacted me. I wasn't cut, but it shook me up for a few moments. Incidentally, I was sure glad to have my sunglasses on to protect my eyes from flying glass particles."

"My goodness, Paul. That was certainly more than enough for one day."

"I thought so too, Shirley, but that wasn't the case. When I arrived in Toronto, dispatch first had me take my damaged bus down to the

Gray Coach bus barns where the windshield was replaced, then he turned me back out as a second section on a local run from Toronto to London. But I did had a couple of hours to relax before I started that run.

"I completed that trip without any complications, but no sooner had I arrived in London than Bill, the terminal manager, told me to pull to the other side of the terminal and load for a return trip to Toronto. This time I was a third section on an express run from London to Toronto. I don't think I'd ever seen the London terminal so busy with people.

"I'll say one thing for the travelling public, they were handling the situation quite well. With that many people elbow to elbow, you'd think there would be some pushing and shoving, but there wasn't any of that all, Shirley.

"This run would soon come to an end as I was now travelling south on Highway 427. Traffic was very light considering it was Sunday late afternoon. As I approached the large overpass where I travel up and over the westbound lanes of the QEW in order to access the eastbound Gardner, a car came toward me from the top of my bridge. He was on my roadway. I had basically nowhere to go but did a quick stop and pulled over on my right side and placed the bus within a couple of inches of the bridge abutment.

"Was the driver of that car suicidal? Fortunately for him the other cars behind me were able to clear a path for him. I couldn't believe it, Shirley, he just kept driving the wrong way. He didn't even attempt to stop and turn around."

"I hope you had a decent trip home, Paul. What you have just described is more than enough for one day, humph, more than enough for one week."

## Swamping the Canoe

"Hey, Dude, why are we sitting here drinking coffee on your veranda when we can be out on the lake chasing those big rollers?"

My buddy Smitty and I both worked out of Windsor, on Eastern Canadian Greyhound Bus Lines as intercity bus drivers. Since we both had the day off, Smitty had come over to my place to shoot the breeze.

July 1975 was a beautiful month. It hadn't rained in a week or so, and the weather had been great with mild temperatures, and long, sunny days. Beautiful Lake Saint Clair was just a few steps from the front of my property where I lived on the south side of Ross Beach Road.

Living just outside the eastern town limits of Belle River, on the south shore of Lake St. Clair was absolutely ideal. It was always great looking out on the lake, and because it was a shallow lake, storms could really generate huge waves.

Today was one of those days. The northwesterly winds were strong, and the waves were big. We called them rollers.

From our perch on the front steps of the veranda, I had to admit it and with excitement in my voice said, "Yup, let's do it, Smitty."

Shirley, my young bride, with a concerned look on her face asked, "Why would you two guys want to endanger yourselves in such rough water?"

"Oh, come on, Shirley. You know Smitty and I are good swimmers. We need to practice swamping the canoe, and then getting back into it, and what better time is there to do that then when the lake is rough like it is today?"

With my canoe on my shoulders, and Smitty leading the way and carrying our gear, which amounted to two life jackets, two paddles, and one bailing container, we angled down the narrow path to the sandy shore.

Standing at the water's edge, and already getting his feet wet, Smitty excitedly yelled out, "Dude, those rollers are pretty good-looking. They must be at least five feet in height."

"We can do it," I yelled with both excitement and anticipation over the roar of the crashing waves. "But we've got our work cut out for us because we need to get to deep water. Those rollers look like they're sweeping the lake floor because it is so shallow here."

We readied ourselves, just waiting for the right moment. The crashing waves were deafening. Adrenaline was pumping through our veins. Our muscles were tense. We were ready to spring into the waves with the canoe. "Count the waves off, Smitty! Make sure to get it right." I had to yell and hoped he heard me.

The sequence was always the same. Look for the highest wave then count each succeeding wave until you count seven. The seventh wave is always the highest. We had to put in on the next wave. It would be the smallest.

"Seven," screamed Smitty. Like a Bobcat waiting to pounce upon its prey, we leapt into the water with my canoe and managed to keep it upright while endeavoring to get in.

Knees braced against the sides of the canoe, we pulled hard on our paddles. These rollers were tough. Smitty, my bow man, was eating those rollers as they broke over the bow. In less than five seconds he was thoroughly soaked.

In the stern, it was all I could do to maintain direction. "DUDE," he screamed back to me, "Steer us left. We need to hit the next roller square on."

"Smitty, I'm doing the best I can, and I can't get us straightened out. Help me out. Stroke on the right side with me."

We were screaming at each other giving directions. The ride was incredible. It felt like a roller coaster out of control. One second the prow was in the air as we crested the wave. The next second the stern was in the air.

"Dude, are you still with me? I feel like I'm doing it all by myself." I'm not sure that last scream from Smitty was pure excitement or pure terror.

"Smitty, this is crazy. I don't know if this is fun or if we're absolutely nuts." I realized there was a mounting tenseness in my stomach. Was that a sign of fear?

Then it happened. A rogue wave caught us off guard. Slamming into our left side, we were lifted up on its crest and brutally tossed out of the canoe. Sinking in the gray frothing, angry water, I was aware of an incredible undertow. I felt it dragging me on the lake's bottom toward deeper water. Struggling with all the strength I could muster, I thrust my way to the surface. At that moment I was indeed very thankful that I chose to wear a good life jacket.

"Dude, you gave me a scare. What took you so long to surface?" Smitty actually sounded concerned. I was touched, well, not by very much though. He knew I could swim.

Coughing, I sputtered, "Smitty, I hit the bottom. There's a serious undertow happening."

With all the strength we could muster, we bailed the canoe until we thought it safe to reenter.

"Hold the canoe on the left side, Smitty, and I'll pull myself in on the right side. Then get over here on the right side, and I'll offset the balance to the left while you pull yourself in."

This was crazy. I was getting hoarse from yelling. I know Smitty was as well. Yet we continued. We were driven by both fear and the desire to conquer. We had bailed the canoe in rough water, and while we were trying to get into the canoe, we were taking on more water. But we did get in and again readied ourselves to head into the angry waves.

"You want to keep doing this, Smitty, or have you had enough?"

"Sounds like you're a big suck, Dude."

That was really funny, and that was all I needed. Smitty called me a suck. No one had better want to call me a suck, least of all him. I didn't need to think that one through for a long time. Leaning into the strong winds hitting us on the left side, I dumped us into the drink. This time I swamped the canoe, not the waves, not the wind, just me. Call me a suck would he?

I surfaced before Smitty did. I didn't hit the bottom. No way was I going that deep this time. But where was Smitty? He sure was taking his sweet time. When he surfaced, he came up behind me about thirty feet away, sputtering and coughing. It took him another moment or so before he could even yell at me, but when he did yell, you could have heard him in the next county.

"Dude, I owe you for that. What are you trying to do? Drown me? You're crazy. You're a real nutcase. You pot-licker, I ought to swim over there and . . ."

I cut him off in mid-sentence and yelled back to him, "You are too cantankerous. You won't drown that easily. Anyhow, Smitty, you know how to swim, so start swimming. Which way are you going to go? Back here to the canoe or to the beach?"

Well, Smitty did swim back to the canoe, and we did both safely get back into it, and although we did this crazy swamping exercise a couple of times more, we had basically run out of energy, and being fully clothed and wet, we were beginning to experience some initial degree of hypothermia. Oh, and we'd yelled so much we could hardly speak audibly let alone yell anymore.

"Let's head her back to shore, Smitty. I'll watch for the next high wave, and we can surf its crest right onto the beach."

Now that was a thrill. We caught the next roller, and riding its crest to the beach, we covered the five hundred or so feet in a matter of a couple of minutes.

We both looked like a real sorry mess. Here we were lying on the beach, wet and cold and laughing our fool heads off.

With what little energy he had left, and his hoarse voice barely audible, Smitty croaked out, "Wow, that was real crazy, Dude. Do you think we mastered the art of getting back into the canoe while in rough waters?"

My voice was just as hoarse, and all I could muster was something similar in a pathetic croaking sound. "What do you think, Smitty? Do you want to go out and try it again for a while?"

Smitty just gave me the look. I knew what that meant.

# TEN

# DANGER ON THE PETAWAWA RIVER

IT HAD BEEN a long winter. As far as I was concerned, winter was always far too long. Winter 1976–1977 had finally come to an end, and at the moment, even spring was fast coming to an end. Summer was a couple of weeks away.

Shirley and I had moved from Belle River back into Windsor, Ontario. We bought a row house condo at East Gate Estates. And in the backyard, you guessed it, was the canoe.

I just loved that canoe. It was a lightweight seventeen foot aluminum Grumman and Smitty's canoe was also an aluminum Grumman; but his was a white-water model. We'd had our canoes out a few times already, and had been practicing our skills because we were getting ready to take an epic canoe trip.

Poking me in the ribs, Smitty said, "Dude, we need to take this canoe trip before the Petawawa River slows down. Spring runoff is nearly done, and the river height could be receding."

Smitty and I had been sitting in a couple of lawn chairs in my backyard this early June Thursday afternoon.

When I spoke again I said, "Smitty, I know you're right. Our plans are made. Let's make it happen. We'll leave early this coming Saturday morning the eleventh just as soon as Greg and Jack get the time off late Friday night.

"Here's the way I see it, Smitty. You and Jack will run your canoe, and Greg and I will run my canoe."

Pausing just for a moment to catch my breath, I continued, "Greg and Jack both said they'd be ready early Saturday morning. If we leave early, we'll be able to make it to Brent Lake on the north boundary of Algonquin Park before nightfall. Bring your canoe over here tomorrow, Smitty, and we'll load both yours and mine on my car's rooftop carrier, put our gear in the trunk, and when those other two guys get here, we can get going."

We were an interesting party to be sure. All four of us lived and worked in Windsor, Ontario. Smitty and I had a long history of friendship going back to our young childhood days, and both of us were employed at Bondy Cartage. Jack and Greg were mutual friends of ours. Jack worked in the automotive manufacturing industry while Greg worked as an appliance repairman. The four of us and our wives socialized with each other.

We were all experienced canoers, and the Petawawa River running through the northern parts of Algonquin Park toward the town of Petawawa, Ontario, was a good river to test us on our canoeing skills, as it had some good rapids and lots of fast-moving water.

"That's the last of the gear, guys. Let's hit the road. I figure it will take us about seven hours to get to Brent Lake, and probably another five or six hours to get ourselves staged for heading out on the trip on Sunday morning. Smitty, you can drive first, and we'll all take a turn at it with me driving the last stage from North Bay to Deux Rivieres on Highway 17, then into Brent Lake on the gravel road."

What a bunch of lucky guys we were with four lovely young ladies (our wives, of course) kissing us goodbye at 4:00 a.m. With lots of hugs and kisses and quiet whispers into our lover's ears, we finally settled in for a long ride.

"Hey, Dude, the trailer with my motorcycle on the back is coming along really well. It pulls great. I hardly notice it at all."

Smitty had a nice motorcycle and a good, solid cycle trailer. We planned on taking the bike to Brent Lake. We would leave our gear, the canoes, and Greg and I would remain at Brent Lake. Smitty and Jack would go back out to Highway 17, and with the bike and trailer in tow, they would go to the town of Petawawa where they would leave both the car and the trailer. They would come back to Brent Lake on the bike. When we set out on our canoe trip on Sunday morning, the bike would remain there at the lake, and upon completion of our trip, we'd all pack everything back into the car, which remained at Petawawa, go back to Brent Lake, and fetch Smitty's bike.

"We've rehearsed our plan several times, Jack. Do you think we've left anything out or forgotten anything?"

"I don't think so, Smitty. I'd ask Greg, but look at him . . . already sleeping, and we've only been on the road an hour. Oh yes, Dude has passed out too."

"Dude, wake up. We've been moving along pretty good and we're making great time. Traffic on the 401 is really light this morning. I say we stop at the Fifth Wheel Truck Stop at Milton and get some breakfast. We'll be there in a few minutes."

"Sure, let's do that, Smitty," I responded, rubbing the sleep out of my eyes. "I can smell the bacon and eggs already. Jack can take over after breakfast and run us up to North Bay on Highway 11. We'll need to get fuel at that point, and then I'll take over and drive to Cedar Lake in Algonquin Park. We can stop at the Fifth Wheel Truck Stop at North Bay. The next stop will be Brent Station on Cedar Lake."

Arriving at the Fifth Wheel Truck Stop in Milton, we noticed there was quite a few rigs parked, probably many overnight, and the car parking lot was quite busy as well. Early vacation season had begun, and there were plenty of people dressed casually for their holidays, so there was a good mix of people in the truck stop, some in work clothes, and others like us four guys who got out of that light blue 1976 Ford Custom 500, shorts and T-shirts were the norms.

We found a good table in the center of the restaurant, and soon, our conversation was full of laughter. It looked like we were having more fun than anyone else. From the looks we were getting, it seemed that at least a half dozen truckers were listening in on our conversation. They weren't doing a very good job of hiding their laughter as we continually cracked jokes and teased the waitress.

Our waitress, Suzy, was enjoying the good-natured banter, and kept a close eye on us to make sure our coffee never ran out. Of course, this gave us the opportunity to tease and flirt with her too.

Suzy knew both Smitty and me, the dude. This was our favorite truck stop, and the last one before we got into the heavy traffic of Toronto.

"Smitty, what are you and Dude doing today. You sure don't look like you're driving your big tractor-trailer rigs dressed like that. Are you guys on a holiday or a vacation?"

"That's what we're up to, Suzy. All of us are heading to Algonquin Park. We're going to take a week to canoe the Petawawa River from the north end of the park out to the town of Petawawa, where it runs into the Ottawa River."

"Oh wow. I love to canoe, and I'd sure love to do what you four guys are doing. I have my own canoe too. It's a sixteen foot fiberglass. When you guys get back from your canoe trip, will you stop in here at the truck stop? I work days next weekend, and I'll want to know how your trip went."

"We'll do that, Suzy, if we can get Dude to stop and let us have a break."

Going through Toronto that Saturday morning at 8:30 a.m. should have been easy. You'd think everyone would still be having a leisurely breakfast. But such was not the case. Highway 401 was anything but quiet at that early hour. Jack, who was doing the driving, wasn't a *happy camper*. The traffic was heavy right then, and we were moving along much slower.

"Did you just see that? That pickup who just passed us cut off the car in front of us to take an immediate exit for Highway 400, and he forced the car to take the shoulder. Man, oh man, what kind of idiot is driving that truck?"

In a nonchalant manner, Dude responded to Jack's startled comment, "Yes, I saw that. Typical Toronto drivers. They're always cutting each other off. You have to keep your eyes open everywhere. Toronto drivers are so aggressive anymore."

"I'm just not used to driving like that or expecting drivers to drive like that, Dude. Give me Windsor any day." Jack said this while shaking his head.

Traffic settled down after our run through Toronto, and the rest of the trip up to North Bay was uneventful. After a coffee break at the Fifth Wheel Truck Stop, located a couple of miles south of North Bay, we settled into the last leg of our trip which was on Highway 17 heading east.

"Hey, guys, we're here . . . at Deux Revieres, that is. Now the fun begins. We have a few miles of gravel road, but at about the ten-mile mark, we have to run on something more like a moose trail for the next fifteen miles until we reach Cedar Lake. Smitty, we'd better check on your bike and trailer, and make sure everything is stable and secure. This trail will tax your stuff and my car to their limits in places."

"Everything is good to go, Dude. Bike and trailer are A-OK, and the canoes are lashed down tight and secure as well."

"Here is what comes next, guys. After we've run those ten miles of gravel, we will stop at the Park's Natural Resources office located right there at the junction with a road to Wendigo Lake. I'll go into that office and get our interior camping permits, some maps, and I'll ask them how the Petawawa River is flowing at this time."

Climbing back into the car with excitement in his voice, Dude said, "The word is that the Petawawa River still has a good amount of water flowing basically because the spring runoff was excellent this year. It sounds like we've made a good choice coming up here. This is going to be a great canoe trip, guys."

However, everyone had a different view of the next portion of the trip to Cedar Lake and Brent Station.

"This trail has to be the roughest I've ever driven over. I hope my muffler is still on the car, Smitty, when we get to Brent Station."

"Why did we choose this place to set into our canoe trip, Dude? Remind me because I've forgotten. And I hope my bike is still with us when we get there, we if we do arrive at all. I nearly think we'll get hung up on some seriously large rocks embedded in the middle of this forsaken trail."

"Smitty, we're doing it in my new car as well. What a way to break it in."

After about one hour of driving dead slow on, without a doubt, the park's worst road, we finally arrived at Brent Station on Cedar Lake. The car and trailer somehow survived the trip, and the bike and canoes were just as secure on arrival as they were when we started. That had to be a testimony to the great skills that Smitty and I had at lashing down freight. What else can you expect from two professional truck drivers who *know their beans*? However, we were nowhere done for the day.

"Smitty, we'll leave the trailer attached to the car while we remove the canoes and all the gear. We have enough time in the day for you and Jack to run the bike and car to Petawawa. Once you find a safe place to park the car and trailer, and permission to leave them for several days, head back here to our campsite. Greg and I will set up both our tents. Don't leave any gear in the car or we'll be up the creek without a paddle for sure."

With that send-off, Smitty and Jack left Brent Station in less than one hour after we had arrived. They had to retrace our steps back out to Highway 17, and do it in such a manner as to preserve both car and trailer with Smitty's bike still lashed down.

"It took us about one and a half hours to get in here off Highway 17. We spent nearly one half hour unloading everything we needed, and now Smitty and Jack left at 2:00 p.m. Greg, I think they'll be gone for six hours. The way I figure it, they will take one and a half hours back to the highway, and one hour to Petawawa. Once the car and trailer are parked, coming back on the bike will take about three hours, if they take a short break."

"So what you are saying is that they'll not get back until 8:00 p.m. I figure you're off by an hour, Dude. I predict they will be back here by 7:00 p.m. Do you want to make a wager on that? Let's say that whoever loses has to buy coffee for everyone when we get out of here, and we're heading back to Windsor."

"You're on, Greg, but right now we'd better set up camp. It looks like we are in a good place to pitch both tents. Smitty and Jack will be over there beside those rocks, and you and I will take this spot just a few feet away from them."

The tents were soon pitched, and the appropriate gear for each guy was placed in their tent. Smitty and Jack didn't have any say in the matter as to where the tents were pitched. But the ground was flat, so if there was any rain overnight, everyone's gear would survive nicely in the tents without getting wet.

"Well, it looks like you won our little wager, Greg. Those guys are back right on your money at 7:00 p.m. I guess I'm buying coffee at one of the truck stops when we're heading back home."

"Now that I think of it, Dude, I should have wagered you breakfast or lunch or whatever meal time it would be back at the Fifth Wheel Truck Stop at Milton."

"Greg, you're greedy. Like you'd have gone for that if I'd have won."

The evening had started to cool down, but Greg and I had made a small campfire, and were just hanging around when Jack and Smitty returned.

"What have you and Greg made for us for supper, Dude? We're hungry, you know. We had to do some serious work while you two guys sat around and watched the grass grow."

"I know you're right, Smitty. But I bet you guys ate before you got back here. How do I know? You're still wearing it on your beard. Looks like you had a spaghetti dinner because you've got a piece embedded in that scraggy beard. Or were you saving that for a midnight snack?"

"Smitty, if you and Jack are hungry, go make yourself a sandwich or something. Greg and I made ourselves a couple of sandwiches three hours ago. Or would you rather roast marsh-mellows around our campfire while we all sing 'Kumbaya'?"

"Well," muttered Jack, "I'm a bit hungry, so I'm going to make myself a sandwich. Where did you stash my stuff, Dude?"

"You and Smitty have your stuff in your tent, Jack. Have at it. What are you going to make? A peanut butter and honey sandwich?"

"I just might do that, but don't expect me to share any of it with you, Dude."

Jack made himself a delectable peanut butter and honey sandwich. The rest of us sat around the fire a wee bit hungry, watching him wolf it down. By then it had been a long day for everyone. We'd all been up by at least 3:00 a.m., and it was 8:30 p.m. at the moment. There had been a lot of activity, and we were all pretty well tired out.

There is a little secret you need to know when you are camping out in the wild. You don't leave any food stocks in the open overnight. You protect your food by keeping it well wrapped, and in this case, because there were no trees around, you'd keep your food in the tent with you.

Stashing your food in the open really works when you have some trees fairly close together. You string up a rope line between two trees high enough, so the bears can't reach it, and just let it swing in the wind all night from the rope. Sure, you still have to wrap it well, so it is hard to smell by the wildlife, but it would be safe swinging on the rope.

Greg and I knew that, so did Smitty, but Smitty didn't clue Jack in even though he saw Jack leave his backpack of food stocks just outside their tent.

"Greg, I think we just may have some wildlife activity tonight. Did you notice that Jack left his food backpack outside the flap of their tent?"

"Dude, don't talk too loud. Jack will hear you and then figure it out, and put his food in the tent. If he leaves it out all night, we're likely going to have a good laugh. What I can't figure out is why Smitty didn't clue him in. Smitty's a seasoned camper. He should know better. Guess he was walking around with his eyes closed on that one."

Sure enough, sometime after midnight, Smitty and Jack were making a real loud ruckus. Could you believe, two grown men were yelling and screaming like a couple of scared school-age children? Seems that they were visited by a couple of raccoons. Jack swears it was a bear. With the noises they were making, and the peals of laughter coming from Greg and me, whatever it was, it sure beat a hasty retreat.

Smitty got up with a dour look on his face on Sunday morning, and it didn't take him long to respond with a retort aimed at Greg and me.

"All right, you smart alecks, why didn't you clue Jack and me in last night when he left his food outside the tent?"

"Sure, Smitty, and miss all the fun we knew would happen? We needed a good laugh, and why not at your expense?"

"Your talk is cheap, Greg. Jack and I will get you and the dude back for that."

Well, that just made Greg laugh all the more as he walked away using his thumb and pointer finger and rubbing them together to mimic a violin.

"Jack, you and Smitty know what this is, eh? It's the world's smallest violin playing a mournful tune for you two winners, or maybe it's you, two whiners."

It was a beautiful morning in the park, best described as absolutely stellar. A clear sky and a light northwesterly wind made it ideal for canoeing on Cedar Lake. This was important to us because having a tailwind meant we would be able to easily cross Cedar Lake from where we were at Brent Station through a long stretch of deep open water for a little over four miles. We would head on a generally easterly direction, and after skirting around three islands, which were close together in the middle of the lake, we'd have a straight line to navigate to a small bay where the mouth of the Petawawa River was located.

It is important to mention that most of the lakes in Algonquin Park can be fairly deep, and without exception, the water is quite cold and clean. In fact, it is so clean, one only has to dip a canteen to a depth of about two feet of water, in less than a hundred feet off the shore, and enjoy a nice cold drink.

Because Smitty and I had camped and canoed in Algonquin Park over the years on several occasions, we were familiar with the most efficient way to camp and also do a successful canoe trip. Weight was always an issue because there would be several portages regardless of a particular trip one might take.

With total weight in mind, I carried a complete set of lightweight nesting pots. Our food stocks were dried items such as flour, eggs, meat, soup, even vegetables and fruits. Water and heat were only needed in order to whip out an edible meal. Items, such as whole eggs, bread, and jars or cans of fruit or vegetables, would not be included in this trip. All garbage had to be transported out of the park. Nothing was to be left behind. A favorite item all four of us included in our food stores was dried meat, such as beef jerky, lots of beef jerky.

"I think we did a great job, Smitty, of setting up our gear and food stocks. Your canoe weighs about seventy pounds with the shoulder yoke, three paddles, and two life jackets. When we weighed out your food stocks and two-man lightweight tent, they came in about seventy pounds as well. I know that Greg and my gear along with the canoe, shoulder yoke, three paddles, and two life jackets are about the same in weight."

"Greg and I will take turns carrying the canoe. Will you and Jack do the same thing, Smitty?"

"I think that is a good idea, Dude. One thing that we won't change though is who the bowman is and who the stern man is when it comes to paddling. Jack will always paddle in the bow. Because I'm a bit heavier than him, I will be best situated in the stern."

"We will adopt the same pattern in my canoe, Smitty. Greg will be in the bow, and I'll be in the stern. I'm a bit heavier than Greg, so the stern's for me."

With gear stowed safely amidships, both canoes set off from Brent Station in the early morning sunlight. The day was warming up nicely, and with our life jackets on, we were all soon warm and comfortable, setting a leisurely pace in paddling. I think we were averaging about one stroke every three to four seconds. That was a good combination as we would not become tired for a long time.

"Hey, Dude, when you looked at the guide map this morning, what did you determine would be our goal for today? What all did you have in mind?"

"Smitty, there is a small bay which we need to find, and head for on the eastern end of the lake. When we get into that bay, we will find the mouth of the Petawawa River because there will be a dam located right at the river's mouth.

The dam isn't too high, maybe eight to ten feet high. It isn't a large or wide dam as the river isn't very wide at that point.

"My guide map indicates that we will have to do a portage around it, and that the portage continues for 940 yards because there are three sets of rapids fairly close together right beyond the dam.

"I think the biggest reason that the dam even exists is to regulate the amount of water flowing into the Petawawa River, especially with the springtime runoff.

"Another fact that we will have to pay attention to is where we can set up camp each afternoon. There has to be adequate room for all our gear, tents, and canoes, and there may be other campers and canoers at the location we choose, so pickings might get a little slim."

"Yes, that's right, Dude. What did you say the elevation drop was on the river from where we enter the river off of Cedar Lake?"

"We will run the Petawawa for about six miles before we come to the next lake, which is Radiant Lake. Between Cedar Lake and Radiant Lake is a drop of ninety-three feet. When we drop that much in the space of six miles, we will have a fast-flowing river in several spots for sure. In fact, the biggest drop will be at a set of rapids called Devil's Chute. I'm not kidding, guys. That's the name. Sounds to me like there are some serious rapids at that location."

With lots of banter going on between the two canoes as we traversed Cedar Lake, it didn't seem very long before we arrived at the mouth of the Petawawa River.

True to the map's detail, there was a lengthy portage getting around the dam and two sets of rapids. Looking around and assessing this location, Greg said, "Here's a great spot to set our gear and canoes down right at the dam. Let's walk along this portage and check out the two sets of rapids that the guide map shows are coming up. It would be nice to take a break here too."

"I like your suggestion, Greg," Dude said. "That's a good idea to check out the rapids before we run them."

Smitty was quick to respond as well, saying that he and Jack liked that idea.

"OK, guys, this is what I think. We've walked the 940-yard portage, checking out these two sets of rapids, and they look tame to me. I think it would be great running them. What do all of you think? Are you game to run them?"

Without exception, Smitty, Jack, and Greg immediately responded to the dude's challenge with boisterous affirmation.

Arriving back at the dam, it looked like all four of us were thinking the same thing, but Greg was the one to verbalize it.

"I'm feeling like I'd like to take a nice shower under the dam. You all know we didn't pack deodorant when we set out yesterday, because that scent will attract bears. Well, I'm up for a shower. How about the rest of you?"

"Right on, Greg, I've been behind you all the way . . . cough . . . cough . . . cough . . . and you sure do need a shower."

"Dude," laughed Greg. "I've got the best spot on the canoe. I get to breathe lots of fresh air."

"Over in my canoe, I'm feeling the same way paddling behind Jack."

"Sure, Smitty. You know my sweat don't stink."

"Tell that to the judge, Jack."

It was settled we would camp here just beyond the dam at the mouth of the Petawawa River. The ground was nice and flat, and it was easy to set up two tents. There was still room to pass by if other canoe trippers should happen along.

In no time, tents were set up, gear was stashed in the tents, clothes came off and four guys ran into the river right under the dam. Believe me, there was a lot of shouting and yelling going on. That water was cold, but it was also invigorating. There we were yelling and hollering up a storm, and likely scaring the wildlife for several miles around.

OK, maybe I exaggerate a bit, but I'm sure we scared off a few birds, raccoons, and skunks or possums. Smitty told me there weren't any possums that far north. I told him to mind his own business. That was my story, and I was sticking to it.

"Wow, that cold shower under the dam sure gave me an appetite, Greg. I could tear into a T-bone right about now."

"That would be fine with me, Jack," Greg said while moving closer to Jack for emphasis's sake, "as long as you brought four T-bones. I know Dude and Smitty and I would create a riot if we didn't get any."

Jack didn't have a T-bone that he had somehow managed to sneak into the camp, and we knew it. But that didn't stop us from quickly setting up a campfire and preparing a good meal of bannock, some vegetables, and fruit from our dried stocks and, of course, some beef jerky.

What do you think four guys would do after they had an early evening meal cooked over an open fire? Because it was decided that camp would be set up right where they had parked their gear earlier in the afternoon, it was Smitty who rousted us from our daydreams and lethargy.

"Do you three fellows think it might be a good time to set up our tents before darkness closes in? Come on, you lazy bums. Let's get 'er done."

"I know you're right, Smitty, but I'll pay you really well if you set up camp for all of us. I'm thinking maybe a couple of bucks would be good wages, eh?"

"Oh sure, Dude. That'd be good wages for you, but I'm a professional. I'd expect way more than a couple of bucks. I'm thinking . . ."

"Whoa, you two lug nuts. Cool your jets. Do you need to have Jack and me show you how it's done?"

We all knew Greg was right, so we got to it and set up camp. Once the tents were secure and a rope line was stretched between two trees that were close to where we'd set up camp, and our food stocks were swinging safely out of reach of any wildlife, we all headed in different directions, looking for some good kindling wood. Dried fallen branches were the best we could find, but we gathered lots of them, so we knew we'd have a good fire that night.

"I've been looking at our guide map again, guys, and we have these two rapids to run, which we looked at earlier. We all agreed that we wouldn't have a problem running them, that they looked tame enough.

"There are another two sets of rapids, probably about a mile downriver after we've run these two sets. I think it would be a good habit to stop above each set of rapids, and scout those rapids out. If we think it would be a piece of cake running it, then we'd just have to put back into the river and do it. If it looked more serious, we'd best empty the canoes of all gear and maybe run the rapids light. We'd portage our gear around the rapids before we ran them, so we'd be ready to continue once we got through the rapids. We'd just pick up our gear and away we'd go."

"Sounds like a plan, Dude."

"Thanks, Smitty."

Night came on and with it complete darkness. The moon wouldn't rise before 2:00 a.m., so when it got dark, it got really dark. Funny how you see shadows when you're sitting around a nice bright campfire. The bush around us seemed to come alive with ghosts moving quickly through the nearby trees. That made for some interesting conversation as we verbalized what we thought we were seeing.

Wouldn't you know it, as if on cue, Smitty started howling like a wolf. It's funny how real his wolf howl seemed when we were sitting in a dark bush on a moonless night.

We all took turns howling, and it wasn't only a few minutes and we got a good response from a couple of wolves, maybe only a half mile away.

"You're doing that howling pretty good, Smitty. If you keep that up, we'll no doubt have a visit from those wolves howling back at us. Do you think we should get a couple of pieces of beef jerky ready for them and give them a little treat?"

"Huh. You do that if you want, Dude, but it'd better be from your stash of beef jerky. Lay your hands on my beef jerky, and I'll throw you to the wolves."

We all got quiet for a while, probably each thinking about the rapids we'd seen earlier. The idea of running them created an inner excitement in all of us.

"Would you look at that? Is everyone asleep already? I haven't heard so much as a peep out of Smitty or the dude. What's the matter with those two? They can't be that tired? It's only nine o'clock."

"You're right about that Greg. Those two need their beauty rest, and they're trying to get a head start on it. Look at them. Their eyes are glassy and their mouths are open. I'll bet you they are sleeping. This is the scary thing. Do you think that if they can do that spaced-out look so easily here, that they can do that when they're driving their big rigs as well?"

"Jack, that's a scary thought. I'd never want to find that out. I mean, I hope that would never happen."

"You will have to ask the dude that question, Greg. Ask him if he's ever fallen asleep when he was driving. I know he has because he told me once when he was driving for Greyhound back in 1973 that actually happened to him. But, hey, don't ask me to tell you the story. Ask him."

"You got to be kidding me, Jack. Are you serious? Did he really fall asleep when he was driving a bus?"

"No, I'm not kidding you, Greg. But I think the best time to ask him about that episode is when we're traveling back to Windsor and he's driving. That ought to keep him wide awake while he tells us about his sleepy-time driving habits."

"I think I just might do that, Jack. But what do you think about now? Let's stoke the fire a bit and wake those two sleeping beauties. We're going to have a fun day tomorrow, and I want to get a good head start on that real early."

"Hey, you two sleeping beauties. Wake up. Get your butts in gear, and let's call it a day. We've got some rapids to run tomorrow, so you two lug nuts better be well-rested."

"Aw . . . shut yourself up, Greg. I heard every word you and Jack said about Smitty and me. I won't deny some of what Jack said, but I'm not about to tell you my driving habits right now. Maybe later."

In just a few minutes, the four of us had crawled into our sleeping bags and soon were fast asleep. Nothing disturbed our sleep that night. Maybe it was 3:00 a.m. when Smitty crawled out of his sleeping bag and stoked the fire, putting more kindling on it. But nobody else stirred, and he was back inside his sleeping bag before you knew it.

*Bang, clang, bang. Clang, bang, clang.*

"Whoa, what's going on out there? Who's the smart-aleck banging the pots this early in the morning?"

"How would you rather I wake you up, Dude? Do you want me to drag you in your pretty green mummy sleeping bag feet first, and throw you in the river?"

"Smitty, it'll take more than you to do that. You better get yourself an army. Anyhow, Greg and I are already awake, so I guess that'll put a damper on your cockeyed plans."

I assure you, washing your face in a cold river at 6:00 a.m. in the morning will wake you up in a hurry. And with a few gulps of fresh cool air, you'd be motivated too. I know I sure was—motivated that is—motivated to get a nice, hot breakfast going on the campfire.

In no time, the four of us were enjoying a breakfast of fresh hot bannock, scrambled eggs, and of course, you guessed it, some dried beef jerky.

"What do you think Jack, are we going to have good weather today?"

"Well, looking at the sky, Smitty, I'd say we're in for a good day for sure. I'm aware there is a bit more humidity in the air today, and there is high-level faint cloud cover. The wind is still out of the west-northwest, but judging by what I've seen so far this morning, I think we may be in for a storm tomorrow."

"I hope you're wrong, Jack, but I was looking at the sky, and I agree with you. What do you think, Smitty?"

"Not sure, Dude. I'll leave the weather forecasting up to you two experts. Ho-ho, expert weather forecasters indeed. I think you and Jack are just wannabe weather forecasters."

When there are four happy campers who would rather be running the rapids than sitting around a campfire, eating breakfast, you can imagine that they wolfed it down in a hurry. Breaking camp seemed to happen almost immediately and without anyone poking at anybody else. Strange how behaviors change.

"Who is going to be first running these two sets of rapids?"

"How about you and Jack be the first, Smitty? Greg and I will give you a couple of minute's head start, then we'll follow."

With gear properly stowed at the center of the canoe for good weight distribution, Smitty and Jack shoved off and soon had disappeared around the bend.

"The river sure is running fast, Greg. Look how quickly they took off and disappeared. Let's get going. We'll follow their same track, running between those two larger rocks in the center of the river. It's going to get real noisy in the center of the river, so if you need to tell me something, yell it out."

In no time, we were centered in the river and moving fast. Greg was the first to yell out, "Dude, steer us to the right. A big rock is coming up. Harder to the right. That's it, you've got it."

"Greg, pull it left. I can't steer it fast enough to the left," Dude yelled back."

Then it was Greg yelling. "There's a couple of shallow spots here, Dude. Steer us to the left again. We made it. That was a hoot.

"That sure was fun, Dude. We traversed through that set of rapids in a hurry. The water is moving pretty fast too."

Smitty and Jack were waiting for us just after the first set of rapids, and laughing their heads off. They must have had a good time running the rapids. Greg and I were laughing just as hard.

"Hey, Greg," I yelled, "talk about getting the ole heart beating fast and the adrenalin pumping through the body. Those rapids sure did that, eh?"

"Yes, they sure did, Dude."

"What do you think, Smitty? Is your white water Grumman canoe doing what you expected it to in white water?"

"I'm happy with it, Dude. Let's take on this next set of rapids. The river looks wide enough so that we should be able to go through the rapids together."

Can you imagine four guys in two canoes running the rapids together? The yelling and laughing meant only one thing. They were having a hoot.

Smitty and Jack were in the lead at that point when Smitty yelled back to Greg and me, "Hey, guys, we better read this sign coming up on the right shore. Let's pull up to it and get out for a break. Things are quiet right here on the river anyhow."

"Dude, check your guide map will you?" Smitty asked. "Where are we? This sign says we have a 940-yard portage."

"The guide map indicates we are at a place where it's going to get crazy. What is ahead of us is a set of rapids that is called Devil's Chute.

We better walk through this portage, Smitty, and check it out. I want to know what's ahead of us before I take it on."

I continued speaking, "This looks like a safe spot to park our canoes, guys. There is lots of room right here at the beginning of the portage. They won't be in the way of anyone who might be coming behind us and wants to use the portage. I think we can trust anyone who is coming through here to leave our equipment alone. That seems to be the unwritten code for working through the portages."

Leaving our gear, our supplies, and the canoes behind in a safe spot at the beginning of the portage around Devil's Chute, we moved along easily eastward through the portage even though the underbrush was fairly dense.

It was only 100 yards or so, and we came across the first indication that there was some wild water ahead.

"Would you just listen to the roar of this set of rapids? It has really increased a lot. There has to be some serious stuff going on over there to the left of us. We better check it out, Smitty."

"I know, Dude. Follow me. I see a bit of a trail that will likely get us to a place where we can check out what we might be up against if we run this set."

What we saw made us realize that this set of rapids was really serious and would be extremely challenging.

Jack spoke up first and practically had to yell above the noise of the cascading water. "The river is really beginning to drop in elevation at this point. The water is moving at an incredible speed, but I don't really see any rocks. It appears to be a smooth riverbed here."

"It's no wonder the water is moving so fast, Jack," Smitty yelled back. "The width of the river right here is probably not more than twenty-five to thirty feet wide. There were a few places we've already come through where the river was as much as one hundred feet wide. The speed of it here is to be expected. But I think, at this point, we could still run the river as there are no real rocks that could hang us up."

"You may be right, Smitty," Jack yelled back to him, "but let's walk along here right at the edge of the drop off as far as we can, so we can check out what's happening downstream. Things can change quickly, and I don't like surprises."

"I don't like surprises either, Jack," Greg yelled.

Changes did happen fast. It wasn't more than another one hundred yards downstream as we were walking along the cliff bank when we came to the spot, that spot where this whole story hinges on. As we looked down from our vantage point, at least eight to ten feet above, it seemed like everyone held his breath.

"I see why they call this the Devil's Chute, Dude." By that time Smitty was literally screaming. "The water is racing here at an incredible speed, to begin with, and that huge rock at least as high as this cliff bank causes the water to split into two fast-moving streams. The chute of water before it hits the rock must be at least forty feet in length. Look at the depth of the V in that chute. The walls of that V must be nearly four feet high, and the width of the V at its top must be a good four feet wide."

"The water splits evenly to the right and to the left of that huge rock," I yelled back at Smitty. "But what makes it really challenging is that there's another chute on the right side of the rock, and the rock cliff we are standing on. Smitty, you would have to navigate that chute and get into the next chute to the right of the rock. That would take some serious work because the water is moving so fast. You'd have to be on top of your game, or you'd lose it right at that point."

"Well, Dude, what would stop us from going to the left of that huge rock? The way I see it, if we went to the left, we wouldn't be in such swift water, and I don't see a similar chute of water on that side."

That seemed like it might be a good plan. It appeared at first glance that it would be easier to navigate around that huge rock if we went to the left of it, but as we continued to walk past the rock and scrutinize the river, our plans began to change.

Jack was the first to yell out, "Hey, guys, going to the left of the rock will be very dangerous. Look at that field bed of seriously sharp, protruding rocks. If we get hung up on those rocks, we'll lose our canoes for sure. The frothing water would indicate that the water depth is very shallow."

Greg was right at Jack's elbow and hollered back with no uncertainty in his voice, "You're right, Jack. Our choice at this point is to stay on the right side of the rock, and run that chute out. It seems to peter out just a few yards further down the river."

The river continued to drop in elevation, but not to the same extreme as it had back up there where the two chutes were located. There were, however, more rocks to navigate around or over in some cases.

"I think this set of rapids stops just up ahead, Smitty," Greg said as he looked back at him. "Look how calm that pool of water is just around the next bend. I'm sure the water is still moving fast, but that calm pool would make you think the water isn't moving at all."

After taking a short break at the calm pool beyond Devil's Chute, we retraced our steps, walking back upstream. Arriving back at our canoes, we debated whether we should run the Devil's Chute or walk by it on the portage trail.

"Let's take a vote," I said. "All in favor of running the Devil's Chute, raise your hands. Well, it's unanimous. We'll run it, but let's figure out the best way to do it. Anybody with some suggestions?"

"Go ahead, Greg. What are you thinking?"

"Dude, I suggest we run them light—no gear and our pockets empty. No extra paddle strapped in the canoes. Just our life jackets and one paddle each. We could take all our equipment through the portage first, and leave it down at the pool somewhere safe. Then come back here and run the rapids."

I spoke first, responding to Greg's suggestions, saying, "Those are great suggestions, and I see them as practical and the safest approach."

I next turned to Smitty, who had been quiet, and asked, "How about you, Smitty? Do you concur with these suggestions?"

Smitty's response was immediate and affirmative, "Greg and Jack covered all the bases, Dude. We have to really focus on staying in the V of both chutes. I don't know how things would work out, if we didn't stay in those two Vs."

I looked at all the guys for a brief moment before speaking. These decisions were going to be very important, and we needed to be certain we had covered all bases. Then I said, "I'm with you on that, Smitty.

Greg and I can start out first. You and Jack wait maybe three or four minutes, then you guys start out. That should give Greg and me enough time to run both chutes and get downstream a few hundred yards beyond Devil's Chute. I saw a place just before you round the second last bend, and we could stop there. The cliff isn't very high, and there are some tree roots we could hold on to while we wait for you guys."

Discussion done, we all jumped into our canoes. Where we set in at the beginning of the portage, the water was calm, so what happened next is hard to explain. I guess I'd chalk it up to nervous jitters.

"Yeow! Greg, the water is cold. What just happened?"

Smitty and Jack were still at the portage and hadn't pushed out into the river yet, but you could hear them laughing hysterically.

Smitty seized the moment to give Greg and me a good dig in the ribs, and laughing at the top of his lungs, bellowed out, "Dude, I thought you knew how to canoe? What are you and Greg doing in the water? We're not even near the rapids, and you two lug nuts are swimming."

Laughing his response in return to Smitty's jab at us, Greg yelled back, "No, we just wanted to get a feel for the water, so we wouldn't be surprised if we dump ourselves somewhere in the rapids."

"Oh sure, Greg, like I'll believe that," chortled Smitty.

"Suit yourself, Smitty," Greg yelled back.

Somewhat chagrinned, I said, "Come on, Greg. Let's get it done. I'd rather be in the canoe than in the water."

Getting back into the canoe, Greg and I headed for the rapids. I don't even think we tried to explain to ourselves how it came to be that we dunked ourselves while settling into the canoe. Some things are just better left unsaid, because there were more important things to think about. The water was moving fast, and some partially submerged rocks were just ahead.

"Dude, from here on, we'd better yell at the top of our lungs so we can hear each other. We can't afford any mistakes because we were unsure of each other's directions."

"You got it, Greg."

I didn't need to be encouraged to yell. With adrenalin racing through my veins, the only thing I could do was yell.

Greg yelled back to me in the stern, "Help me pull to the left. Big rocks in front of us. Keep pulling left. More rocks dead ahead. OK, steer us to the right, Dude. A series of rocks coming up in front of us. There's a better path to the right of them."

That's how it went for maybe three hundred yards, Greg and I yelling instructions back and forth. Being the bowman, Greg could see what was ahead of us better than I could, so I relied on his directions.

"First chute coming up fast, Dude. Steer us right down the slot. Hold it steady, Dude. OK . . . now help me pull her right. Harder, harder. PULL HARDER."

Greg was literally screaming as loud as he could over the roar of the rapids.

I had never gone so fast through the water in a canoe. I felt like we were flying. The din was deafening. The adrenalin was pumping. I think I was nearly standing as I was pulling right so hard. There was no time to think. We were acting instinctively.

"Dude, help pull left . . . Hard left. Harder, harder. Keep pulling. OK, steer us straight now. Easy does it. We made it. Steer us straight. That was crazy. I've never been on the water that fast." Greg was not just screaming, he was doing so ecstatically.

At that point, I didn't need to scream quite so loud, but it just seemed natural to continue yelling because I was so excited. Finally, I was able to settle down somewhat and loudly, but not screaming, said, "That was crazy, Greg. Looks like a piece of cake from here on in. Water's fast but nothing serious right now."

Greg and I covered the next few hundred yards easy enough. Sure, we had to paddle, and Greg still shouted out steering orders, but we were so high on adrenaline from the ride we just had through Devil's Chute, everything seemed less than climatic at the moment.

In just another moment, Greg called back to me, "Here's a good spot to hold back now, Dude. Steer us into that clump of roots a few yards in front of us to the right. We should be able to hold on tightly to them, and be safe enough while we wait for Smitty and Jack."

With some alarm beginning to register in my voice, I said, "Greg, we've been waiting now more than five minutes. What's happened to Smitty and Jack? They should have come by us a couple of minutes ago." And with the next lung full of air, I yelled with serious anxiousness in my voice, "Oh no. Look, Greg, there's one of Smitty's paddles floating by out there in the rapids. This is not good."

Greg was fast to respond to this new situation, and yelling, said, "Let's climb up on the cliff here, Dude, and beach the canoe. We can get up on the cliff easy enough here and pull the canoe up with us. We can then run back upstream, looking for Jack and Smitty. They must be in trouble."

Yelling, I responded, "I'm with you, Greg. Something must have definitely gone wrong."

We beached the canoe, and left it and the paddles safely on the cliff's bank. We didn't take off our life jackets. When I thought about it after, we probably didn't even think about taking them off. But it was good that we didn't. You'll see.

It wasn't very long, only a couple hundred yards around that last bend, and we saw Jack. I yelled back to Greg, who was just a couple of yards behind me,

"Greg, I see Jack holding onto a rock or root just up ahead. I can only see his head. Do you see him?"

"Yes, I see him, Dude," yelled Greg.

We covered the last few yards in a matter of seconds. How long had Jack been hanging on to that root? There was no time to waste. He could become so fatigued, he would indivertibly let go of that root.

"Jack, grab my hand . . . Hold on tight," I yelled. "Greg, grab my left hand and anchor yourself as best you can. OK . . . Pull hard. Come on, Jack. Get up here. Pull, Greg. Pull, pull."

I slipped on the wet rocks and ended up in the rapids with Jack. It was a good thing Greg had a death grip on my hand and I still held on to Jack's hand. It seemed, with superhuman strength, Jack and I were pulled back onto the cliff that was above the spot where we first found Jack. Greg told me later he'd never pulled anyone as hard as he pulled Jack and me at that moment.

Experiencing that cold water again had taken my breath away. I couldn't imagine how Jack had held up so long. I was glad my life jacket was still on right then.

Greg had managed to pull two dead weights, Jack and me, up on the bank and, with his next breath, had yelled out to Jack, "Where is Smitty? Did he get past you on the rapids? Where is he, Jack?"

Jack was still trying to get his breath, but he pointed back up the river. Without waiting for Jack to answer his question, Greg started to run back up the portage trail, which was adjacent to where we'd pulled Jack in from the river. Jack and I jumped up and ran as hard as we could, following Greg, who was several yards ahead of us. We had to run right back to that huge rock, which created the Devil's Chute.

"There's the nose of the canoe, Dude," Greg yelled back to me. "I see the nose right there at that huge rock. I don't see, Smitty. Where is he?"

There he was, hanging on for dear life. Smitty was in the center of the canoe. The canoe was breached on the rock at the waterline. The keel was on the rock, and the canoe was open to the water, pinning it hard on the rock. It had to be perfectly balanced. The water pinned the canoe hard. Smitty couldn't unbalance it to shift it off the rock, and it was all he could do to keep his head above water.

"Smitty, can you hear me?" I yelled as loud as I could. "You have to let go of the canoe. You have to let go. You have to get free of the canoe. You are going to have to ride the chute down feet first. Use your arms and hands to steer and to stabilize yourself. Keep your feet together. Smitty, Smitty, you have to do it. You can't stay in the canoe. We can't get you out of the canoe."

"Greg, Jack, run down the cliff. Find a place where you can make a human chain. You're going to have to get into the rapids and catch Smitty as he rides the rapids. Go now!"

Constantly yelling and waving my arms, I held Smitty's attention. "I'm going to run on the cliffs above you and try to keep up with you as you ride the rapids. Back paddle as much as you can. Keep yourself going as slowly as you can. Greg and Jack are going to be waiting for you in a couple hundred yards. Watch for them and grab at them as you start to go by. They'll catch you and pull you out."

"Now, Smitty. Now! Let go. Go! Go! Go!"

Smitty did let go, and he did ride the rapids by the seat of his pants, feet first. He had to be absolutely freezing. It must have been a crazy ride. It didn't really look like fun either.

In just a couple of minutes, Jack and Greg saw him coming, and they braced themselves to catch him as he was going by. Smitty was eager to get out, and he wasn't going to get caught passing Jack and Greg. No way.

Laying on the ground at the cliff's edge, no one spoke for a few minutes. We were all breathing hard and our minds were going a mile a minute as they say. Finally, Smitty spoke first.

"Guys, thanks for fishing me out of there. I thought I was a goner for sure. I don't think I've ever been so scared and cold all at the same time. I could hardly keep my head above water, and I was getting so cold, I was afraid I'd lose my grip on the yoke while I was trying to get the canoe free of the rock."

Finally, we caught our breath and got up. We were just too cold and wet to lie on the ground any longer. We had to do some physical activity to warm up.

"Dude, what do you think we should do now?" asked Smitty.

"First thing I think we have to do, Smitty, is go further downstream and get my canoe. Then we need to go further down the portage to the end where we left all our gear and gather it all up. Then we need to get back to your canoe, Smitty."

Continuing, I asked a general question, "Anybody got some ideas how we can get Smitty's canoe off that rock?"

"I packed a small portable saw in my gear," Smitty said. "I think it will come in handy. We could cut down a sapling, maybe ten to twelve feet long."

"We could then all push on it at the bow of my canoe to try to off-balance it. If we could get it off-balance, it would take off down the rapids, and we could probably run along the cliff fast enough to keep it in sight, and then get it when it got to that pool where we left the gear."

"That sounds like a good plan, Smitty," Greg said. "We might as well leave all our gear and Dude's canoe where it is then. We'll just get the saw and go back up to the rock."

"Greg and Jack, why don't you two guys just head back up to the rock, and Smitty and I will get the saw and be back to the rock in no time."

When Smitty and I got back up to the rock where his canoe was impaled, Greg and Jack had selected a good size sapling, and we were able to cut a good strong pole at least fourteen feet long.

Smitty took control of the situation at that point and gave some directions. "Let's all get on this end of the pole, and maybe with all of us pushing together, we can get the canoe off-balance enough to cause it to shift and be pushed by the water force off the rock. If it is off-balance, it will move quickly with the strong force of the water. We'll run after it down to that pool."

Smitty's idea was a good one, but it didn't work. As much as we pushed, we couldn't budge that canoe. We tried and tried for at least a couple of hours but to no avail. You never saw a more dejected bunch of fellows. Nobody said a word for a long time. We just sat on the cliff and looked at that canoe.

Finally, Greg broke the silence. "Guys, it's almost three o'clock. Maybe we should set up camp right here and try to figure this out. If we get a better idea, we could start again in the morning."

"Good idea, Greg," Smitty said. "At least I think so. Does anybody else have a different thought that might work?"

"No, Smitty. Greg's idea is a good one," Jack said.

Camp was set up on the cliff adjacent to Smitty's impaled canoe on the rock. Hunger wasn't mentioned, but when Jack rifled up some hot grub, it was devoured in no time at all.

It was a quiet meal, but the dude spoke up as he was cleaning the last of the food off his plate, "Here's the way I see it, guys. If we can get Smitty's canoe off the rock, everything will work out OK. But if we can't get it off the rock, we'll have to retrace our steps out of here and get back to Brent Station. I don't think there is any other choice that we have. There may be someone who could help us, or maybe has a better idea than anything we've come up with."

"I think you're right, Dude. I sure would hate to leave my canoe here."

Campfire talk focused on the impaled canoe. But as much as we talked about it, there didn't seem to be a good workable plan to free it up. Neither Greg nor I asked how it came to be that Smitty and Jack got into that predicament. I figured we'd all know about it soon enough.

Tuesday morning came in cool and muggy, and as the somber bunch of us worked at breaking camp after a quick breakfast of bannock and instant porridge, our conversation continued to center on Smitty's canoe.

With the sound of dejection in his voice, Smitty said, "I don't think we have any chance of getting my canoe free today, and I've resigned myself to that fate, so let's just make plans on how to get out of here and back to Brent Station."

"Smitty, I think you are right," Jack spoke with resignation in his voice as well.

Greg and Dude agreed with Jack and said as much.

In a sense, the ball was hit into Dude's court, so he resolutely spoke up. "OK. This is what we'll have to do. We will load Greg and my gear in my canoe, and we'll go back upstream to the first set of rapids right there at the dam where we camped out last Sunday. I will drop Greg off there, and he can set up camp with our gear. It will take more time going back up the river because we will have to portage around the five sets of rapids."

"I'll come back down here light and pick up Jack next. Jack and I will throw your gear, Smitty, in my canoe, and we'll go upstream to where Brian will be waiting at the dam."

"Jack will set up your camp beside Greg, and I'll come back down here light again. Smitty, you'll be the last to leave here. We'll have all day to do this, but I don't think it will be a pleasant day. It feels like a storm is coming."

It did take nearly all day to follow through on my plans, and it rained much of the time as well. It wasn't pleasant canoeing in the rain, but at least the rainwater wasn't nearly as cold as the water in the Petawawa River.

Arriving back at the dam after struggling at points going upstream, I said with some degree of satisfaction in my voice, "Well, Greg, you're the first to set up camp, so you'll be the first to dry out. Hopefully, you'll find some good wood dry enough to burn. That ought to make you feel a lot better once you're dry."

"Yes, you're right, Dude, and you'll get to enjoy the rain all day by the looks of it," Greg said with a cockeyed grin on his face.

Even though I was canoeing alone and I was going downstream, I had five sets of rapids to run before I arrived back at the quiet pool just before the Devil's Chute. I could handle these rapids alone, and it was a bit dicey, but by then, I was familiar with each set of rapid's peculiarities.

Smitty and Jack had carried their gear to the quiet pool upstream from Devil's Chute. It was just a matter of minutes, and Jack was my bowman. Both Smitty's and his gear were stashed in the center of my canoe and we were heading back upstream.

"Jack, you're doing well as a bowman. What happened at the chute?"

"We started into that first chute, Dude, and we weren't quite in the grove. We were up on the left bank of the V, not much, just a bit, but we were having a hard time getting into the center of the V. We were trying as hard as we could to get straightened out, but as we got just about to the rock, we started to roll over to the right. I was trying to pull us hard to the right, so we wouldn't crash directly into the rock face, but the force of the water was too strong.

"Smitty was also pulling to the right, but because we now were way off-balanced, neither one of us could steer around that rock. We hit it nearly straight on. But because we hit on a bit of an angle, it was just enough to send the canoe toward the right side of the rock. When the canoe hit the rock, it started to ride up onto the rock. We stopped suddenly, and because we were tipped over at the same time, the incredible force of the water hit us broadside. The force of the water was so strong, we remained impaled on the rock. We tried to move the canoe but to no avail.

"My first thought was that we'd still continue to ride the rock and come out on the right side of it, but that wasn't the case. We were pinned down against the rock by the force of the water. I was soon swept out of the canoe and started down the chute headfirst. I guess it was at that point I lost my paddle.

"I didn't know what had happened to Smitty either. I was underwater for a brief time, going down head first, and that was incredibly scary. I managed to come up, grab some air, and get myself turned around, so I was then going down the rapids feet first. It must have been when I was going down the rapids feet first that my right foot hit a submerged rock with incredible force. It jarred my whole body. I noticed later that my right boot had lost its heel. That probably happened when I hit that submerged rock. But it wasn't just my boot that took a beating. In that short time, my body took quite a beating on a few submerged rocks. I'm glad it was feet first, or I'd have smashed my head in for sure. I'm also glad I didn't break any ribs in those tumultuous moments.

"I thought Smitty would be right behind me, but at some point before you and Greg pulled me out, I turned around to see if he was behind me. I didn't see him, so you can imagine I feared the worst. I have to tell you, was I ever happy to see him still in the canoe when we got back to the rock."

"Jack, that is one incredible story. I can't tell you how glad I am you both made it out of that situation alive and in one piece."

We paddled in silence for a long time after Jack told me his story. I guess we were both lost in our thoughts even when we had to portage around the five sets of rapids. Finally, the camp Greg set up came into view.

Jack was carrying the gear and was ahead of me on the portage when he yelled back to me, "I see Greg's camp, Dude. We've only another hundred yards or so to portage and we'll be there."

This was the second time I'd run this trip back upriver, over the two portages, and returned downriver, so you can well imagine that when I hollered out to Greg if he'd gotten any grub rustled up, his affirmative response warmed my heart.

"I figured you'd be hungry, Dude, so I made some stew. It's been kept warm on the fire, so it should still be good even though it's been raining steadily for quite a while."

As I was sitting down on a large rock close to the fire, I happily said, "I can't tell you how happy I am to sit down for a while and have that stew. Thanks, Greg. You're the man."

By the time I'd regained some strength and had a good helping of hot stew, I was ready to turn around and go back downriver and fetch Smitty.

As I began to get the canoe ready to put into the rapids, I piped up and said, "I'll see you guys a bit later. Hey, Greg, how long was it when I left you and came back up here with Jack?"

"You were gone a good two and one half hours, Dude."

"Thanks, Greg. I guess I'll see you guys in two and one half hours, eh?"

Just like before, I ran all five rapids going downstream. By then, I was getting used to it and really quite enjoyed it even though the loss of Smitty's canoe still played heavily on my mind.

"Ahoy there, matey," was my greeting when I saw Smitty. I was trying to be cheery with that greeting, but I realized, at the look on his face, it didn't come across as being cheery at all.

I didn't say anything for a few moments after I'd tried to be cheerful. I just sat on a rock nearby and looked at the river. Then speaking with resolve in my voice, I said, "Finally it's your turn, Smitty. We should move along fairly well and we'll be somewhat lighter without any gear. Greg and Jack have set up camp so when we get there, hot food will be waiting for you."

After a few minutes of paddling and neither of us saying a word, Smitty opened up first. "Dude, I feel real bad about wrecking our canoe trip. When we hit the chute a little to the left of center, I knew we were in for some trouble. I figured we'd be able to steer and pull ourselves back to the center of the grove, but we were going so fast. It happened before I could change our course. It was like the rock jumped right up in front of us.

"The water pulled Jack out of the canoe, and it would have pulled me out too, but I got my arms around the yoke and hung on for dear life. I don't know what made me hang on for so long. I guess I feared more about riding the rapids without the canoe than with it. The force of that water was incredible, and it was all I could do to keep my head above water. I was just about to let go when you guys showed up."

"That was incredible that you hung on that long, Smitty. You must have been absolutely numb by the time we showed up."

"Half frozen was more like it. But my mind was numb. I'd just about given up any hope of seeing any of you. I was wondering if you and Greg had made it through to the end. Sure was hoping you had made it."

"Even if we'd made it out of there, Dude, if we had gotten the canoe off the rock, would we have continued our canoe trip? Both Jack and I had lost our paddles."

I now spoke up in a matter-of-fact sort of way, saying, "Well, I guess we could have continued, Smitty. We still had our two extra paddles down by our gear at that pool, but the better question would have been, would we have wanted to continue our trip? Of course, the answer to that question rested on our ability to free your canoe up. We couldn't do it, so here we are heading back home, minus one canoe, but a whole lot wiser and very happy that you and Jack didn't experience any serious injury or even death."

We had made a portage over the first set of two rapids and were soon back in the canoe. The water was moving along at a good clip, but with Smitty and me paddling as hard as we could, we were still making good time.

"Dude, did you hear that thunder? Out of the corner of my eye, I thought I saw a flash of lightning just to the southwest of us, low on the horizon. We're going to get a storm."

"I saw it, Smitty. Keep a close eye on it. If it is coming this way, and I think it is, we'll have to run the canoe aground. There is no way I want to be on the water in an aluminum canoe with lightning popping off all around us."

"I'm with you, Dude, and I think we'd better head for shore right now. This storm is moving fast, and the wind has picked up considerably. We're not making any headway at all in this wind, and now it's starting to rain again."

"Head for that open patch to the left of us, Dude. It looks like a good place to beach the canoe. We should be safe enough there. Just don't crawl under the canoe to stay dry. If lightning hits the canoe, we'll look like fried bacon."

We made it to the shore in short order, got the canoe out of the water, and ran off a few feet to get under a couple of good-sized cedar trees. We stayed dry, and the storm passed quickly.

Back in the canoe, Smitty verbalized what I had been thinking. "Dude, what do you think of that? The storm rushed by us and cleaned up everything. The humidity is gone, and it sure is nice to see lots of blue skies."

"I'll always take fair weather over foul weather, Smitty, and I'll always like a good hot sun shining down on my parade rather than it raining on my parade."

Soon enough we'd covered the last portage and were approaching the camp. Smitty was carrying the canoe at that point when I yelled back at him, "We made it, Smitty. The guys have a good fire going, and I can smell some baked beans and maybe some stew too."

Yelling back to me, Smitty verbalized his feelings succinctly, "Dude, you'd better stay out of my way and keep your spoon out of those baked beans. I'm so hungry, I could eat that whole pot of beans all by my lonesome."

It had been a long day for all of us. We hadn't covered a lot of the territory, but you have to remember, we were retracing our steps all the while moving upstream. The work is harder going upstream than riding the waves going downstream.

"Wouldn't you know it, guys," spoke up Greg while we were sitting around the fire after we'd eaten. "Another storm is coming at us. More rain and lightning for sure. I just saw some flashes of it over Cedar Lake to the northwest of us. Probably around where Brent Station is located."

Sure enough, within fifteen minutes, it had broken over us as well. We made a hasty retreat to our tents to ride it out.

Hunkered down in our tent, Greg and I were discussing the storm that was breaking all around us. "I think it's going to take a lot longer to ride this storm out, Greg. The wind is strong and the rain is heavy. The lightning is really close. Listen to how quickly the thunder comes after the lightning flash, just a second or two. Wow, the thunder literally shakes the bush all around us."

Sometime later, the rain and the lightning passed by but the wind remained. All night it continued. But I think we were all so tired, we slept the sleep of dead men, oblivious to the wind or rain or the mysterious noises coming from the depths of the bush behind our tents.

"Hey, come on, you guys. It's time to get up. Are you going to sleep all day?" I was yelling because the wind was still strong, and it was easily drowning me out with its noisy assault.

Sticking my head back into the tent, I said, "No use in making a fire, Greg. The wind will blow it out before it takes hold. Guess we'll be eating cold cereal today."

Jack had come up behind me as I was telling Greg it was a cold cereal morning and said, "I think you're right, Dude. Dry cereal washed down with cold water. Sounds absolutely delightful, don't you think?"

Climbing out of his and Jack's tent, Smitty hollered back at us, "I'm heading down to the lake. I want to see how it looks this morning."

"I'm with you, Smitty," I said as I started to head in the same direction toward the lake. Turning around, I loudly exclaimed, "Hey, Greg and Jack. Come on. Let's all walk down to the lake. I have a feeling we're not going to try running the lake today. With that strong wind all night, the waves will be intense. We'll have five miles of open water with the wind right in our face. But let's take a look at the situation anyhow."

After arriving at the lake and observing it for a moment, I said to all the guys, "On this deep lake with the waves at least four feet high, it will be quite a struggle to make it to Brent Station. I'm not too excited about that prospect, so I'm recommending we sit it out for the day."

"Well, it's your canoe, Dude. I guess we're all with you" piped up Smitty. "And even if we did make one trip across the lake, you'd still have to come back and pick up Greg and Jack. I mean I could help you on that, Dude, but it would be a tall order."

Jack, who was standing to one side of the rest of us, put his arms in the air and his hands behind his head and nonchalantly said, "So we're sitting it out then. I might as well find a nice comfortable spot to rest awhile, put my feet up, and daydream, eh?"

"Go for it, Jack. I'll join you." Greg had made up his mind already and yelled back to Smitty and me, "You and Smitty going to do the same, Dude?"

"Not much else to do, Greg," replied Smitty.

The ground was still quite wet from the heavy rains we had yesterday, so Smitty and I parked our butts on a couple of rocks down by a quiet spot on the bay.

"You keeping track of the days, Smitty? Doesn't seem like we've gone too far or done too much canoe tripping, but we've really done a lot when you think about it. We just haven't covered that many miles."

"I know, Dude. We left Windsor last Saturday, the eleventh. Sunday, we came to this point and camped at the dam. Monday, we lost my canoe at Devil's Chute. Tuesday, it took all day to get back here. It looks like we'll be stuck here at the dam for the day. Hopefully, we'll get back to Brent Station tomorrow on Thursday. If we can keep at it, we should be back in Windsor by Friday night, the seventeenth."

"If I ever do another canoe trip in the future, Smitty, one thing I'm going to do is pack a fishing rod and some tackle. Here we are, sitting around doing nothing. Wouldn't it be great to get a good fish fry going?"

"Dude, you're always thinking about food, but I must admit I wouldn't mind a good fish fry right now as well."

Long about midafternoon, the wind had died down, but it would be several hours before we'd see calm waters return to Cedar Lake. So what were four guys supposed to do? Greg's suggestion, well more like a command, was acted on pretty much immediately.

"Look, you guys. You're all beginning to stink. I mean, when was the last time you had a shower? Nothing is living if it's downwind from you. I'm heading for the dam right now."

"That's right, Greg. You know that a skunk smells its own smell first, eh?"

"Sure, Smitty. I know that but I also know that even a skunk is going to run away from you. You're that bad. Hahaha."

No imagination was needed here. How else were you going to get clean than to strip down and run into the waterfall falling over the dam? I suppose you could say that the water was *dam* cold because it really was.

While we were sitting around our evening campfire, I mentioned to everyone what I'd read on my guide map earlier.

"Hey, fellows, I noticed on my guide map that Cedar Lake is one of thirty-nine lakes here in Algonquin Park where motorboats are allowed. Let's work out our escape from the dam tomorrow in this fashion. I'll take Smitty over to Brent Station, and if there is anyone who has a motorboat at the campground there, I'll ask that they help us. I'd come back with the motorboat, and Smitty could get his bike running and head for Petawawa and bring back the car and trailer."

"If there isn't a motorboat available, then we'll have to do it like we did the other day. I'll come back light and get Greg and our gear. Once Greg and I are back at Brent Station, Smitty can take my canoe and go get Jack and their gear. Doing it that way will take us the better part of the day. If there is a motorboat, we'll be done that much sooner."

We all agreed my plan should work, and soon, it was growing dark. Our campsite had been cleaned up. Food had been strung up between two high trees, and the utensils had been put away. The night had grown quiet with no wind. The only sound was the crackling of the campfire as we sat around it, seeking its warmth. Smitty broke the silence with his astute speculation. "Guys, the water is calm and the wind is calm. The weather is clear with very little humidity. As a professional weather forecaster, I predict that it will be a good day tomorrow. As the dude would say, it will be a CAVU day, a clear and visibility-unlimited type of day."

It wasn't too much later before Greg set more wood on the fire and then stated in a matter-of-fact way, "Guys, I'm heading for bed. I want to get my beauty rest."

We all thought that was funny enough to laugh at, so we gave it a feeble attempt. The real joke was that Greg needed more than a little sleep. Beauty wouldn't come that easily.

Smitty was first up the next morning. His anticipation must have been sky high as he wanted to waste no time getting back to Brent Station. He was like a pit bull terrier. Once he latched on something, he didn't let it go. So he made breakfast for all of us.

Wiping his lips with the back of his hand, Greg verbalized what Jack and I felt, "Smitty, you're the man. That was a good breakfast you scrambled up. Scrambled eggs and beef jerky, bannock and hot porridge should keep us all going good for the day."

Washing down the last of my scrambled eggs, I spoke up, saying, "Jack, would you and Greg clean up everything and break camp? Smitty and I will leave now and head for Brent Station. With any luck, one of us should be back here within two to three hours."

You would have thought Smitty and I were in a canoe race. We were paddling like there was no tomorrow. We covered that five miles from the bay on the southeastern end of Cedar Lake back to Brent Station in record time, or so it seemed.

"Dude. What a nice sight to behold. Here comes Brent Station. Let's pull up where we set off last Sunday. Doesn't look like there is anyone here though. Hold on a minute. I think I hear an outboard motor. Sounds like it's coming from our right. Let's change direction and stroke toward that rock protrusion, Dude."

"You're right, Smitty. I hear the outboard too."

With some powerful stroking from both of us, we both simultaneously saw the motorboat nestled up to a short dock once we cleared the rock protrusion.

"I think it's going to work out, Smitty," was my brief comment as we pulled the canoe up to the dock.

An elderly gentleman was in the boat, bending down over the outboard motor. He had the top off and was adjusting something with his screwdriver, so I tried not to scare him when I approached and greeted him. "Excuse me, sir. May we talk with you?"

He appeared to be in his fifties, and with a casual smile turned to greet us, "Hi, fellows, how are you doing? My name's Rick."

Smitty spoke up for both of us. "Good morning, Rick. This is Paul and I'm Don. We're doing quite well ourselves, but we could use your help if you are able?"

"If I can be of some help, Don and Paul, I'll try. What is your situation, fellows?"

Briefly, I described the predicament we had found ourselves in. "Would it be possible for you to run your boat over to the bay on the southeast end of Cedar Lake with me, and we would pick up two other fellows, Greg and Jack? We also have some gear. We'd be happy to pay you for helping us, Rick."

"Hey, boys, I'd be happy to help you and you don't need to think about paying me. Give me a couple of minutes to finish tuning up this old girl. These Johnson outboards just seem to run forever, but they do need some tuning every once in a while."

"See you later, Smitty," I called out as he jumped back into my canoe and started to head toward the spot where we initially were prepared to beach the canoe.

"See you, Rick and Dude. I'll be leaving for Petawawa before you get to the middle of the lake."

Rick had a quizzical look on his face as he asked me, "What are you fellows up to? And Smitty called you Dude? Is that your nickname, Paul?"

"You are correct, Rick. Smitty's real name is Don, and my real name is Paul, but we grew up together and always used our nicknames, Smitty and Dude."

"Smitty's motorcycle is over in the campground, and he's going to ride it over to Petawawa where we left my car and trailer. He'll come back here and pick us all up. Our canoe trip came to an unfortunate end, but we still need to get back to our homes in Windsor."

"Fill me in on your canoe trip, Paul, or is it OK if I call you Dude? What happened? Sounds like you had to abort the trip. Is everything going to be alright?"

For the duration of the short trip to the bay, I painted a rough picture of our canoe trip fiasco, concluding with, "So that's how it happened, Rick," just as he nudged the bow up on a section of sandy soil near where Greg and Jack had been standing.

Before Rick could shut down that old Johnson outboard, he looked over to me and said with some real awe in his voice, "Man, oh man, Dude. You guys sure came through a knothole backwards. That must have been one scary situation you all found yourselves in."

After introducing Greg and Jack to Rick, we all set about loading Rick's boat with our gear, the two extra paddles, and two life jackets.

"Looks like we got everything, boys," was Rick's response as we stood on the shore next to his boat. "Let's get going, and I'll get you, fellows, back to Brent Station in no time."

Rick was true to his word. We were finally back at Brent Station, and he wouldn't take any money for helping us. We all shook his hand in parting as Jack spoke up, "Rick, thanks for your help. You don't know just how much you have made our day. We won't soon forget your kindness, and we hope you have a great day too."

The next couple of hours passed quickly while Dude, Jack, and Greg were lying around on the grass down by the beach. At one point, Jack asked Dude a question, but got no response. With a quizzical look on his face, Jack again asked a question, and again Dude just continued to stare into space as if no question had been asked.

Now with raised eyebrows, Greg asked Jack, "Didn't you tell me he could slip into a spaced-out state of mind, and not hear anything when spoken to?"

Nodding his head, Jack said, "Greg, it was back when we had set up camp at the dam before we ran any rapids. We were quietly sitting around the campfire, and you noticed he had that spaced-out, glassy-eyed look with his mouth open."

"Now I remember, Jack," Greg said. "You told me I'd have to ask the dude if he ever did that when he was driving. Give him a poke, Jack, and wake him up because that is what I'm going to do."

"Ouch! What's that all about, Jack? Why are you poking me in the ribs? Can't you see I was meditating?"

"That's got to be the funniest thing you've come up with yet, Dude. You were sleeping with your eyes open." Jack continued, "Greg wants to know about you sleeping with your eyes open when you drove a Greyhound bus back in '73."

"Seriously, Dude, did you really do that?" Greg asked in mock concern.

"Tell me about that story. It will be a constant reminder for me to keep my eye on you when you're driving."

"Like you're going to watch me drive every moment I'm behind the wheel. Greg, trust me. I'm a professional driver, or did you forget?"

Greg now became emphatic with his facial and body actions as he made a weird face and threw up his arms. "Spare me the jazz, Dude. Let's hear the story."

"It was a dark and stormy night on the prairie as the wind wiped up the waves on the ocean. I'd just gone to bed in my igloo after spending all day laying on the beach. I had this royal sunburn and couldn't wear my parka."

"Dude! Knock off," Greg spoke while laughing and looking exasperated.

"OK, guys. Here's the real story as it happened. In '73, Greyhound became very busy when both Canadian National and Canadian Pacific railroads went on strike. Their passenger services ceased, and it fell on various bus companies to pick up the slack, moving people on various intercity corridors throughout Ontario.

"I had probably been driving each day for nearly a month. I was extremely busy, and my times for rest had diminished. I was at a point where I was driving, but my head wasn't in it. I was doing everything the correct way—stopping, starting, steering, passing, and all that—but I'd slipped into a state of mindless driving."

"Where did that happen, Dude?" Greg asked with genuine concern.

"Guys, I remember passing through some construction on Highway 401 eastbound in the Kitchener/Cambridge area. But then I don't remember anything after that. I must have driven for over an hour, and I did everything I needed to do in order to be safe, but it wasn't until I'd crossed over the Humber River Bridge on the Gardner Expressway

Eastbound into Toronto where I became aware of what I was doing. I was startled because I didn't know where I was nor where I was heading. Had I missed a terminal where I should have stopped to discharge or pick up passengers and what run was I on?

"Finally, I remembered what run I was on and where I was going. Needless to say, I booked some time off and got some serious rest and downtime. That little episode really put the fear of falling asleep right up front and personal to me."

Everyone fell silent for a long time after that while their thoughts were on the fact that it could happen to any one of them if they were to push themselves beyond their endurance level.

Finally, it was Greg who spoke up. "I hear your car, Dude. There he is just coming into the clearing. Smitty doesn't have the trailer or his bike though."

"Smitty, where are your bike and trailer?" the dude hollered as Smitty got out of the car.

"Motorcycle and trailer are back at the Natural Resources office, Dude, where the turnoff is for Wendigo Lake. They said it would be safe there."

We were all lost in our thoughts again as we loaded up my car with our gear and only one canoe. "This really sucks, Smitty. I sure wish we had your canoe on the racks with mine."

Smitty said nothing, just nodded his head slowly with a serious look on his face.

"It's only taken us about five hours since we got up this morning at six until we're ready to head back home guys," I exclaimed. "All in all, I'd say we did OK. It sure went a lot faster with Rick's help. If we push it, we'll be back home in time to watch the Late Show with Johnny Carson."

"Hey, Dude. That sounds like a plan. "I was looking at your fuel gauge when I was coming back from Petawawa with my motorcycle. We'll have to stop for fuel at North Bay. The Fifth Wheel Truck Stop should be a good place to fill up the fuel tank, and we can grab some snacks to go."

"Good deal, Smitty. After North Bay, I'll continue driving and get us to the southbound Highway 400 Esso Service Center just before we get to Toronto. You can take over from there and run us into Windsor."

A few hours later, after we'd fueled up in North Bay, we all were looking forward to that break at the Esso Service Center. At that point, Smitty said to everyone, "Guys, I don't want to stop at the Fifth Wheel Truck Stop in Milton. I want to push it right through to Windsor. Are you all good with that? I hope you are, so you'd better get what you want for a snack or two now before we leave."

"OK, Smitty. I'll make a phone call to Shirley, and tell her we'll be back at my house around eight o'clock. She can tell the girls, and they'll be waiting for us by then."

"Hey, Dude. You're forgetting something," Greg yelled from the other side of the car. "Are you trying to skip out on the bet we made last Sunday?"

"What bet did you and the dude have Greg?"

"Smitty, we bet you and Jack would return at a certain time from Petawawa last Sunday, after you dropped the dude's car and your trailer off somewhere safe. I said you would be back at Cedar Lake by seven o'clock, and the dude said you'd be back by eight o'clock. The payout was that the loser would buy coffee for everyone when we were returning to Windsor after our canoe trip. Well, you guys were back by seven, so I won the bet."

"Yes, so the dude owes us all a coffee," Smitty growled while looking at Greg. "He was going to try to skip out on us, eh? Alright, you lug nut, how about that coffee, and while you are at it, buy a dozen donuts also. Payback time, everyone, and Dude is doing the payback."

With a helpless look on his face, Dude muttered, "I wasn't trying to skip out on you, guys. I was going to come good on my bet with Greg when we stopped at the Fifth Wheel Truck Stop in Milton. But since Smitty and the rest of you wanted to run through and not stop at Milton, I figured I was off the hook on that bet."

"We don't want to hear any lame excuses from you, Dude. You're nothing but a pot licker trying to skip out on a bet and stiff us all," sneered Smitty.

"OK, Smitty," I said, as I began to sing that song by Johnny Nash, "'I can see clearly now the rain is gone. I can see all obstacles in my way.' Come on. Let's get some coffee and donuts. Guess I'm buying."

True to his word, Smitty hammered away at it until four and one half hours later, he broke the silence with words we all wanted to hear: "The Walker Road exit into Windsor is in my view. Here we are, guys. We'll be at the dude's home in less than fifteen minutes."

Our wives were happy to see us, but they had quizzical looks on their faces too. Kathy, Smitty's wife, spoke up first, "We weren't expecting you for another couple of days, and where is your canoe, Don?"

"I'll tell you all about our trip, Kathy, when we get home." Then looking at the rest of us as we were also listening to hear what he would say to Kathy, he directed his comments to us and said, "Maybe all eight of us could get together in a week or so, and we'll tell all you ladies our story."

Whatever Smitty would say to Kathy later wouldn't be a happy conversation, but we knew he wouldn't get any sleep until Kathy heard his unhappy story.

Smitty and I switched his trailer from my car to his while everyone else gathered up those items that belonged to them. Conversation among us all was low-key. We all knew our wives would pump us for every bit of information when we all had the opportunity to be alone with them.

All four of us went back to our jobs with memories still fresh in our minds. However, it would be a long time before any of us would just get together with each other, and recount our experiences on the Petawawa River.

## Get in, Get it Done, Get Out

It was a surprise when Smitty called me on the phone on August 13, Saturday morning, and just blurted matter-of-factly the following statement, "Dude, I will need your help. I want to get my canoe back."

He quickly caught my attention with that serious request, to which I asked, "What do you have in mind, Smitty?"

Though I asked that question, I already knew what his answer would be. We'd be going back to Cedar Lake.

"Dude, you know I want to get my canoe back because that's all I ever think about or even talk about. I think it is still hung up on that rock, and I have an idea that will work so that I can get it freed up."

"OK, Smitty. You've got my undivided attention. What's your plan?"

"Well, since we are both driving for Bondy Cartage, I'll tell them my story and ask for the weekend of August 20 and 21 off. You do the same, Dude."

"We can leave early Saturday morning, the twentieth, at midnight and run straight to Cedar Lake. We'll take my car. We should get there early enough in the morning so that we can canoe into Devil's Chute, get my canoe, and be back at Brent Station's campground early enough in the evening to set up your tent before the sun goes down. We can leave Brent station on Sunday morning, the twenty-second, and be back in Windsor by early evening if everything goes according to my plan."

"OK, Smitty, I see how your plan will work logistically; but how are you going to get your canoe off the rock?"

"Look at it this way, Dude. We tried with the pole to shove it off the rock, but that didn't work. I will rent a come-a-long or a hand winch with some cable to anchor it to a solid rock or large tree and a good length of chain with a hook."

"OK, Smitty, sounds good so far. But how are you going to get hooked onto the canoe? We can't just lean over and reach it with our hands, and we won't be doing any swimming to get to it."

"That's the simple part, Dude. We will strap the chain to a pole, maybe the pole we cut down, and with the chain's hook at the end of it, we'll reach out to the canoe and try to catch the nose of the canoe with the chain's hook."

Now, I was excited and with anticipation already beating within me I spoke up quickly, "Brilliant, Smitty. That sounds perfect. We'll get it done in no time."

Friday evening, August 19, Smitty came over to my house. Sure enough, he had a two-ton come-along and at least twenty-five feet of chain. There was also enough cable to anchor the come-along to a good-sized tree or a large rock.

"Looks like you put it all together pretty good, Smitty. I've got my tent packed as we agreed earlier. I've got the two life jackets we'll need, our two paddles with a spare just in case and some grub. Oh yes, I'm bringing my nesting pots along, so we can cook our grub over the fire."

Early Saturday morning, as planned, shortly after midnight, we left my house. My gear and Smitty's rental equipment were stowed in the trunk of his car. As we settled in for a long ride, I said, "Got to tell you, Smitty, my canoe looks pretty sitting up there on those racks."

"It will be even nicer if my canoe is still up there at Devil's Chute, and I can get it back. Once it's back on my car, I'll be a happy camper."

Smitty took the first shift driving. The halfway point was more or less Milton, and it was an easy exit off Highway 401 into the Fifth Wheel Truck Stop.

"I had a good snooze for a couple of hours, Smitty. Let's take a coffee break at the truck stop, and I'll drive to Deux Rivieres. I'll let you run your car over the moose trail. That way, if you take a muffler off, I'm not to blame."

"Sure, Dude. I didn't take a muffler off your car when I ran over that moose trail, so I wouldn't expect you to take one off my car. But since you're a wuss, I'll drive it into Cedar Lake."

We didn't see Suzy at the truck stop, but of course, it was too early anyhow. I suppose if she had been waitressing that early in the morning, we'd have spent too much time joking with her, and not enough time trying to get to Cedar Lake.

The coffee break behind us, Smitty and I settled in for another long stretch of driving.

"Dude, I'm going to get a snooze so keep the radio down, eh?"

Nighttime driving can be boring. It's dark outside. The radio always seems to play only sad love songs. Anybody else in the car was sleeping. To pass the time, I looked for wildlife to run over. Not. I'm just kidding.

Equally bad would be me trying to sing. I just decided to be quiet, and my thoughts went back to the canoe trip. Leaving Smitty's canoe behind caused us all a lot of unspoken sorrow. It's like your canoe is an extension of your character. It reflects the type of person you are. You like nature, and you want to keep your life simple and esthetically pleasing. Canoeing can be challenging, but there is also a romantic side to it as well. What better way is there to enjoy the company of your wife than on a quiet lake, surrounded by private coves and bays where one can secretly enjoy the sweet solitude of lovemaking?

"Dude, are you awake? I asked you a question twice, and you were just staring off into space. How do you drive a car and zone out like that? Was anything running through your pea-picking little mind, or are you in total lockdown?"

"Huh? Oh hi, Smitty. I didn't know you were awake. I was just thinking about . . . hum . . . Never mind. It wouldn't interest you anyhow."

"No kidding. I asked you twice where we were and all you did was keep staring into space. So I'll ask you again, where are we you lug-nut?"

"I don't know where we are either. Oh, hold on. We just passed that tree on the north side of the road that looked vaguely like you. Hahaha. We are about one half hour before Deux Rivieres exit. You can jump in the saddle when I turn off the highway."

Smitty shut up for a while, and my thoughts went back to canoeing. This time, I determined that on my next canoe trip, it would be with Shirley. Forget about the guys, and all the macho stuff. I'd dial it down big time so that my pretty lady, my beautiful auburn-haired Shirley and I could enjoy some tender, loving, on that private cove I was daydreaming about.

Interrupting my daydream, I poked Smitty in the ribs and said, "Your turn. You can run us on the moose trail up to Cedar Lake. We should be there about eight, and we can get right to it and go fetch your canoe. Don't forget you need to get a permit at the Natural Resources office. That'll only take a couple of minutes."

"Do you think they will be open this early in the morning, Dude?"

"Smitty, a notice on the door last time we were here said, 'Open 6:00 a.m.'"

The Natural Resources office was open, and in less than one hour, and we had traversed that disgusting moose trail and arrived at Brent Station on Cedar Lake. It was déjà vu all over again.

"Are you hungry, Smitty? I know I am. Let's dive into the sandwiches our wives made us. We'll have to pack some food with us as well, even though we expect to be back here by evening."

Looking out over the lake as he climbed out of his car, Smitty happily said, "The water sure is calm. I hope it stays that way all day, Dude. We can make good time under those conditions. I don't see a cloud in the sky. For sure, the weatherman is our friend today."

With light chitchat between us, we soon had our fill of sandwiches, and my canoe was loaded with everything we needed. "We've got the spare paddles, some food, and the gear you brought, Smitty. We have the come-along, the cable, and the chain. Looks like we're ready to push off and get this job done. Let's go."

We were familiar with Cedar Lake, portaging around the dam, the five sets of rapids, and the portage around Devil's Chute. And we made it in record time.

"Not bad, Dude. We made the trip here from the campground in just over two and one half hours. Let's portage the canoe and all our gear right up to the rock at Devil's Chute."

With the chain, the good length of cable, and the come-a-long hung over Smitty's shoulders and down his back, his gear must have weighed a good seventy-five pounds. My canoe, and a backpack with food, and some other junk we might need must have come in at about seventy-five to eighty pounds as well. All in all, though, we were traveling light.

"We'll make this a sting operation, Smitty. Get in, get it done, and get out."

Arriving at the site of the big rock, Smitty angrily exclaimed, "What the dickens is that, Dude? There are two guys where my canoe is located, and it looks like they're trying to salvage it. Let's drop your canoe here behind these cedars and take my come-along and gear over there."

As we approached these two guys, we noticed that they had somehow attached a good length of strong nylon rope to the bow of the canoe. Smitty spoke up first.

"Hey, you guys. This is our canoe, and we're going to get it off that rock."

They both turned around in unison, and the taller one yelled back at us. "This canoe is ours and we're going to get it off this rock. You two can just disappear back from where you came."

I looked at Smitty and he looked at me. I was the first to whisper, "Let's just retreat back to my canoe for a couple of minutes. I have a plan."

As we were retreating from the site where Smitty's canoe was impaled on that rock, he asked me, "What are your plans, Dude?"

"Look Smitty, you have a hunting knife with a six-inch blade on your belt, and I do as well. Let's just leave all our gear here for a few minutes, strip down to our pants, no shirts, and charge those two clowns with our knives drawn.

"We can yell our heads off as we charge them. Smitty, I'm willing to fight those goofballs for your canoe. I'm not leaving here without it."

Smitty agreed with me, nodding his head while muttering something under his breath. When he spoke, it was more like a snarl, "You take that shorter one, Dude. I'm going for the big mouth. If he doesn't beat a path out of here, he's not going to look pretty."

Those guys must have thought we departed the area because they weren't looking behind them when we silently approached within thirty feet. Then all hell broke loose. We were running and yelling at the top of our lungs. Our knives were drawn. Bare to the waist, we must have looked like a couple of Indians on the warpath. But it worked. There was no shed blood. They split out on a dead run.

Their words were few but were heard clearly, "It's your canoe and you can have the rope too."

We never saw them again. We must have scared them good. Incidentally, that rope was a ¾-inch nylon rope, and it was strong, so Smitty suggested, "Let's try with the rope first. Maybe we can winch the canoe with it."

With a loud snap, the rope broke. "Dude, that rope was strong, but we broke it. The force of the water on the canoe was too much for the rope. Let's get back to my plan. I saw the pole we cut down from before, so let's strap the chain to it and see if we can't snag the bow with the chain's hook."

"We did it. We got the chain's hook firmly locked onto the bow of the canoe, Dude." Smitty was really excited now as he continued, "Give me a couple of minutes to make sure the cable is firmly wrapped around this rock."

Struggling, Smitty began winching slowly. "Dude, there is an incredible force working against this come-along. I can't believe how difficult this is. I hope the canoe moves and not this rock I've got the cable lashed around."

"For sure," I said. "I hope your rock is stronger than the force of the water. Smitty. I'd hate to see that rock come flying out of the ground. It would take you with it right over the side of the cliff."

"What kind of morbid mind do you have, Dude? Are you some kind of thrill seeker? It isn't the rock that is moving. Look. The canoe seemed to move a couple of inches."

"You're right," I said excitedly. "I just saw it move a little as well. It's going to happen. We're going to get your canoe back. Keep winching. It's working."

And work it did. With a few more arm-length winches from Smitty, and that canoe found freedom. I mean, it really found its freedom. Smitty explained it this way. Well, more like he yelled it excitedly this way, "Wow! Would you look at that? The canoe just exploded into the air.

"It seemed to shoot up at least fifteen feet. It went straight up and right over that huge rock. It landed in the rapids behind the rock, Dude. Let's get out of here and chase it down the rapids. I hope we can catch it down at the pool."

We ran hard, but the canoe had a good head start. When we got to the pool, there was a guy and girl standing over the canoe. They had pulled it out of the water and were looking at the extreme damage which had been done to it.

Smitty was all smiles when he yelled out his greetings. "Howdy. Thanks for beaching our canoe for us."

The fellow hollered back to us, "You guys must have had a serious accident with this canoe. The damage is unreal."

Yes, Smitty's canoe was extensively damaged. To hear his commentary on the damages was heartbreaking. "Would you look at that? The keel is pushed right up to the level of the gunwales. Only a huge force of water would do that.

We're going to have to get that keel pushed back down as much as we can before we can get it out of here."

"You're right, Smitty. Let's balance the canoe upright on these two rocks. They're far enough apart so that we should be able to balance it. If we jump up and down inside the canoe, maybe we'd be able to send the keel back down."

The two people who had fetched Smitty's canoe out of the quiet pool of water had not departed, but remained listening and observing the conversation and actions the ensued when we arrived on the scene. Turning toward them and directing my question to them, I said, "If you two people help us by stabilizing the canoe while my buddy and I jump up and down inside of it, I think we might get the keel back down a bit."

With the help of those two people, we were able to bend the keel back down nearly a foot. It still had quite a curve, but the keel was considerably straighter than before.

"Now the easy part, Dude. We have to pull the sides of the bow back together. The hook on the chain opened the bow up like a can of sardines when the canoe was released from the rock's grip. There's a new roll of duct tape in my backpack, and we can wrap up the bow until it is watertight. We'll do that when we get back to where we left your canoe and the come-along gear."

Thanking the guy and girl who helped us, we headed back up the portage.

As we wrapped the bow of the canoe with a whole roll of duct tape, Smitty couldn't help but remark about the damage, "It is incredible. In the two months since I impaled the canoe on the rock, the force of the water bent the keel right up to the level of the gunwales. It's hard to believe, but here's the evidence."

"It was a good idea to bring your camera along, Smitty. Not only do you have some good pictures of the canoe on the rock, but taking pictures of the damages before and after we did a makeshift job of getting it seaworthy will be helpful. Grumman has a lifetime warranty on their canoes to the original owner. Your canoe got hung up on the rock doing what it was designed to do. It is a white-water model, and you were running white-water when everything went sideways."

"I'll have to follow through on that, Dude. This canoe will never see white-water again, and I sure do want to have another canoe to replace this one, so I hope their warranty is everything they say it is."

We finished the makeshift repairs to Smitty's canoe and soon we were pulling it backward behind my canoe with a twenty foot length of the ¼-inch nylon rope I'd brought along for just that purpose. By then, it was getting on to three o'clock, and we still had two portages ahead of us. The first one we'd encounter going back upstream was a 750-yard portage, and the second portage was a 1,050-yard portage. That would bring us to the dam, and the small bay at the southeastern end of Cedar Lake.

Arriving at the first of the two portages, Smitty exclaimed, "Whew. Our work is cut out for us, Dude. We each have a canoe to carry on these portages and our gear as well. That come-along, chain, and cable aren't light, and your pack is a few pounds as well. I know I'm going to be bagged by the time I see Cedar Lake."

With sheer guts and determination, Smitty and I did it. We hauled everything through those two portages in one trip. I helped by carrying the chain. I strapped it to the canoe. It was just too much to expect Smitty to carry it all.

Arriving finally at the dam, Smitty exclaimed. "I've had it, Dude. I'm going to cool down and take a shower at the dam. I need to get my strength back, and a cold shower will do that."

With that comment from Smitty, he just removed his boots and walked straight into the water beneath the dam. "Why didn't you take your clothes off before you jumped in under the dam?" I asked Smitty in astonishment. "It's like this, Dude. My clothes will be wet for a while as we paddle back to camp, and that will keep me cool. You, on the other hand, will work up a new sweat faster than me because you skinny-dipped and your clothes are dry. I'm the one with the built-in air conditioner. I guess we know who the smart guy is, eh?"

With a smirk on my face, I said, "Yes, I concede you're the smart one. Just don't waste all your energy bragging about how intelligent you are. You need to pull your weight here too."

Not satisfied, Smitty had to rub it in a bit more by saying, "Aw, Dude. You're just sore that I am way smarter than you."

Out on the open water of Cedar Lake, paddling was much easier while pulling Smitty's canoe behind mine. We had done a good job wrapping the bow with duct tape as no leaks had been evidenced thus far. There was, however, an interesting dynamic that we observed. Because the keel of his canoe was still very warped, the only spots where the canoe touched the water were at the stern and the bow. Smitty's canoe lacked the ability now to track true while being towed.

"It's a good thing, Smitty, that the breezes are light on the open water. If we were to experience a good headwind or a wind off our quarter to the port or starboard, your canoe would be tracking dramatically on its own tangent. It would make a harder pull for us. As it is, your canoe is constantly zigzagging."

"What about this scenario, Dude? If we were to have a strong tailwind, the fact that my canoe lacks directional stability because its keel is above water and it is light while we have maybe a bit over five hundred pounds in gear and human weight in your canoe would suggest that my canoe would probably pass us. Then I'd say, 'Let the fun begin' for sure."

Well, with lighthearted back-and-forth banter, the trip across open water seemed to pass in mere minutes. It was Smitty who verbalized his observations. "We're doing a good job staying the course, Dude. We'll be running aground right where we put in this morning in just a couple of minutes, and we've done it all within eight hours."

"We make a good team, Smitty. Let's get both canoes strapped down on your car's roof racks and then we'll pitch our tent and think about getting some grub put together."

When the gear was stowed in the trunk, the canoes strapped down, the tent pitched, and hot stew bubbling in the pot over the open campfire, Smitty finally let it all out. "Dude, I prayed that we'd be able to get my canoe. I was concerned that it wouldn't be there when we arrived, and I guess that is why I waited two months before I dared to ask you to help me retrieve it. God sure did answer my prayers in a big way. Even the weather was fantastic this weekend."

Smitty and I did not remain around the campfire too long that evening. Basically, we'd been up and active for the most part since Friday morning, the last day we'd worked. Any sleep we did get was just a couple of hours each while traveling. Now it was Saturday evening, and finally, standing up and yawning, I said, "I'm going to dowse the fire, Smitty. I'm passing out just sitting here. I'm going to sleep like a dead man tonight."

Sunday morning broke early with clear skies, fresh temperature, and a beautiful calm lake, so when Smitty spoke up, he was echoing my sentiments exactly. "If we didn't have to be back to work tomorrow morning, Dude, I'd be tempted to suggest that we just hang out here for a few days and enjoy canoeing around the lake."

"I'm with you on that, Smitty, but it isn't going to happen. I will make a suggestion though. Why don't we just pack up the tent and get out of here? Forget about cooking breakfast over the fire. That would leave us with more work, and we'd not get free to leave for a couple of hours. This way, we can stop at the Fifth Wheel Truck Stop in North Bay and let them cook us up a really good breakfast. We're bound to save a good hour doing it that way."

It was a good idea, and Smitty liked it as well, so he offered another great idea, "After breakfast at the Fifth Wheel in North Bay, Dude, we could run straight to Milton and stop at the Fifth Wheel Truck Stop there for a coffee break before continuing on to Windsor."

That Sunday morning, Smitty was so happy to have his canoe back, he actually bought my breakfast. I just had to thank him for his generosity, but being that we were always digging at each other, it was a bit of a backhanded compliment.

"Smitty, you're a true gentleman and a scholar." It worked, I got the facial reaction I fully expected him to give me—a big sneer out of the right corner of his mouth while he curled up his nose and directed his eyes skyward.

Time passed quickly as we journeyed south on Highway 11 toward Toronto. At one point, I verbalized something I'd remembered from a conversation we'd had, "Smitty, remember when we were coming up here and we'd stopped at the Fifth Wheel in Milton? Susy was our waitress. As I recall, she said she worked days on the weekend. She is going to want to know how our canoe trip went, and if she sees your canoe, you'll have to tell her the whole story."

"Hey, we'll stop at the Fifth Wheel Truck Stop for sure, Dude, but I'll only give the *Reader's Digest* version. I want to get to Windsor by suppertime."

Sure enough, Smitty was true to his word. Suzy was our waitress, and he only gave her an abbreviated, condensed version. Even at that, she was spellbound as he recounted some of the tangles we got ourselves into. It made me wonder, while I was listening to him if we shouldn't get ourselves a gig and go on tour. We could embellish our story and tell it to sellout crowds.

Smitty gave me a poke in the ribs and laughingly said to Suzy, "Look at the dude, Suzy. He's daydreaming. It's like that guy can totally zone out sometimes. We should check to see if he's still breathing or even has a pulse.

Dude, you're daydreaming. Come on. We need to get going."

"Home at last, Dude." Smitty woke me up by poking me in my left arm. I'd been dreaming again, reliving our canoe adventures. "Let's get your canoe and gear off. I'm heading home for a good rest tonight, and I'll not be dreaming about canoe trips either."

## The Warranty Honored

It was a year later, just about to the exact date, June 9, 1978, when Smitty and his dad, Cecil Smith, left Windsor for Marathon, New York. Marathon is located on Interstate Highway 81, south of Syracuse, before you get to Binghamton. This was where Grumman had their manufacturing plant. The beautiful seventeen-foot, lightweight whitewater models were made there.

Smitty had been planning to take his battered and busted canoe back to the Grumman plant because the warranty on Grumman canoes was for life to the original owner. The stipulation was that the canoe had to be involved in the activity it was designed for, in this case, whitewater running.

As was told to me later by Smitty, this was a memorial journey. He and his dad had been planning this trip for a couple of months. Up until then, his canoe had been sitting behind his house, weeds growing all around it. It was a forlorn sight, and every time he looked at it, Smitty grimaced.

When he called me on the phone that Friday morning, his exact words were, "Dude, I'm going to get a new canoe. I'm going to Marathon with my dad. I have my warranty in hand. Everything lines up good. I'm entitled to get a new replacement for my busted-up canoe. We'll get there later today, and I should be back home by tomorrow. I have to take my old canoe with me because I'm sure they'll want to see what happened to it."

Receiving another phone call from Smitty later that day, he excitedly told me, "Dude, Dad and I are at the Grumman plant in Marathon. You know I took a lot of pictures when we were trying to get the canoe off the rock and then later when we did. Well, I showed them those pictures and told them the complete story. They had a couple of executives listening in while I showed the pictures and told what had happened, and more than once they exclaimed that our trip was certainly a harrowing one. Dad and I were in their boardroom for a good hour.

"When I had completed my story, the sweetest words I could hear were 'You get another canoe, Don. We always stand by our warranties.'

"The only downside to our trip down to Marathon was that because we were Canadians and I had purchased my canoe in Canada, we would be unable to get a new canoe in Marathon. We have to return to Canada. We are to go to their distribution center at Napanee, Ontario.

"We'll go back up Interstate Highway 81 right to the top past Watertown, NY, and cross over on the international bridge into Ontario just east of Gananoque on Highway 401. We'll get a motel room for the night after we've arrived in Gananoque."

Saturday, June 10, about noontime, I got another phone call from Smitty.

"Dude, I've got it. I've got a new canoe identical to my old one. I left my old one here in Nappanee where Grumman has their distribution center. Dad and I are heading back to Windsor. You've got to know it, Dude. I'm one happy camper."

Smitty and I never did take another canoe trip together. We often talked about doing another trip, and sometimes, we would even draw up a few plans. But it never worked out.

A couple of years later, just before Christmas time of 1980, I moved my family from Windsor, Ontario, to Winnipeg, Manitoba. It would never happen again. Our canoeing days together had come to an end. Well, maybe that would end, but the stories of Smitty and me, they never ended.

## ELEVEN

# FISHING AND FIGHTING A FOREST FIRE

"PAUL, GET THE alarm, please. It's been going for over a minute already."

Rubbing my eyes with the back of my fists, I mumbled, "Oh sorry, Shirley. I guess I was dreaming about going fishing."

"You're funny, Paul. Why are you dreaming about going fishing when you are supposed to get up out of bed early today, so you and my dad can go fishing, or did you forget?"

"Oh yes, now I remember. Dad and I are supposed to leave by 6:00 a.m. We're going to canoe and fish on Black Lake in Nopiming Provincial Park. It should take us about three hours to get there. I guess if I don't get up now, it will take longer than three hours to get there."

Shirley and her mom had already been up at least one half hour earlier and the aroma of bacon and eggs was stimulating. It didn't take long to arrive at the kitchen table, but I was still the last one there. My father-in-law, Dan, was already halfway through his breakfast when I sat down.

"Well, well, well. Look who's the sleepyhead. I thought maybe I'd leave without you," he jokingly said.

"I can choke down this breakfast in short order, Dan, and we'll leave on time. The car is loaded with our gear and the canoe is strapped down on the roof racks."

Stopping long enough in my rush to get going, I kissed Shirley goodbye and gave her a good squeeze. But I was still the last one out the door. Dan was already waiting beside the car, trying to look impatient, but it wasn't working, and I told him so.

"Knock off the impatient look, Dan. I'm still two minutes early. We're not going to be late leaving. Did you forget I used to drive for Greyhound? I know how to keep a schedule. If you were that impatient, you'd already be in the car and likely tooting the horn." I said this with a laugh, knowing full well he'd never take me seriously.

Without a backward glance to the ladies standing at the front window, Dan and I stuck our arms out the side door windows and waved goodbye to them.

"Fishing trip here we come, Dan."

"You said earlier, Paul, we'd be going to Black Lake. Have you ever been there before?"

"No, Dan. I've not been there, but a friend where I work at Gravure Graphics told me the fish were always biting when he fished there back in June of this year. If you like pickerel, I'm told that Black Lake is well-stocked. I can't imagine that we'll come away without any fish. Fishing season is still good. After all, it's only August the fourth."

"Bear in mind, Paul, this is a long weekend because of the Civic Holiday on Monday, August 6. There will likely be a lot more fellows on the lake because of the holiday."

"That's likely true, Dan, but there are many lakes throughout Manitoba. Not all fishermen are going to head for Black Lake. I would expect many more will be fishing the lakes in Whiteshell Provincial Park. That park is much closer to Winnipeg than where we're going."

"I hope you're correct on that one, Paul. I haven't had any pickerel since you and I went fishing up on Georgian Bay back in 1975. This is 1984. Can you believe it? It's time for a good fish fry today. Nine years is too long to wait for fresh pickerel frying in my hot skillet over an open fire."

"I know you've gone fishing a few times over the past nine years, Dan, but no pickerel? What were you catching?"

"I've caught catfish, perch, bass, salmon, and a couple of species of trout either in the Thames River, down at Lake Erie, or in some of the lakes in Eastern Ontario."

"I remember our fishing trip quite well when you and a couple of your buddies and myself went up to a small island near Manitoulin

Island on Georgian Bay. We drove into Killarney, coming off Highway 69. That was a slow-winding, third-class road we were on once we left the main highway."

"Paul, do you recall that it was a rather stormy day as well? The sky was overcast with low clouds that threatened rain. The waves on Georgian Bay were quite a good size, and the boat I'd rented felt a wee bit too small when I was facing it into the waves and wind."

"Yes, I do remember that now, Dan. Your buddy Ken had a much larger boat, and we decided I should ride in his boat and not with you. I had a cast on my left foot as I'd torn ligaments in my ankle a few weeks earlier. I couldn't drive for six weeks and was on workman's compensation from Greyhound."

"I believe we thought it best for you to be in the bigger boat as there would be less chance of you getting the cast wet. If you had stayed in the boat I was operating, you would definitely have gotten that cast wet from water spraying off the bow," Dan said this as he was scratching his chin in a gesture of trying to bring back old memories.

"That was a good fishing trip, Dan. We were gone four days, and what really sticks in my mind was the fresh fish fry we had each evening. Another thought that just crossed my mind was that you had a terrific batter you cooked the fillets in. Did you bring that batter with you today?" I said in a hopeful questioning voice.

Dan looked at me with a bit of a cockeyed grin and said, "I never leave home on a fishing trip without it, Paul. Oh, by the way, you said you'd never been to Black Lake before. Where is your Manitoba map? I'd like to see the route you're taking."

"Great idea, Dan, and I'll let you be my navigator. Right now we're heading north on Highway 59. Just ahead maybe five miles is Highway 44. We'll turn east on it and go through Beausejour. Highway 44 will T-bone with Highway 11. We'll turn north at that point. I can get you to that place well enough as I've run through there a time or two on 44. However, I've not been north on 11."

"OK, I have 44 and 11 pinpointed on the map. How far do we run north on 11, Paul?

"Here, Dan, I've written the route that my friend gave me on this piece of paper. Follow it and it should be no problem getting to Black Lake. Oh, by the way, Dan," I asked in a quizzical voice, "why didn't we go fishing that time in the summer of 1978 when two of my friends, Brian and Gord, and you and I went on that canoe trip in Algonquin Park? Do you remember we started at Canoe Lake, and it took us approximately a week to get to Opeongo Lake?"

"It doesn't stick in my memory, Paul, that we had a reason for not fishing while on that canoe trip. Possibly, it was because we had to take a fair amount of gear with us and there were many portages we had to navigate."

"You're probably right, Dan. That was a good canoe trip though, wasn't it?" I asked in a happy, questioning voice.

"Oh yes, Paul, and I remember we came to this one portage. I was carrying our gear; and you had the canoe, paddles, and life jackets on your shoulders. It was a fairly long portage, as I recall. And about halfway through it, we came to a small, shallow pond that some beavers had created. You were some distance behind me, so I wasn't actually communicating with you. But what I did was walk around that pond and picked up the portage trail on the other side."

I started laughing as I lightly said, "Oh boy, now I remember that portage, Dan. When I came to that beaver pond, I thought I'd just walk through it as it wasn't very wide at the point where the portage trail intersected it. I did give thought briefly to putting the canoe in the pond and paddling over to the far side, but there were so many trees. I figured I get hung up trying to get the canoe back on my shoulders. My decision made, I just stepped into the pond with my clothes and boots still on me and, of course, the canoe on my shoulders."

Dan started laughing and could barely speak for a moment. "I had made it completely around that point, so I was just standing at the edge of the portage trail, watching for you. I didn't say anything to you, I guess, half expecting you to walk around the pond like I had done, but before I could tell you that option, you just stepped into the beaver pond and started walking through the water to the other side. You looked a bit surprised though once you got about halfway through that pond, Paul. It was likely deeper than you thought as it came right up to your chest."

"That was funny, Dan, and when we caught up with Brian and Gord, they had a good laugh as well."

"Oh, by the way, Dan, we must be getting close to our turnoff from Highway 11. What is the highway number again?"

"Slow down, Paul. We're coming up on Highway 313 right now. You need to turn east. The map shows 313 as a secondary road, which you will only travel on for several miles before you turn north again, this time on Highway 315. Highway 315 is paved only for about five miles. At which point, you'll continue on gravel. You'll have to turn north on Highway 314, about ten miles into highway 315. Highway 314 will be a good twenty miles before you come to Black Lake."

"Pretty much all the roads heading north, Dan, especially on the east side of Lake Winnipeg are gravel. You'll notice on the map that, as you go further north, the roads become winter roads only. But where we're going today, we won't experience anything like that. These roads are maintained year-round."

For the next hour, we slowly made our way north. With gravel to drive on, we were now more concerned about rocks being kicked up by oncoming cars. The last thing either vehicle would want was a cracked and broken windshield. Thus everyone reduced speed substantially.

Excitedly Dan broke the silence, "Paul, Black Lake, one kilometer ahead."

That excited comment created an immediate response in me, and with a sigh of relief, I spoke up, "I'm glad to see that sign, Dan. We'll be there in a moment. I see a campground just ahead on the right side of the bridge we're crossing right now. We'll turn in there and park. My friend told me we'd have to canoe east just a short distance from Black River to reach Black Lake."

"I'd say we made good time, Paul. You said we'd need about three hours for travel time before we reached our destination, and we're right on the money. We made it in two hours and fifty minutes."

It didn't take us long to unload the canoe and put our gear into it. While holding on to the dock as Dan stepped into the bow, I made a comment based on what surrounded us that delightful morning, "It sure has turned into a beautiful day. Warm breezes and calm water are greeting us here on Black River. I expect it will be the same as we enter Black Lake. We will follow the northern side of the lake as we've decided earlier. It lies in the southeastern/northwestern direction. There is a slight northerly breeze, so the northern shore will be the calmest."

Dan was the expert fisherman, and I left it up to him to decide where to drop our lines. So it wasn't too long before he sang out, "Paul, let's just stop here for a while. This looks like a great place to start fishing."

We'd come to within twenty feet from shore and had stopped paddling. Both our lines were quickly dropped in the water. Then about ten minutes later, I noticed wildlife on the shore adjacent to us. It sent a shiver down my spine.

Quietly but clearly, I spoke up, "Dan, I think we'd best move from this location. There is a large black bear giving us the evil eye, and I'd like to put some distance between us and him."

Dan looked over his left shoulder and gave a bit of a grunt when his eyes focused on that black bear. Speaking softly, he said, "I'm in agreement with you, Paul. Let's just quietly paddle back out into the lake and continue down the shoreline. I'm sure we'll find another good spot. I'd like to get some fresh pickerel without having a black bear think we'd done that fishing just for him."

We could have chosen several good spots to stop and begin fishing, but both of us wanted to put some space between ourselves and that black bear.

After several minutes of paddling, we came around a slight point, and Dan optimistically said, "I like this spot right here, Paul. It's not too deep, and the water is calm. Let's drop our lines."

Our quietness was broken after several moments when Dan presented a question to me, "Paul, I recall that you and Shirley had an incident with a black bear. Didn't it have something to do with one of your children when you were camping?"

"Actually, Dan, it did have something to do with our oldest child, Colleen. Shirley and I had taken the four kids for a weekend camping trip to Whiteshell Provincial Park. It was an early fall weekend in September 1982, just a few days before the end of the month.

"We had two good-sized tents and had placed Colleen, Connie, and Charles in one tent. Shirley and I and our little two-year-old Catherine were in the other tent. But let me back up a wee bit here.

"Shirley and I were going to camp at the West Hawk Lake campsite. I had been there earlier in the summer with my son, Charles, and my friend, Imre. At that time, the three of us had spent a couple of days there. I liked that campsite, and since the lake had a nice beach, I chose that site for our family camping weekend."

"Was there any good fishing in that lake, Paul?" Dan had asked that question in a rather jovial voice.

I responded to Dan with laughter in my voice, "There is no end to good fishing on the eastern side of Manitoba. You pick the lake, and I guarantee the fish will pick your line to get reeled in on."

"Sorry, Paul. I just had to ask. Once a fisherman, always a fisherman. Please go back to your story."

"The family and I had arrived early that Friday afternoon. Once I'd pitched the tents, we all had a pleasant swim in the lake. The consequence of that was that everyone was really hungry and could hardly wait for me to grill some hamburgers. But what was really surprising was that, just a couple of hours after they'd eaten and just before Shirley and I sent everyone to bed, each kid, in turn, said they were still hungry.

"What to do? The remaining food had been repacked in the cooler, and it was placed in the trunk of our car. The purpose of that was really quite simple. I didn't want to leave any food stock out overnight, because I knew the scent of food would attract wildlife, and most likely, that would be skunks, raccoons, or bears."

"That certainly makes sense, Paul, that you'd remove any food from remaining in the open."

"Well, the children wouldn't stop complaining that they were still hungry, so I suggested to Shirley that we make each of them a peanut butter and honey sandwich. They were indeed hungry and wolfed down those sandwiches in short order. After which, we cleaned up the camp again, redeposited the food back in the cooler, and placed it back in the trunk. Then we cleaned any food that remained on the kid's faces or hands."

"Hold those thoughts, Paul," Dan called back to me with exuberance, "I've got a bite. I think I've got a good-sized fish. There is a good pull on the line. Get ready with your net, and I'll reel it in so you can scoop it up."

Dan caught the first fish of the day, and it was a good-sized pickerel. That fish lying there on the floor of the canoe would be a good start for a lunch of pan-fried fresh fish. We'd certainly need another couple of pickerel, but at the moment, we were optimistic that we'd picked a good spot.

Back into the water, Dan cast his line while at the same time calling back to me, "OK, Paul, get on with your story. Don't leave me hanging. You did get all traces of food off of the kids, didn't you?"

"I certainly thought so, Dan. Shirley and I were attentive to the younger two kids, Connie and Charles, but I guess we must have thought our eldest, Colleen, would be able to attend to her own face, and make sure it was clean from any traces of food. In retrospect, that was my mistake. I should have made sure Colleen's face was as spotless as her siblings were.

"The kids were then sent to bed, and Shirley and I retired for the night soon after. It must have been around midnight when I was awakened with a start. I had heard some grunting, and rightly assumed it was a bear. I yelled out to Shirley that there was a bear outside our tent. At the same time, I yelled to Colleen, to ask her if there was something going on over at her tent. She responded with a lot of fear in her voice, saying that something was trying to pull her out of the tent.

"Dan, it seems comical now, but at the time, it wasn't funny at all. I had a mummy sleeping bag, and do you think I could get the zipper down and extract myself from it? No way. Shirley, on the other hand, was quick at jumping out of her sleeping bag, and with a lot of screaming from both of us, we scared the bear away."

"Hey, Paul," Dan said, laughing loudly, "I remember that mummy sleeping bag. It was green, wasn't it? You used that bag when we were on the canoe trip where you walked through the beaver pond."

"Indeed, that was the green mummy sleeping bag I was using when the bear came to our campsite."

"Get back to your story, Paul. What happened next?"

"When I did get out of my sleeping bag, Dan, I ran to the other tent. There was a small hole in the tent, into which I'd placed a dirty sock to keep the mosquitoes out. That hole had been created by mildew from repacking it while there was dampness on the canvas. Evidently, the bear was attracted to the sock and to Colleen's face. He had pushed his paw and head through that hole, making it much larger, and with his paw, he was trying to drag Colleen to the side of the tent. He had shredded her sleeping bag above her torso, and had begun to chew on the top of her bag next to her face. I believe now that Colleen must have still had some traces of peanut butter and honey on her face, and it had rubbed on the top of the sleeping bag.

"Hey, Dan, I've got a bite," I interrupted my own story to exclaim in excitement. "It's a good tug I'm getting on the line. Get the net ready because I'm reeling this fellow in."

Soon we had two beautiful pickerel on the floor of the canoe, and both were a good size. At that point, with excitement, Dan echoed my thoughts completely, "It's looking good, but let's try for one more. Three will make a great meal. I can already taste fresh pan-fried pickerel wrapped in my secret batter right now, Paul, but I'll be patient for a bit longer."

"Get back to your story. There's more isn't there, Paul?" Dan asked in a raised voice.

"Well, to put a cap on the story, Dan, Shirley and I didn't want another visit from the bear, so we packed up the kids and put them in the car for the remainder of the night. I'm not sure they had a good sleep, but they were safe from another bear attack. Shirley and I and baby Catherine remained in our tent, but when it came morning, after breakfast, we decided we would cut short our camping trip. Colleen's sleeping bag was destroyed, and the tent now had an L-shaped rip that extended nearly two feet in both directions.

"On our way out of the campground, I stopped at the camp warden's office and explained what had happened the prior evening. He told me that the bears have been attracted to the campground because of so much human garbage, much of which has been cast around the various campsites. Once a bear becomes used to humans and their garbage, they will not leave the campground but become nightly intruders and pests to the campers."

"You folks were certainly fortunate that Colleen never suffered any direct mauling from that bear. That event could have taken a much worse turn and caused some lasting grief, Paul."

"You're right, Dan. I believe the Lord was watching over all of us that night."

No sooner had I put a cap on the bear story than Dan sang out in excitement, "Got me another fish, Paul. Let's get it in the canoe and head for shore. Fish fry here we come."

It wasn't maybe more than ten minutes of paddling further down the lake when we came around a point of land jutting out into the lake and noticed that there was a nice little clearing ahead, which would be perfect for a place to have our fish fry.

As we pulled the canoe up on the shore, Dan exclaimed excitedly, "Would you look at that, Paul? There is a spot right here on this big flat rock where we can fillet the fish, and right over there is a good-sized grate over a spot where we can set up a small fire."

While Dan was filleting the three pickerel we'd brought ashore, I set about finding some suitable firewood to build a small fire beneath the grate. By the time I had a fire going well, Dan had battered the fillets, and put the skillet on the grate. The sound of the fish fillets frying was mesmerizing. Both he and I stared silently at the battered fish, lost in our own thoughts.

The silence of that moment was soon disturbed as Dan arose from the log he was sitting on, and took his spatula and flipped each fillet over. In a satisfied voice, he said quietly, "Paul, get ready for a good feast of freshly fried pickerel in my secret batter. We'll be ready to eat in just a few moments."

Indeed, those fresh battered and fried pickerel were excellent. I thought it was hard to compare the taste to anything else that might cross my mind. Maybe a grilled T-bone steak might come close.

We sat around for another half hour while the fire died down, lost in our own thoughts, but it was me who broke the stillness of the moment with a yawning comment, "Dan, what do you say we put this fire out, and head back out on the lake? We haven't got any fish to take back home to our wives."

A few minutes later, the fire was extinguished, the canoe put back on the water, and Dan and I started to paddle now across the lake. It was early afternoon, around one o'clock, and we'd planned to fish until four or five o'clock. By then, we hoped we'd have several pickerel, and be ready to head for home.

It was Dan who caught my attention with a rather loud exclamation, "Paul, look ahead and to the right. Coming from behind that island is a considerable amount of smoke moving low on the water. What do you think might be causing so much of it?"

Staring at the low-moving smoke coming from our right, I said with some concern and hesitation, "Dan, I don't like the looks of that. There is far too much smoke for a small campfire. The amount of smoke that we are seeing is being generated from a much larger fire. We'd better pick up our pace and check this out. That much smoke doesn't bode well."

Coming around a protruding point of land of the island adjacent to us, I exclaimed without hesitation, "Dan, look over to the next island which is to our left. At the far end, it certainly appears that the whole tip of that island is on fire. We best get closer to that fire. We'll have to make a quick assessment, and as quick as we can, we'll have to return to the campsite where we parked and report this fire. There is no time to waste."

We soon traversed the distance from our first observation to the point where we were now abreast of the fire. The whole tip of this island appeared to be burning. And quite suddenly, we were startled when a voice called out very loudly, "Ahoy, the two men in the canoe. Come ashore immediately. We need your help to fight this fire."

Without a moment's thought, I pointed the canoe toward the shore and then spoke quickly to Dan. "We are obligated to help fight this fire. We are able-bodied, and if we were to refuse, there could be legal ramifications brought against us by the Province of Manitoba."

Dan didn't respond, but in a way, he did respond because he pulled even harder and faster on his paddle. Quickly, we covered that short distance and nimbly dragged the canoe ashore beside the boat these men had arrived in. We were met by a tall man who introduced himself briefly.

"Men, my name is Kyle. I'm in charge here. I have four other men helping me fight this fire, but we need your help as well. This fire is getting away from us. Here are two shovels and two hand-pump fire extinguishers. Fill them with lake water and move over to that area to your left. You will need to use both the shovel and the extinguisher. Shovel the earth and peat moss off the rocks and blast it with water. It is important to get the fire while it is still on the ground. Once it gets into these pine trees, it will run away on us faster than we can run to keep up with it or to escape from it."

With those somber words from Kyle, and not speaking a word to each other, Dan and I began to do exactly as we were instructed. Back and forth from the fire to the lake we ran while observing that the other five men were doing exactly the same thing. But our best efforts were in vain. This fire was getting away from us rapidly, and heading into the interior of the island. It had begun to get into the pine trees.

At one point, I had stopped for a brief moment just to wipe the sweat from my eyes. Mistakenly, I was standing next to a pine tree possibly fifteen feet high. Without warning, the tree ignited. But the source for its igniting was from the peat moss on the ground. With a loud swoosh, the pine tree went up in flames from its roots to its tip. I jumped back in dead fright. I could feel the heat of that flame singe the hair on my arms.

Dan happened to be looking my way as this happened, and yelled over to me with concern in his voice, "Paul, are you alright? Be careful, son."

We continued to fight valiantly for possibly another hour. I don't know, maybe it was more maybe it was less. It was hard and it was scary. It was hot and it was exhausting, yet we fought on. Sometimes we fought close to each other; sometimes we were a hundred or more feet away from each other, but Dan and I reconciled within ourselves that we'd fight until we dropped.

Hearing a new sound other than the roar of the fire as it raced through the tops of the pines all around us, I stopped. It was the distinct *whump-whump-whump-whump* of the blades of a big helicopter. I knew it was racing toward us. The sound of the helicopter was loud as it approached at a low level. If it were to pass by, the sound lost its distinct *whump-whump* suddenly.

Catching Dan's attention, I yelled out, "There is a helicopter approaching. He's coming in low and fast. I've just seen him above those pines over your right shoulder. We're going to get some help. That is one big, sweet-looking yellow helicopter."

Within mere seconds it seemed, that helicopter hovered over the lake, maybe twenty feet out from the shore. Rappelling ropes were thrown out the open doors, and several men in quick succession rappelled into the lake. Immediately, heavy firefighting equipment was lowered into the lake behind the men.

These firefighters were professional men. They had lengthy hoses coupled to high-powered pumps. No little hand pumps for these guys. Within moments of arriving, they began to blast burning peat moss clean off the rocks, and also hit the pine trees with extreme jets of water. Dan and I just stood there, dumbfounded. What a beautiful sight it was to see as professional firefighters began to slowly regain control of this runaway forest fire.

Running up to Dan and me just a little while later, Kyle, with relief in his voice, said, "Men, we have all the help we need now with these forest firefighters and their gear. We'll regain control and have this fire extinguished before nightfall. I sure do appreciate your willingness to help fight the fire."

Dan spoke up and said, "Kyle, I'm glad you were able to catch us. I hope our little contribution was in some way a bit helpful."

"Believe me, fellows, you were very helpful. Thank you so very much."

Before we parted, I asked Kyle, "Would you give me directions for the shortest way back to the parking lot at the campground that is located at the mouth of the Black River to Black Lake?

Kyle pointed us in the right direction, and with his parting words, said, "You should be able to get back to the campground within a couple of hours with reasonable paddling."

Dan and I bid Kyle goodbye with encouraging words, "You've got some good men working with you. They are truly an asset with their professionalism."

True to his words, Kyle was right on the money. We arrived back at the parking/campground within two hours. My, oh my, were we ever tired. Without talking, Dan and I both lay in the grass beside the canoe and tried to recapture some strength.

Finally, I spoke up, "Dan, we'd best prepare to go back to Winnipeg. I just looked at my watch, and it is after 6:00 p.m. We have a three-hour drive ahead of us, and it is going to take all the strength I have left in me to get us there safely."

Without a word spoken, Dan just nodded his head, and we set about to load up the car with our gear and the canoe.

About an hour into our return trip, I think Dan and I both noticed at the same time that we were rapidly running out of energy. Our stamina had left us, and we were running on raw determination. We had not spoken to each other in the last hour. I suspect Dan was running the immediate past over and over in his mind. I know I certainly was. It seemed I was reliving every moment of the fire.

"Paul, how are you doing?" Dan finally asked. "You are beginning to look like you are losing your concentration."

"I am losing it, Dan. You'd better keep me engaged in conversation. Otherwise, I may have to pull over to the side of the road and catch a few hours sleep."

"I'm sitting in the same spot as you, Paul. I'm just about spent for the day. Look, you always have a story to tell. Belly up to the mike, and let's hear a good, stimulating story. No holds barred. Let's have all the details."

"Thanks for the vote of confidence, Dan. I'm sure I can tell you something, but you, in turn, may have to tell me a story or two as well."

"Beauty before age, Paul. Although I must say you look anything but beautiful. You have a rather disgusting, smoky-smelling, charcoal sweat-streaked countenance."

That comment brought a good round of laughter from both of us, and I, in turn, complimented Dan on his disgusting excuse for a good-looking man.

"OK, Paul, we're done with the pithy comebacks. Let's hear something that will do the trick. We need to stay awake and aware of everything on this dark road. I'd hate to see a black bear or a moose or even a deer right now, and not be quick enough to respond with evasive actions."

"Right you are, Dan. I have another fire story for you. This one happened just a couple of years ago in the summer of 1981. I had gone to Lynn Lake, Manitoba, to drive for a company called Mid North Hauling. Basically, they ran hopper service between two different mines and the railhead in Lynn Lake. The Canadian National Railroad ran that service into Lynn Lake.

"Mining back in the early '80s was still going strong in Northwestern Manitoba, and in the area surrounding Lynn Lake, there were two mines that Mid North Hauling serviced with their hopper service. Basically, as drivers, we would go empty to one of these two mines and be loaded with either copper ore or zinc ore. Copper was hauled out of Leaf Rapids, which was south and east of Lynn Lake while zinc was hauled out of Fox Mine, which was south and west of Lynn Lake. The loaded hoppers were brought back to the railhead in Lynn Lake where they were unloaded of their ore onto railway hopper cars.

"On this particular trip I'm going to tell you about, Dan, I was working the night shift, which was comprised of twelve hours from 8:00 p.m. to 8:00 a.m. I'd left Lynn Lake shortly after the start of my shift as dusk was fast approaching. Highway 391 was a winding-up-and-down road where often you wouldn't see too far into the distance. In this instance, I had just crested a hill, and was letting my Jake Brake hold me back as I idled on the downgrade. A set of headlights alerted me to the fact that a vehicle was down in a rock cut to my left about a quarter mile ahead. At that point, I couldn't tell if it was on its roof or on its wheels, but that isn't where you would want to be as there was a substantial ravine, which had been filled in by a large amount of rock. As I approached, I felt I should stop and investigate. It appeared that this pickup truck was still on all four wheels, and as night had set in, I was able to see that the interior lights were on. I was possibly as much as twenty feet above it as I stopped, put my hazard lights on, and set my brakes. There were no real shoulders upon which to pull over on, so I had to remain on the highway.

"The rocks, Dan, were very large that I had to traverse down, so it took me a couple of minutes to get to the pickup. When I peered in through the driver's door window, I saw a man lying face down on the full seat with his feet under the steering wheel and his head against the right side door. I opened the driver's door and yelled several times, but got no response from the prostrate man. It was at that point I could smell alcohol and noticed a whiskey bottle on the floor still with a small amount of booze lying in it. I tried shaking this fellow's legs but to no avail.

On the other side of the pickup, I did the same. I opened the door and started to yell at this guy. There did not appear to be any visible injury to this individual, so I began to shake his shoulders. It was at that point he regained consciousness and tried to sit up. He began to yell back at me incoherently. I held my hands up and told him to settle down. I was there to try and help him. He struggled to get out of his vehicle, and when he was able he asked me for some matches. I told him I don't smoke and don't have any matches. Even if I did have a book of matches with me, it didn't seem like a good idea to give him any. That proved to be the right approach to take, and I soon saw why."

"That was a strange question to first ask you wasn't it, Paul? I would have expected he'd have asked you to either help him get his truck out of the rock cut, or take him to the nearest community where he'd be able to seek further help and assistance."

"That's correct, Dan, and that was my first thought as well. I asked him why he wanted matches and no further assistance from me. His answer caused immediate concern on my part. He wanted to ignite his truck and burn it to a crisp. I didn't have to be a brain surgeon to figure that one out. He wanted to get insurance money for his destroyed pickup. It was a Ford F150 and of very recent vintage, possibly a year old at the most. I could well imagine that the underside of his truck was utterly destroyed by the large rocks it had careened over on its way to the bottom of that rock cut."

"My response to him was an immediate no. I would not be a part of his insurance scam. I turned and started to climb back up the rock cut to my truck. At the same time, a northbound Silverwood's Dairy eighteen-wheeler stopped beside my rig, and the driver jumped out and came around to the ditch side of his rig. Seeing me trying to climb up the rock cut and that drunken fool trying to chase me, he asked if I needed any assistance. I told him quickly what that fellow was trying to do, that he wasn't hurt, just drunk as a skunk, and that I was getting out of there forthwith. The Silverwood's driver agreed with me, and we both jumped in our trucks, and left the scene just as that drunk got to the pavement."

"I've got a feeling that isn't the end of the story though, is it, Paul?"

"No, Dan, there is still more to come. I continued on to Leaf Rapids where I was slated to pick up a load of copper. It took quite a while to get loaded. There were a few trucks ahead of me, and as I recall, there had been a small breakdown in the loading process, which had backed things up somewhat. At any rate, I did get my load of copper, and once I'd pulled the tarps down over my loaded hoppers, I pointed my rig west and headed back to Lynn Lake. Incidentally, Dan, I was running with a set of B trains, and had five hoppers to re-tarp, so that took about an hour.

"About halfway between Leaf Rapids and Lynn Lake, which would have been about an hour's drive in either direction, was the location where the pickup had gone into the north side of the highway's rock cut. It would have been very close to a small lake called Adam Lake. It was now early morning daylight, and as I got within sight of the pickup, I observed that it was indeed on fire and burning brightly.

"I shook my head in disgust and muttered to myself, 'That clown must have siphoned some gas out of the fuel tank and banged two stones together to get a spark.' At the same time, I now saw him standing by the side of the road beginning to wave for me to stop."

Dan started to laugh and jokingly said, "So I presume you were a Good Samaritan, eh, Paul, and you stopped?"

"Yes, of course, Dan. *Not*. Traffic is light on that road, and he would likely stand there for a while longer before someone would pick him up, but it wasn't going to be me. What I did though was continue to Lynn Lake, and stopped at the local Royal Canadian Mounted Police precinct, which was located at the edge of town. I went into the cop shop and told the desk sergeant what I had observed last night, and what had transpired between that first encounter and the second encounter when his truck was on fire as I passed him by though he was waving me down."

"What was the cop's reaction to your statements, Paul? Do you think he believed everything you told him?"

"Yes, I do think he believed me because he said that kind of thing has happened a time or two before. Somebody trashes their vehicle and gives an alibi that he was cut off and ended up in the ditch. Obviously, the truck is damaged beyond repair, so the insurance scam gets him a fresh pickup. But today, he continued, that sucker isn't getting a fresh pickup. And with that brief explanation, he called on his radio to a car somewhere out there to proceed to Adam Lake and give that fellow a ride to town.

"After the desk sergeant took a brief statement from me, I continued to the railhead and released my load to the receiver. They have a huge fork truck that can pick up each hopper in turn and run it over to a dumpsite. One flip of a switch, and the hopper is upside down, and the loaded ore is dumped, and then the empty hopper is quickly returned to my trailer."

"I'd say you played that story out very well, Paul. Look ahead. There are the lights of Winnipeg. I think I can stay awake a little longer now, knowing we'll be parked in your driveway soon."

"We sure will, Dan. I don't have any more really short, short stories to fill in the gap between here and the driveway, so why don't I just turn on the radio and get the late news from CJOB."

Arriving shortly thereafter, Dan and I clumped into the house to be greeted by two very astonished women.

Shirley spoke up first with a wide-eyed and quizzical look on her face as she cautiously asked, "Paul, Dad, what have you two been up to? You look an absolute mess. Don't move any farther from the door. Stay where you are, and get out of your dirty boots. Your faces and hands are black with filth, and I'm sorry to say, but you both stink like soot."

Dan was a bit of a comedian at this point, and holding his arms outstretched, he laughingly said to Shirley's mom, Kay, "Come to me, my dear, so I can give you a hug and a kiss."

She responded with a disgusted look on her face, "No way, buster. You're heading for a shower to get cleaned up before you get any hugs and kisses from me."

Before Dan or I could retreat to a quiet spot where we needed to get cleaned up, the obvious question was asked by Shirley for the second time, "What have you two been up to, and why are you so dirty? And where are the fish you caught?"

While Dan and I were both giving a brief explanation, the girls were wide-eyed and slack of jaw, with mouths wide open in disbelief. It might have been hard to believe such a tale had it not been for the fact that Dan and I both did look and smell the part. We were firefighters that day and proud to be as much.

Shirley clapped her hands together and proudly exclaimed, "Paul and Dad, Mom and I are proud of you both. You both are our heroes. Now go and get cleaned up. You look awful and you stink."

## TWELVE

# MY FIRST JOB DRIVING SEMI-TRUCKS

"HI, SMITTY. I'M back in St. Thomas. The college graduation exercises were last night at the Masonic Temple in Toronto, and now, my one-year college experience and life on campus are done."

"Well, how about that, Dude. What are you going to do? Do you have any job prospects lined up?"

"I'm not exactly sure how I'll get into trucking, Smitty. I've never really driven anything larger than a three-ton straight truck, and that was with P.K. Hardware Wholesalers. I left them in September 1969, and went back to work on the railroad. I was with the CNR for a year up until September 1970 when I went to college. That pretty much brings you up to date, here and now."

"Dude, I would wager a bet that you'd have no trouble getting into trucking. You just need a break."

"So how am I to get a break, Smitty? I'll just walk into a trucking company and proclaim loudly, 'It's me. I'm here. Let the bells ring out. O'Brien will save the day. Give me a semi-truck and I'll get 'er done.'"

"Sure. That'll get you a job, you pot licker. You need some experience driving a big rig. Once you get that experience, you won't have any trouble getting that perfect job."

"Yes, I know that I need some experience, you purple pimple of puss, but how will I get it?"

"That's where I come in, Dude. It's Smitty to your rescue. Oh, and by the way, where did you come up with that crazy and disgusting phrase, 'purple pimple of puss?'"

"When I was sleeping last night, it just came to me in a dream, Smitty. When I woke up, I wondered where would I ever be able to apply such a disgusting phrase, and I immediately thought about you. I figured it would be a perfect fit. When the opportunity comes to use it, I'll just out with it. You got to admit, Smitty, it really is a perfect fit, eh?"

"Nice, Dude, real nice. I thought I'd help you get a trucking job, now I'm not sure about helping you after all."

"OK, Smitty. I'll be nice to you for a little while. What's your plan?"

"You better learn to respect your elders, Dude. You don't ever want to forget that I'm a year older than you. So here's my plan. The next time I get a night run, say down to Windsor, I'll take you along. When it's dark and Highway 401 hasn't much traffic, I'll teach you how to drive my rig. One lesson, and you'll be a qualified trucker."

"That simple, eh, Smitty?"

"Yes, it's that simple. The rest is up to you. You just have to know how to present yourself in the best possible light. You'll make yourself so attractive that any company will be begging you to come to work for them."

"Seems simple enough, Smitty. I shouldn't have any problem getting a job then. I'll just rehearse a few lines until I believe them and then I'll stand before the firing committee, I mean, the hiring committee, and *buda bing, buda boom*, the job is mine."

"That's pretty much it. But first things first. I have a trip to Windsor coming up tomorrow evening. That's Tuesday, the fourth of May for you, Dude. I'll leave Waldie Trucking's yard shortly after 7:00 p.m. I want you to be waiting for me at the Flying M Truck Stop just north of the Ford plant on Highway 4. Your car will be OK there. I'll drop you off there on the way back from Windsor."

"Got it, Smitty. I'll be waiting for you. I'll grab a couple of coffees to go too. So we're going to Windsor then."

"Yes, we're going to Windsor, but I have a delivery in Tilbury before I get to the Ford engine plant in Windsor. I was thinking I'd give you a driving lesson when I'm on the return leg of this trip to St. Thomas."

"What will you be hauling, Smitty?"

"I'll have a two-part load of cardboard boxes out of Consolidated Bathurst. Easy to haul and easy to unload. I'll gross out at 60,000 lb. Not too heavy, so we'll make good time."

The rest of Monday went fast, and Tuesday moved along quickly as well. I was anxious to get on the road with Smitty that night. It would be the first time I'd have a ride in a semi-truck, and I was plenty excited about it. I'd even grabbed a few hours of sleep earlier in the afternoon, so I'd be well-rested and fresh. I sure was looking forward to my driving lesson with Smitty.

I arrived at the Flying M Truck Stop at about 7:00 p.m. and immediately bought two large coffees to go. It would only be a matter of a few minutes, and Smitty pulled up in the truck parking lot. He was driving unit number 303, a 1968 Ford F900 conventional tractor with a 534 cubic inch V8 Ford Super Duty gas engine. The transmission was a ten-speed, and it was called a short forth regarding the shift pattern. It was a single-screw or a single-drive axle with a tag axle, or an axle that didn't have power but was used to better distribute heavier load weights. The trailer was a 40-foot Com-Car dry van.

Once onboard, I handed Smitty his coffee. There was a coffee cup holder that Smitty brought along, and it fit rather nicely on the dash.

"Let's rock 'n' roll, Dude. Thanks for the coffee too. We'll stroke this old girl to Tilbury, and I'll make a brief drop off. Well, I hope it'll be brief. You never know ahead of time how many rigs are ahead of you, waiting to get unloaded."

"Everything is good with me, Smitty. I'm as fresh as a cucumber. I must have got about four hours sleep earlier this afternoon."

I was going to enjoy this ride. It was a bit rough at times, but I expected that. After all, this was a big rig. I was going to drive a semi-truck as well, so I'd better get used to the characteristics of a tractor-trailer's ride.

As Smitty drove his rig through the exit ramp from Highway 4 onto the entrance ramp to Highway 401, I began to closely watch his every move. I needed to learn how this tractor was shifted gear by gear. It seemed simple enough. Smitty was light on the clutch, and pulled the gear shift effortlessly through the gears.

"Hey, Smitty, I notice that you are pushing the clutch pedal twice for every gear you shift. What is that all about?"

"It's called 'double clutching,' Dude. It makes for a smooth shift without any grinding of the gears. This tractor doesn't have synchromesh gears. If it did, you'd only have to depress the clutch and pull the gear straight through on that one clutch depression. Simple, eh?"

"Simple enough, Smitty."

"Where do you think you might apply for a job driving truck, Dude?"

"I was thinking about Thompson Transport. You know where their yard is, Smitty. It's just past Centennial Avenue, going east on Highway 3. They appear to have a substantial amount of equipment, both tractors and trailers. I also thought about Waldie Transport where you found your job. At this point, I was only thinking about local trucking companies. I'll have to check the yellow pages for London. I expect I could find a few trucking companies located in the London area as well."

"That sounds like it would work, Dude. When do you figure you will start your job search?"

"I figure that Thursday this week will be a good date to start my truck driving job search. Wednesday is just a little over three hours away, and while I don't know when we'll get back to St. Thomas, I expect it won't be until early in the morning. I'd probably be best advised to rest up tomorrow, and hit the ground running on Thursday."

"I'm impressed, Dude. It sounds like you've given this some thought."

"How about you, Smitty? Has Waldie Transport treated you well since you hired on with them?"

"Yes, they have, Dude. I've been given steady work since day one. I've had to learn on the job, so to speak, but I've watched how other drivers do things, and listened to them chatting with each other in the driver's room at the yard. On occasion, I've asked a couple of drivers how to do a particular task when I've been unsure. They are a good bunch. Nobody has refused to help me when I asked for help."

When you're having a good time, it seems that time passes quickly. I was enjoying my first experience in a tractor-trailer, and Smitty was a good teacher.

Yes, he did brag a bit about his driving expertise, but I pretty much ignored that.

The miles passed by in quick succession, and it seemed that in no time at all, we'd arrived at Tilbury. Pulling into the yard of the company where Smitty had a small delivery, he said to me, "Dude, you'd best come with me, so you can see how to talk to the receivers. You need to surrender your bills of lading to them. They'll then direct you to back your semi-truck into a dock where they'll unload your trailer. Sometimes, receivers and shippers will have an appointment time for you. You need to be there by that time, and actually, you need to be a wee bit early. That gives them time to do any necessary paperwork and still have you in their dock by the appointed time.

"These people are easygoing in that regard. They wanted this product tonight but didn't specify a delivery time, so we're good whenever we arrive."

The paperwork was done for the moment. The bills would be signed off when the load was counted and inspected on the receiver's dock. The next step was for Smitty to back his rig into the dock that the receiver opened for him.

"Everything is pretty straightforward, Smitty. I don't see any great issues here. Just follow the receiver's instructions and get your rig unloaded."

"Dude, use your mirrors carefully when you back up. Be sure to have them adjusted properly before you leave on a trip, and they will work well for you through the whole trip. It is especially important that they are properly set, so that you don't back into any other object, be it another trailer or a fixed object, such as a post or wall or stairs."

I'd like to think that I was a fast learner. In reality, I rapidly latched on to whatever Smitty showed me or instructed me to do or not do. I felt that this brief lesson in the middle of the night would do me in good stead.

When we arrived at the Ford engine plant in Windsor, the very steps Smitty had gone through at the Tilbury plant were repeated. These docks were inside the building; whereas, the docks at Tilbury were not enclosed whatsoever. It became immediately evident that backing into a well-illuminated dock in the middle of a dark night was immensely easier than backing into a dark outdoor dock.

Here again, there was no need for a delivery appointment. The receiver made note of the order that trucks arrived with deliveries, and we thus awaited our turn to back into a dock. Everything was done in an orderly fashion, and it was possibly about an hour, and a dock was opened up for us to back into.

"It sure seems evident, Smitty, that backing into a well-illuminated dock is far easier than backing into a poorly illuminated outdoor dock like we had back in Tilbury."

"Yes, that's a fact, Dude, but let me tell you another scenario where it can be difficult backing into a dock that appears well-illuminated when you are inside that dock, but when you are on the outside looking in, it is very dark."

"OK, Smitty. You've got my attention. Let's hear it."

"It is the middle of the day. The sun is shining brightly and you need to back into an enclosed dock. Sure, they have interior lights on, but the daylight is so much brighter, you can barely see beyond the entrance doorway. Now you've got a problem. Most receivers and shippers know that, so they have installed on the cement floor a strip of reflective material that reflects light. If you back your trailer up beside that reflective tape whether it is placed on just the driver's side or on both sides of your rig, you'll stay safe. If you cross that reflective tape, you're in immediate trouble. You will hit some stationary object or another trailer quickly."

"Thanks for the heads up on that, Smitty. I'll remember that for sure."

Our delivery completed and the bills of lading signed by the receiver, noting everything was in order with no damages or shortages, we pulled out from the dock, closed the trailer's barn doors, and proceeded to leave Ford's property. In a short amount of time and just a few miles through the city of Windsor, we were out on Highway 401, heading east toward St. Thomas and Waldie's yard. By then, it was 1:00 a.m., Wednesday morning.

"It's your turn, Dude. You get to drive my semi-truck. I hope you're a fast learner because I'm only going to give you one lesson, and this is it. You've seen everything I've done, how I've shifted under acceleration, and how I've downshifted when I've needed to slow to a stop or proceed at a reduced speed. You've seen how the paperwork is done, simple really, and you've watched how I've backed this rig up using my mirrors. You've listened to all the tips I've given you. Now it's your turn."

Well, that was quite a mouthful coming from Smitty. He gave a splendid speech all the while as he was downshifting and applying his air brakes, and as he maneuvered into a parking position at the Tilbury Service Center on Highway 401 eastbound.

"We've been running along for the past several hours, Dude, and now it's time for a break. Let's go into the service center restaurant and sit down. I need to replenish my starving body with some really good junk food."

"Sure, sure, Smitty. Your idea of healthy sustenance is probably a Coke and fries or a coffee and a donut. Well, I suppose I could go along with that. I'm personally thinking of a hamburger and fries, so I guess my idea of healthy replenishment isn't any better than yours."

I was soon enjoying my hamburger, and all the while, I was giving some thought to Smitty's motive for stopping for an extended break because that's exactly what it was. We were there for at least one hour. Was he hoping I'd forget some of the truck driving skills he'd shown me? I think he was hoping to get a couple of laughs, if and when I flubbed on my nonexistent truck driving skills.

"OK, Smitty. Let's get at it. I'm going to end up sleeping here at the service center if we don't get the show on the road. Maybe you'd better get another coffee to go. I don't want you to become bored and fall asleep while I'm driving."

"I don't think that'll happen, Dude. I'm taking a big risk here letting you drive my rig. If you screw up, we'll both be in some serious hot water. Here are the keys. Treat my rig with love and respect."

It got real quiet all of a sudden as I climbed into the cab of Smitty's semi-truck. He wasn't going to let me get away with anything. He was giving me the beady eye, as I started up old 303 and sat for a minute while waiting for the low air indicator to deactivate. Once the air was built up to 120 psi, I slipped the gear shift into first gear, eased out the clutch, and as they say in the movies, the rest was history.

Not a word was spoken for the next ten or twelve minutes while I flawlessly went through all the gears as I smoothly accelerated. Once up to highway speeds, we both settled in for a nondescript ride. Nothing out of the ordinary happened. I steered the semi-truck flawlessly. I mean, how could I not? The highway was nearly always straight. The lanes were plenty wide enough. The traffic was light. We weren't hauling anything except a load of sailboat fuel. I actually cast a few sideways glances at Smitty, and at one point, he'd nodded off and got himself forty winks.

Driving that truck was like stealing candy from a baby. It was downright easy. I could have driven right back to the yard, but of course, that wasn't going to happen. What if someone saw me driving Smitty's rig while he was snoozing with his head up against the right side window. We'd prearranged that I would stop at the Dutton Service Center, and he'd get back in the saddle as the real truck driver while I'd jump back in the right-hand seat and ride shotgun back to the Flying M Truck Stop where I'd left my car.

Just as I dynamited the air brakes, Smitty woke up from his power nap and asked, "What? Are we at the Dutton Service Center already?"

Now it was my turn to take a shot at Smitty. "What happened to you? You fell asleep fifteen minutes after I'd hit high gear. For nearly an hour, you were out cold. What's that telling you, Smitty?"

"OK. You're a bona fide truck driver, Dude. You can chalk that up to me being a really good driving instructor."

"I know you're right, Smitty. You're a really good driving instructor. The best in the business no doubt . . . Not. The fact is, I'm a natural at driving semi-trucks. I'm happy you lent me your semi-truck, so I could prove that to you. Mucho gracias."

Now back at the Flying M Truck Stop, I bid Smitty adieu and headed for home in my old reliable van. I had a bit of a smug smile on my face, and knew I'd be able to prove to any trucking company I was a semi-truck driver.

It wasn't as easy as I thought it would be. Getting a job as a truck driver was my sole ambition, and I was relentless in my pursuit. As I'd planned, I arrived in Thompson Trucking's office bright and early on Thursday morning.

I was a bit cocky, and had a swagger when I walked. I was living the part. I was a bona fide semi-truck driver. But I didn't have any resume.

How would I prove that I was a semi-truck driver if I didn't have any records of previous employment as a semi-truck driver?

What it amounted to was a bold, barefaced lie. I'd have to be very convincing in my determination to be employed as a semi-truck driver. So when Jerry Thompson came into the office and asked what he could do for me, I bluntly stated I wanted a job as a semi-truck driver.

"We don't need any drivers. What was your name again?"

"I'm Paul O'Brien. I live nearby. I want a job driving one of your semi-trucks." There I'd said it again.

Jerry sort of escorted me or pushed me out the door. Wow, that was a short interview. Well, basically, that wasn't an interview at all. So much for cold calling. I muttered to myself as I walked back to my van. "You haven't seen the last of me, Thompson. I'll be back."

That's exactly what I did. Every second day for a couple of weeks, I returned to Thompson Trucking and asked for a job driving trucks. And every time, Jerry escorted me to the door.

"I don't need any truck drivers. You're wasting your time coming here."

After a little better than two weeks of applying for a job every second day, I upped it by applying for a job every day. Would you believe it? After doing this for four days, on Friday, May 28, 1971, Jerry Thompson said in a very frustrated voice, "I'm sick and tired of you coming in here every day, looking for a job. I don't believe you know how to drive a truck, but today, I'm giving you a road test, and when you fail that test, I don't want to ever see your face again."

Jerry reached over and grabbed the phone on his desk and spoke into the receiver. "Van, come to my office. I want you to give this guy a road test."

Jerry told me to go outside and wait. His dispatcher, Van, would be out there in a couple of minutes to give me a road test.

Van approached me where I'd been waiting outside the shop doors. He wasn't the chatty type of person. Basically, he spoke in one or two syllables, "I'm supposed to give you a road test. We'll use that tractor over there. The unit number is 2601. I want you to check the tractor over then we'll hook up to an empty trailer."

Smitty hadn't shown me how to inspect any equipment, but I'd learned how to check out trucks when I had driven for P.K. Hardware a year ago.

Van stood behind me and watched me check out the tractor. It was the same when I hooked up to an empty trailer. Smitty had told me how to hook up the glad hands, and look under the trailer to make sure the kingpin on the trailer was locked into the fifth wheel. I made a thorough inspection and got no comments from Van, so I assumed he approved my inspection.

Van was brief and to the point. There was no extra chatter on his part. "OK, let's head into town. I'll tell you what to do as we go along."

I took my cues from him. If he didn't want any chatter, I'd keep my mouth shut. "Mum's the word" became my instant headliner.

"Turn right at the next intersection."

I followed through on his directives and completed a right turn perfectly. My trailer didn't jump any curbs, and I didn't cut off any cars.

I continued to drive for a couple of city blocks before Van spoke up again, and when he spoke, all he said was, "I want you to stop beside that dark gray manufacturing plant on your left side. You will back the trailer, turning it to your left so that you are beside this plant on the south side. Then make another left turn of 90 degrees. There is an outdoor dock that you will see once you have completed your second left turn backing up."

I had driven through a residential area, but quite suddenly, there were more factories as I looked further down the road. We had arrived at an industrial section of St. Thomas.

This was new territory for me. I'd never backed up before. Smitty had let me drive one time for about an hour, but he'd not let me back his semi-truck up.

However I will say this. I had closely observed Smitty when he'd backed his rig up, so I felt that was something I'd be able to do as well. So that is what I did. I backed that semi-truck up flawlessly, and I did it in one attempt. I had made two left-hand turns backing up, and I'd bumped into the dock perfectly. I did this all with one attempt. I did it easily and efficiently.

"Humph! Jerry told me you didn't know how to drive a semi-truck. That was perfect the way you backed up. I don't know anyone who could have done it any better than you just did. As far as I'm concerned, you have the job, and I'll tell Jerry to hire you immediately when we return to the yard."

Those were the most words Van had said that day when he'd constructed a few full sentences and basically hired me right on the spot.

Once I'd parked and dropped the trailer and put the tractor back in the same line as the other tractors, his last statement to me was, "OK, Paul. Meet me in Jerry's office."

Walking into the office a few moments later, Jerry stood up and came around from behind his desk. He extended his right hand to shake mine and said, "Van tells me you know how to drive a tractor-trailer. I'm a man of my word. If Van says you can drive, then you have a job. Be here Monday, May 31 at 7:00 a.m. You are hired on as a city driver, and you will report to Van in dispatch each morning when you come to work.

"Before you leave, see Beth in the front office. She has a few forms you will need to complete and sign."

Jerry turned on his heel and returned to his desk. That was it. No fanfare. Just the best words I could ever want to hear, "You're hired."

I truly believe that God had given me the skills I needed in order to drive a semi-truck. Incidentally, I have believed that all my life as a truck or bus driver.

In my long career spanning more than forty-five years behind the wheel and more than four million miles, I have never had a driving lesson other than the one Smitty gave me in the middle of the night back on May 4, 1971.

# THIRTEEN

# AN IMMINENT HEAD-ON CRASH

"Catherine, I'm so pleased that you and Cheyne and your two children, Andrew and Elaina, were able to come to Canada and spend some time visiting with mom and me. I know, my dears, that you and your family will be leaving today, but before you go, would you walk with me for a little while? I have three stories I wish to tell you.

"Cheyne, you may have heard parts of this first story if Catherine has recounted any of it to you, but I don't believe either of you have heard the second and third story I will tell you today as we walk together.

"Any time, Catherine and Cheyne, when I tell this story, it causes me to pause and reflect. I expect even now, as I recount it to you, I may have to stop in order to regain my composure.

"Cheyne, Catherine was a key player in this first story, yet she had only a very small part to play. In fact, were I to put a time element into this story, Catherine's part took only a nanosecond.

"I was so very tired—gut tired, emotionally tired, physically tired—to the extreme, yet I felt I had to push on. What would motivate me to push myself to this point? I'm not sure I can fully answer that question. Was it overconfidence in myself that I could drive beyond the screaming personal identification markers? 'Stop, Stop, Stop!' I screamed silently to myself. 'You will kill yourself if you continue.'

"But I continued, Catherine. I resolutely determined that my willpower was more than a match for my physical endurance."

"It was mid-September 1980. The day had been stellar. Warm sunny weather blanketed the State of Minnesota. I was driving my big rig north on US 59. In the near distance was Halstad. I had left Moorhead less than one hour ago."

"Cheyne and Catherine, I was driving double. This is a trucking term that is used by drivers to describe a particular type of trucking operation. There would be two drivers in the truck. One driver would be on duty and driving for a few hours. At the same time, the other driver would be resting in the bunk, hopefully, sleeping."

"My partner, Ron, was in the bunk, sleeping. He had an amazing ability to sleep when the truck was rolling. I found it difficult to sleep. I was into the fourth hour of my shift. We usually ran five-hour shifts. At the conclusion of that shift, we would switch out, take a break, possibly fuel up, and then hit the road again.

"Cheyne, I was slapping my face, pinching my legs and arms, trying to stay awake. The window was open. Fresh air was blowing on my face. The question in my tired mind kept repeating itself, 'Why was I hell-bent on working like this?'

"Catherine, I was dead tired. I had lost my ability to concentrate. Several times, over the past four hours, my mind had flipped into a place where I saw things, but nothing registered. That would sometimes last for several seconds. I would suddenly come out of that state, and realize I was sleeping with my eyes open.

"I was inwardly, silently, yelling at myself, 'Paul, STAY AWAKE! There is a southbound truck approaching.' Then it happened. I passed out. No. I didn't fall asleep. I passed out. When my head dropped to my chest, it hurt. My neck was stiff, and the jolt of my chin hitting my chest hurt. I snapped awake.

"'GOD!' I screamed in absolute desperation, Catherine. That scream for help spent my last breath. There was no air left in my lungs. With less than one second to a head-on impact, I knew instinctively, I was dead."

"Oh, Dad."

"His truck was a cab-over GMC Astro of mid-seventies vintage. I saw right into his eyes, Cheyne. His face had the look of death. His eyes were extremely wide open. His gasping open mouth revealed the absolute horror of that split-second moment. Eternities' hand clouded his face.

"I'm not talking several seconds here, Catherine. This all happened in the space of one second. My whole life flashed before my eyes. In that nanosecond, I saw past events in my life that were significant—childhood and teenage memories, my wedding to my beloved Shirley. I saw many personal life experiences that I had forgotten over my thirty-one years of life.

"In that brief nanosecond, Cheyne, I experienced every emotion a human would experience. I felt happiness and joy. I felt grief and sorrow. But the greatest emotion was immense sorrow.

"I instinctively knew I would never see you grow up, Catherine. You were my baby, the fourth of my children. You were so small, so tiny and fragile. I loved you so much. But my pain and sorrow were real. You would never know your daddy. He would only be a small picture you might look at once in a while.

"It is hard to explain something so personal, my dear ones. It is hard to place those vivid memories before my eyes and relive that moment. I feel it even now so fresh in my mind as if it had just happened."

Tears flooded my eyes as I spoke. My cheeks were wet with tears unabated.

"Something happened that was so dramatic and life-changing. Life had stopped for me, and I knew I was stepping through a portal into eternity. But it was as if hands had grabbed me and brought me back from the brink of death.

"Was it the hands of an angel sent from heaven's shores to thwart that impeding head-on crash? I personally believe it was. In extreme slow motion, that southbound truck came to my very windshield, yet we did not collide. I distinctly remember this and expecting metal and glass to shatter, I was surprised when the two cab-over trucks were parted by mere inches. His truck passed on my left side . . . in slow motion, Catherine. I looked into his side window and saw a look of utter amazement on his face. I'm sure my face reflected the same amazed look.

"His rig continued in slow motion to pass on my left side but didn't go into his right ditch, nor did his rig touch my cab or trailer. Yet I remained in his lane. He didn't stop but disappeared from my sight.

"Oh, Catherine. What happened in that brief moment of my life on the highway will be forever indelibly stamped within my being. I deserved to die, yet I was spared from death. I have often asked myself, 'Why did God spare my life? Why did He rescue me from the very brink of death?' Those are questions I will ask once my life is over and I stand on heaven's golden shore.

Another question I have more recently asked myself, Cheyne, was the fact that God spared the life of that other driver. Why? Both of our lives were spared. We were both on the brink of eternity, yet we lived.

"Is it hard to believe that God not only had a purpose for my life that I should continue to live, but that He also had a purpose for the other driver's life? Then we can compound this a little further, Catherine.

"Ron was sleeping in the bunk behind me, totally unaware of the immediate events unfolding before him, yet he was also spared imminent death. Again I ask the question, 'Why?' My only answer to those questions is that God's purpose in each of our lives had not yet been fulfilled. Only in eternity will those questions be answered.

Perchance, Catherine, that in eternity, I will have the delight and honor to meet those other drivers and learn of their lives after that moment when we each faced imminent death, yet we lived.

"Arriving back at my base terminal in Winnipeg, Manitoba, later that eventful afternoon, I walked into the terminal manager's office, and explaining what had transpired just a few hours ago, I resigned. I quit. I vowed within myself as I walked out of his office that I would never again run double.

"I didn't really want to quit, Catherine and Cheyne. I prided myself in not being a quitter, but this event was not the first time I had fallen asleep behind the wheel.

"I'm a little tired of walking for a moment, Cheyne and Catherine. There is a nice shady spot just up ahead, and the bench that is under that tree is a wonderful spot to stop and take a rest."

"This is a beautiful spot, Dad. Lake Ontario is so peaceful today, and the gentle breeze coming onshore is refreshing as well. Just enjoying the quietness and serenity of this place puts me in a very meditative mood."

"I often come here to sit and meditate, Catherine. It is one of my favorite places to become introspective.

"Allow me to continue, Catherine, and I'll recount to you and Cheyne my second narrative. The first time I had fallen asleep behind the wheel when it was my turn to drive had a lot of similarities to the story I just recounted to you.

"It was a warm summer night in August 1980, probably about the middle of the month. My partner, Ron, and I had picked up a load in Minneapolis, Minnesota, earlier that evening. This load was destined for Winnipeg and needed to be there by the next morning. We could easily do this trip within ten hours. I took the first shift, and Ron jumped in the bunk. Boy, that fellow could sleep.

"It's true. I was sleepy, but I felt confident that I could beat this momentary tiredness and handle my driving responsibilities with the professionalism that was expected of me. But it happened, Catherine. I fell asleep."

"This is how that event unfolded. Ron and I were traveling westbound on Interstate 94. Before we had passed the exit for St. Cloud, I had thought about going into the truck stop there and getting a coffee to go. But I didn't want to disturb Ron and so continued westward.

"Somewhere before the exit for Sauk Centre, about fifteen minutes after I had passed the exit for St. Cloud, I fell asleep at the wheel.

"When I think about it, Cheyne, it seemed easy to fall asleep. The evening had been warm, the highway was smooth and wasn't busy with traffic, the night was dark as I don't recall there being any moonlight. Suddenly startled, I inwardly screamed, 'What's happening?' Wow, was this ever a rough road. Again I screamed inwardly, 'Where is the road?' I was yelling these questions in quick succession in my mind.

"Can you believe this, Catherine? I was actually looking out the windshield and was completely lost. I didn't see any road in front of me. What I did see as I became aware of the situation unfolding before my tired mind was that there wasn't any road, but only grass and a fence running beside my right-side door.

"Now I was in a complete panic. Where was the road? What road? Where was I? Believe me, at that moment, I was completely lost. Catherine, I was so confused in my clouded mind, all I could think was that I was lost. Then suddenly looking out my left-side door window. I saw the road. There it was, the road, the road I was supposed to be on, but it was above me. I was driving fifty-five miles per hour in a ditch as I had not involuntarily taken my right foot off of the accelerator.

"I can assure you Cheyne, without even thinking that the truck might tip over, I took that big rig up the incline on a dangerous angle to the left and brought it onto the road.

"Catherine, do you think that moment, I was wide awake? I can assure you, I certainly was. I was very wide awake, and I stayed wide awake. It was then only a matter of driving for a few more miles before I pulled off at the Sauk Center exit, and went into the truck stop on the south side of that interchange.

"What do you think I bought Cheyne?"

"That's a no-brainer, Dad. You bought the largest coffee they sold to go."

"That's correct, and I never shared it with Ron either. Incidentally, Ron never woke up during that rough ride in the westbound ditch of Interstate 94.

"God had protected both Ron and me from certain calamity, and if you are thinking about the timeline here, Catherine, this near-disastrous event took place when you were barely three months old.

"Both of those events, which I have just described, happened in the summer of 1980 when I was driving for Canadian Great Western Express. Their head office was in Winnipeg, Manitoba, but your mom, you, Catherine, and your siblings and I were still living in Windsor, Ontario, at that time, so I was running out of their regional terminal located on Walker Road South in Windsor.

"I think we'd better turn around and head back to the house, and I'll tell you about this next story while we're walking back to the car.

"It doesn't happen every time a driver falls asleep that there is a traumatic event that immediately unfolds. This next event, Catherine, happened in the late fall of 1994. While brief and not like the other two events I just told you and Cheyne about which happened in the summer of 1980, it is nevertheless of a serious nature.

"When I think about it now, you were about fifteen and a half years old, and we were living in Niverville, Manitoba. I had graduated from Providence Theological Seminary in April of that year, and we had moved to Niverville from Otterburne. I had been driving for Jade Transport, out of Winnipeg, Manitoba, since May, and it was now November. Snow already lay a few inches deep in the fields and ditches, but thankfully, Interstate 29 southbound in North Dakota was cold and dry.

"Winter always seemed to come early in the west, and North Dakota was settling in for a long and cold one. I was running tanker service, and I'd picked up a hazmat chemical load earlier in the day in Winnipeg. This load was manifest for St. Paul, Minnesota, and as was so often the case, the bills of lading demanded an early morning delivery.

"Clearing United States Customs at Pembina, North Dakota, had been easy. My paperwork was all in order. I had a clear shot through to St. Paul. My intention was to run this trip nonstop as far as Rogers,

Minnesota. I would pull into the Union 76 truck stop on the north side of the Rogers exit, off Interstate 94, and enjoy an early breakfast before running into St. Paul for a seven o'clock delivery.

"Catherine, you would think that some of the lessons I'd learned many years ago as a younger driver would stick with me, but such was not the case in this event. I was running tired, and my workday would eventually extend to more than twenty-four consecutive hours on duty.

"I had been up all day. In fact, I had arrived at Jade's terminal early that morning and got my rig set up. But the shipper was slow in loading me, and I spent several hours waiting for this load of hazmat liquid chemical. By the time my paperwork and customs manifests were completed, it felt like I'd put in a full day and gone nowhere.

"There is no other way to describe it, Cheyne. North Dakota's highways were boring. They were flat. They were straight for miles and miles, and traffic was always light. I had gone through the weigh scales at Joliette, just a few miles south of the Canadian and United States international border. No problem there. Now the boredom set in. And with boredom, so often, sleepiness follows close behind.

"What was that? What had just flashed by the right side of my truck? I know you can't answer that question, Catherine, but I certainly can. It was a bridge abutment. I had just gone under the Burlington Northern Railway overpass, and I was far too close to this abutment for comfort. In fact, I was on the shoulder of the highway just a couple of inches from crashing the right side of my rig into that abutment, and at 60 mph too.

"Here is what had happened. I had fallen asleep several miles back. I really do not know how many miles I had driven with my eyes open, but I was not connecting the dots as they say. I guess you could say my head was on autopilot.

"God had spared my life yet again, Catherine and Cheyne. However, there were other times during my work history as a long-distance transport driver or even as an intercity bus driver when my life was spared as were those who were with me or near me.

"I'll try to make this story short, Catherine and Cheyne, because the car ride back to my home will not be long. This takes us back to

1973. I had only been driving as an intercity bus driver with Eastern Canadian Greyhound Bus Lines for a short time when we were suddenly very busy. I would experience working for the first time in my life seven days a week for a period of several weeks because both the Canadian National and the Canadian Pacific Railroads had gone on strike. Each railroad still operated passenger trains at that time. Soon the influx of passengers wishing to ride on Greyhound buses throughout Southern Ontario where I drove on scheduled runs with magnified many times over.

"Catherine, as I just mentioned, I was running back and forth from Windsor to Toronto and various points in-between. I had been doing this for at least a couple of weeks and not getting much rest either. Consequently, I was becoming fatigued. Yet the work was there, and the dispatches were relentless.

"I remember this one run very clearly even though we're stepping back in time more than forty-five years ago. I was on an express run from Windsor to Toronto in the middle of the day. I had gone by the Kitchener exit on Highway 401 and had also navigated through some highway reconstruction near the Cambridge exit. It was shortly after that point when I have no memory whatsoever.

"Cheyne, driving a bus with approximately forty-five people on board, I fell asleep. None of the passengers were aware that I was sleeping because I was still in control of the bus. Or was I? From that point where I last have any memory of driving the bus until I became aware of my surroundings would have spanned at least one hour. It is fair to say that I was sleeping, yet I had not closed my eyes. My head had not dropped to my chest, Catherine. I still controlled that bus through turns and passed slower vehicles, yet I was unaware of that.

"I had taken the 427 exit, off the 401, and traversed that road in the southbound lanes for several miles at which point I would have taken the eastbound exit to get on the Gardiner Expressway. That road would take me to downtown Toronto. I had just crossed over the Humber River Bridge when, all of a sudden, I seemed to come out of a trance or something like that. I was startled and confused. For a couple of moments, I couldn't remember where I was or where I had been or where I was going. Had I missed a couple of scheduled stops? What was my destination?

"I'll tell you something, Catherine and Cheyne, that kind of fear not knowing where you are or where you are going, yet you are operating equipment at highway speeds is very unnerving. Then it happened. All of a sudden, my memory kicked back in. I was going to Toronto, specifically the bus terminal on Bay and Dundas, and I would be there in just ten minutes.

"Dad, what did you do after that scare?"

"I did the most sensible thing that could be done. I called dispatch when I arrived in Toronto and told them I was extremely fatigued and wanted to cushion home. That meant that I just wanted to ride on the bus back to Windsor and not drive it. I didn't tell dispatch what had transpired, but I did emphasize I was too tired and wasted to be able to drive. I then took a few days off."

Shaking her head, and solemnly speaking to me, she said, "Dad, you have been protected many, many times over many, many years by God who loves you more than we could ever love you." She then squeezed my arm as we walked up the sidewalk to my home.

"I'm not entirely sure, but I do believe there were also times when I was unaware of God's provision of safety. Yet God stepped in and provided a way of escape from what would have been an inevitable crash or other dangerous situation.

"I marvel at the blessings and the safety I have received from God. I once saw a plaque somewhere in my travels, and the words written on it have never faded from my memory. It read, 'Safety is of the Lord.'

"I could never dispute that saying, Catherine and Cheyne. In all the many years and many miles I have driven commercial vehicles, whether they be bus or semi-truck, whether they be on the highways and byways of North America or even in the fields or rocky terrain of oil pipeline construction, I am constantly reminded that each mile I travel is with the presence of the One who created me."

# FOURTEEN

# A DIFFICULT SITUATION AND OTHER TRUCKING STORIES

**Going Through Hell**

"I WAS BEGINNING TO think that you weren't going to answer your door, Smitty. What are you doing, just lazing around? I know we got shut down today because of the rain, so does that mean you are going to just sleep the day away? If nothing else, come with me, and let's go to that '50s rock 'n' roll diner on Eighth Street, and enjoy a coffee and a piece of their famous strawberry-rhubarb pie. You know the restaurant I'm referring to. It's called Stuie's Place."

"Aw, come on, Dude. Since we arrived here in Dawson Creek in the middle of June, the sixteenth to be exact, we've been running seventy hours a week hauling gravel or sand or pit run rock all over the area, and as far away as Tumbler Ridge, British Columbia. Wes has kept us really busy hauling for John Dyck Trucking. Now it's Friday, July 13, and we finally get a rainy day. Why don't you chill out, Dude, or better yet, go bother the waitresses in the Voyageur Motor Inn Restaurant? I'm sure they'd be excited to see you."

"Sure, Smitty. You and I will be there soon enough for supper, and we can both jazz them with our wonderful charm and wit. But it is 2:30 p.m., and are you just going to sleep your day away? Seriously, I'm getting in the pickup and driving over to '50s diner in a couple of minutes. Get your shoes on and get in the truck."

It was the summer of 2012, and Smitty and I had flown out to Dawson Creek, BC, to work for a local trucking company, hauling sand and gravel from their own gravel pit, as well as at least a half dozen other pits in the area, from Dawson Creek to Tumbler Ridge, from to Chetwynd to Fort St. John, and even back into Alberta over to Grande Prairie.

We had indeed been busy, but we really did love the work. Most Sundays were off, so we had great opportunities to go to church. We had begun to establish ourselves at the First Baptist Church over on 113 Avenue, but this was Friday and a great time to grab a piece of pie in the middle of the afternoon.

Smitty happily exclaimed, "I'm glad you rousted me from my slumber, Dude. I'd probably have slept the whole day away otherwise. And this pie is to die for.

"I'm enjoying our summer work out here in British Columbia, Dude, but sometimes I miss hauling steel back in Ontario out of Windsor and Chatham. I just really don't know why the market was dropping for steel. But anyhow, we're getting to see some great mountain country, and I haven't run into any dull moments yet with our work. Speaking of steel, did you ever haul any steel, Dude?"

"Yes, I did, Smitty, on more than one occasion. I used to haul coils for Frederick Transport out of Chatham for a short while back in 1980, but I didn't really enjoy it because I had to load the coils in their dump bodies. That was awkward at best. But let me tell you of the first time I hauled iron beams back in the summer of 1988.

"I was running for Big Freight Transport out of Winnipeg, Manitoba, at that time, and I'd been dispatched from London, Ontario, where I'd dropped off a load of large air conditioners for a mall construction project. I had to run with my 48-foot empty flatbed over to Laval, Quebec, for a load of iron beams to bring back to Winnipeg.

"I get into this place to make my pickup, and I surmised by the questions I asked, the shipper assumed I was a greenhorn when it came to hauling beams. Anyhow, the boys loading my trailer screwed me up, and at the time, I didn't realize it."

"What did they do, Dude? How did they screw you up? Isn't it pretty straightforward loading iron beams?"

"Well, when you know what you're doing, it's pretty straightforward, Smitty, but I didn't know what I was doing, and so I totally depended on the shippers to load my trailer properly and in the safest fashion."

"You should have called me, Dude. I'd have told you how to load those beams."

"OK, Smitty, I'll remember that when I run into a problem I can't solve on my own."

"OK, OK. Let's hear your story, Dude. I'll try hard to keep my mouth shut for a couple of minutes. If you make your story go too long, you'll have to buy me another piece of strawberry-rhubarb pie."

"Smitty, stuff your napkin or something in your mouth, so I can tell you my story without you interrupting every time I need to catch a breath.

"These iron beams were all the same length at 50 feet, but there were several different widths. Some were quite wide while others were much narrower and lighter in weight. The shipper must have thought it would be humorous to load the larger iron beams at the sides of the trailer and the smaller iron beams in the center of the trailer. Bear in mind, these iron beams were all the same length, but their width dimensions were vastly different.

"I chained down this load in an appropriate fashion. These beams would not fall off the sides of the trailer while in transit. But some serious mistakes were made. While my chains touched the larger beams on the sides of the trailer, the chains did not touch every beam contained within the larger beams. These smaller, lighter beams were therefore not being restrained by chains."

"Oh boy, Dude! I think I know where you're going with this story and it doesn't sound pretty."

"Right on, Smitty. I know that you know where I'm going with this story, but let me continue.

"When I stopped to examine my load after just a couple of hours in transit, I realized to my horror that one lighter beam in the center of the trailer was beginning to squirt out at the rear of the trailer. It had already moved about three feet rearward. I knew that this was extremely dangerous. If this was to continue, my load would soon be lying on the highway. I couldn't even begin to envision the damage and possible loss of life to other motorists sharing the road with me."

"So what did you do, Dude?"

"Smitty, let me describe it this way. You know that I have always been self-taught. I have never taken any official lessons or courses on how to drive class 8 trucks. I have hauled virtually every kind of load which can be put on a semi-truck. I learned how to chain down large dimensional loads by reasoning within myself that certain forces would constantly be applied to the load when it was in transit.

"Did I ever make mistakes? Did I ever screw up? Yes, many times. And this time, I really felt like I was going through hell. What was I going to do? One thing for sure, I had to keep going.

"There was a phrase that was ringing in my mind as I looked at the predicament I was facing. I know you remember hearing about Sir Winston Churchill. He was the prime minister of Britain, back during the Second World War. Well, I idolized Sir Winston Churchill. He was a man's hero to me. I was not quite sixteen when he died on January 24, 1965, but I felt like I knew him well. I had read every book I could get my hands on pertaining to his involvement in the war effort. Did you know, Smitty, that Sir Winston Churchill was a key player in the success of Britain in defeating the Axis powers?"

"I think I remember hearing about him, Dude, but where are you going with this history lesson? I thought you were telling me about that iron beam load squirting out the rear of your trailer."

"Hang in there with me, Smitty. When I was looking at this load and wondering how to correct it, I remembered reading about a speech Sir Winston Churchill gave. This speech became very famous and was often quoted over the years. When he was the prime minister of Britain on October 29, 1941, he spoke to the boys at Harrow, his old school.

"Listen, Smitty, this is part of that speech which many have quoted over the years: 'Never give in, never give in, never, never, never—in nothing, great or small, large or petty—never give in except to convictions of honor and good sense. Never yield to force; never yield to the apparently overwhelming might of the enemy. If you are going through hell, keep going.'"

"OK, Dude. I think I've heard some of that speech in times past. So how did that speech work for you? How does that speech of Churchill's play a part in your iron beam load going south on you?"

"Let me answer your question this way, Smitty. I have practiced daily the fine art of keen observation. If others could do it, then I could do it. The *it* in this case was what to do with my load of iron beams.

"After carefully examining my load situation, I decided to make a pocket out of several chains so that I could contain this slipping beam, and with the proper tension on the chains combined with the movement of the trailer over the highway bumps and rough sections, my expectation that the beam would move forward was realized. However, my problem with this beam was only partially solved."

"I know where you are going with this, Dude. I expect that wayward beam was going to squirt out the front of your trailer. Am I correct in saying that?"

"You're right on, Smitty. That is exactly what happened next. That wayward iron beam began to squirt out from its containment with the other beams, in a forward movement. Now I had another real danger, and it was imminent. This beam, if not contained, would continue forward and puncture through my cab. I was in danger.

"Once again, having observed how my rear containment was successful, I created a new pocket with several chains, and again, the motion over bumps and a rough highway brought this wayward iron beam back to safe confinement with the complete load."

"Hey, that was good thinking, Dude. If I say so, I couldn't have done better myself."

"Coming from you, Smitty, that's a real compliment. I suppose now you'll want me to buy you another piece of the pie because you patted me on the back."

"I'd thought about that already, Dude, but I do need to save some room for the homemade meat pie special tonight at the Voyageur."

"So to cap off my story, Smitty, I arrived at my destination with a load of iron beams that had been safely transported over many miles and several days."

"What did you learn from that experience, Dude?"

"It's like this, Smitty. Stop and observe the situation. Think it out by playing before your mind all the different scenarios that could develop and what would be their ramifications. Be creative and inventive. Act accordingly and, if necessary, repeat the above steps as often as necessary until final success is realized."

"I got it, Dude. Let me put a cap on your story: 'NEVER! NEVER! NEVER GIVE IN! If you're going through hell, keep going!'"

**Night Run to Denver**

I'd been driving for Precision Truck Lines out of Woodbridge, Ontario for one year having hired on in October 2003. It was now December 2004, and Shirley was with me on this run from Toronto, Ontario, to Denver, Colorado. I had a morning delivery in downtown Denver, and this demanded that I run through the night to honor my appointment.

"Aren't you getting tired, Paul? I don't want you to push yourself beyond your limits. You have done that many times, and lest you forget, you have fallen asleep more than once. Your guardian angel has a busy job looking out for you and keeping you from harm."

"Shirley, I did get a couple of hours' rest late in the afternoon when I was waiting to get my partial load taken off the trailer back there in Omaha, Nebraska. I'm feeling well-rested as we speak, but how about you? Why don't you crawl into the bunk and get some sleep? If I continue to make good time as I have to this point, I may be able to get another couple of hours sleep and still make my appointment on time."

"If you're awake, Paul, then I'm awake. I'll tell you what. Why don't you tell me some of your trucking stories? That will keep both of us awake."

"You've probably heard all of my stories many times over, Shirley."

"I doubt that to be the case, Paul. I've heard you go on for hours with your stories, and it seems to me most of them are ones I've never heard before."

"OK, Shirley. Let me ask you if you've ever heard my short story about a B-52 bomber?"

"Come on, Paul. I don't even know what a B—whatever is."

"I'll give you a little history about the B-52 bomber, Shirley. It's a long-range American subsonic jet-powered bomber built by Boeing from 1952 to 1962."

"I'm not much with statistics, Paul, so get on with your story."

"OK, Shirley. But just to let you know, a B-52 bomber is huge. We're not talking about a small jet here.

"I was driving for Gravure Graphics when we first moved to Manitoba. This was in 1983 when I saw this B-52 bomber. I'd picked up a full load of large rolls of paper from Thorold, Ontario, probably around 45,000 pounds and was heading back to the plant in Winnipeg. Quite often, I drove a northern route through Michigan, Wisconsin, and Minnesota and would cross into Manitoba at Emerson from Noyes, Minnesota."

"I remember, Paul, that you had taken that road when I was riding with you on a few occasions. We went through some pretty country in Michigan and Wisconsin too. I especially liked going through Bemidji,

Minnesota. Wasn't that where the statue of Paul Bunyan and his giant blue ox named Babe were located?"

"Hey, that's correct, Shirley. I'd forgotten about that. Anyhow, I liked driving that road for some of the same reasons.

"I'd left St. Ignace, Michigan, on the Upper Peninsula less than a half hour earlier. The day was stellar. Blue sky and mild temperatures enhanced the beauty of the magnificently colored autumn leaves. At this point on US 2, the highway ran beside the north shore of Lake Michigan. Without exaggeration, the lake was less than 200 feet away to my left.

"There was ample bush country on the north side of the highway but mostly sandy shores on the south side. Suddenly, a deafening *whoosh*, and a B-52 bomber flew over the highway less than 200 to 300 feet in front of me. To say I was startled would be an understatement."

"Wow! Paul, did that bomber crash into the lake?"

"My immediate thought was that it was going to crash, but it didn't. Shirley, it leveled out just mere feet above Lake Michigan. It continued to fly south, and in a matter of a moment or two, it disappeared from my sight. As long as I could see it, the flight tangent did not change."

With a sudden degree of alarm in her voice, Shirley yelled out, "Paul, what is that directly in front of us on the highway?"

Immediately, I was in a state of high alert and yelled back, "Hang on!"

With an incredible thump and a loud scraping and tearing sound, I drove over a mattress and box spring lying directly in my path.

Continuing to show alarm, Shirley asked, "Paul, what just happened?"

"I noticed a car pass me just a couple of moments ago, Shirley. On his roof was that mattress and box spring. Evidently, it was ripped from his roof because it wasn't properly secured."

"Why didn't you try to miss it, Paul? I can still hear something scraping and dragging under the truck."

"Look out your window, Shirley, and focus on the mirror. Do you see that huge rooster tail of sparks? I believe the mattress is hung up under our tractor, and the springs are scrapping on the asphalt creating those sparks. I can see the same out of my side mirror as well."

When I ran over that mattress and box spring, my truck and trailer created a huge amount of debris from the broken box spring, but I couldn't shake the mattress out from under my tractor.

I was completing a pass of another eighteen-wheeler and so could not dodge the bed lying in my path. But the driver quickly noticed my situation, and slowing down quickly, he yelled at me on the CB radio, "Precision, bring your truck back into my lane. I'm slowing down, so you can get your rig off the highway."

I wasn't sure he'd actually seen me hit the bed on the highway. I figured he must have thought I'd lost a critical part from my tractor, and it was dragging and sending up a huge amount of sparks that basically cleared the top of my trailer. Bear in mind, my trailer was 13 feet, 6 inches high. That was a serious amount of sparks, and to another driver, it would look like my tractor was on fire.

It seemed that, almost immediately, several trucks heading eastbound on Interstate 80 lit up the nightlife with emergency CB warnings that my rig was on fire. To further create impact and importance to their warnings, they were fiercely blinking their lights to catch my attention.

"Paul, are we going to be alright? Are we safe? What's going to happen?"

Shirley was clearly worried, and I could hear that in her anxious and loud voice.

"Shirley, it's OK. I have full control of my rig. Sit tight, babe. I'm pulling off the highway."

I grabbed the mike of my CB and thanked that other trucker who gave me room to safely pull off the highway and, in the next breath, told Shirley to "sit where you are. Do not exit the truck. We are not on fire."

Climbing back into the truck several minutes later, I informed Shirley of our situation. "It is exactly as I suspected. The mattress got hung up on some suspension parts, and I am dragging at least three quarters of it. Furthermore, I can't free it up from under the truck, and I don't like working on it while on the side of the highway. It is dangerous anytime but more so in the dark. I feel like I'm an accident looking for a place to happen."

Now revealing fear in her voice, Shirley asked, "What are you going to do, Paul?"

"We've just gone by Kearney, and the exit for Odessa is maybe five miles ahead of us. I can make it to that exit without any problem. I've been there before, and a small truck stop is on the north side of that exit. When I get there, I'll figure out how to get rid of that mattress."

Back on the interstate, I drove at a greatly reduced speed with my hazard lights flashing. It became quite comical actually. Every rig that passed us, whether eastbound or westbound, had to excitedly inform me that my rig was on fire. I just gave up responding to their emergency proclamations. I was becoming hoarse of voice, trying to get back to them to inform them I wasn't on fire.

Odessa came into view, and I could hear Shirley's audible sigh of relief as she spoke to me. "Paul, I can't tell you how relieved I am to see that truck stop."

I made my way to the farthest reaches of the parking lot where I found a decent stretch of open gravel next to the weeds and the fence. Through patience and persistence, I was able to extract my rig from that stubborn mattress. Then I dragged that offending piece of junk to the nearest refuse container, and unceremoniously deposited it into the dumpster's dark open cavern.

"You still awake, Paul?" Shirley laughingly asked me.

"Hahaha! I have no problem in that department, Shirley. But I'm losing time, so I better get the show on the road. We still have a long way to go and a short time to get there, and I don't want to be a day late, and a dollar short."

Back on Interstate 80, heading west, both of us had entered into a quiet spell. It was Shirley who finally broke the silence.

"You never did finish your story about that bomber, Paul. Was that all there was?"

"You're right, Shirley. Where did I leave off when we busted up some poor fellow's mattress and box spring?"

"You said you saw that bomber disappear into the horizon, and it was just above the water as it vanished."

"That's correct, but I couldn't figure out why it was so low and flying so fast. When I arrived back in Winnipeg, I phoned our friend, Hillford, and asked him what he thought might have been happening with that B-52. Remember, Shirley, Hillford had a commercial pilot's license and flew a DC-3 out of Winnipeg into Canada's far north, to Nunavut and the Northwest Territories, as well as the northern parts of the three prairie provinces."

"I do remember Hillford. What did he think about that B-52?"

"Something I hadn't thought about, but Hillford suggested that the bomber was on a training flight and was endeavoring to fly beneath Chicago's radar, after which, at a point close to the Windy City, the pilot would pull up to a safe height. He was working on an element of surprise. Hillford further suggested that Chicago knew what was happening, and was working with the pilots of that B-52."

"Paul, that seems like a plausible conclusion, which I will accept."

Both Shirley and I had grown quiet, and as the miles passed beneath us, and I had settled into a state of lethargy. It was my sweetheart who noticed my fixed stare and startled me with her loud exclamation, "Paul, you're drifting off into Never-Neverland. Pay attention to your driving!"

"Oh yes . . . right," I exclaimed. "Thanks, Shirley."

"You used to tell me, Paul, about the times you'd take our family pet dog Peanuts with you on some of your trips. Didn't he just sit on the floor over here by the right side door and watch you? If you appeared to be sleepy, wouldn't he get up and come over to you and start pushing on your leg with his snout?"

"You're right, Shirley. He'd do that as many times as he thought I was getting sleepy. When I stopped and crawled into the bunk, he'd crawl in after me, and we'd both get some sleep."

"Well, I'm not your pet dog, Paul, but you'd better stay awake. I'll tell you what. Give me your tire thumper, and I'll keep you awake with that when I thump it on your leg."

"That's not going to happen, my dear. I guess I'll just have to tell you another story or two."

"They'd better be good stories, Paul, or you'll talk me to sleep."

"I don't think I've ever told you this story, Shirley. Charles was just ten years old when he wanted to spend the summer trucking with me. This was back in 1988. I'm not sure of the month, but it was during his summer holidays, and I'm thinking it was in August."

"Get back to the details, Paul. You're just waxing eloquent on fluff."

"Boy oh boy, Shirley, if I ever write a book, I'll get you for my editor. You'd take all the fat fluff and turn a big book into a scrawny quick read."

"The story, Paul, the story please."

"I was driving for Arnold Brothers Transport out of Winnipeg, and I'd just picked up a load destined for Vancouver. I'd checked my load, my rig, and my paperwork. Everything was in order. The trailer had just been repaired. It had been brought into the garage with two leaking hub seals, both of which were on the left side. The repair order stated everything was restored and in good condition.

"My trip was going along smoothly as we crossed the prairies from Manitoba, through Saskatchewan and through Alberta. With the Alberta foothills behind me, I'd now crossed into British Columbia and pulled off into a trucker's brake check area.

"It was evening, maybe nine or ten at night, and Charles was asleep in the bunk, so I tried not to disturb him but quietly climbed out of my rig. I checked all my brakes and all were temperate, not cool or hot. There were no hot brakes which might indicate an improper brake setting.

"At this time in trucking history, Shirley, drivers still had to go under their trailers and manually check and set their brakes. I had done this in Winnipeg. The prairies are flat, and the traffic was relatively light. I had no reason to use a heavy brake application at any time thus far on this trip. This of course would now change. I was going to pull some heavy upgrades, and the downgrades would demand appropriate braking to maintain greatly reduced speed and good control.

"There was a couple of times it felt like my brakes might be fading, but I was operating my semi well within its capabilities. It wasn't until I came down the last steep grade westbound into Golden, BC, on Highway 1, and had pulled into the provincially run weight station, that

I noticed in my rearview mirrors I had a problem. Actually, it appeared to be a serious problem.

"Stopping on the scales, and with more than sufficient lighting both the scale master and I noticed an incredible amount of smoke coming off what appeared to be all my brakes, tractor and trailer. The scale master just shook his head with a look of disgust. I'm sure he thought I was a greenhorn, a flatlander from Manitoba. However, he did give me a green light to proceed."

"What did you do, Paul? Were you having some serious brake problems or were you not paying attention to the downgrades, and using way too much brake?"

"No way, Shirley. I'd driven that road many times. I knew when to brake and what speed to enable me to maintain control. But what I did do was pull into the Husky Truck Stop, which was just mere yards from the weigh station.

"It was then I discovered that the garage in Winnipeg had not changed out the old brake pads, which had become soaked in hub oil. All they had done was replace the seals and top up the hub oil."

"How did you figure that out, Paul?"

"Really, it was quite simple, Shirley. I crawled under the trailer, and with my torch, I looked at the brake shoes and smelt them too. I could see some oil saturation on them, and the smell was not of burning brakes but rather that of hot oil."

"Was that making the smoke, Paul?"

"That's exactly what it was, Shirley. The brakes were smoking from hot oil on the pads, not misapplied braking."

"But I also noticed brake smoke from my tractor brakes and knew exactly why they were smoking. I wasn't getting sufficient braking from the trailer brakes, so the tractor brakes were being overworked causing them to get very hot and smoke."

"Did you have to find a repair garage and get your trailer brakes fixed again?" Shirley asked, visibly concerned.

"No, I didn't, but what I did was get under my tractor and reset my brakes. Then I notified dispatch in Winnipeg and apprised them of my situation. Of course, they asked me what I wanted to do.

"We both knew that repair facilities did exist, but I would lose considerable time getting repairs, which would consist of new brake shoes on the left side of the trailer. I suggested taking the Thompson Canyon route on Highway 1, rather than going over the Coquihalla Pass on Highway 5."

"Paul, what would have happened if you were unable to control your rig on the downgrades?"

"That wasn't going to happen, Shirley, because I reduced my speed even more than I normally would. With my Jake Brake and good tractor brakes, and of course, good brakes on the right side of the trailer, I arrived safely in Vancouver.

"There are runoffs with a huge amount of soft gravel at the base of several steep downgrades, and their purpose was to get a rig safely stopped if the driver was unable to control his equipment at a safe speed. I was determined, Shirley, not to use a runoff."

Shirley, bless her heart, kept me awake and operating in my right mind. I'm left-handed, of course. But I digress. After a rather exciting night run, the early morning sun lit up the Denver horizon. We'd made it. Then to get unloaded. Some serious time in the bunk never looked so good.

## First on the Scene of an Accident

"Hi, Paul. I woke up and noticed you weren't in the bunk with me. Where did you go?"

"I just got a message on my Qualcomm from dispatch in Toronto. Qualcomm is a satellite-based mobile communications system, which provides real-time messaging and position reporting between a rig and the home base. We are going to Salt Lake City for a reload, and it is destined for Toronto. That means we should be home in time for Christmas, Shirley. So I was just outside, giving my rig a good pre-trip inspection. Everything is copasetic. We're on our way."

December is cold in Colorado and Wyoming, but on this particular day, the late afternoon sun seemed to have a little warmth in it as Shirley and I began to make our way west on Interstate 80.

We'd left Denver and run north on Interstate 25 to Cheyenne, Wyoming.

But it was, at the moment, a dark, moonless night when we arrived in Rawlins, stopping for fuel and an evening meal.

Once we were back in the truck and on our way, Shirley had quietly asked, "Paul, how come we seem to be running more in the dark these past few days? It is much more delightful to be able to see all the different terrain, but all I'm seeing is our silhouettes in the windows."

"I prefer running during the daytime as well, Shirley, but once a trip gets established with nighttime running, it can be hard to break that cycle. And when dispatch gives you a morning pickup appointment with the shipper, you can really become locked into running through the night."

"I looked at my atlas earlier, and we had approximately 310 miles to run from Rawlins to Salt Lake City. I should be able to do that in six hours. It was 9:00 p.m. when we left the truck stop. We could be there by three in the morning, but what I'm thinking is that we'll shut it down at Evanston, Wyoming, in about four hours. We'll be pretty much on the state line with Utah at that point. That would give us about five hours' rest, and we'd still be on time if we left at six in the morning."

Between two big yawns, Shirley managed to blurt out, "You're the truck driver, Paul. I'm glad you know how to figure all that stuff out."

"Crawl in the bunk, Shirley. I'm good for driving at least four more hours."

The miles quickly passed beneath me as I relentlessly pushed my rig ever westward. I had covered at least 150 miles when Shirley poked her head out between the curtains of the bunk and startled me with a comment, "Paul, sorry to startle you, but I just couldn't sleep, knowing you might be getting tired. I'm coming back out into the cab. Maybe you could tell me another trucking story?"

"Aw shucks, Shirley. I was hoping you get some rest. But come on out. You know I just absolutely love your company, my dear. Make yourself comfortable, and I'll tell you about the time I nearly froze."

"You just made me shiver when you said that, Paul, and it is cold outside, so maybe you'd better put a bit more heat in this truck because I don't want to freeze," Shirley laughingly said.

"This was back in 1984 when we were living in Winnipeg, and I was running for Gravure Graphics. It was bitterly cold, probably around -15°C. That cab-over Freightliner had been giving me some problems. The alternator was starting to self-destruct, and I knew it but I also knew I had strong batteries, and I'd be home in less than two hours. What I wasn't expecting was that I'd get pulled into the weigh station at West Hawk, Manitoba, right on the provincial line with Ontario. The scale master said I was overloaded on my drives.

"Wouldn't you believe it, Shirley? While I was discussing my weight problem with the scale master, he pulled in an Arnold Brothers Transport rig with the same problem. He was overweight on his drives as well.

"The scale master was firm. We couldn't leave until we were able to scale out legal. It was Saturday night, and if both of us ran back to Kenora to get our loads restructured to make us legal, that wouldn't happen until Monday."

"My goodness, Paul, your alternator was malfunctioning. Didn't you say it would be nip and tuck just getting your rig to Winnipeg?"

"Shirley, I was running without lights. Mind you, it was still daylight when I was stopped at West Hawk, but I was also running without heat. I had put on extra clothing, so up to that point, I wasn't too worried about the cold. Oh, and by the way Shirley, the Arnold Brothers driver was our neighbor Jim who just lives in the next block on our street. Well, Jim called his dispatch, and asked if they'd send out an empty trailer with a Tow-motor, so he'd be able to reorganize his load. His dispatch said it wouldn't happen until Sunday morning. Jim said he was OK with that.

"I mentioned to Jim at that point that I'd be willing to pay for the other driver to take a couple of pallets off my trailer and run them to Winnipeg with his extra pallets. He was sure that would work out.

"By then it was dark. I was going to stay in my truck through the night, and I didn't want to run the heater. The alternator had quit by then, and my tractor was running on batteries that were slowly losing their charge."

"I remember now, Paul, some of that situation there at the weight station in West Hawk. Didn't your truck eventually shut down and left you stranded?"

"It wasn't quite like that, Shirley. Jim woke me up just after midnight. The weigh station had closed for the remainder of the night, and this was something they rarely did. So he came over to my truck and knocked on the driver's door. When I opened the door, he said, 'Let's get out of here. We can forget about being overloaded. Let's make a run for it and get to Winnipeg tonight.'"

"But you were basically broken down, weren't you, Paul?"

"That old Freightliner was still running, so I asked Jim to run behind me to Winnipeg. By then, I was extremely cold. I had on two parkas and a couple of pairs of jeans. I said to him that I had to run without headlights and heater, but that if he was good with it, I'd run ahead of him. If I pulled over to the side of the road, it would mean my engine would have finally shut down because the batteries had fully died.

"Jim assured me he'd follow me and not leave me stranded if it came to that."

"You were crazy, Paul. What made you think you could run a dark highway in the middle of the night without headlights? Not only that, but run without a heater in some very cold weather when you were already very cold?"

"In retrospect, maybe I was crazy or stupid or both, but I knew that my tractor would die, and then I'd have to get a wrecker from Winnipeg to come out to West Hawk and tow me into a repair facility back in Winnipeg. I just figured that if I could run, I'd have a better chance of making to Gravure Graphics, than if I remained parked at the weigh station. And of course, the over-riding factor was that, if I did run, I wouldn't need to worry about my overload situation.

"So that is what I did, Shirley. Jim stayed behind me and used the high beams on his headlights to shine past my rig, so I'd be able to see some of the road before me. That was a bit nerve-racking, to say the least, but I pressed on. I'd become so cold I'm not sure I was thinking everything through appropriately. When you get that cold, you can't think straight, and you can end up doing some crazy things. What I was doing was crazy, and I will admit it."

"Paul, didn't you rationalize that if you were stopped by the Royal Canadian Mounted Police, you'd end up paying a pretty hefty fine?"

"I wasn't rationalizing anything, Shirley. I was so cold, I could barely fix my mind on what had to be done. I just wanted to stop and crawl in the bunk and sleep."

"I remember more of this event now, Paul. You didn't make it to Winnipeg with that Freightliner, did you?"

"No, I didn't make it to Winnipeg. My tractor finally gave up the ghost. I ran the batteries dead. About two miles west past Highway 12 exit to Steinbach, I finally coasted to the shoulder and set the brakes. Jim pulled over to the shoulder behind me and helped me get into his truck."

"He knew I was freezing, so he grabbed a heavy blanket from his bunk and got me to wrap up in it. He set his cab heater on a high setting and drove in his shirtsleeves while I basically shook uncontrollably."

"I was so cold, Shirley, I couldn't talk. I tried to say something a time or two, but my voice was so hoarse and my lungs hurt so much. I just sat still and prayed I'd make it home."

"If Jim had not been there to help you, Paul, you would have frozen in your truck before the light of day Sunday morning."

"I believe that would have been the case, Shirley. Jim got me through that night and got me safely home."

"I remember that I was away for the weekend at a ladies' retreat, and had a babysitter stay with the kids Friday night, all day Saturday, and Sunday until I arrived home that afternoon."

"Do you remember the name of that babysitter, Shirley?"

"No, I don't, Paul."

"Her name was Marlene. When Jim dropped me off at our home, I tried to get in, but I'd forgotten my keys in the Freightliner. I banged and banged on the door. She wouldn't open it. I guess I made so much noise, I awakened our oldest child. Colleen came to the door and asked who was there. When she knew it was me, her dad, she opened the door."

"Paul, I truly believe your guardian angel was working overtime that night."

"What is the temperature outside our truck tonight, Paul? I saw that it was about minus twenty degrees Celsius when we left the truck stop back in Rawlins."

"It's still about the same, Shirley, minus twenty degrees Celsius. We are just fifteen miles away from Evanston where I'll shut down for a few hours."

We fell silent for a few miles, both of us lost in our own thoughts. I was happy this Kenworth W900L had some good heaters, and I was looking forward to taking a few hours' break at Evanston. Little did I know that, within a couple of minutes, my thoughts of a warm sleep would vanish.

"Shirley," I loudly said with a great deal of alarm in my voice, "I don't like the way that eighteen-wheeler just passed me. He was way too close to my side door mirror, and he nearly side-swiped my semi. He's driving erratically, and has pulled back into the right lane too quickly putting his right side onto the gravel shoulder. Now he has drifted back into the left lane just as suddenly."

That driver must have realized he was drifting back into the passing lane, and tried to pull his rig back into the right lane. But he ran onto the left lane's gravel shoulder, and then overcompensated in his steering trying to get his rig back on the asphalt. That's when the inevitable happened. His rig started to lay over on its left side.

"Shirley, hang on," I yelled. "I'm going into emergency braking. We have to make a sudden stop. That rig in front of me lost control and laid his truck down on its side. He is sliding into the right-side ditch."

I was so close to that sliding semi that I couldn't stop until I'd passed by about one hundred feet. I placed my emergency hazard lights on, and yelled at Shirley, "Stay in the cab. Don't get out. I need to get back to that accident, and render any assistance I'm able to give."

I grabbed my parka and bailed out on the run. The other driver's semi had turned one hundred and eighty degrees as it slid into the right-side ditch. His trailer was facing west and his cab was facing east.

I quickly covered the one hundred feet, and found that the driver was trying to sit up on the ground. He was maybe ten to fifteen feet from his overturned cab. The cab of that Kenworth T2000 had split wide open just behind the driver's seat. There was another driver in the bunk who was trying to extricate himself from the cab when I ran up. I assisted him and got him to sit down beside his partner.

It was at that point I realized the driver had some formidable head injuries. His co-driver appeared to be unhurt. I told the co-driver to keep his partner sitting up but not to let him try to stand up. Both drivers were beginning to enter into shock and were shaking violently.

I grabbed my cell phone out of my pocket and called 911. I was able to tell the emergency 911 operator where this semi-truck had overturned, and stressed that there were obvious head injuries on one driver. The other driver appeared to be without any visible injury.

I was able to walk right into the truck through the huge separation in the roof. The cab and bunk were a one-piece unit, but they had parted by better than two feet. I found some blankets in the dark and quickly returned to cover up both drivers.

The co-driver who had been in the bunk asked me if he could use my cell phone. I remember he called a California number and talked with his company briefly.

Emergency first responders arrived on the scene and were able to attend to both drivers. They were placed in the ambulance and taken to Evanston's hospital.

Wyoming state troopers asked me if I'd witnessed this accident, to which I affirmed I had. A brief discourse took place, and then a state trooper said I could leave.

As I climbed back into my own rig, I was met with a wide-eyed stare from Shirley, who questioned me in a halting voice, "Are those drivers going to be all right, Paul?"

I assured her that they were in good hands, and then blurted out, "My feet are frozen. I was driving in my slippers, Shirley, and I didn't even think to put on my boots before I jumped out of the truck."

"I have no doubt your feet are freezing. You have been out there for nearly one hour, Paul. And, Paul, you were telling me about the time you nearly froze back in Manitoba when your truck broke down on Highway 1. Do you have something going on with the cold that I should know about?"

I looked at Shirley with resignation written all over my face, and humbly said, "I think I just learned a much-needed lesson tonight. I will never again drive in my slippers. From now on, I will always wear appropriate footwear."

"Paul, explain to me what appropriate footwear is for you."

"Boots, Shirley, boots."

# FIFTEEN

# A BUFFALO STAMPEDE AND MORE TRUCKING STORIES

### A Stampede on the High Plains

"HELLO. HI, SMITTY, where are you calling from today?"
"Hi, Dude, how are you doing? I'm down in Ohio, on Interstate 75, just north of North Baltimore. I was wondering where you were as well. Actually, I'm going to stop at the Petro Truck Stop and grab a late lunch."

"Aw shucks, Smitty. I wish I was near you because I'd make a stop there as well, and have lunch with you. It would be good to say hi to Jessie, our favorite waitress. I haven't seen her since I started running contaminated nuclear to Utah. Fact is, I made my delivery yesterday at Blanding, and I'm up in Wyoming right now. I've been running some US highways, working my way north, and right now, I'm on US 20, south of Thermopolis."

"Guess I won't see you at the Petro today, Dude. You sure do get around. When were you last home in Cobourg?"

"Hum . . . let's see. I left with the load of contaminated nuclear waste from Port Hope about three days ago. Now I'm heading for Saskatoon, Saskatchewan. I'll pick up a load of yellowcake for Blind River, Ontario. Then I hope to get something back in Sault Ste. Marie, Ontario, for Toronto. From Toronto, I'll head home for a couple of days in order to reset my logs."

"You're sounding pretty good, Dude. Did you get that new Bluetooth headset you were talking about?"

"I'm talking to you right now on it, Smitty. It's worth every dime I spent on it. Your voice is clear, and the sound quality is great."

"I'm thinking I'll get one as well, Dude. Well, I'm just getting off Interstate 75 right now, so I guess I'll say goodbye."

"Wait a minute, Smitty. I'm seeing something strange up on the horizon. It looks so small, but there are so many black dots moving quickly from my right to my left. I must be at least a mile away. I can't really tell what it is yet, but hang on a bit before you jump out of your truck."

"I'll hang on, Dude. Let me know what's happening."

"I can't tell yet, Smitty, but there is no way I can count how many there are. I'm thinking maybe wild horses. I'm not sure cattle can run like that.

"Smitty, I think they are buffalo, and they are moving very fast. Oh wow, they are looking more like buffalo as I get closer to them. I believe this is a buffalo stampede happening right before my eyes.

"There is a bridge up ahead, Smitty. I'm sure I'll get there before the buffalo, and I think they are going to run right through under that bridge. Hang on a minute more. I'm stopping now.

"Smitty, I've never seen anything like this. The bridge is over a dry gulch, and they are moving incredibly fast toward it. It is wide enough for me to stop my rig on it without impeding any traffic from either direction. I've jumped over to the right side of my rig, and got the side window down. You're not going to believe this, Smitty. These buffalo are moving fast, and as they approach the bridge, they're starting to line up to run under it. They were spread out, now they are cramped together, but they haven't slowed down one bit."

Then I was screaming in excitement, "I've shut my truck off, Smitty, and the noise is deafening as they're approaching the bridge. This is amazing. They've narrowed down to about six running abreast from maybe a couple of dozen abreast. They haven't slowed down and they aren't running into each other.

"Smitty, they're now beginning to run under the bridge. Wow! The noise is incredible. There must be two or three hundred buffalo. They're running flat out, and the only ones that can see where they're going are the six buffalo in the lead.

"This is hard to believe, Smitty, but I'm witnessing something I've never seen before. The rest of the buffalo are basically running blind. Their noses are maybe as much as a couple of feet behind the tail of the buffalo in front of them. That is all they are seeing, the rump of the animal in front. And another thing, Smitty, their strides are all the same. They are keeping perfect pace with the one in front of them and the ones beside them. Their front legs are extended in unison as they propel themselves with their hind legs which are also in unison.

"Smitty, six buffalo were leading at least a couple hundred or even more, but I looked out my left side window, and they are spreading out again to run maybe fifteen or twenty abreast after they've passed under the bridge.

"It's hard to tell exactly how fast they are stampeding, but I'm estimating that they are running flat out at a minimum of 30 to 35 mph. They are extremely agile as they turn to run under the bridge. I'm so amazed they don't crash into each other."

"Dude, are you taking some pictures of this stampede?"

"Oh nuts, Smitty, I didn't even think to grab my camera. It's too late now. I don't want to leave the window and get it. I'll miss some of this stampede if I do.

"The dust is intense, the noise is intense, and the stampede of a couple hundred buffalo is intense. I know I'll regret not using my camera, but I doubt I'll forget this scene anytime soon, Smitty. I only wish we were running double and you could see what I'm seeing."

"Dude, you don't wish that as much as I wish it. What a sight it must be to see so many buffalo stampede and to be on a bridge right above them as they stampede through that dry gulch just a few feet below you. I'll tell you right now, Dude, I'm one jealous trucker."

"Believe me, Smitty. This is one of the most awesome sights I have ever seen. They are gone now, and the last one to run under the bridge was still running in unison with the very first ones leading."

"Dude, you're going to regret forever that you weren't able to capture with a movie camera the sight you just saw. I don't think I'll ever have an opportunity to see what you have seen."

"Smitty, I doubt that I'll ever see a stampede of buffalo again in my lifetime either. Something like a buffalo stampede just doesn't happen every day, and besides, what are the odds of witnessing something like this again, and being so close to it as it happened? I felt like I could have reached out and touched their heads as they ran under the bridge.

"Oh say, Smitty, would you say hi to Jessie for me. Tell her I'd send her a postcard of what I just saw, but I don't know where I'd find one."

"OK, Dude. I'm heading into the restaurant now. I'll tell her that the wiener says hi."

"Talk to you again soon, Smitty. I'll call you tomorrow morning. Stay out of the snowbanks today if you find some. Being that it's July, I doubt you'll find any."

"Yes right, Dude. If you go swimming, you'd better wear your parka so you don't get a sunburn, and better yet, take your ice saw so you can cut a hole in the ice.

"July. Did you say July, Dude? Had me scared you were thinking it was December. Hope you don't develop any serious head problems from all that buffalo dust you were breathing a moment ago."

## The '97 Blizzard That Beat all Blizzards

"Sweetheart, can you grab the phone? I'm just getting out of the shower. Thanks, Shirley."

"It's OK, Paul. It's Kooistra dispatch. He asked that you call him back in fifteen minutes."

"Dispatch, please, Paul O'Brien speaking. Hi, Conard. What do you have for me today?"

"Paul, I've got a trip for you from Swan River, MB, to Pittsburgh, PA. The load will be ready for you at 11:00 a.m. today. Can you make it to Swan River by then? The load is in the yard, and the paperwork is at my desk. I hear that the roads are good for bobtailing up from Dauphin."

"Hey, thanks, Conard. I'll be there by 11:00 a.m. What have I got for a load?"

"Your load is cedar shakes. Tim brought it in early this morning from Maple Ridge, BC. The weight of your CLT Ford with full fuel and chains, and this load of cedar shakes weighing in at 44,000 pounds, should keep you legal at just under a gross vehicle weight of 80,000 pounds."

"Sounds like a plan, Conard. See you soon."

"Shirley, I'm heading for Pittsburgh. I'll bobtail to Swan River after breakfast. I'm picking this load up at the yard at 11:00 a.m. I'll be grossed out at about 80,000 pounds, so it should be a good run."

The day had just begun and already I had a trip. I had just taken a week off after four weeks on the road. Spring was supposed to be here, but in Manitoba's parkland, it hadn't really arrived yet. Sure, the snow was mostly gone. There were a few dirty snowdrifts lying in the ditches and up against the side of many buildings, but lots of brown grass was also exposed in everyone's yards in Dauphin, Manitoba. With daytime temperatures just below zero degrees Celsius and nighttime temperatures hovering around -10 degrees Celsius, in our minds, we still considered it winter.

I bobtailed up to Swan River, and the roads were indeed clear and dry. I sure did like to see that. I'd just about had enough of winter for a year.

Arriving in Swan River, approximately ninety minutes after I left the house in Dauphin, I was whistling a happy tune as I walked into the dispatch office.

"Hey, Conard. Good to see you. What's my trailer number?"

"OK, Preacher. Your trailer is K-48097."

Of course, my name is Paul, but I had a nickname at Kooistra Trucking. The nickname, Preacher, had been given to me by a couple of drivers who knew that I had been the minister of a small country church in Gilbert Plains, Manitoba.

"Hum . . . Conard, you're giving me a short trailer today, eh? Just a forty-eight footer. Are you going to be able to get me a good reload out of Pittsburgh or wherever?"

"Preacher, have I ever let you down? Come on. I'm the best there is. I'll get you a good reload. I'm already tracking one right now that ships out from Pittsburgh back to Toronto, ON."

"It's the fifth of April today, and you have a delivery appointment for the eighth, Tuesday morning at 9:00 a.m. I'm giving you lots of time to make your run. I heard that we're expecting some snow for the next couple of days. It's supposed to be a Colorado low, but I don't think it's going to amount to much. You should likely make it to Fargo, ND, this evening before you see any of whatever they are expecting for a snowfall."

It generally takes about half an hour to hook up to the trailer, and do an inspection of both the tractor and trailer. I was able to do it in twenty minutes, so when I had my paperwork and logs in order, I was pulling out of Kooistra's Swan River yard exactly at 11:30 a.m.

"Hi, Shirley. I know my cell phone signal isn't the best up here in Swan River, but I'm just leaving the yard now. My delivery appointment is for next Tuesday at 9:00 a.m., so I shouldn't have too much of a problem getting there on time. I did hear from dispatch that we are in for some snow, but I'm grossed out at 80,000 pounds, so I should be able to get good traction in the snow and keep her on the road."

"Drive carefully, sweetheart. It sounds like a good trip ahead for you. The kids and I are going to miss you, so drive safe and hurry back."

"I'll drive safe, Shirley. Of course, you know that I won't be back for at least three to four weeks. When I stay out that long, the company doesn't mind me taking a week off. So I'm likely going to make it a target for taking a week off in the first part of May. Hey, there should be green grass by then and leaves on the trees. Ha, we'll likely already be cutting the grass."

"Well, Paul, I was listening to the weather channel on television, and they are saying to expect a nasty snowstorm in this area today from the Colorado low."

"Oh, I guess the weatherman is changing his mind. What I heard up in Swan River was that it wouldn't amount to much. Oh well, I guess I'll take whatever comes along. I've got chains and lots of food and water. You know me, babe. I never leave home without at least 80 liters of potable water and two weeks' worth of canned or dried food. Well, that's if I don't pig out. But remember, I use that food in an emergency. I don't eat from my food stock otherwise."

"OK, Paul, but you be mindful of the weather. You know that it can change very quickly at any time in Manitoba. I love you, so come back home safe to me."

"I love you too, babe. Talk to you again before the day is done. I'm hoping to get to Fargo, ND, before I have to shut down for the day. Love you, bye-bye."

That phone call only took a few moments, but in that short period of time, I noticed that the snow was beginning to come down just a bit heavier. The road was cold, so the snow wasn't sticking to it yet. But if the weatherman was changing his mind, I would expect to see more snow, and maybe some of it sticking to the road. The other noticeable change was that the wind had begun to pick up. Nothing serious, just a light wind out of the southwest.

The load of cedar shakes was well-placed in the trailer, and 097 was tracking well behind my two-story Edsel. I'd passed Dauphin two hours earlier and was thinking I'd need a break soon. I'd been driving for a total of a little more than three and one half hours, and right then, the roads were beginning to plug up with snow. I was losing more time every hour because this Colorado low was beginning to foul things up. Neepawa was up ahead on the horizon, but there wasn't a truck stop there. The little truck stop just east of town had been closed for about a year. They had good food and coffee, but just not enough business.

Visibility had been reduced sharply within the past half hour, and the wind out of the southwest had picked up substantially. I wasn't worried about my load, but I realized that I'd not likely even make Fargo, North Dakota, anytime soon, let alone Winnipeg. There were several truck stops in Winnipeg, but basically nothing between Neepawa and Winnipeg. I might have to work out a plan B.

But what was plan B? The way I saw the situation, this Colorado low was catching everyone in Manitoba by surprise. Had I known it would amount to a full-blown storm before the day was done, I would have rebooked a much later delivery time for my load and gone back home to Dauphin to ride the storm out.

Oh boy, not a good time to have a cell phone call, but I noticed that it was Shirley calling me.

"Hi, sweetheart. What's up?"

"Paul, this storm is really starting to break wide open here in Dauphin. Where are you and are you experiencing the same storm intensity?"

"Well, I've just passed through Neepawa, and the storm is starting to get very serious. The roads are bad, and are plugging up with snow and drifts. I'm going to make a run for it to Portage la Prairie. My goal is to get to the Royal Plains Mall on the west side of town. I'm hoping I can keep this rig on the road and not get stuck. It's hard to see where the road is at times, and I don't need to end up in the ditch because my visibility has become so impaired by the blizzard. I'll get off the road when I arrive at Portage."

With genuine concern in her voice, Shirley said, "Paul, keep in touch with me and let me know what's happening."

"I will, babe. Do me a favor and call Conard at dispatch, and inform him you were just talking to me. I just passed through Neepawa, and I'm going to try to make it as far as Portage. I know I'll not make it as far as Winnipeg, and it's even a bit of a long shot to make it as far as Portage.

"Shirley, the wind is getting stronger by the moment, and if I'd had a light load, I'd be all over the road. As it is, this wind is keeping me down to about sixty kilometers per hour."

"Conard will be going home for the weekend by 5:00 p.m., and it's now past 3:00 p.m., so call him right away, babe. Got to go, Shirley. Love you."

At that point, I was heading due east, but once I got past Gladstone, I'd be running on a southeast tangent, and the wind was out of the southwest. It would be hitting me broadside. This was going to be difficult keeping my rig on the road without having my trailer being blown into any opposing traffic when a strong gust of wind would want to blow it sideways.

By then, as I was crossing the CNR railway tracks just north of Highway 1, the visibility was down to less than fifty feet. I had dropped down to fifth gear and was keeping the speed down at about 25 to 30 kilometres per hour. Even at that, I felt like I was going too fast. Blinding snow and poor visibility will fool you into thinking you are speeding. The sensation of speeding right then was equivalent to running at one hundred kilometres per hour.

I assure you, I was praying that I'd be able to keep my semi on the road and not have a vehicle or truck stalled out in front of me. If I had to stop, I wasn't sure I'd get rolling again.

The wiper blades were beating the windows as hard as I could get them to go, but they were barely making any headway. The snow was building up on the windshield and both the wipers. But I couldn't stop to clean either of them. If I were to stop, I wasn't sure I'd get rolling again, and sure as shooting, someone would run smack-dab into the back of my trailer. That's not a pretty picture to dwell on.

"Oh, shoot. There goes my cell phone. Nuts. It is Kooistra phoning me. It must be Conard. "Hello. That you, Conard?"

"Hello, Paul. No, this is Cliff. I sent Conard home a couple of hours ago. Your wife Shirley just called me. Sounds bad by what she said. Where are you?"

"Hi, Cliff. I've just made it to Highway 1. I'm off Highway 16 now. I'm hoping to make it to the Royal Plains Mall on the west side of Portage. I'm down to running in fifth. I've got the diff's locked up, and slippage is minimal. It's my vision that's compromised by the thick snow on the windshield and the wipers. The defroster is barely keeping up with the demand to clear the windows."

"Take it easy, Paul. As long as you can keep it rolling, even if you are in low range, you should try to make it to the mall. You're looking at only a handful of miles. When you get to the mall, phone me back. I want to make sure you've made it. If I don't answer from my office, call me at my home. You have my number?"

"Will do, Cliff. Yes, I have your home phone number."

It took me another forty-five minutes to run those few miles, approximately six miles at the most, but I made it. What a forlorn sight welcomed me when I arrived at the Royal Plains Mall. The parking lots were basically empty. McDonald's restaurant at the far west end of the parking lot was closed. All the lights were out. By then, it was dark, and the mall was in total darkness as well. Evidently, everyone working there had gone home early. Shut down, dark, tight, and cold, and I was at that point the only big rig parked at the mall. This had the makings for a long cold and lonely night.

When I phoned back to Cliff, he came on the line right away. "Paul, did you make it to the Portage Mall?"

"Cliff, I made it. Now that I'm stopped, I'll undoubtedly get buried by the snowdrifts in short order."

"Is anything open there, like maybe McDonald's?"

"No, Cliff. Everything, the mall, McDonald's, even the establishments across the highway are closed. At this point, I think I'm the only one here. I can't see very far, so there may be others here but visibility is at worst down to thirty to thirty-five and, at best, maybe as much as forty feet."

"Have you got some emergency supplies, Paul?"

"No problem there, Cliff. Lots of water and two weeks' worth of canned and dried goods."

"How much water do you have Paul?"

"I've got four, twenty litre containers full of potable water. I'm in good shape, Cliff."

"You're a wise man to run with that much emergency rations, Paul. Listen, I'm going to let you go but stay in touch. I'm going home now because it is about as bad up here in Swan River as it is down there in Portage. You've got my home number, so don't hesitate to call me if you run into any kind of a situation."

"Thanks, Cliff. I'm not worried about anything. This old two-story Edsel is running very well. Right now, I can say I appreciate the fact that you look after your equipment very well. I'll let you go for now, Cliff."

"OK, Paul. I'll call you in the morning, and see how you made out through the night. Take care."

The blizzard raged unabated. In fact, it only got worse toward 7:00 p.m. The truck began to shake violently at times when there were strong gusts of wind. Fortunately, the wind was hitting my right rear quarter. Had it been totally broadside, I think I would have feared that a super-strong gust of wind had the potential to blow me over.

Long about 9:00 p.m., my cell phone rang again. It was Shirley.

"Honey, how are you doing? I figured you made it to Portage because you haven't called me. So did you make it there?"

"Hi, babe. Yup, I made it to the Royal Plains Mall on Highway 1A, at the west end of Portage. This is the strongest blizzard I think I've ever been stuck in. I'm going to get rocked to sleep tonight if it doesn't blow me over."

"Do you really think the wind could blow you over, Paul?" Shirley asked this question with a lot of concern in her voice.

"No, actually I don't think that, Shirley. Anything is possible, of course, but the storm has not been increasing in fervor or intensity for a couple of hours. I basically have no forward vision, and looking in my mirrors, I can't even see the backend of my trailer.

"Well, I'll be a monkey's uncle. Shirley, a car just pulled up beside me on my left side. He will be blocked by my rig from getting the full force of the wind. That was a smart move on his part. I'm going to get out of my truck and speak to the driver of the car. I won't get lost in the blizzard because he is basically just below my door."

"Call me back, darling. I want to know what is happening."

"OK, Shirley. I'll call you back soon."

I put on my parka and climbed down out of my truck. Boy oh boy, did it look like a strange sight. So much snow was pasted against the side of the trailer and even the tractor, I couldn't tell the color of my rig; just basic snow white.

The lady driving the car rolled down her window a bit when I knocked on her door.

"Good evening, madam. I'm the driver in the rig right beside you. I have a warm truck, lots of potable water, and food. And if you would care to spend the night in my rig, you are welcome to."

"That's very kind of you, driver. I think I'll be fine for now. But if it's OK with you, if I seem to be having some problems after a while, I will come knocking on your door looking for help."

"That's OK with me, madam. I hope you will be able to stay warm and safe. I'll remain right beside you if you need help."

"Just calling you back, Shirley. I spoke with the driver of the car beside me just a few moments ago. After that, I looked as best I could around the parking lot. But I didn't see any other vehicles or trucks here at the mall. The woman driving the car said she'd be alright and would remain in her car."

We talked for a few more minutes and then blew each other a kiss with a promise to talk again in the morning.

The storm raged on throughout the night even into the morning. Awakening from a fitful sleep, I noticed the car still beside me. It was still running, and the snow had melted from the roof and windows, indicating that the car certainly had a good heater.

In the early morning light, while the blizzard still raged, I began to notice several rigs scattered about nearby. I could see a little further in the distance, so I realized the wind had died down somewhat, but it was still strong enough to be considered a blizzard. It was definitely one mean Colorado low, which had blanketed all of Southern Manitoba.

I needed to make two phone calls, so I got to it. "Hi, babe. I made it through the night with no problem. The storm still rages on, so snowdrifts are becoming very tall and huge."

"I'm glad you are OK, Paul. I knew you'd call me if you ran into problems."

"Everything is fine. I've just enjoyed a can of stew for breakfast. I'm sure glad I have lots of water and food. How is everything back in Dauphin?"

"The storm hasn't died down at all, Paul. My car is absolutely buried under a huge snowdrift. It is certainly going to take some time cleaning all the snow off when the storm dies down."

"Get the kids to help you, Shirley. But don't even think of going to church today. I dare say Pastor Bob has canceled the service anyhow."

"Actually, Paul, Bob just called a few minutes ago to tell us that the morning worship service was indeed canceled. I'm still going to keep the kids indoors today. I don't want them wandering around in a blizzard.

It's too easy to get disorientated and lost when you can't see a horizon or even a couple of buildings away from where you are standing."

"Right on, Shirley. I'll let you go for now. Stay warm and dry, babe."

Later that Sunday morning, I talked with Cliff Kooistra. He stated, "Let me assure you, Paul, I don't want you taking any risks. You will likely be staying in the mall parking lot for a day or longer. Don't worry about your delivery appointment. When you are finally clear of the mall parking lot and on your way, and who knows how long that will be, give me a call. You'll likely not be clear of anything until Monday sometime at the earliest."

"Yes, Cliff. It certainly looks like I'll be here for quite a while yet. This blizzard hasn't really died down much at all."

All-day Sunday, the storm raged on, and it wasn't until early evening that it began to die down. I was anxious to get going, so prematurely I kicked her into gear and started to creep forward. Even with substantial snow all around the rig, I was able to move, so I kept giving that two-story Edsel more power, and she kept moving. I was indeed thankful that I had the weight to keep all the wheels solidly on the ground and gain decent traction.

But as I said, I moved from the mall parking lot prematurely. The road had not been cleared. Snowdrifts were everywhere. I was trying to get through Portage on the main drag, and I wasn't able to. I was getting bogged down pretty much as soon as I left the mall parking lot.

After pushing my rig painfully slow and not making any headway to speak of, I made it to the center of town. That's as far as I went. I stopped in front of the post office and shut it down for the second night. It wasn't so much of a blizzard at that point, but it was still snowing quite heavily, and the road was basically impassable at this point.

About the time that I stopped in front of the Portage Post Office, my cell phone rang. It was Cliff on the line.

"Hello, Cliff. How are you doing up there in Swan River? Have you been getting as much of a blizzard there as I've been getting down here in Portage?"

"Pretty much the same, Paul. You making out all right?"

"Doing fine, Cliff. The CLT is running good. No troubles at all. The heater is good. I'm comfortable and well-fed. Looks like I'll be spending another night in Portage."

"Paul, the last thing I want you to do is trying to be a hero and leave the safety of Portage too quickly. In the morning, Conard will call the receiver in Pittsburgh, and inform them of the situation. Once you are on the road, we'll reschedule your delivery time. By the way, how are you doing for fuel?"

"Fuel's OK, Cliff. I've still got better than a half tanks, should be able to run for a couple of days yet before I need to pay any attention to my fuel condition. I expect that I'll likely be able to get out on the highway sometime tomorrow. The storm has died down substantially. I think we are over the worst of it.

"I'll check in with Conard first thing in the morning. Have a good night, Cliff."

"Good deal, Paul. You have a good night as well. Stay safe and warm. I understand that it got down to minus 28 degrees Celsius last night, and it'll probably be a cold one again tonight. So long for now."

I spent Sunday night in front of the Portage Post Office. Basically, the main drag was not passable. I didn't have any other choice.

"Hi, Shirley. I'm still in Portage la Prairie but tonight I'm parked right downtown in front of the post office. I prematurely decided I'd try to get out on the highway and head for Winnipeg, but that didn't work. I was only able to get to the center of Portage, and even then the main drag was nearly impassable."

"Are you going to be alright where you are? The police won't come along and tell you to move will they?"

"I don't expect any visitors tonight. Likely, most police have resorted to snowmobiles to get around the town."

"Do you think you'll be able to leave tomorrow, Paul? I sure hope you won't have to spend a third night shut down in Portage."

"I've seen a couple of front-end loaders running around, so they're likely breaking through the biggest drifts, getting things ready for the snowplows. I hope you and the kids are OK, and be sure to keep them indoors until things have settled down in Dauphin. I'll bet you they are anxious to go out and play in the snow, and build a couple of snow forts. The snow won't melt for a few days, so they'll have an opportunity to build igloos, I'm sure. Shirley, I love you, and I hope you have a good sleep tonight, so I'll say goodbye for now."

"You sleep well too, Paul. Stay warm and know that I love you too. Nighty-night. Sleep tight. Don't let the bedbugs bite."

When I awoke Monday morning, April 7, I noticed that the street had been cleaned, and I'd have no problem getting my rig in gear and heading for the highway. Before I could release the brakes and begin to roll, the cell phone rang. It was Kooistra Trucking calling me.

"Hello."

"Good morning, Paul. Conard here. I hear you're still in Portage. What are you waiting for? Spring has already come."

"Good one, Conard. Your lazy brothers down here are slow at clearing the roads of a little bit of snow. I guess their union says they don't have to work in bad weather. Kind of like Kooistra dispatch. I understand you got off early last Saturday. Was the snow real that scary, Conard? Hahaha."

"Touché. Let me know when you're rolling, Paul."

"I was just about to kick it into gear when you called, Conard. Better mark me down as on the road again."

"I expect that the roads won't be too good yet, Paul, so when you've cleared customs at Pembina, ND, give me a quick call. That'll help me when I talk to Pittsburgh, and try to re-establish a new delivery time for your load."

I no sooner came to the edge of town when I was forced to stop. The grader type snow-plow had become stuck in a drift that was at least 10 feet in height.

He was slowly working his way back out of his predicament. Evidently, this would be a slow day getting out of Portage la Prairie.

Finally, the drift had been cleared from the road, and the grader led the procession of several rigs, and a couple of cars as we looked at Portage in our rear-view mirrors and bid its inhabitants adieux.

"Oh, nuts! What now?" I yelled at myself as my rig slowly lost speed, and I coasted to the side of the road right in front of a mom-and-pop gas station barely three miles from the western edge of Winnipeg.

Speaking to no one but myself and the truck, I growled out unrepeatable comments, "Come on, old girl. What are you doing to me? How come you lost power, and I can't get any gears? Are you going to be cantankerous this trip, and give me more grief?"

Shaking my head and grumbling to myself, I picked up my cell phone, and placed a call to Kooistra Trucking. "Hello. Paul O'Brien speaking. I'd like to speak to Conard in dispatch, please."

"Paul, what's up?"

"Conard, this two-story Edsel is giving me some grief. I lost power, and all my gears as well. I can't get it into gear. The clutch seems to work, but the gear shift is just sloppy, and all over the place."

"Paul, I'll put you over to the garage. Maybe they can give you an idea of what might be going on. Keep in touch with me."

"Thanks, Conard. Will do."

"Hello, garage. Paul O'Brien speaking. I'm running number twenty-eight, and I've run into a snag. Rather suddenly, I started losing speed, and couldn't get a gear. The gear shift is sloppy and doing nothing. I can't select any gears whatsoever."

"Hello, Paul. Mike here. Can you crawl under your tractor and examine the transmission linkage? Maybe you might see something that appears out of order."

"OK, Mike. I'll call you back in a few minutes when I see something."

I put on my parka and my coveralls. Mind you, it was still cold outside, and I was going to crawl under my tractor to do a brief inspection.

Back in the truck, I phoned Kooistra's shop. "Mike, I can't see anything out of the ordinary. The problem must be internal."

"I'm going to call the wreckers, Paul. Give me your exact location on Highway 1."

"Mike, I'm eastbound on Highway 1, just west of Headingly, and right at the junction of Highway 26, north to Francois Xavier."

"Thanks, Paul. I'll get a wrecker to you as soon as possible."

I was only waiting a couple of minutes, and Mike called again.

"Paul, the wreckers are all very busy this morning as you could expect. The blizzard has sent them into high gear. They are indicating to me that they won't be out to tow you into Winnipeg until sometime this evening after 7:00 p.m. I gave them your cell number, and they'll call you when they can give you a definite time. Hope that works for you."

"I guess it'll have to work for me, Mike. This two story Edsel has lots of fuel and the heater works well, so I'll just curl up in the bunk and have a snooze. Not like I haven't had lots of time over the past two days, in order to get my beauty sleep."

Midway through the afternoon, I got a sharp rap on the driver's door. There was a fellow standing outside my truck, waiting for me to speak to him. I thought as I rolled down my window that somehow I recognized him.

"Hello, driver. Are you broken down and need assistance? Hey, I think I recognize you. Aren't you, Paul? I believe that I studied with you at Winnipeg Bible College during the freshman year of 1987–1988?"

"That's me, and I'm sure I recognize you as well. You're Vic, aren't you? Wow. We haven't seen each other in quite a few years. I'd say about ten years to be exact, Vic.

"I'm broken down, but a wrecker from Winnipeg will be coming for me a bit later today. What have you been up to, Vic?"

"Paul, I got married after college, and my wife Tammy and I are farming not too far from here to the west. And I see you are trucking. Have you been trucking for a long time?"

"Vic, I pastored for a while after I graduated from Providence Theological Seminary in 1994. I was up in the Parkland Area of Manitoba at Gilbert Plains. I've since left that church, and I'm back trucking. I haven't been at it too long, and have actually just started driving for this company the first of March this year."

Well, it was nice to meet up with someone from the past, and Vic and I stood beside the truck and had a good chat for a few minutes. But it was cold outside, and because there wasn't anything Vic could do specifically for me to help me get rolling again, he was soon back in his pickup, and heading east toward Winnipeg.

What a pleasurable experience meeting up with an old college mate. I mused about my old college days for a while but soon decided I'd better get some up to date information regarding this blizzard.

Listening to CJOB Radio Winnipeg, I learned that this Colorado low was being recorded as the worst blizzard Manitoba had ever experienced. There were sustained eighty-five kilometre per hour winds for more than forty-eight hours and wind chills that exceeded minus twenty-eight degrees Celsius. The blizzard had caused Manitobans to endure eighty hours of incredible winds, snowfall exceeding forty centimetres, and many snowdrifts exceeding ten to twelve feet in height. As a consequence of this blizzard, all roads in Southern Manitoba from north of the Parkland to the United States border had been closed. All vehicular transportation was suffering from an intolerable gridlock.

It wasn't until 8:00 p.m. that I was able to get the wrecker's assistance to tow my rig into Winnipeg. By Tuesday evening, I was finally able to slip my two-story Edsel into gear, and leave the city lights of Winnipeg behind. I now set my eyes and hopes on a favorable trip to Pittsburgh. I would not experience any other detainments or delays. Indeed, it was a joy to see the city lights of Pittsburgh, and make my delivery time for 7:00 a.m. Friday morning.

Within a couple of weeks once the blizzard of '97 had passed, the weather turned springtime warm. The sudden change resulted in the worst recorded flood in Southern Manitoba in five hundred years. The Red River south of Morris created a lake forty miles wide. The major highway running south out of Winnipeg, highway 75, was shut down so that access to the Canadian and the United States border at Emerson, Manitoba, and Pembina, North Dakota, was not accessible. This resulted in huge detours for many truckers like myself, who ran back and forth from Canada to the United States.

## A Nasty Three Blizzard Trip

How would I not remember this trip? Can you imagine that in the space of one week in January 2008, I drove through, or shall I say I suffered through, not one blizzard but three blizzards, before I could return to my home in Cobourg, Ontario, from Blanding, Utah, by way of Wyoming, Montana, Saskatchewan, Manitoba, and ultimately Northern Ontario?

"Paul, would you answer the phone? It looks like you are going to probably get the dispatch you've been waiting for, because it's RSB Transportation in Saskatoon on the line."

"Thanks, Shirley. I just stepped inside from shoveling the snow in our driveway. Tell them to hold for a couple of seconds while I take my parka off."

"Hello. Paul speaking."

"Hello, Paul. This is Murray in dispatch. I've got a trip for you. There is a load ready for pick up in Port Hope, at Cameco. It's a hazmat load destined for Blanding, Utah. Delivery for Monday morning, the fourteenth, at 5:00 a.m. This load will be on RSB's trailer V53120."

"Thanks, Murray. I'll get on it right away and send you a message with the load particulars when I'm ready to leave Cameco."

I'd done this run, Port Hope to Blanding, Utah, several times over the past year. It was always a straightforward trip with no complications. This trip would be without any exceptions as well, but where it got really interesting or shall I say challenging was the return trip.

I could never count on a return trip from Blanding, to Port Hope, to be the same as any I'd had before. From Blanding, I was always dispatched to some point in the western United States to pick up a load destined for Canada. Likewise, there was never a repeat of the same Canadian destination. I would, however, eventually return to Port Hope. That made each trip interesting in its own right, and afforded me the opportunity to see so many different places, both in the United States and in Canada. Suffice to say, I was never bored.

I'd left Port Hope, on January 11, noontime, and had arrived in Blanding, at the appointed time of 5:00 a.m. The weather had cooperated throughout the whole trip to Blanding. Sure, it was cold; it was January, of course, but nothing I wasn't prepared for. It was mildly cold in Blanding, not nearly as cold as it had been running across Iowa, and Nebraska. I'd stayed on Interstate 80 westbound out of Chicago, and it wasn't until I was in Wyoming, where I'd turned south to run on a state highway into Colorado, and ultimately southwest into Utah, that I noticed a distinct weather change. It had become noticeably warmer. Possibly a chinook was moving in from the west.

I'd released my trailer to the receivers, and they'd hauled it to a location unknown to me. This was standard protocol. That's just how this company handled their business. It was probably about one hour later, and my trailer was back on my tractor and my bills were signed.

The standard way of communicating with my dispatch was through Qual-comm, which was a satellite uplink. My rig was equipped with a keyboard, much like a computer laptop keyboard. I would receive a message from dispatch on my monitor, and I'd type my response and hit send, and that message would then be transmitted via satellite back to my dispatch.

The present message from dispatch indicated that I had a pickup in Cody, Wyoming. The pick would consist of a trailer load of an agricultural product, namely canola seed destined for spring planting somewhere in the Canadian prairies. I would deliver this load to RSB's main terminal yard in Saskatoon, Saskatchewan, three days hence. While there was no specific arrival time set for Saskatoon, this trip should only take about three days.

Right after I'd received this new dispatch, I grabbed my cell phone and called Shirley.

"Hey, sweetheart. I've made my delivery in Blanding, and I've just got a new dispatch to pick up a load in Cody, Wyoming, destined for RSB's yard in Saskatoon. This load will be ready for me tomorrow morning anytime. I'll retrace my route back up to Interstate 80 then run east to Rawlins, Wyoming."

"Paul, I remember Rawlins. I was trucking with you and we were there back in June 2003 on a Sunday when you called your mother, and she told you that your Uncle Edgar had just died."

"Yes, you're correct Shirley. You have a good memory. Any other news from home?"

"Smitty called for you yesterday, Sunday. He was just wondering how you were doing. He'd said that he couldn't get through to you on your cell phone. He figured you were running in dark territory."

"I'll call him later today, Shirley. There are a lot of territories out here where it is hard to get a cell phone signal. I'm going to let you go, babe. Got to get the show on the road as they say. Love you."

The weather stayed mild and the roads were dry, so I made good time retracing my route until I arrived at Rawlins, Wyoming. I needed fuel and food. Both my rig and I were running low on sustenance.

Funny how you can sometimes get a premonition of impending danger. I had just such a premonition while I was fueling up. I checked my emergency supplies, and was gratified to note that I still had ample potable water, and my food stocks were down somewhat, but not significantly. Nevertheless, I went back into the truck stop, and purchased several items of food that would remain fresh in my fridge.

With the fueling done, and the food stocks restored, I released my brakes and moved out, heading east on Interstate 80 for just a couple of miles. My route called for me to exit onto US Highway 287 north. I would run through high plateau country over to the junction of State Highway 135.

I had good cell phone coverage at this point, and being that I was so close to Rawlins, I took advantage of it and called Shirley.

"Hi again, sweetheart. I'm just leaving Rawlins now. I'm somewhat concerned about this weather. It has turned warm since yesterday, and it seems that when it turns warmer in high plateau country, you can expect a storm on the horizon. I don't see anything resembling an approaching storm at this point, but I have a feeling I'll be running into something. That's just a premonition."

"Thanks for calling back, Paul. Drive safely. I want you to come back home safe and sound to me and the kids."

"I'll try to stay in touch with you. I know that cell phone coverage is often very sparse up here in backcountry Wyoming. There just isn't the population base to warrant better coverage."

It wasn't very long before my cell phone lost any coverage, and my conversation with Shirley ended rather abruptly. By the time I got to Muddy Gap where there is the junction of US Highway 287 with State Highway 220, it had begun to snow. It was what I had expected.

This was warm, wet snow, and it began to stick to the road and to my rig. The wipers on my W900L, Kenworth, began to beat out a familiar tune as they endeavored to clean the windshield. For a while, the wipers worked well enough, but soon, the snow became dense, and I was forced to slow down. My forward vision was being compromised by both the increasing buildup of snow on the windshield and on the highway.

I hadn't run US Highway 287 before, so I was in unfamiliar territory. I had just passed signage on my side of the highway, which, if the lights were flashing, would have indicated that I needed to shut down immediately, and put tire chains on. There was a pullout where this would be possible. The signage said that there was a dangerously steep downgrade ahead. This would not be the time to negotiate a downgrade of ten percent. But the signage remained dark. I continued onward the remaining length of 287, and quickly passed the junction of State Highway 135.

Within a couple of miles, new signage indicated that I had to pull out in order to check my brakes. I had arrived at the serious ten percent downgrade. I stopped and indeed checked my brakes and all tires, as well as all lights, and while just walking around my semi, the snow increased in density yet again.

I made a quick decision. I would not run this downgrade. The road was getting boxed in with dense snow, which, right then, was at least four to five inches thick, and it was building rapidly with each passing moment.

When I had passed the junction of State Highway 135, just a couple of miles back, I had noticed through the blowing snow, that there was a small state picnic park, equipped with washrooms. More importantly, there was enough room to get into that safe haven, so I turned my semi around, and retreated those few miles back to the state picnic park.

I carefully negotiated a couple of tight turns to get into the small parking space, and with that maneuver completed, I set my brakes. I had made the correct decision to park, and ride out the storm in this state park, because the storm had abruptly taken on the dynamics of a full-blown blizzard. The winds had picked up considerably, and the snow was now blowing more horizontally than falling vertically.

I decided to use the washroom while I could still see where it was. Upon entering the washroom, I read some Wyoming State signage, which said this location was referred to as Sweetwater Station.

Quickly, I returned to my truck, and it seemed that, in a matter of just a few moments, this blizzard broke completely open. I could not see more than ten feet to the front or rear of my equipment. My trailer literally disappeared in the blinding snow. If I were to wander more than a few feet from my rig, I would be hopelessly lost and disorientated. The seriousness of this thought hit me hard. If I left the safety of my cab, I would perish if I moved more than ten to fifteen feet away from its safety.

It's funny how a blizzard will make you feel cold even when you are in a safe haven. I remained in my warm cab; it was my safe haven, but I felt the chill of the storm, not so much physically but more psychologically. I involuntarily reached over and turned the heat up more.

The blizzard raged ferociously, so much so that it seemed to darken the daylight to what would be equivalent to dusk or nightfall. This wasn't the first blizzard I'd ever had to endure while in my truck, but I will assure you it was one of the most intense.

About that time, my cell phone rang. This surprised me because I had tried several times over the past couple of hours to phone Shirley, while I was locked down at Sweetwater Station. Can you believe it? My buddy, Smitty, was trying to get me on the cell phone. The signal was very poor, yet he got through to me.

"Hello, Smitty. I am really surprised that you were able to get through to me on my cell. I've been trying for a few hours to get a signal, so I can call Shirley, but to no avail."

"Hi, Dude. I've been wondering where you're at and what you are up to. I've tried to get through to you a couple of times in the past couple of hours. You don't have a strong signal, so where are you?"

"I'm shut down in a small state picnic park in high plateau country in Wyoming. The name of the place is Sweetwater Station. I think it is rather a nice name, but it is anything but nice right now."

"How so, Dude? I'm betting you're stuck in a blizzard because nothing much else gets you shut down. You're like a rolling stone which gathers no moss."

"You called it right on, Smitty. I'm stuck in a nasty blizzard. The fact is that it is so nasty, I can't see more than ten feet beyond my windshield. When I look in my mirror, I can't see the front of my trailer. If I was to get out and start to walk around, I'd get totally lost if I strayed more than ten feet from my rig."

"Hey, Dude, that reminds me of a story my dad told me a long time ago. You know, my dad was from Saskatchewan, and when they'd get a bad blizzard, if they didn't have a cable running from the house to the barn, they'd get lost in the blizzard and perish. They held the cable even when they couldn't see but a few feet in front of them. They'd always get to the barn or back to the house safely, as long as they didn't let go of the cable. I wonder if that saying, 'I walked the line' meant the same thing? Probably not but it sounds cool anyhow."

"Smitty, that phrase, 'I walked the line' is the title of the song by Johnny Cash, and meant that he'd behave himself and stay true to his lover.

"But that idea that your dad would have to hold onto the cable, or walk the line is true here right now in this blizzard, Smitty. I would get lost if you were parked here as well, and were more than ten feet behind my rig. As long as I'm in the comfort of my cab I'm safe. If I had to walk around my truck, I'd not let my hand off the equipment at any time for fear of wandering away in the blinding snow and then be truly lost."

"I knew you'd gone to Blanding, Utah, Dude, and you'd said your delivery time was early this morning as I recall, so you're in Wyoming now. That must mean you are heading for a pickup somewhere in Wyoming?"

"You're right on the mark, Smitty. I'm supposed to be in Cody, Wyoming, tomorrow morning for an early morning pickup. I have a gut feeling that isn't going to happen even though I'm maybe two hours away from my pickup. The way this blizzard is blowing, I'll probably be parked here until Wednesday, the sixteenth."

"I've sent a Qualcomm message to dispatch in Saskatoon and told them I'm shut down in a blizzard, and their only response to that message was, 'Let us know when you are mobile again.'

"Say, Smitty, what are you up to? Are you on a run right now or are you parked at home?"

"I'm down in Ohio, just north of Cincinnati, near Munroe, Ohio. I'm heading for Beaverdam, Ohio, where I'll pick up some fuel at the Flying J and shut down for the night.

"You said you were going to Cody. Where are you heading after that, Dude? You're not doing LTL, less than trailer load pickups are you?"

"Smitty, I don't recall doing any LTL pickups with RSB since forever. I'm getting a full trailer load of canola seed destined for Saskatoon. From there, I'll likely get a load back to Blind River, Ontario, with some yellowcake."

"Oh right. Most of your loads out of Saskatoon are back to Blind River with that yellow uranium ore, aren't they? Then where do you figure you'll go from Blind River?"

"Not sure where I'll get a load after Blind River's drop, but the last time I was in Blind River, I got a reload in Sudbury, for New York City. It was some sort of chemical out of CIL as I recall."

"I remember you telling me about that load, Dude. But you didn't take to New York City, did you?"

"No, I didn't. RSB had a fresh driver waiting for me when I arrived in Port Hope, so I was able to drop it, and he hooked onto it and was gone in a few minutes. Must have been a tight schedule he was on."

"Dude, you've been dropping your signal for the past few minutes. I'm only getting part of what you're saying. I should probably let you go."

"Smitty, would you do me a favor? I've not been able to reach Shirley. Would you call her, and tell her where I'm at? Tell her I'm all right, but just shut down for a while because of the blizzard. She already knows I was heading into a storm at some point. Thanks. I really appreciate that, Smitty."

"Be happy to do that for you, Dude. Stay safe and warm. I'll try and get through to you sometime tomorrow morning."

I was happy to get that phone call from Smitty. We go back a long way, and it's always a pleasure chatting with him. But now with the phone dead again, and the storm howling and raging outside my windows, it just seemed to be doubly lonely. I was tired of looking out the window and seeing nothing, and it was dark even in my cab except for my dash lights, which I always leave on when I'm running the engine.

What do you do when there is nothing to do? Well, of course, you get sleepy, and soon, I was semi-asleep, just sitting in the driver's seat. But that's a waste of a good bed when you're just sitting upright and dozing. The logical thing to do was to jump into bed and get real sleep. So that is what I did.

I don't know how long I had been asleep, but I certainly awakened with a start when the alarms started going off. There is a shrill alarm behind the dash up against the firewall, and it was making a terrific noise. Jumping out of bed, I stumbled into the cab from the bunk. I immediately noticed my engine was beginning to overheat. That is something you just don't want to have to deal with. If I had to shut the engine down, I'd soon become cold enough that I'd eventually enter into hypothermia.

I wasn't going to idly sit by, but I would endeavor to find out why the engine was overheating. I shut down the engine, and putting on my parka and boots, I was soon pulling the hood open to reveal the complete engine. The problem was easy to fix. Snow had packed in around the radiator and the radiator fins. I hastily cleared the snow away, and the radiator was free again to cycle the coolant and keep it at an appropriate temperature. Job done, and I was quickly back in the cab. The engine started up easily, and the alarms ceased to sound. Ah, the heat was luxurious.

The blizzard didn't slack off at all but raged on with intensity all night. The strong wind shook the cab considerably. This actually had a positive effect on me. I slept like a baby, being rocked in the cradle all night.

Awakening in the morning, I immediately realized I was in for a longer wait before I'd be able to leave the state picnic parking area. Visibility had improved somewhat. I could now see, possibly to a distance of twenty-five to thirty feet.

Certainly, not good enough to attempt to get back on the highway. The other fact I had to also contend with was that I didn't have a load on the trailer. I was empty, and would be subject to losing control if the wind remained strong. It could actually blow me off the highway where I running on slippery surfaces.

I guess you could say I made an executive decision. I was parked and was going to stay put. The visibility needed to improve, and the roads needed to be cleaned. I certainly didn't want to leave my safe haven at Sweetwater Station. I was not going to venture into a situation that could go south very quickly.

I was enjoying a cold breakfast of BBQ chicken, which I'd purchased the day before when I'd stopped for fuel at the Flying J Truck Stop in Rawlins. All I needed to wash that chicken down with was a good big mug of steaming hot coffee. Oh well, I could dream, couldn't I?

While I was still daydreaming about a hot cup of coffee, there was a sharp knock on my driver's door. That rather startled me as I wasn't expecting to receive company in the midst of a blizzard. I will admit the blizzard was slowly dying down, nevertheless, well, I'll be a monkey's uncle if it isn't a state trooper looking at me.

Opening my door to let him speak, he initiated his conversation in a terse manner. "Get your parka on and come over to my 4X4. I want to talk with you."

Funny how you get a feeling this wasn't exactly a social call. Meeting terseness in the same kind, I responded simply with a grunt that sounded like "Yup." The reason I hadn't been aware of his presence before the knock on my door was the simple fact that he'd driven up beside me, coming from the rear.

Once I was in his 4X4, he rather bluntly asked me, "Why did you drive past the signage back up the road a couple of miles when the lights were flashing?"

Of course, I remembered that signage. Its simple message was "Stop, chains required beyond this point." This would indicate to any knowledgeable driver that there would be a steep down or upgrade ahead.

My response to his question was a simple denial. "When I went by that signage yesterday, the lights were not flashing. Had they been flashing, I would have stopped. However, as I said, they were not flashing. I continued until I came to a pullout indicating a brake check was necessary. In that short period of time, the snow had begun to fall more earnestly. It was at that time I decided to turn around and return to this state picnic park."

"I can give you a ticket for going by the signage when it was flashing."

"Officer, before you hand me a ticket, you need to be aware that I have a recording of everything I do, and the time it was done. It is recorded on my Qualcomm when I stopped at the check brakes pullout. It was recorded when I turned around and arrived back here at this picnic park. It was recorded when I shut this truck down yesterday.

"If you want to write a ticket, go ahead. However, you'd better be aware that my lawyers will ask when that sign was turned on. Furthermore, that information will have to be recorded electronically. They will then compare your information, which had better show that the signage was on before my recorded information indicates my location relative to the signage at that particular time.

"Let me suggest that you are wasting your time and mine as well. Everything that happens in that truck is recorded according to Greenwich Mean Time. Take those facts into consideration before you act prematurely."

He responded with a simple request, "Let me see your commercial driver's license."

My response was equally simple, "I don't have it on me. It's in my truck."

It would appear that he wanted to save face and have the last say, "Alright, driver. You can return to your truck. Just be aware that I could have written you a ticket."

If a scowl on my face could have said anything, it would have said what I was thinking: "Hey, Smoky Bear. Don't push me around while you go fishing for something to hang on me."

Letting him look at my scowl for a long minute as I stared unblinking at him, I then exited his 4X4, and without a backward glance, climbed back into my rig.

As his taillights disappeared in the blinding snow, I just shook my head and spoke loudly to no one in particular, "Hey, bucko, if you're going to write a citation, you'd be best advised to substantiate it with real facts, not innuendos."

Nothing like a little drama to get the blood boiling. The upside of that is that now I wasn't just daydreaming, I was wide awake and ready for anything. All of a sudden my senses had become keener, my vision had become sharper, and my hearing had become more acute to any external noise or audible stimulation.

But what could I do with that heightened sensitivity to my surroundings? Actually, I couldn't do anything. I was still sitting out a blizzard. After checking the gauges on the dash, I did what any sane driver would do. I pushed my driver's seat back as far as it would go, took my boots off, leaned back, and put my stockinged feet on the dash. Speaking loudly to no one, I said, "Aw . . . the good life, riding out a little blizzard. Bring it on."

The rest of the day, January 15, passed without further excitement, or external stimulation from man or machine. Any previous situation was now just a memory. I had long ago given up on trying to reach anyone on my cell phone. It just wasn't going to happen.

Night had turned into day, but before I could rub the sleep out of my eyes, I heard a welcomed rumble. Looking out my driver's door window, I was pleased to see a snow-plow move past the left side of my rig.

"Oh, happy day. I'm being released from my prison of multiple snowdrifts." was all I could say as I quickly put my boots and parka on.

Doing the required circle check of my equipment, I found no situation demanding any attention. Everything was in order. My gauges indicated substantial fuel remained in both tanks, engine temperature was normal, and as I released my brakes, my air pressure gauge indicated no problems in the air system.

The snow had stopped. The roads had been cleared and salted or sanded while I slept. The parking lot in which I had remained for nearly two days was adequately cleared so that I could make a safe exit. And I began to sing loudly that familiar song Willie Nelson had immortalized, back in 1980, "On the road again, just can't wait to get on the road again, my life is trucking with my friends, I just can't wait to get on the road again."

OK, you know what I mean. Those weren't the exact words from my old buddy Willy, but they sure did apply to me the way I sang them. I was a trucker, and whether it rained or snowed, whether it was cold or hot, whatever, I felt best doing what I loved most, trucking.

"Cody Wyoming, here I come." And just like that in less than three hours, I'd arrived at Cody Feed and Seed, Inc.

In my Qualcomm message to dispatch, I indicated that I'd loaded on my trailer forty-five thousand pounds of canola seed. In our transmissions back and forth, dispatch had given me a delivery time for my load. I was to be in the company's yard in Saskatoon, Saskatchewan, by midday of January 18. With a good load, the sun shining in a clear blue sky, and the wind at my back, "No problem," was my verbal response to an inanimate machine.

Sitting in my warm cab at the truck inspection/weight station located approximately ten miles west of Billings, Montana, on Interstate 90 East that evening, I was once again waiting out a new blizzard, as I mentioned to Shirley on my cell phone, "Honey, it's like this. 'The best laid plans of mice and men' is what is happening to me this trip. It seems I'm like that old cartoon character in *Li'l Abner*, 'Joe Btfsplk.' If I recall correctly, it seems wherever he went there was a storm cloud over his head."

"Well, my dear," exclaimed Shirley, "being in a hurry isn't the most important thing in trucking. It's being safe that's most important. And you're safe sitting out a blizzard, not trying to drive through it."

Shirley was always the practical one, bringing me back down to earth. I'd get caught up in events, she'd find a way to bring sanity back into my life.

"I know you're right, my dear. I was so looking forward to steak and eggs tonight at the Flying J Truck Stop in Billings, MT. Like they say in the movies, 'Close but no cigar.'"

Shirley laughingly responded, "You don't smoke cigars, Paul. Enjoy your cold cereal tonight, and maybe you'll get lucky and have your well-earned steak and eggs tomorrow morning."

This blizzard, while categorized as one, was nevertheless a wimpy little blizzard. It blew hard, and the snow was thick for about six hours, then as suddenly as it came, it left.

Looking out the windshield when I awakened about five in the morning, I realized the blizzard was not only gone but the parking lot at the truck inspection station had been cleared, and the snowplows had done their magic to the interstate. It was also cleared and salted.

"Steak and eggs, here I come. I'll be chowing down at the truck stop in no time at all."

No one heard me say that out loud, but when you are alone for long periods of time you find yourself talking out loud to yourself, or am I the only one?

"Ten miles to go, and I can get out of this rig, stretch my legs, have something to eat, and even take a shower after I fuel up. Ah, this is the good life. Oh, oh, I hope nobody heard me say that. I really don't need another blizzard right now."

I guess I figured I could jinx myself by speaking out loud to no one but myself. I really did need to change gears soon, and get out of this rig. Well, at least talking to oneself either out loud or under your breath did help to pass the time, and before I knew it, I was at the truck stop.

"Get organized, Paul. First things first, fuel up and get that out of the way."

Oh, the simple joy of a long hot shower, which I sure needed after spending so long in my rig, thanks to Mr. Blizzard. Steak and eggs couldn't have tasted better even if my darling wife would have prepared them for me.

Fuel, shower, food—check. Whistling my favorite country and western tune, "On the Road Again," by Willie Nelson, I happily climbed back into my W900L Kenworth, released the brakes, and eased her into gear.

The miles moved quickly past my window as I now drove on good cold and dry state highways and US highways toward my destination of Saskatoon, Saskatchewan. How quickly I forgot the past few days when I had experienced two blizzards, treacherous roads, and even a run-in with Smoky the Bear.

How best would I describe a good trip? I'd describe it as a trip that was without drama. It's nice to do a trip where you really get to enjoy the passing scenery without any external stimulus. You can just sit back and listen to the radio while the tires hum a tune that compliments anything and everything that the satellite radio has to offer.

Saskatoon was on the near horizon. I wanted to be in and out of the city in short order. "Just let me drop this trailer and hook onto the next load and be on my way," I muttered to myself. And wouldn't you know it? It happened just as I wished.

With a few hours of daylight left, I quickly saw Saskatoon disappear in my rear-view mirrors. Oh, happy day, I was on my way to Blind River, Ontario, with a load of yellowcake ore fresh from the mine.

They say time flies when you're having fun. Well, it certainly does, and this part of my trip was enjoyable. I was now pointing my rig toward home. Sure, home was still many miles away, and I first had to drop my present load of yellowcake in Blind River, but it was a good feeling to know I was going to be home by the twenty-second.

At least that was the plan. But by now you probably would have guessed correctly, if you thought my plans would get changed again, and I'd be stuck in another blizzard. Hum. Just thinking, but maybe my title to this engaging story gave it away. Hahaha.

The roads had been good, the weather had been good, and I had seen Winnipeg and Thunder Bay pass by my windows. It all looked so good, seeing those two cities disappear in my rear-view mirrors. The next major city would be Sault Ste. Marie. Then, just an hour later, I'd make my delivery in Blind River, and maybe, just maybe, I'd get a load out of Sudbury, destined for Toronto. Home was just an hour and one half east of Toronto.

But oh, what was that I was seeing falling hard and fast upon my windshield? What was that sticking to the roads? Highway 17 had been great as I had traveled toward Thunder Bay, but at Thunder Bay, that the highway had changed directions and was following the north shore of Lake Superior, and heavy snow was blowing in off the lake.

Lake Superior very rarely, if ever, froze over, so with a southwesterly wind blowing onshore, a lot of snow would be created in short order, and it was quite common to run with heavy snow from Thunder Bay to Sault Ste. Marie. Today was just such a day, but when the winds are much stronger, a blizzard is in the making. And so it was that day.

A blizzard came hard against all traffic on Highway 17, and I barely made it to Nipigon. I would go no further. It was far too risky. Visibility was extremely poor, and traffic was always heavy because Highway 17 was the major artery east or west through Northern Ontario.

Here I was, stuck again in a blizzard. It was by then January 20. I had wanted to be home by then, and I would on a good day, but I was still about a day and a half away from my own bed. At least, I was in a safe place. I had made it to the Husky Truck Stop in Nipigon. There would be lots of good hot food. Showers were readily available, and of course, good conversation if I sat at the counter in the restaurant. That was indeed my favorite place to sit when enjoying a meal. Inevitably, other drivers would be sitting nearby, and there would always be the opportunity to tell your story, or listen to another driver's story.

That's how it was as I sat at the counter the evening of January 20. Another driver had sat next to me, and when I'd introduced myself, telling him my name, Paul, he had, in turn, introduced himself as Rob.

"Rob, which way are you heading today?"

"Paul, I've been heading west. I have delivery in Calgary in a couple of days. It sort of looks like I might be a day late and a dollar short on that one though as this storm is coming in pretty heavy. The fuel desk says to expect it to last for at least the next twenty-four hours."

"I hadn't talked to the fuel desk myself, Rob, so I'm glad you told me that. I'm not happy about the next twenty-four hours being parked, but at least the food is good here, and I'm off the road. It sucks when you have to shut down in a blizzard, and basically you're the only one parked. No other traffic is passing by, and it gets really quiet in a hurry."

"I know that story all too well, Paul. I've had that experience as I'm sure every driver in this restaurant has had. That's the lonely side of trucking, isn't it?"

Well, you can imagine that I told Rob my story. Sure, I tried to abbreviate it somewhat, but the impact was still the same. "Rob, this is my third blizzard on this trip."

Rob told me about his experience with blizzards; I told him mine. We had a good chat with each other for more than an hour.

"You know, Rob, that's one of the nice things about us truckers. We get into a situation like this, and we all become instant friends. We'll share some stories and have some good laughs. Even though we have to go through hell or high water sometimes, we're all on the same page. We'll probably never see each other again, but we won't forget our stories."

"That's a fact, isn't it, Paul? I know I've had some good times sitting in a restaurant just like tonight, and laughing at the jokes going around, or listening to the other drivers' stories."

"Right on, Rob. The fact is we actually look forward to getting together around a table, or at the counter with other drivers, just so we can have some laughs, or just so we can blow off some steam."

I don't remember who called it a night, whether Rob did or maybe it was me, but after we'd drunk at least a gallon of coffee each, one of us decided it was time to head for his truck.

I looked out through my windshield when I awakened on January 21, at about 3:00 a.m., and would you believe it? The blizzard raged on. The snow was still coming down heavily, and the wind had not abated.

Checking my watch, I thought I might just as well crawl back into my bunk and sleep this storm away.

Have you ever had this happen? You awaken and then determine you might as well get some more sleep? You have nothing else to do, so why not? But it just doesn't work. You look up at the darkened ceiling or at the darkened curtains. You close your eyelids. You try to clear your mind of any stimulating thoughts. Nothing works. It's like your mind has shifted into high gear, and is going a hundred miles an hour.

"This isn't working. I'm getting up. I might as well go into the restaurant and get an early breakfast. Hum. There I go, speaking out loud to myself again. Bad habit that."

It was 5:00 a.m., and the restaurant would probably be empty, but to my surprise, there must have been at least twenty other drivers who couldn't sleep either. Every seat at the counter was taken, and just about every table was fully occupied.

At a table near the entrance to the restaurant, a driver caught my attention by waving his arm. He called out to me, "Hey, driver, if you're by yourself, we have an empty chair at this table. Come on over and join us."

I waved back and nodded my head, affirming I was alone. An empty chair awaited me, so as I sat down I introduced myself, "Good morning men. My name is Paul. I drive for RSB out of Saskatoon."

Each driver in turn mentioned their name as well. "Hello Paul. I'm John, and I drive for Tri-Line Freight Systems." John sat across from me.

"Hi, Paul. I'm Glen, and I also drive for Tri-Line." Glen sat beside John.

And the driver who had called me over and who was sitting beside me introduced himself, "Howdy, Paul. My name is Dave and I also drive for Tri-Line."

Right away, I felt like I was among friends, and said. "Gentlemen, I'm pleased to meet you all. You fellows drive for a good company. I was once driving for Tri-Line before Laidlaw took it over. I'd started in Winnipeg back in 2000 with them while driving a broker's truck. He sold that truck, so I lost that job but rehired with them in Winnipeg a few months later. Tri-Line leased many of their semi-trucks, so I drove one of their leased rigs. I was always treated very well by Tri-Line, and ended up working out of Toronto."

Dave asked, "Paul, why did you leave when Laidlaw took Tri-Line over?"

"I'd mentioned that I was driving a leased tractor, Dave. Laidlaw fired all the drivers running with leased trucks. They did offer to hire me and give me the opportunity to drive a Laidlaw rig, so I went down to Guelph where Laidlaw had a yard and talked to them.

"I'd be running equipment owned by Laidlaw but still with the Tri-Line name on the door. That all sounded very attractive until it came to their answer to my question. How much per mile were they willing to pay me? I would have to take a beating on that one. They were offering, if I recall correctly, five cents less per mile. I told them thanks but no thanks.

"How about you, gentlemen? How long have you been with Tri-Line and what yard do you run out of?"

Glen replied for all three of them, "Paul, we all run out of Woodstock, which is one of Laidlaw's yards. Tri-Line doesn't have a yard in Toronto now, and Laidlaw's yard in Guelph is now a different division basically with just Laidlaw paint on the doors.

"Paul, all three of us hired on about the same time back a little over three years ago in 2004. We all operate in Tri-Line's dry van division. We're happy enough with Tri-Line's ownership by Laidlaw, but we understand that Tri-Line paint on the doors is going to change at some time in the future. The name will disappear, and Laidlaw's paint and name will then be applied to all former Tri-Line painted equipment. We're told nothing else will change. Pay rate and other company distinctive remain intact."

It was always interesting what news one picked up as he traveled down life's highway. This latest news from my new friends, Glen, Dave, and John filled me in on some blanks that had been in the back of my mind for a few years.

"I had enjoyed those years I drove for Tri-Line, guys, and sort of wished it hadn't come to an end the way it had. But I had moved on, and now and I'm hauling a lot of nuclear products, something I had not done before. It is very interesting, and I've experienced a different dynamic in the trucking industry."

"I think all of us here, Paul, have heard a few things about your work with RSB, when you haul those huge cylinders. By the way, what is in them?"

"John, the product in those cylinders is uranium hexafluoride. Rather deadly stuff to be exact. Where have you seen RSB hauling them, John?"

"I've been delayed at the Blue Water Bridge between Sarnia, Ontario, and Port Huron, Michigan, when you fellows have hauled those cylinders from Canada to the United States. As I recall, once my delay was nearly one hour. I guess it wasn't just your uranium hexafluoride because a couple of semi-trucks came in right after you with two loads of cobalt. That product is radioactive too, I believe."

"I know that story well, John. That has been my regular run for a few years now. I'm doing a different trip, still nuclear, but I'll be back on the cylinders shortly. Something to do with some shipping problems from the source."

Well, the conversation between John, Dave, Glen, and me continued for probably another hour, as we compared notes on a variety of transportation subjects. We weren't paying attention to the weather as we were so engrossed in our conversation, until we were interrupted by our waitress who informed us of some very welcomed news.

"Drivers, you'll be happy to know that the storm is pretty much over. We expect that the roads will be cleared up soon, and things will get back to normal. That's good news, eh, boys?"

Sunny skies, good highways, and a load that pulls well are always good news. To make that news better was the fact that I'd be on my way again, heading for home.

I voiced my delight after receiving that good news as did Glen, speaking for the other two Tri-Line drivers. "I've heard that as we go further west, it gets colder and drier. That's good for us. We've been here about twenty-four hours, so we've got to make some time. We all have a delivery in Edmonton, so we've still got a few miles to run."

"I'm glad you fellows will have some good roads ahead of you. I left Saskatoon a couple of days ago, and the roads in the west have been good for a couple of weeks. I'm heading east with a delivery for Blind River on Highway 17, so I've got a lot of miles to cover with Highway 17 running beside Lake Superior, and then basically on the north shore of Georgian Bay. I'll be keeping my fingers crossed that I don't experience another storm."

Our conversation came to a close, and we parted company. Glen, Dave, and John headed west, and I headed east. We all left the Husky Truck Stop in Nipigon at about the same time in the early morning hours. I looked at my watch as I slipped my transmission into gear. It was seven o'clock right on the mark.

Later that day, I was indeed happy when I arrived at Blind River, with no more storms coming in off the lake or bay either. Because I had lost so much time getting to Blind River, from Saskatoon, I'd lost my reload, which I would have had out of Sudbury.

Murray, my dispatcher, contacted me on the Qualcomm and indicated that I would run empty from Blind River, to Port Hope. That was good news, which I relayed to Shirley when I checked in with her by cell phone.

"Hi, sweetheart. I finally have some good news. I've delivered my load at Blind River, and since I couldn't make my pickup time in Sudbury, the load was given to another driver. I'm running empty back to Port Hope. I hope to be home late tonight or early in the morning. I sure am looking forward to getting some hugs and kisses from you."

Both Shirley and I were excited that I'd be home on January 22, even if it was late in the evening.

"Paul, that's delightful news. I've missed you a lot. I thought you'd be home a few days ago, but I'll be happy whenever you do get home."

I lost count of how many times I sang that old country song I'd heard many years ago first in 1963. "Six Days on the Road" (and I'm gonna make it home tonight) was sung by Dave Dudley. I liked his raspy voice. He had a good strong trucker's voice, I thought.

I sang with one slight modification. Could anybody fault me for this slight change? My rendition was just as good as Dave Dudley's. Twelve days on the road, and I'm gonna make it home tonight.

I'm happy to report that the rest of that trip, the trip I had three blizzards to contend with, went without a problem whatsoever. The skies cleared up, and the sun shone brightly on the freshly fallen snow, making it glisten and sparkle like acres of diamonds.

Port Hope was a welcome sight as I pulled into Wakely Transportations' yard where we kept RSB equipment. And I made it home to Cobourg just as the clock struck twelve, midnight.

"Twelve days on the road, and I made it home tonight." Funny that. I sang that one line as I walked into the arms of my beloved wife.

## Working with Smitty in Dawson Creek

I'd been working in transportation, driving a shuttle bus with highway coaches for Diversified Transportation in and out of Fort McMurray, Alberta, during the fall and winter months of September through December 2011.

Starting in the New Year, January 2012, I'd left Diversified and started work with O.J. Pipelines, also out of Fort McMurray. It had been a good job as was Diversified, but toward the end of April, we had to shut down the pipeline construction as spring thaw had arrived in earnest. And we had to be off the land as the Cariboo would soon begin their annual migration.

Shirley had come out to Fort McMurray, to spend time with me after my work with O.J. had ended, so we took our time visiting with friends and relatives throughout Alberta and Manitoba. We'd enjoyed a month-long vacation together during May and had arrived back home in Cobourg the first part of June.

I had anticipated going back out to Alberta in July for more pipeline construction work, but one phone call had ultimately changed the whole direction of my life before July could come.

"Paul, Don is on the phone. Can you pick up in the office?"

"Thanks, Shirley. I've got it."

"Smitty, how are you doing?"

"Dude, glad to hear you made it back home to Cobourg. When did you arrive?"

"Just a couple of days ago, Smitty. I'm just settling in for a few days of rest and relaxation before heading back out west to Alberta. There's a lot of pipeline construction going on right now. What's on your mind?"

"I'm not getting enough work over at T.D. Smith, Dude. I'm starving, and I can't make this month's truck payment. Fact is, I couldn't make last month's payment either. It's a good thing I have a line of credit, or I'd have lost my truck by now. I'm really unsure to know where to turn for work.

"I remember you had mentioned to me back last September, if I accurately recall, that you had some work hauling gravel if you wanted it out in British Columbia. I don't remember where it was or who it was with, but you'd said it was a toss-up whether you'd go to British Columbia or return to Alberta, and work with Diversified Transportation in Fort McMurray. Do you remember who had an opportunity you could have taken if you'd gone to British Columbia?"

"Yes, I do, Smitty. I'd heard about a good job up in Dawson Creek, BC, hauling gravel for a company called John Dyck Trucking Limited. They basically haul gravel out of their own gravel pit, as well as several other pits in that area. They could pretty much supply me with work for the most part of the year. Of course, spring breakup would mean that the trucks would be parked for a couple of months probably mid-April to mid-June, but after that, it was steady work with lots of hours and good pay."

"What do you think, Dude? Should I get your contact information and give them a call? Do you think they'd hire me even though I'm in Southern Ontario, a long way from Dawson Creek, BC?"

"Well, that's a call you'd have to make, Smitty. I know you'd have to park your tractor. That is something to consider. You still have to make payments on it, so you'd need enough in wages out in British Columbia to cover that, as well as yours and Kathy's living and home expenses."

"That's a lot to think about, Dude. I'm not too sure I want to take that risk?"

"Smitty, it can't hurt to call them, so ask for Wes Dyck. If I'm not mistaken, he runs that outfit with John, who is his dad. Here's the phone number. Give them a call. I want to know how it works out for you, so call me back right away."

It wasn't very long, probably less than half an hour, and Smitty called me back.

"Dude, they've offered me a job, and basically, I can start with them as soon as I get my butt out there."

"Smitty, that's good to hear. I'll tell you what. I've just been thinking about it as well, and I'm going to call Wes Dyck also. If he'll offer me a job, I'll get on a plane with you, and we can go out together to work there. Give me a few minutes, and I'll get back to you."

That's exactly what I did. I gave Wes Dyck a call, and it was he who answered the phone.

"Wes, this is Paul O'Brien. I talked with you last September, and although I enjoyed talking with you, I chose to work in Fort McMurray for a while. My buddy, Don Smith, was just talking to you, and I'm glad you gave him a job. Wes, if you have room for one more driver, I'd like to be that driver."

"I remember our conversation last fall, Paul. The fact is I can use another driver, and since I've hired Don and since you and he are buddies, I'd be happy to hire you as well. Both of you get here as quickly as possible. I'd suggest flying West Jet to Grand Prairie, Alberta. I'll have someone meet you at that airport, and bring you back to Dawson Creek."

"Thanks, Wes. I'll call you back with flight reservations and times as soon as possible."

My phone sure was getting a workout. I was excited by now. I'd be going to British Columbia to work, hauling gravel for the next several months. The pay was extremely good, and John Dyck Trucking would cover our flight expenses, give us each a room at a local hotel, and a Ford Super Duty 250 pickup to get around in.

Calling back to Smitty, I relayed the complete information I'd received from Wes Dyck. "Smitty, we're going to work together with John Dyck Trucking. We'll get a flight with West Jet to Grande Prairie, and be picked up there by someone from the trucking company. I've got a feeling this is going to be a really good summer and fall. Wes actually said we'd probably work right through the winter as well, because there's a lot of gas plant construction happening at this time."

"Wow, Dude, that's great. I'm really looking forward to this. You know what I'm thinking I'll do? I'm going to put my Kenworth W900 up for sale. If I'm working out west for a while, I don't need to be making payments on something I'm not driving. It should sell easy enough. I've often been told I have a good-looking tractor, and you know, it's given me good service too."

"I know you've had both good and bad times as an owner-operator, Smitty, but I think it's a good move on your part. You've just not been getting the miles, and the loads you've needed for the past three or more months."

"I know what I'll ask for it, Dude. It shouldn't be a problem to sell that Kenworth for what I'd like for it."

"Here's the deal, Smitty. I'm going to book a flight, hopefully for Friday, June 8, with West Jet out of Hamilton. That should give both of us time to get our gear together and catch up with each other."

The flight was booked easily enough. Both Smitty and I would fly out of Hamilton early Friday morning, and although we'd have to change planes in Calgary, we'd still get to Grande Prairie at a decent time late in the afternoon.

When I relayed this information to Smitty, he had a good suggestion as well.

"Dude, why don't you and Shirley meet Kathy and me at my daughter Carrie's home in Hamilton. We can get there Thursday afternoon, and Carrie or her husband can drive us to the Hamilton Airport early Friday. Shirley could return to Cobourg in her car, and Kathy would return to Bothell in her car."

"That sounds like an excellent plan, Smitty." After a few more details were worked out, we said goodbye. It was at that point that I filled Shirley in on all my new plans. No pipeline work for me. I'd be working with Smitty in Dawson Creek.

Shirley was as excited as I was. She knew that Smitty and I had always been the best of buddies, and once again, we'd have the privilege of working together. That was something she knew we always enjoyed.

It was actually beautiful the way our plans came together so quickly and so well. I believe Smitty and I were both quite amazed that everything had worked out wonderfully. I know that Smitty and I both realized, that it was the Lord who had orchestrated these events, which had happened and which would happen over the next several months, as we enjoyed working together once again.

Both Smitty and Kathy, and Shirley and I, had arrived in Hamilton mid-day Thursday. We had enjoyed visiting together over a delightful picnic in a local park. Now it was Friday morning and our excitement had escalated. We'd be in British Columbia before the close of the day.

"Smitty, it looks like we'll have a good flight to Western Canada today. The weatherman is our friend too. He is calling for fair weather throughout British Columbia and Alberta, for the next several days. I think we'll get off to a great start with John Dyck Trucking."

"This will be quite an adventure for me, Dude. I know you've been working throughout Alberta for a couple of years in pipeline construction, but I've not had the same opportunity until now to work at a steady job in another province for a longer period of time like you've experienced."

Our flight from Hamilton to Calgary went smoothly. We had a brief one-hour layover in Calgary, and then a direct flight to Grande Prairie, Alberta. Arriving midafternoon in Grande Prairie, we were met by Wes Dyck's father-in-law, Carl. Carl quickly filled us in on several trucking contracts that the trucking company had set up for the next several months. This was good news for Smitty and me. We'd be busy right through to winter. Carl was even hopeful that winter work would keep most of the drivers busy as well.

Within an hour and a half, we'd arrived in Dawson Creek, BC. Pulling into a large parking lot, Carl cheerfully spoke up, "Here we are, guys. You both will have your own room, and you'll be staying here at the Voyageur Motor Inn. Wes will cover the room expenses, as well as one meal a day. My suggestion would be to take the evening meal. Voyageur Motor Inn has a great restaurant as part of their establishment.

"I'll wait while you unload your gear in your rooms, then we'll go out to the yard where all the semi-trucks are parked. Wes should still be there, so I'll introduce you both to him. He'll get you established, and there is the usual paperwork you'll need to fill out. He'll explain how we work our system here, and get you both up to speed on all the details you'll need to know, once you start to drive for him."

It was just a short ride to the yard of John Dyck Trucking. In less than fifteen minutes, Smitty and I were standing in Wes's office. Wes introduced himself to us, and for the next hour, we filled out forms, talked with Wes, and were shown around the yard.

"Don and Paul, we start at 7:00 a.m. daily. We work Monday to Friday, and sometimes Saturday, depending on the contract. The odd time we will work on Sunday, but that is the exception, not the rule.

"Tomorrow, Saturday, we will be working so be here before 7:00 a.m. I'd suggest that you be here by 6:30 a.m. as you will want to inspect your rig and get your paperwork in order. We'll be hauling gravel from our pit to Tumbler Ridge where we're installing a large gravel pad upon which a gas plant will be constructed. I'll have my dad, John Dyck, run with you. He'll show you how we do things at the pit, as well as run with you back and forth to Tumbler Ridge. He'll be there to answer your questions or make suggestions, which will help you get a good firm grip, on what we do and how we do it.

"Don and Paul, you each will be assigned your own semi. It's up to you to keep it properly serviced and in good working order. Our shop here will help you with anything that needs repair. One last thing, here are the keys to that pickup sitting outside the shop doors. It is unit number eighteen, and it will be your source of transportation while you are employed with John Dyck Trucking."

"Well, Smitty. It sounds and also looks like this ought to be a good place to work. The equipment appears well maintained, and even the pickup we'll be running around in is a very respectable ride. The people we've met so far are also pleasant to talk to."

"I'm impressed with their setup as well, Dude. Let's get on back to the hotel. I'm famished. We'll have time to set up our gear tonight and maybe even watch a movie."

It had been a long day for both Smitty and me, so we wasted no time getting to the restaurant at the Voyageur Motor Inn. What we quickly noticed was that not only was the restaurant busy, but that most of the customers were working type folk just as we were.

"That was a good meal that I had, Dude. I've always enjoyed liver and onions. It looked like you enjoyed your meal as well. Oh, by the way, the hotel's restaurant has some pretty sharp-looking gals for waitresses, eh?"

"I think we're going to enjoy our evening meals here, Smitty. We'll have to start our good guy–bad guy shtick. Our comedy routine ought to bring more than a few laughs, eh?"

"We'll have lots of good laughs, Dude, but don't you try to set me up for a fall. Don't you ever forget, I owe you for life because of that cream puff caper you pulled off on me back in '75."

"Smitty, get over it. That was thirty-seven years ago. But I have to admit, I'll never forget the cream puff stuffed in your mouth, nose, and even up to your ears."

Life was good. Smitty and I had great jobs hauling gravel in the surrounding district, probably in a radius of about 150 miles. We were busy twelve hours a day, Monday to Friday. Most Saturday's we worked until noon. If we had a rainy day during the week, we'd almost always end up working a full day on Saturday and, sometimes a half day on Sunday. But that only happened a few times.

There were a few notable events that happened to me during my time working in Dawson Creek. One such event was when my tractor broke down and was towed into the shop for repairs.

Wes approached me while I was in the shop, and he'd said, "Paul, we've ordered the parts needed to repair your tractor. They won't be here for three or four days, maybe a bit longer. These parts have to come in from Indiana. I'm sorry, but I don't have a spare tractor. You'll have to sit this one out, I'm afraid."

I immediately retorted, "No way, Wes. We've been spreading gravel on the Old Edmonton Highway for a couple of weeks, and I'm able to run your packer. Take the young fellow who is your packer operator, and put him somewhere else for those days that I'm waiting for repairs. I'm ready to start tomorrow."

"Hum. Hadn't thought of that, Paul. But I do like your suggestion so that is what I'll do. Henry is a good lad, and I can keep him busy for a few days with the ground crew."

That was an easy job. Running the packer was like a pleasant walk in the park. I had an umbrella over my head. I sat in the open air, enjoying the breezes that came off the nearby mountain range. Maybe it was a bit boring, just running the packer back and forth over the fresh gravel that was laid down by Smitty and the other drivers, but I didn't mind. If I wasn't busy, I'd stop near one of the flaggers and enjoy a good old chat for a bit.

"Dude, you look like you're enjoying running that packer. Putting your feet up and your hands behind your head every time I drive by with my load of gravel suggests you're trying to bug me."

"No way, Smitty, I'd never try to rub it in, even if I was having a good time lazing about while you were busy working your buns off. Oh yes, and still getting the same rate of pay per hour as you are, even though I've been away from my rig for three days. No way, not me. I'd not rub that in."

"You pot-licker. What are you doing right now if you're not rubbing it in?"

"Just stating facts, Smitty. Just stating facts. So sorry if that bugs you."

But I do have a bit of a scary story as well, and it's about broken glass from the windshield of my tractor. This is how that played out. It was a beautiful day in the middle of August. I was heading back to our company's open gravel pit for another load of pit run.

Pit run is the first aggregate usually dug out of a new section of an existing gravel pit. It consists of large and small stones mixed with sand or even some sub-soil. It is used first when starting to build a gas site. Upon it would be placed other sizes of rock to ultimately create a solid pad, often more than several acres in size. I was working alone on this particular day. Smitty was elsewhere, running out of another pit and hauling rock on another company contract.

I was west of Dawson Creek and had just turned off Highway 97 to head south on Highway 52. I would run on Highway 52 for about five kilometers before turning west again to run on a secondary gravel road for about ten kilometers.

When I work alone sometimes, I will audibly respond to situations that impact me whether positively or negatively. That was the case in this event.

"That car coming toward me is traveling at an incredible speed. He must be crazy. There's a stop signal just ahead for him," I yelled loudly to myself.

Just as the speeding car passed me, my windshield erupted in a million pieces of shared glass with a huge bang!

"Oh no," I yelled loudly to myself. "He picked up a large rock, and his tire spun it into my windshield. I've got glass all over me."

But I had more than glass all over me; I had something in my left eye. My eye was immediately irritated. It felt like something was scratching under my eyelid. I realized to my horror that I did indeed have some glass in my eye.

What was I to do? Speaking aloud again, I said, "Paul, you have to keep your left eye closed. Try not to move your eyes to the right or left but stare as much as possible straight ahead."

That was easier said than done, but I did it as best I could. I had to make three rather sharp turns before I could enter the company gravel pit, but I accomplished that task, and then I parked my rig as best I could beside the weigh scale's shack.

I then grabbed my cell phone and called the company dispatch. George, our dispatcher, picked up immediately.

"George, Paul here. I'm at our pit and I'm parked by the weigh scales. I had a rock come through my windshield from a car traveling north on 52 just after I got off 97. I have some glass in my left eye, as well as glass all over me. I'm OK other than the glass in my eye. I need someone to come out to me here at the pit and take me to the Dawson Creek Hospital."

"Just turn around, Paul, and run back to our yard, and then someone will take you to the hospital."

"No way, George. I'm not moving one inch. I have now closed both eyes so that I won't be tempted to look about. I'm going to sit right here in my truck, until you or somebody else, comes out here and picks me up, and takes me to the hospital. I will not open my eyes again until I'm sitting in front of the emergency doctor on call at the hospital, and I'm told to open my eyes."

"OK, Paul. We're really busy here today, but all right, I'll bring our mechanic with me, and he'll drive your truck back to our yard. I'll get you into my pickup, and then I'll take you to the hospital myself."

About an hour and a half later, with my both eyes still closed, George helped me to navigate the steps and doors, and I found myself in the emergency waiting room of the Dawson Creek Hospital. George explained to them why I was there with my eyes closed, so I didn't have to surrender any ID immediately. The intake nurse said she'd get it from me later after the doctor had attended to my needs. And with that, I was immediately placed in a room with the doctor.

"Mr. O'Brien, that was a smart move on your part to close your eyes as soon as you were able to do it. You have a lot of tears, and that is a good sign. I'm very confident that you have washed that shard of glass from your eyes when you opened your eyes before me. I do notice some degree of scratching, and that would have happened immediately upon the glass entering your eye.

"It's interesting to note, Mr. O'Brien, that your eye wants to heal itself almost immediately when something like this, when a foreign particle like a shard of glass enters your eye. I can already see some healing taking place on those scratches.

"I've rinsed your eyes carefully, and I want you to wear this eye patch for a couple of days. You will not see from your left eye, but your right eye will adjust to your needs very well. You won't stumble or walk into objects just because you have one eye closed. It would be a good thing to take a couple of days off before you get back to work."

"Thanks, Doctor. I'd like to request that you prepare a note of some sort that explains your requests for me to follow. This will help the company to establish a BC worker's compensation file for me. It will also allow me to take those days off without any hassle from my company."

As we were leaving the hospital, I spoke to George. "Drop me off at the Voyageur Hotel. You have all the proper paperwork that the doctor has given to me, so I really didn't need to return with you to the company office.

"The doctor said to take a couple of days off. Today is Friday, and it's nearly done, so I'll take tomorrow and Sunday off. I should be ready to go back to work Monday morning."

Later that evening, when Smitty came back to the hotel after work, he banged on my door.

"Dude, I heard you had a bit of a mishap. The word around the shop is that you had some glass in your eye, and you'll not be back to work tomorrow."

"That's the word and it's correct, Smitty. I'll be getting a couple of days' pay while you work your butt off, Saturday and Sunday."

"Oh yes, you sure do know how to work the system, Dude."

"You know that old adage, 'Jealousy will get you nowhere,' Smitty, so don't crash and burn over my good fortune.

Would you care to read about another broken glass story?" Oops, there I go again, speaking out loud to no one in particular.

Barely a month had passed, and another window in my tractor was shattered. This one happened when my own drive tires picked up a large rock, and projected it through the back window of the cab. Sometimes a large rock will get stuck between the dual drive tires of the tractor. When the truck is up to highway speeds, the rapid rotation of the wheels will often spit that rock out. It is anybody's guess as to where that rock will fly, but in this case, it flew right through the back window of that International day cab.

Here's how this event played itself out. I was northbound on Highway 52 and just shy of the intersection with Highway 2. I was gearing down as I had a good solid load of gravel, which I'd picked up at a gravel pit back south on 52, about fifty kilometers. All of a sudden, *bang*!

"Not again. What's with rocks and windows?"

Nobody heard me yelling, but it felt good nevertheless to verbally express myself. Immediately, I was covered with broken glass. This time it was all over the back of my hat and head and on the back of my shirt, and what a mess it was. Incidentally, the large rock made it past my shoulder without hitting me, and crashed into the dash. It was raining quite heavily, and I became saturated with dirty, muddy water that was being sucked up behind the cab. Not only was I covered in wet, dirty water sprayed up by the drive tires, but the inside of my windshield was likewise covered.

Lest you think that was all that was polluted with dirty water, my glasses were also awash with that filth. I now had to drive without my glasses. The wiper blades did a respectable job of clearing the rain off the outside of the windshield, but trucks don't have wipers on the inside of the windshield. I had to grab a rag off the floor and continuously wipe the windshield so I could see.

On this particular day, Wes Dyck, my boss, was working on site. We were under contract to rebuild the Old Edmonton Highway. In just a few kilometers, I arrived at the worksite and spread my load of gravel, all the while enjoying a wonderful bath of muddy water.

Seeing Wes just up ahead sitting in his pickup, I stopped beside him and yelled down to him from my cab, "Wes, a large rock shattered the back window of my cab. I need to get this fixed immediately as the inside of the cab is now completely saturated with spray off the drives."

"Paul, didn't you check your duals on the tractor and the trailer before you left the gravel pit? That's what happens when you have a rock stuck between the duals. It'll spin off, and today, it went through the back window. Maybe tomorrow it would spin off and go through someone else's window."

"Hold on, Wes. I did check all my duals before I left the pit. There weren't any rocks stuck between the tires at that time. As I was approaching the intersection of Highway 2 and Highway 52, there were several large rocks lying on the pavement. I couldn't avoid them because of oncoming traffic. Evidently, it was one of those rocks that found its way into my cab."

"Yes, right. OK, OK. Take your rig back to the yard. I'll call the shop and have them get Speedy Auto Glass to come out to the yard and replace the window. It is 3:00 p.m. right now, so you won't be able to finish the day out here. Sign yourself out at 7:00 p.m. as usual, but before you do sign out, be sure and get over to the fuel pumps and fuel up for tomorrow's work."

That night back at the hotel, I had to listen to Smitty whining again.

"Dude, what's with your driving skills? I thought you knew how to manoeuver your rig? What's the idea about running through a field bed of rocks? You're always looking for a way to get out of work, and still get paid."

"Shut up, Smitty. Don't bother trying to bug me because you know it won't work. I'm like Teflon. Nothing sticks to me, so let's go and get dinner, and you can bug Violet, our waitress. You do that Mr. Bad Guy so well. I'll have to mop up after you, and smooth out her ruffled feathers. I'm Mr. Good Guy to the rescue."

"Hey, you. Yes, you, whoever you are reading this story. Here's a funny little story of Smitty and me, the dude. This ought to put a big smile on your face."

It was the end of a good day. Both Smitty and I had been hauling out of the same gravel pit up near Fort St. John, British Columbia, where we were under contract to rebuild some side roads just south of the Fort.

Neither Smitty, nor I ever rehearse what we're going to say or do when we play this bad guy-good guy shtick. It just happens spontaneously.

On our way back to our yard in Dawson Creek, Smitty got ahead of me by a couple of kilometers, when he was able to pass through some highway construction on the green light. I had to stop. The light turned red just as I approached it. Yuk. Oh well. Stuff happens.

By the time I arrived back in Dawson Creek, Smitty had fueled up and already left the fuel pumps. That meant he'd be in the yard at least ten minutes ahead of me, and for that matter, so would three other company semi-trucks who had been running with Smitty and me all day.

Fueling up didn't take long, and soon, I was pulling into our yard. I realized I was the last rig in for the day. The other drivers, as well as Smitty, were standing around outside the office door, just talking with each other. There was one spot left for me, but because the yard was so plugged with other rigs and several empty trailers, I was having a bit of a difficult time getting my rig turned around and pointed for the gate. That's how we did it. When we'd arrive in the morning, we'd be ready to leave without trying to maneuver around the yard to make our exit.

As I finally make my last maneuver and parked beside Smitty's rig, he left the other drivers and approached my tractor. He began yelling and waving his arms like a madman.

"What's the matter with you, Dude? Haven't you learned how to drive yet? I thought I'd taught you well back there in '71, but you're driving like a little old lady. You don't even know how to back up yet, and it's taken you at least ten minutes to get into that parking spot. You suck at driving. You ought to get on the next plane and fly home. Why don't you give up trucking, and go drive a taxi? You think you could do that without driving into curbs or other parked cars? Did I tell you that you really suck at driving?"

This was too funny. I knew exactly what was happening. Smitty was setting me up for a good shtick. He played the bad guy so good. But today, I was going to play the bad guy as well. This was going to be a lot of fun, and we had a ready-made audience. There had to be at least four other drivers standing around.

Jumping out of my truck, I approached Smitty quickly. "Shad up, you purple pimple of puss," I yelled while waving my arms wildly. "Where do you get off on telling me how to drive? You want to make a big deal out of how professionally I was operating my rig, and executing some very good maneuvers to park beside that beat-up piece of crap you call a truck? I've been watching you, you left-handed lug nut, and I noticed you got stuck at the pit today. The front-end loader had to pull you out. Only a dolt who doesn't know how to drive a big rig would get stuck in the only place where you could get stuck in that whole big gravel pit. You had more than forty acres to get that sorry-looking piece of junk you call a semitruck turned around, and there you go and drive in a sump hole. You sure do know how to drive 'em, Smitty."

Well, we carried that shtick on for a couple more minutes, yelling at each other and wildly waving our arms. When Smitty winked at me, I knew we'd finished our two-man show.

I turned on my heel and walked down the left side of my rig. I still had to finish a post-trip inspection. Smitty walked back to the group of men who hadn't moved an inch. A couple of them stood there with their mouths still open in disbelief that Smitty and me, two good buddies, could just about come to duking it out in the yard.

Smitty later told me, as we rode back to the hotel in our pickup, "Those guys didn't say a word to me. I think they probably thought I'd light into them as well. Too funny, Dude. I think we pulled off a good shtick tonight, eh?"

"It was beautiful, Smitty. We played those guys really good. I was watching them out of the corner of my eye as we were lighting into each other. They were, without exception, wide-eyed and open-mouthed. They must have believed that we'd back up our verbal bashing of each other with our fists."

Our laughter and happy comments about our "fight" in the yard captivated us all the way to the hotel. We were still laughing about it as we sat down to eat. And wouldn't you know it, Smitty began another shtick just for the waitresses that usually hung around our table, if they weren't too busy.

It wasn't a busy evening in the Voyageur's restaurant, so there were two waitresses sitting at their table nearest the kitchen doors. Maggie and Belinda were just nursing a coffee each when Smitty and I came in, and sat down beside them. Violet was immediately beside Smitty and happily spoke to both of us.

"Well, well, well. Look what the cat dragged in. If it isn't Mr. Nice Guy and Mr. Sour Puss. You two bad actors look like you're starving. Would you like what's on the house tonight?"

Putting on his best exasperated face, Smitty said, "Violet, whatever has been put on top of the house, or wherever it has been put can stay there. I want to eat some good food at this table, not sit on the house, and eat whatever it is that's been put on the house."

"Cute. Real cute, Smitty," Violet said as she stuck out her tongue at him, and then turning to me, she smiled demurely and asked, "Dude, it's our famous meat pie loaf that is the house special tonight, and I know you like it. Would you care to order our special?"

"Violet, I'd enjoy the house special tonight, and I especially enjoy anything the cook whips up when you are here, because you are my favorite waitress and your smile always makes everything taste the best."

That comment got me a big smile from Violet, but as she turned back to Smitty, her countenance changed, and she sort of growled as she asked, "OK, Mr. Grumpy, what do you want to eat, or are you just going to sit there and be a real pain in the butt?"

Before Smitty could open his mouth, Maggie got into the conversation with a sarcastic comment directed toward Smitty, "Hey, you old crank. It sounds to me like you've had a rough day, eh? Did your boss fire you for being a big grump?"

Belinda got in on the act too, and turning toward me, said with a pleasant smile on her face, "Dude, none of us understand Smitty, but you are just the sweetest, and in fact, you are our favorite customer as well."

Smitty knew he was out numbered, basically three to one, so he turned toward Violet, reached for her hand, and holding it, said, "Please forgive me, and I would like the meat pie special as well."

That is how it went most every night when Smitty and I came into the restaurant. We enjoyed playing our little game, and the waitresses enjoyed playing along with us. And when it wasn't busy, the cook and the dishwasher would join all of us at that special long table at the rear of the restaurant. It would be lots of fun, as all of us would enter into excited and animated conversation.

As Smitty and I were finishing up a delightful dessert of hot apple pie and ice cream, Violet sat down beside us for a quick little break. While enjoying her coffee, with a big smile, she said, "You know what, guys, every night when I go home after work, my husband always asks me about you two. He says, 'Well, tell me what Smitty and Dude did tonight? Did they do their Mr. Bad Guy, Mr. Good Guy shtick?' Of course, I have to tell him everything that happened. I know he likes you, guys."

In retrospect, I think those evenings spent around that long table at the back of the restaurant in the Voyageur Inn were some of the most delightful times, Smitty and I had when we worked in Dawson Creek back in 2012.

How much fun can two guys have anyway? It seems as one gets older, reminiscing about the past becomes a more dominant theme in one's life. Such was the case with my time working in Dawson Creek. Smitty and I had enjoyed many wonderful times working together, but this would be the last time we were able to do that. We didn't part ways and deny our friendship; we just went down different paths for the next three years. I returned to work in pipeline construction, and Smitty retired from driving during the next spring.

Smitty came home from Dawson Creek for the Christmas season of 2012, but returned in January 2013. That period of work was cut short soon after his return. While helping the shop mechanic fix a broken part on the dump body of his truck, he fell to the cement floor, and busted his left shoulder rotator cup. He returned to Ontario severely injured, and unable to continue his driving career.

We were the best of buddies right up to the end. We laughed at life, and we laughed at ourselves. We enjoyed doing things together so much, and were often seen together, that even when we'd meet strangers, they would ask if we were brothers. We had a one-liner we always used when that question was raised. Sometimes one of us would respond, usually me, but most often we'd respond with the same words together in unison, "Yes, we're actually twins, born on the same date, one year apart by separate mothers."

That comment always elicited confused looks.

I had ceased working in Alberta in pipeline construction during the Christmas of 2014, and had picked up a local job, driving for a trucking company in Peterborough, Ontario.

As spring time ran into the summer of 2015, my three younger brother and I organized a grand birthday celebration for our mother, who was celebrating her ninetieth birthday. Smitty and his wife Kathy were invited, but really, he didn't need an invitation. He had always been a part of my family, and always called my mother his mother too.

It was interesting to note that Smitty and I wore identical shirts at my mother's birthday party, which was held in the lovely Pinafore Park, that park in St. Thomas where we spent so much time in our youth. Unbeknown to either of us, we'd purchased the same shirt just a couple of months earlier, me in Edmonton, and Smitty in Chatham.

We had some good laughs as many came up to us at the birthday party, and told us we looked like brothers. Of course, we gave them our one-liner: "Yes, we're actually twins, born on the same date, one year apart by separate mothers."

In the fall of that year, I began driving for Highlight Motor Freight out of Concord, Ontario. It was about that time, the middle of October, when I paid Smitty and Kathy a visit at their home in Bothwell, Ontario.

Smitty took me aside, and in a somber and broken voice told me, "Dude, the doctor told me a few days ago that I have six months to live. The cancer that was in my prostate has spread to other parts of my body, and it is also in my spinal cord."

We hugged each other and we both cried. I knew Smitty had prostate cancer. He'd had it when we were working out in Dawson Creek, BC, back in 2012. But it was still hard to hear those words – "Dude, I have six months to live."

"Smitty, I need to get back on the road, but I'll call you often, and I'll stay in touch with you and Kathy."

During the last full week of December, I asked Highlight's dispatch for a load which would take me to Edmonton, Alberta, at Christmas time. Dispatch responded by giving me a load, to be delivered in the Greater Chicago Area at Orland Park. Then I had a reload to pick up south of Chicago, at Kankakee, Illinois, which was destined for Edmonton, to be delivered Monday, December 28.

I wanted that load to Edmonton, because Shirley was going with me. She would be able to see her sister, Karen and brother-in-law Bob. They resided there.

We had arrived in Edmonton, December 25, and one day later, while Shirley and I were sitting and visiting with our loved ones, I received a phone call from Donna, Smitty's youngest daughter.

"Uncle Paul, I'm Donna. Dad has been in a coma now for nearly two days. The doctor says he will die in the next day or two."

"Oh Donna, Smitty told me he had six months to live, not six weeks."

"I know Uncle Paul. I guess he didn't want you to know his time was so short."

"Donna, please do this for me. I can't be at his bedside, I'm out in Edmonton with Shirley, but I want you to place your cell phone with the speaker on beside your dad's ear. When I'm done talking to him, you will know, and then be able to close off my conversation with him."

"OK Uncle Paul, the phone is on speaker mode and is beside his ear."

"Smitty." I spoke that nickname I gave him over sixty years ago. Then I paused.

Immediately, Smitty came out of his coma. His response was clear, albeit very weak. "Dude."

"Smitty, you know you are close to death. You and I have talked about death many times over the years. When you die, Smitty, you will immediately be in the presence of Jesus Christ. The Holy Bible assures you of this, because you accepted Him as your Lord and Savior."

Smitty, with a barely audible voice responded, "I know Dude."

"Smitty, your family is at your bedside. They love you and they will be with you until you are in the presence of your Lord.

"Smitty, when you arrive on that golden shore, you will see and experience the love again of those who have gone before you – your mother and father and your grandmother. There will be others there who will also greet you."

Again, Smitty responded weakly, "I know Dude."

My conversation with Smitty, was personal and somber, yet I didn't want it to be very long, because of his weakened state. So my few parting words to my best friend, my buddy who I grew up with, who I shared so much life with, was a simple farewell.

"Smitty, when you get to Heaven's golden shore, will you watch for me? I'll be coming soon."

Again, Smitty responded weakly, "I'll be watching for you, Dude."

With a choking voice, I spoke these final words. "Smitty, I won't say good-bye. I'll just say, see you soon."

I will never forget his final farewell to me, and the last words he ever spoke in his lifetime, when he uttered in a clear and quiet voice. "Dude, drive safe."

Why were those three words so touching to me? Why did they move me to tears? Those three words were always the last words Smitty ever spoke to me, and I to him, as we parted company, or as we closed off a phone conversation. Smitty was a trucker to his dying breath.

And so it was, that two lads who knew each other from their earliest days, and had grown up together, and spent their lives entwined in each other's lives, had come to the end of a long and beautiful relationship. Smitty died and passed into eternity on December 31, 2015.

"Rest in peace, my friend. I'll see you later."

# SIXTEEN

# PIPELINE CONSTRUCTION CAN BE DANGEROUS

**Brandon, Manitoba with Banister Pipelines**

"PAUL, WILL YOU get the phone? I'm not able to get to it."
I was close to the phone and caught it on the third ring. After a brief conversation, during which time Shirley had come into the kitchen and had given me some quizzical looks, I tried to ignore her, and soon my conversation was concluded and the phone replaced on its cradle.

"Shirley, that was the Teamster Union Hall in Winnipeg. They just offered me a job, driving a truck on an oil pipeline construction project in Manitoba. I asked them to give me a half hour to respond back to them."

That's how it all started—a phone call out of nowhere and a job offer in Manitoba. Some history will explain how this all came to be. Events in my past became my history, and what happened in my past had an impact on what would happen in my future.

I became a Teamster Union member more than four decades ago. That all came to pass during the time I was driving intercity bus with Eastern Canadian Greyhound Bus Lines. I had been laid off late in the fall of 1973 from Greyhound, and had hired on with a local trucking company named Bondy Cartage. They were a union company. Thus, I became a Teamster Union member in order to work for them. Incidentally, Windsor had always been a union city because of the big three automakers. I moved my union hall affiliation from Windsor to

Winnipeg in 2000, when I became employed with Tri-Line Freight Systems. I remained in the union to the present time of that phone call.

It was June 13, 2009, and I had been preoccupied with looking for meaningful work as a semi-truck driver. I had not driven for better than a year, because of the nation-wide depression we were experiencing in Ontario. Now, I was offered work in the province Shirley and I had left over eight years earlier.

"What are you going to tell the union hall, Paul?"

"I will tell them I'll take the work. When I asked them how long that term position would last, they said the potential was for at least a year. This is what I want ask you, my dear. Will you accompany me to Brandon, Manitoba?"

Shirley spontaneously agreed to go to Manitoba with me. One phone call later, and I not only had a work assignment, but a starting date of Wednesday, June 17. I would be employed with Banister Pipelines Corporation.

"Shirley, we need to not only prepare to leave but we need to leave within a couple of hours."

"Really? You're giving me two hours to get ready and leave that quickly Paul?" Shirley asked that question with a slightly elevated and quizzical voice.

Not only were both Shirley and I ready to leave within two hours, but we were already on the road and had left within one and a half hours. Our little car was packed to the roof, and with a hasty goodbye to the neighbors, we departed on an adventure, which would be lived out in many different ways over the next ten years.

"I'm really happy, Paul, that we are returning to Manitoba for a while. It will be good to see our daughters, Colleen and Connie, and their families."

I shared this happiness and joy with Shirley as we both looked forward to visiting our daughters and their families. Brandon would be a great place to live as we'd be only a little over two hours away from Grandview, Manitoba, where Reuben and Connie lived. We would also be just three and one half hours away from Rosengart, Manitoba, where Steve and Colleen lived.

Our trip west was uneventful, and we got a motel room as soon as we arrived in Brandon. We would begin looking for an apartment as soon as possible. This was going to be challenging and also a lot of fun. We'd have to buy furniture and the essentials like pots and pans and dishes. Shirley was left with those tasks as I basically started work with Banister the day after our arrival.

I was greeted at the door of the hotel room by my smiling and happy sweetheart. "Hi, Paul. How was your first day with Banister? Tell me all about it."

"Here's a *Reader's Digest* version, Shirley. I am driving a three-ton straight truck, which has large propane tanks on it. Long torches attached to hoses, which are attached to the tanks, provide intense flame which is focused on heating the end of each 80-foot long pipe. Welders follow immediately after we move to the next joint. They weld the two pipe ends together. It's a simple job with two men operating the torches. I remain in the truck as long as the men operate the torches. That's pretty much a complete description of my workday. Sounds boring, doesn't it? But the paychecks won't be boring, and that's why we're here."

Sitting at our kitchen table late one evening in August, after I'd come in from working on the pipeline, I said to Shirley, "Remember, sweetheart, when we left home to come out here, the union hall said this pipeline gig would go on for at least a year?"

"Yes, I remember, Paul. But I get the feeling there might be a change of plans. Am I correct in assuming this?"

"As a matter of fact, you are correct. My position as a preheat truck driver comes to an end with the start of the Labor Day weekend, September 4."

"I feel like we have just arrived in Manitoba, Paul, and now are you saying that we'll be leaving so soon?"

That's exactly what I wanted to talk to Shirley about, so in the course of a lengthy conversation, we decided to remain in Brandon for the foreseeable future and I'd begin looking for work as a semi-truck driver.

"Paul, I have a great idea for what we could do on the Labor Day weekend."

"You've got my attention, Shirley. What might you have in mind?"

"Colleen was talking to me earlier, and she and her family are going to Manhattan Beach Camp for the long weekend. Why don't we see if there is any accommodation still available? Maybe we could go as well. It would be great to see the family there."

It was delightful to visit with family for a few days, but I did have some mixed emotions. I was finished with the pipeline gig I had so thoroughly enjoyed. Now it seemed I was back to square one. Unemployment stared me in the face.

"Shirley, I enjoyed our little break from reality, spending the Labor Day weekend with Colleen and the family here at Manhattan Beach Camp, but tomorrow morning, I either search for meaningful work, or we'll have to go back to Cobourg."

Over the next month, I spent a lot of time in and around Brandon, looking for a work driving a semi, but to no avail. It wasn't until October when something appeared on the horizon, which gave me hope.

"Shirley, somewhere in my job hunting journey, I was given a tip that a company in Portage la Prairie, is looking for semi-drivers. I'll check this out, and hopefully hire on with this company. Then we'll stay in Manitoba, but if I don't land a job, we must return to Ontario. Our funds are getting depleted."

Returning from Portage, I called out, "Shirley, I have great news," the words spilled out of my mouth as I entered our apartment that Monday evening, October 12. "I will start driving for Lark Transport in Portage. They've already given me a trip. I will be one of four drivers, all taking the same loads from the Carberry Distribution Centre down to Laredo, Texas. I'll pick up my semi-truck and get that load on Wednesday, the fourteenth."

Everything went smoothly. I had no trouble with the load, no trouble with the rig, and no trouble staying on schedule for delivery in Laredo on Saturday, the seventeenth. However, Lark Transport didn't seem to be in a rush to get any of the three other drivers and myself a reload. Consequently, a one-day wait became a three-day wait before I was assigned a reload.

"Paul, this is Lark dispatch. I have a reload for you. This load is out of El Paso, Texas, and will be ready for pickup on Tuesday, the twentieth, at 8:00 a.m. This load is destined for Calgary, Alberta, and delivery is scheduled on Friday the twenty-third at 4:00 p.m."

Finally, I had a reload. The destination of Calgary wasn't quite getting me back to Portage la Prairie, but dispatch assured me that they would get me a load from the Calgary area for Winnipeg. That was good enough for me.

I immediately grabbed my cell phone and called Shirley, "Hi, sweetheart.

I've got a reload back to Canada. I'll run over to El Paso this afternoon and get my reload in the morning. I'm taking it to Calgary. From there, I'm told I'll go to Lethbridge for a load to Winnipeg. Depending on reload timing in Lethbridge, I could be home as early as Sunday evening. More likely, I won't get back to Brandon until Monday evening, the twenty-sixth."

I made it from Laredo to El Paso in good time and found a spot to park for the night just outside of town at a rest area. "This is good," I said loudly to myself. "I'll get a good start for tomorrow and be able to make some excellent miles."

But it didn't work out that way whatsoever.

Midway through that night, I groaned audibly. "Oh no, I'm going to be sick."

I was indeed sick. I was never so sick in my life. I had a high fever and became violently sick, vomiting repeatedly into my garbage can. I knew instinctively that I was quickly dehydrating. I tried to drink water. I couldn't keep it down. I tried to drink repeatedly, but the results remained the same until I passed out. I fainted dead away and collapsed on the floor of my bunk. I don't have any recollection of how long a lay on the floor, covered in my own vomit and excrement.

I know, at one point, I came to but continued to lay on the floor, too weak to get up. In my semi-comatose condition, it seemed time had stopped. I thought I was dying.

Was it an hour later that I regained enough strength to sit up? I don't know, but finally, I did get up and tried to clean up the mess. At that point, I was unable to find my cell phone and call Shirley, because I wasn't connecting all the dots.

Speaking out loud, I said, "There it is." I was referring to my cell phone. Somehow, it had got shoved up under the dash against the firewall on the right side of the truck.

I immediately called my wife, and in a weak and trembling voice, I said, "Shirley, I am very sick. I lost all my biscuits and made a total mess of things in the cab and bunk."

Immediately, Shirley showed serious concern in her voice, "Oh, Paul. What did you pick up? Do you think you've had some food poisoning?"

"I've had food poisoning a couple of times over the years, but I don't think this was a case of that."

"Do you feel any better right now, Paul?"

"Maybe a bit better, Shirley." I then proceeded to recount what had taken place over the last few hours.

"Paul, maybe you should check into a hospital. You have insurance coverage, you know."

"I assure you, Shirley, I have certainly given that some thought, but I think I can tough it out. I have a load to pick up in a couple of hours."

"But first, I'm going to drive over to a truck stop just a few miles away. I need to get some cleaning solvent and straighten out the mess I've made."

"Why don't you go into the C-Store or even the restaurant and drink some Coke, and maybe get an order of toast? I think the Coke will settle your stomach, and you need to get some nourishment in you as well."

I listened to Shirley and did exactly what she said. The Coke seemed to help, but I just couldn't eat any toast.

"Hi again, Shirley. I picked up my load, and I'm heading for Calgary. I have lots of water in the truck and some food as well, but I think it best if I just drink for a while and not put any food in my stomach."

I remained in that condition for a couple of days. I'd drink water and have diarrhea, drink water and have diarrhea. My temperature returned to near normal, but if I tried to eat anything like even a piece of fruit, such as an apple, up it came.

That was probably one of the hardest drives I'd ever endured or undertaken. I was entering into an accelerated weakened state, yet I seemed unable to reverse that course.

I guess sheer determination got me through two days of near total collapse. Calgary lay low on the horizon ahead of me. I would make it and I'd make it on time as well.

"Shirley, I've made it to Calgary. I think I'm starting to get over the hardest part of whatever I've had. I still have diarrhea but not as often. I've been able to eat some chicken noodle soup and toast, but that's about the extent of it."

"That's hardly enough to sustain you, Paul. Please look after yourself. You are not made out of rebar, you're only human."

But my diet of soup and toast remained my focus for bodily sustenance even after I'd picked up my reload in Lethbridge.

I talked continuously with Shirley. It was her encouragement that kept me going. I was weak and often realized that I was lacking mental focus. She challenged me to do certain mental exercises, which could help me, and doing that did help.

"I'm going to make it to Portage la Prairie, Shirley. The load is destined for Winnipeg, but I told dispatch I was sick, and they needed to get another driver to finish my trip."

"Where are you now, sweetheart? How close are you to Portage?"

"I'm just passing through Virden, Manitoba. If you leave for Portage in the car within the next half hour, you should arrive about the same time as me."

Portage la Prairie was a welcome sight for sore eyes to be sure. I'd told dispatch I needed some time off in order to recuperate. They certainly had no problem with that.

While I took that week off, Shirley and I discussed our options and decided it would be best to return to Cobourg instead of remaining in Brandon.

It was just two weeks later when I called out to Shirley. "The moving van will be here within the hour. Everything is packed and ready to go. Once they have loaded our furniture, we're out of here."

After Shirley and I had arrived back in Cobourg, I described to a medical health professional what I had experienced and endured for better than a week back in September when I contracted something in El Paso, Texas. I was thus informed that I'd come down with the H1N1 virus, also known as the swine flu. I was assured that I had now built up immunities and would never get the H1N1 virus again.

## Red Earth Creek, Alberta with Louisbourg Pipelines

"Paul, while you were out running errands for me, you got a phone call from Reuben and Connie. Reuben wants to talk to you about some pipeline work, so you should call him right away."

Quickly picking up the phone, I called my son-in-law in Manitoba. "Hi, Reuben. What's up?"

"Dad, are you interested in doing some more pipeline work? There's a winter project happening up in Red Earth Creek, Alberta, and my union hall in Edmonton needs more Teamsters. You've got pipeline experience now, Dad, so you'll be qualified, and I'm pretty sure I can speak on your behalf and get you a job working out of the Edmonton hall."

Later that evening, when Shirley and I were having a conversation about potential pipeline construction work, she said something very positive. "Paul, I think you'd better start packing your gear in order to be ready to go to Alberta. I really believe that Reuben will be able to land you some work in Red Earth Creek."

Shirley and I had returned from Brandon, Manitoba the first week of November 2009, where I had been working with Banister Pipelines. Now it was toward the end of that month was there a good possibility that I could be working again in pipeline construction, this time in northern Alberta.

Barely twenty-four hours later and another phone call from Reuben, and my world took a delightful turn. "Dad, great news. I'll be working with Louisbourg Pipelines up in Red Earth Creek as a sandblast truck driver and bus driver. The hall needed two drivers for the same job, and I asked that they consider you as the second driver. They agreed that would work because you've had some experience already."

One phone call to the Edmonton Teamster Union Hall, and I confirmed with them that I'd be willing to go to work. I then made a quick trip to Staples, and with all the proper documentation I'd need to supply to the hall, I quickly faxed it to them.

Later that evening I was on the phone with Reuben. "That's fantastic, Reuben. Shirley and I were hoping this could happen so I've already packed my gear. I'll reserve a seat with VIA Rail, and I'll catch the next train to Winnipeg. It will leave tomorrow evening from Toronto's Union Station."

Plans were quickly made and finalized. Then I needed to call Reuben back and confirm with him my plans and arrival time. Reuben answered his phone immediately and I imagined him sitting by the phone with his hand hovering over it. With a good degree of excitement in my voice, I said, "I'll catch an early train from Cobourg to Toronto in order to meet the Winnipeg train. I checked out bus service with Grey Goose, and I'll be able to catch a bus to Grandview the same day I arrive in Winnipeg. It will be a slam dunk. I'll see you later that day about noontime, and we can then leave in your pickup for Red Earth Creek."

The VIA train left on Thursday night, the third of December 2009, right on time. It would arrive Saturday morning, the fifth, at 8:00 am. The Grey Goose bus would leave Winnipeg just a short while later and arrive in Dauphin, Manitoba, where Reuben would pick me up. We'd be able to get close to Edmonton that day and finish our trip to Red Earth Creek on Sunday, the sixth. We'd be right on time for orientation Monday morning, the seventh.

But here I was, standing in the main concourse of the Winnipeg Union Station, complaining over the phone, "What's in that saying, Shirley, 'The best laid plans of mice and men'? Well, I guess you could say that about me. All my plans fell apart on this trip. It's not my fault, mind you, but nevertheless, here I am stuck in Winnipeg because the train was four hours late. I've missed my bus to Dauphin. I'm now working on plan B, whatever that is.

"I've called Reuben and told him my dilemma, and he said he'd wait until I have some concrete plans set up. I'll keep you informed as well. Love you, babe."

With that short conversation concluded, I set about to seek a solution to enable me to arrive in Red Earth Creek with Reuben, and on time as well. It was now the time to push back on VIA. After all, it was a situation of their creation that I found myself in. Possibly no more than ten minutes later, and satisfied with the results, I called Shirley back.

"Hi, sweetheart. I think I've got the wrinkles worked out on plan B. I'm in a rush in order to catch the VIA train, so I'll just say for now that everything will work out, and I'll call you later when I have a good opportunity."

It wasn't until late that same day I had that opportunity to speak to Shirley, and when I did, it was with both a mixture of relief and awe. "Here is how my plans played out, Shirley.

"VIA offered to provide me with a coach seat on the train to Melville, Saskatchewan. This was the same train I'd arrived on from Toronto. Reuben said he'd be able to pick me up in Melville, and basically, we wouldn't have lost time heading further west. But can you believe what happened next, even before I was to leave Winnipeg? I had boarded the train and was waiting for it to depart, when an announcement came over the public address system. The train was cancelled.

"The next announcement came almost immediately following that first stunning announcement. Shirley, here's what the second announcement was. 'All passengers traveling beyond Winnipeg, please report to the station's ticket counters.'"

"OK, Paul, I get it now. The train was cancelled in Winnipeg, but how did you end up at the Edmonton airport?"

"Of course, I returned to the ticket counter immediately, Shirley. I told them again how I was unable to catch the Grey Goose bus to Dauphin because the train was late. I told them that I was willing to take VIA to Melville where I could get a ride by truck to Edmonton and then to Red Earth Creek. I told them now that the train was cancelled because of a train wreck in Portage la Prairie, I would miss my Melville connection. I reminded them I still needed to be in Edmonton that evening. And for sure, I told them I needed to be to work in Northern Alberta on Monday morning, the seventh.

"Here's what happened next, Shirley. There were quite a few people who needed to be in Edmonton the next morning as well as me, so it was decided after some consultation with VIA's head office in Montreal that all those who were destined for Edmonton would fly out of the Winnipeg airport early that evening to arrive in Edmonton by 10:00 p.m. mountain time. We made one quick stop at Saskatoon and were soon in the air again. Air Canada was right on time, landing here in Edmonton."

"So that's where you are now, Paul. What is going to happen next?"

"I called your sister, Karen, and Bob, my old buddy Horse Thief, is on his way to the airport as we speak. I'll stay the night with them. Reuben was informed of all the changes, and he is racing toward Edmonton. When he arrives, he will also spend the night at Bob and Karen's. We will then leave early tomorrow morning and should arrive at Red Earth Creek tomorrow, early evening."

"Paul, that's amazing how those plans all worked out when it first appeared you'd be stuck in Winnipeg. That has every sign of the Lord bringing those events together for you and Reuben."

Laughingly, I said to Shirley, "I felt like that Hollywood actor, John Candy, in the movie, *Planes, Trains and Automobiles*."

It was just before midnight when Reuben arrived at Bob and Karen's home in Edmonton. We sat around with Bob and Karen and chatted for a short time, but it was Reuben who said something that promptly cut our conversations short.

"Dad, I expect you're tired. I know I sure am. It has been one very eventful day, and I think we should turn in and get some sleep. I'd like to leave by 8:00 a.m. at the latest. Karen, don't prepare any breakfast for us as we'll grab something from A&W or MacDonald's before we leave Edmonton."

The ride was uneventful from Edmonton to Red Earth Creek on Sunday. One small exception however stands out. We were on Highway

88 northbound, possibly one to one and a half hours south of Red Earth Creek when we approached a pickup truck stuck in the northbound ditch. The pickup's tracks into the ditch were gradual, which might have suggested the driver fell asleep. At any rate, Reuben stopped to see if we might be able to help.

Reuben, speaking to the unknown motorist, said, "I've got a good length of strong tow-rope with me, and I believe I can pull you out of the ditch."

His response, "I'd sure appreciate the help," was to be expected. In no time, Reuben had the stranded driver's pickup safely on the side of the road.

Arriving less than two hours later at the camp on Highway 686, about three quarters of an hour east of Red Earth Creek, we were greeted with the delicious smell of freshly baked hot three meat pizza with cheese and mushrooms. Just what two hungry fellows needed to top off an incredibly interesting, albeit a challenging journey.

Just as the union hall had informed us, both Reuben and I were working the same job. We would each drive a crew bus to the worksite, then each of us would jump in a sandblast truck and proceed from welded joint to welded joint where the sandblast operator would thoroughly strip clean the weld and surrounding pipe of any paint or surface rust. The paint crew was right behind us, immediately coating the freshly blasted area. Incredibly boring, but the pay was more than excellent. It was easy to do a boring job with that kind of coin deposited weekly in my bank account.

A couple of weeks into this work assignment, I responded to some questions Shirley had when I called her on the satellite phone, "We have no other way of calling anyone, Shirley. There is absolutely no cell phone coverage for probably over one hundred miles around us. That is why we can only talk for about five minutes at a time on the camp's satellite phone. Other men are patiently waiting their turn to call home as well."

"Do you enjoy your work, Paul, and is everything working out well for you?"

"The work is boring, Shirley, but I do get to remain inside the cab of my truck all day where it's warm. And of course, you like the paychecks, so that keeps me happy. Oh yes, Reuben and I leapfrog over each other all day. My crew will be working on a section, and Reuben's crew will run around us and set up their workstation, blasting and painting maybe a mile ahead of us. We'll catch up to where they started in blasting and then run around them."

"So sorry to hear it's boring, Paul. Just keep working, boring or not. If you don't make Momma happy, you aren't going to be happy, you get it?"

"Funny girl. Oh, by the way, I'll be spending Christmas with Reuben and Connie and the kids in Grandview. We'll have a couple of weeks off before we'll be expected back in camp."

Christmas 2009 had come, and it had gone. There wasn't any bad weather to complain about, and I'd enjoyed a horse-drawn sleigh hayride from Reuben's home area into Riding Mountain National Park. There must have been a dozen of us, all snuggled up tight together as we followed a trail through the park to a place where we had a robust fire to sit around and warm ourselves up. I was playing the grandpa part with great love as I snuggled with Austin, Cheyne, and Shantel around the fire. Not to mention that the roasted marshmallows and hot chocolate were also delightfully received by the young and the old alike.

Arriving back in camp after a really great time spent with Connie's family, Reuben and I were told to get ready to move. We were to relocate about fifty miles away in a new camp, and we'd continue to do sandblasting working back toward where we'd left off from the last camp.

More than two months later, while sitting around a dining hall table with Reuben and a couple of other fellows, I mentioned to Reuben, "I've heard a rumor that tomorrow is our last day on this gig as bus/sandblast truck drivers."

"That's the word I've received as well, Paul. It's been a good work experience. We've had the best part of three months with Louisbourg, and I for one have thoroughly enjoyed it. How about you? You had a nice piece of equipment to drive?"

"That's right, Reuben. I've had a good bus to drive and the sandblast truck worked flawlessly. But I have to tell you about a bit of a scary situation that happened to me today, when I was bringing the sandblast truck back to the camp."

One of the other fellows at the table asked, "On your second last day and you had an incident?"

"Well, not quite an incident," I said. "It could have been, but I was quick thinking and managed to safely extract myself from a potentially embarrassing situation, which could have had ramifications on future work in pipeline construction for me."

Reuben looked me directly in the eye and, pointing a finger at me firmly, said, "OK, so you've really got my attention, Paul. Let's hear it. What happened?"

"Guys, I was approaching the steep incline at marker 145, and I got about halfway up when I spun out. I had the deferential locked up, but I was unable to continue, and immediately started to slide back down the hill. I knew that braking wouldn't stop the backward slide, and furthermore, I could see that I was beginning to slide toward the pipe and would ultimately slide into it. Before that could happen, I threw the transmission into reverse and powered that old Ford Louisville down the hill backward."

"I hope you didn't have traffic behind you, Paul."

"Well, I did have traffic behind me, but he saw what I was doing and because it was only one vehicle, he was able to reverse as well and stay clear of my rapid, reversing descent."

"That sounded a little hair-raising, Paul. OK, so you backed down the hill. But you couldn't get up the hill in the first place. What'd you do? Did you wait for a D6 bulldozer to tow you up?"

"That would have worked, Reuben, but I was blocking all traffic both up and down the hill. Who wants a traffic jam on the right-of-way under such muddy conditions? I walked back to the vehicle behind me and asked him to back up a good distance. I told him I needed more flat right-of-way in order to get up to speed.

"There was a flagman at the top of the hill, Reuben, and he was concerned about my situation, so he was coming down the hill to talk to me. That hill was muddy because he actually slipped on one occasion and landed on his backside in the mud. A chilly and dirty experience I might add.

"I asked him to get to the top of the hill and clear the traffic back from the top. I suggested he have any vehicles there back up a hundred yards at least. I was going to take a run at the hill in a higher gear. I figured my speed would help me gain the top of the hill. But once up at the top, I didn't want to run into any vehicle nearby."

"When the flagman had accomplished everything I asked him to do, he indicated to me with his flags that he was ready for me to make my run."

"Jumping Willikers, Paul. You had that all planned out pretty good. Did it go according to that plan?"

"With one small exception, Reuben. I gave that old Louisville lots of power, and I did make it to the top of the hill with minimal spinning or slipping. But when I got to the top of the hill, I realized that the flagman could have moved traffic back further than he did."

"Not a good place to be by the sound of it, eh, Paul?"

"I just about bought the farm on the top of the hill, Reuben. I locked up my brakes and started sliding. I was drifting sideways toward the vehicles waiting to go downhill when I hit some hard earth. That was all I needed. I got a good grip on that hard earth and was able to avoid hitting the first vehicle in the lineup of several waiting to descend that hill."

"I'll bet they were holding their breath on that one, Paul."

"No doubt they were, Reuben, but they also looked wide-eyed as I maneuvered past them."

## Fort McMurray, Alberta, with O.J. Pipelines

"Hi, Connie, Mom and I are finally on our way home. We aren't in a rush to get to Cobourg, so we were wondering if you'd have room for a couple of houseguests for a couple of days?"

"Dad, are you planning to stay only a couple of days? You know that isn't enough time to have a good visit with you and Mom. You'd better plan on several days. Reuben and I will want to hear all about your pipeline gig up in Fort McMurray."

"Well, we're not in a rush, Connie, and we do want to see you, Reuben, Austin, Cheyne, and Shantel for a few days, so maybe we could plan on staying with you for maybe four or five days."

Shirley had come to Fort McMurray to spend some time with me when my work with O.J. Pipelines had concluded at the end of March 2012. We had remained in the Fort for about a month until the end of April. While we were together, we'd visited with Bob and Karen Gal in Edmonton, as well as our daughter, Colleen, and her husband, Steve, and their three children, Victoria, Matthew, and Daniel.

It had been a wonderful visit for several days as we visited with family and friends. Now we were headed for Manitoba where we would again visit with family and friends.

Ever since we'd moved from Manitoba to Ontario, back in 2001, we'd missed being close to our two daughters, Colleen and Connie, and their families. That made a visit delightful as we got caught up on family news and events.

Within a day of our arrival in Grandview, Reuben caught up with me, saying, "Dad, I want to hear all about your pipeline work with O.J. I left after my gig was done, driving the sandblast truck, but you jumped over from driving a bus for the main pipe gang to driving crew bus for tie-ins."

Reuben had come to the Fort, the first week of January 2012 and bunked in with me. I'd already been in Fort McMurray since September 2011, driving for Diversified, but had left them in December to work with O.J. Pipelines Canada.

"Boy, Reuben, I had a good work experience with tie-ins and was able to carry that through to just about the end of the season. One event worthy of mentioning was when my bus started to go out of control."

"Dad, those words would put fear in any pipe-liner bus driver's heart. But did it go out of control because you took that bus past its limits?"

"Reuben, have faith in me. Have I ever taken man or machine past its limits? Oh, don't answer that. I already know your answer. However, in this case, no. Let me start at the beginning.

"We were doing tie-ins heading north and approaching a 25 percent downgrade with a sharp right turn at the bottom of this very steep hill, and just mere feet beyond the turn was the Athabasca River. I had gone down that hill, which was about 250 meters long, a day before when the weather was much colder, but on this particular day, I'd stayed at the top of the hill. In my estimation, the hill had become dangerous because warm weather had set in, and the hill was then completely muddy. My foreman, Wyatt, had no problem with me remaining at the top, but evidently, the straw boss took it upon himself to tell me to drive down the hill."

"Sounds like a recipe for disaster, Dad."

"Exactly, but the straw boss wouldn't reason with me. I basically told him that I was regarding the hill as unsafe to traverse under the present muddy conditions. I held out on him for a short time, but he was insistent I take that bus down the hill.

"I kept the bus in the lowest gear and held it back with some brake application, but halfway down the hill, Reuben, my tires became clogged completely with mud, and I lost a firm grip on the hill. The bus broke away on me, and I started sliding toward the pipe on my right side. On the left side of this hill was vertical solid earth reaching skyward. A serious cut in the hill had created this right-of-way. I needed to purchase some solid ground, or I'd slide out of control to the bottom, and wouldn't be able to negotiate the hard ninety degrees right turn. More than likely, the rear right side of my bus would eventually collide with the pipe before I reached the bottom of this down-grade.

"By sheer determination, I was able to steer the bus gently to the left, toward the vertical earth wall. My left front wheel found a solid footing on earth not reached by the sun. It was still frozen. I continued down the hill basically sideways right to the bottom and the ninety degree hard right turn."

"You made the ninety degree right turn safely, Dad?"

"That was a bit of trick as well because there were some work vehicles parked on the left side right at the ninety degree turn, and I had barely enough room to squeeze by them. You see, Reuben, I had obviously picked up some speed while sliding down that twenty-five percent grade, and I was unable to reduce that excess speed in such a short distance. I managed to straighten the bus out and safely cross the bridge over the Athabasca, and as they say in the movies, 'Close but no cigar.'"

"How come I get the feeling your story isn't done, Dad?"

"You know me quite well, Reuben. You're correct. The story isn't done."

"I found my foreman Wyatt, and he and I had a little conversation. I informed him of the overreach from the straw-boss, ordering me down the hill when I suggested it wasn't safe. Basically, I said, 'Wyatt, from now on, you give me orders and keep that straw boss away from me. Furthermore, from here on, I want a D6 dozer holding me back as I negotiate that downgrade, and I want a D6 dozer pulling up that downgrade when I need to get to the top.'"

"How did Wyatt respond to your demands, Dad?"

"Wyatt is a good foreman, Reuben, and he saw that I was sincere about working safely. He agreed with me, and it was as I had demanded."

"Got time for another short story, Reuben?"

It was so typical when two fellows get together and swap stories. There is always just one more, and that leads to just one more.

"OK, Dad, but just one more and no more."

"Tie-ins had come to a close, and Wyatt had approached me and asked if I wanted to continue for a few more days? It seems there was a small sandblast/paint crew that had been formed to correct a few welds that hadn't met muster in regards to paint. Of course, I responded affirmatively."

"I was the truck driver for this small crew. We were on the last repaint. That was it. The gig had come to an end. I was helping to roll up a hose when I slipped in the mud. I'm talking lots of mud, better than two inches of the stuff. I lost my footing and fell. Not on my face, mind you, but on my back. There I lay in two to three inches of cold muck. I had created a vacuum when I fell, and for the life of me, I couldn't roll over or get up.

"The rest of the crew was basically done and were just hanging around until I got the hose back up onto the flatbed of the truck. And were they ever laughing. I mean it was funny, and I was laughing too, but as I said, I couldn't get up. Finally, I got the foreman's attention and yelled at him, 'Dennis, I'm stuck. I can't get up.' A couple of fellows close by came over and pulled me up, and sure enough, you could hear the sucking sound of the mud from the vacuum that had been created."

"That is too funny, Dad. And then you had to drive back to your room all covered in mud. What a nice way to treat the upholstery in your Dodge Magnum."

"Reuben, you know the blue one-piece protective suit that the painters put on when they start painting? They had an extra one, which had never been worn, so they gave it to me."

"Let me get this straight, Dad. You took that PPE and put it on over all your muddy clothes and drove back to your room?"

"No way, Reuben. I opened both doors on the left side of my Magnum, grabbed some cardboard I just happened to have in the back of the car, took my boots off and all my clothes, even my wet underwear, of course, and put the blue protective bodysuit on. And then I drove home with only socks on my feet. My muddy boots and muddy clothes were tossed in the back on another piece of cardboard."

"What a great way to end that gig, Dad, and a great way to end your day. No clothes on except a painter's blue PPE suit, and more than one half hour commute before you got back to your room. And I'll bet you looked like an escaped convict from the local crow-bar inn. Hahaha."

## Mariana Lake, Alberta, with Waschuk Pipelines

Working with my buddy, Smitty, had been a great delight when we'd spent about a half year in Dawson Creek, British Columbia. But it was now late in November 2012, and I was anxious to return to pipeline construction even though I had only arrived home in Cobourg, just two weeks before from Dawson Creek.

"Shirley, I am going to get back into pipeline construction this time with Waschuk Pipeline Construction Company. I'll be up in Mariana Lake, Alberta, in a camp this time. It should be a good gig as I'll be driving a dump truck."

"Where is Mariana Lake located in Alberta, Paul?"

"Mariana Lake is about an hour's drive south of Fort McMurray. It is barren country in that area as there are no communities nearby. But I'll be in a camp that will supply everything I need. If I get a weekend off and the weather permits, I'll go to Fort McMurray for anything I should need plus fuel for the Magnum."

"When do you need to be there, Paul?"

"It's Thursday, the twenty-ninth, and I need to be there by Monday, December 3. That gives me nearly four days if I can leave within a couple of hours."

Kissing Shirley goodbye, I spoke lovingly into her somber face, "Babe, I don't expect to return home until this gig is over next spring. I could be in Alberta until near the end of April."

"I love you, and I'm sure going to miss you, but I promise to phone as much as possible. I'm not sure of the cell phone reception. It may be that I'll only have access to a camp satellite phone, but I'll call you as soon as I'm settled in at the camp."

With a few more longing kisses and hugs, I departed for Western Canada.

Driving hard for four days, I finally arrived and immediately called home. "Hi, Shirley. I've arrived in Fort McMurray this evening, just an hour ago. Tomorrow, Monday morning, I have an appointment to get a drug test at a clinic, and once completed, I'll be heading to Mariana Lake. I expect to be there by noon."

We continued to chat, but I had to keep an early appointment in the morning, so we quickly concluded.

"Hi, Shirley, I made it to Mariana Lake about noon and was able to settle into camp life quickly. A few new safety courses were completed, and I was assigned to an access crew as a dump truck driver."

"That's great, Paul, and I see that you've called me on your cell phone. I guess you'll not have to use a camp satellite phone then, will you?"

"This camp has placed a strong cell phone tower next to it, so I'm set up really well in that regard. I'll not be able to call you when I'm out on the right-of-way, but there won't be any problems here at the camp."

Shirley and I chatted for a few more minutes, and with a promise to call her again tomorrow evening after my first day of work, I blew her a kiss.

I liked camp life. The meals were exceedingly good, and the selection was akin to a top-grade buffet from any name-brand restaurant in Fort MacMurray. So it was that on my first full day of work with the access crew, I had a fantastic breakfast. I met my foreman, Stan, and was assigned a brand-new Kenworth W900 three axle Dump Truck.

After a brief safety meeting, something that was mandatory and done first thing every morning, I was assigned to hauling loads of manmade snow. We would be building snow bridges over frozen creeks and small rivers. It was on my second trip, hauling snow, that I was involved in a head-on collision on the pipeline right-of-way. At that moment, life took an unexpected and dramatic turn.

"Hello, Paul. I notice you are calling me in the middle of the day. I thought you were working until evening and would call then."

"Shirley, I was involved in a head-on collision with another pipeline truck. I sustained some minor injuries, and will likely be off work for a few days."

"Oh no, Paul. What happened?"

"I was empty. I'd dumped a load of manmade snow beside a river over which we would build a snow bridge. I was returning to the site where the snow was made. As I approached a fairly hard left-hand turn on the snow-packed right-of-way, a pipeline work truck coming toward me did not negotiate the turn safely. Because of excessive speed, he slid across the right-of-way into my lane of traffic and collided with me on my left front side.

"The impact of the collision was severe enough to total the complete front end of his truck and cause extensive damage to my truck. In fact, the force of the collision completely destroyed my steering box, and I couldn't control the direction of my truck.

"Because of the angle with which we collided, he ricocheted back into his lane of travel and my truck rolled into a deep ditch on my right side. Braking on hard slippery snow isn't very effective, so no amount of braking would keep me out of the ditch."

"But you said you sustained some injuries, Paul. What happened?"

"The steering wheel of the Kenworth truck is larger than that of an automobile or light truck, and I was unable to avoid a hard impact with it. Consequently, I suffered a few dislocated or broken ribs in my chest. That put me in a lot of pain rather quickly.

"There were other vehicles and people in the vicinity of the accident, and someone immediately called for the pipeline medics. They arrived quickly and gave me an examination to see if they should transport me to a hospital in Fort McMurray an hour away.

"It was determined that my injuries were minor in that sense, and basically, nothing could be done for my comfort. I would just have to tough it out for a few days until the medics were satisfied that I could return to work. That's where I am in this process."

"Will you be getting some time off then, Paul?"

"Waschuk Pipeline Construction has determined that I should get the rest of the week off. I will remain in bed for the most part for the rest of today and tomorrow. They want me to come into the construction office and do some work for them on the computer beginning on Thursday."

"How did they manage to get a work assignment like that for you, Paul?"

"Right after the accident, Shirley, I had to go to the construction office and write out a report of what happened. Obviously, the other driver did as well. But here's the interesting part. I asked that they give me a computer, and I'd type my report out instead of writing it out longhand on loose-leaf paper.

"I guess they found that rather novel that a teamster truck driver could find his way around on a computer. Even though my chest hurt like the blazes, I quickly finished my report to the amazement of some management onlookers.

"They appeared to like my ability to express myself in full sentences, using the Queen's English. One of them actually asked me where I'd learned to type so fast, and express my thought so fully. Once I told them I'd been to university and actually had a master's degree, with wide eyes, they backed up a step or two."

"Come on, Paul, it sounds to me like you were bragging a wee bit."

"Maybe I was bragging too much, Shirley, because now I'm going to have to drive a desk job for a couple of days. Oh well, the upside of this is that I met the head of the safety department. His name is Ken. He is from Ottawa, and when he found out I was from Cobourg, we became immediate friends."

Smashed ribs did hurt, but it would be just a matter of time, and I was back to work in fine form. Waschuk seemed to like me because they transferred me over from the access and ditch crew with Stan and placed me with the truck transportation crew. Norm was then my foreman and he kept me busy on another dump truck hauling snow or gravel. Then I was placed on a water truck.

That was interesting, laying down water over fresh soil that had been turned over when many trees were cut down in order to run the right-of-way through a bush. This was done in order to freeze up the soil faster, so the heavy equipment could move back and forth without breaking through where the winter frost wasn't deep at that point.

I remained in the camp over the Christmas break, and ran the fuel truck to supply fuel to the small crew that remained working. When I wasn't running fuel, I was running the gravel truck or the water truck.

My teeth were really chattering one day early in January when I called Shirley, "Hi, honey. I am so cold today. My dump truck broke down on the right-of-way, and there are no other crews or workers nearby. I'm absolutely freezing."

"Paul, what happened?"

"I was dropped off where I am at this time. I hitched a ride on a crew bus that would take me to where this dump truck was parked on the right-of-way overnight. But the problem came when the crew bus left before I was able to indicate to them that the truck refused to start."

"I'm surprised you were able to get a signal to call me, Paul."

"I thought I'd try, and I am surprised that I got a reasonable signal as well, Shirley. But I can't seem to raise the camp on my cell phone. I need someone out here to provide some assistance. It's about minus twenty-five degrees Celsius, and I'm starting to freeze up. I've been hoping someone would drive by, and I'd be able to get on their two-way radio and call for help. But no one has come by my truck in at least one and one half hours. Unfortunately, the two-way radio in this truck doesn't work if the engine is not working or if the battery is dead.

"I need to hang up, Shirley. A company pickup is approaching, and I need to jump out and stop him. I'll call you later tonight probably."

With that abrupt termination, I climbed down from the cab of my truck and stood in the middle of the right-of-way.

"Hi, Shirley. I'm back at the camp now and just had my supper."

"Paul, I'm so happy to hear your voice. I was worried about you. You must tell me what happened when you saw that pickup approaching you."

"Shirley, that pickup was driven by Waschuk's number one man, the superintendent for this project. He stopped and said he'd call someone to come out from the truck garage back at camp to get my truck started, and he indicated he wanted to continue on his way. But here's the problem. I was at least thirty miles from the camp, and the right-of-way speed limit is only thirty kilometers per hour.

"I told him that wasn't acceptable. I was dropped off better than one and one half hours ago. The bus driver didn't wait to see if I was able to get the truck started. I was freezing."

"What did he do, Paul?"

"He didn't do anything because I told him straight up he'd not be moving one inch until a crew arrived to start the truck. I was freezing, and I was going to sit in his warm pickup until the repair crew arrived, at which point I could sit in their warm truck until my truck was up and running.

"He wasn't especially happy with me telling him to park it and wait. We both knew a crew wouldn't be arriving for at least another hour or even a bit longer. He began to deny that he'd wait that long until I told him this was a safety issue. I was freezing. I'd put him on report if he left me stranded."

"Pretty brave of you, don't you think, Paul? Telling the head honcho what to do, when to do it, and where to do it?"

"Brave or not, I had him by the short hairs, and he knew it."

"Did you think he might retaliate for you telling him to park it?"

"It crossed my mind, Shirley, but remember, I had a good friend in safety, and working safely tops every other aspect of pipeline work. Without safety, the project comes to a screeching halt."

Much later, in fact, it was toward the end of April 2013 when the project I was working on was wrapped up. The frost was coming out of the ground, and we had to be off that land before our equipment would break through and sink where there was marshy soil or even swampy land.

The other reason for the project termination was that we absolutely must clear out before the migration of the caribou. Waschuk would face heavy fines if they were found to be in violation of that mandate.

It had been a good gig. I arrived in Edmonton the same day the project ceased. My daughter, Colleen, and her family lived there, so I visited with them for a few days then parked my Magnum in storage and took the VIA transcontinental train to Toronto. Then home at last into the warm and tender embrace of my beloved Shirley.

## Brandon, Manitoba, with S.A. Energy Group

"Hello, is that you, Connie?"

"Yes, Dad. Mom called me and told me you had to be rushed to the Glenboro Health Centre in Glenboro, Manitoba. She said you had pneumonia or a lung infection. She wasn't sure what you had."

It was September 2018, and I was working for S.A. Energy Group, a pipeline construction company since the middle of July. I had a room at a hotel in Brandon, Manitoba, and that was where I was when Connie called me midday on Saturday, the fifteenth.

"Some kind of nasty bug apparently is going around at this time, and evidently, I've picked it up, Connie. It seemed to hit me quite hard by lunchtime yesterday. I was sitting in the crew bus, trying to watch the workers closest to me, and I found myself beginning to pass out. Probably, I did pass out once or twice. I had a fiercely high body temperature, and several times, I thought I would be sick."

"Oh my goodness, Dad. Were you trying to drive the crew bus when you were sick like that?"

"I had a bad feeling that if I tried to drive anymore that day, I'd probably pass out again, and roll the bus over in a ditch on the right-of-way, or drive into a ditch while on the highway.

"One of the crew came on the bus, probably to get a bottle of water, and I asked her to call Tom, the foreman. She could see I was sick and immediately responded. Tom was nearby, and he came over to the bus quickly. He took one look at me and immediately called the medics to inquire where they were located at that present time."

"Did the medics come to where you were, Dad?"

"No, Tom felt that it would be quicker to take me to them because they were closer to the hospital in Glenboro.

"When we arrived at the medic's emergency vehicle, Corrine, the medic on duty, gave me a quick examination and rushed me to the hospital. She later told me, both she and Tom thought I was having a heart attack.

"I was immediately rushed into an emergency room where a doctor checked my vital signs and quickly determined I wasn't suffering from a heart attack, but that my high temperature needed to be dealt with. I was dehydrated from the high temperature.

"An IV was put into the back of my left hand, and some medication was given to me orally to bring down my temperature. The nurse attending to me also gave me substantial amounts of water when I informed her I was very thirsty.

"Connie, the emergency nurse didn't even get an orderly to take my work boots off. I just lay on the bed with those muddy boots making a mess out of everything they touched."

"Well, Dad, how did they determine you had pneumonia or a lung infection, or whatever it was that you did have?"

"Connie, once they got my temperature down to a safe level, they hustled me off to the X-ray room where they took several X-rays of my upper torso and especially my chest.

"Not long after that, when I was back in the room where they had hooked me up to IV, the emergency doctor approached my bed, and asked me a strange question."

"What did the doctor ask you, Dad?"

"She asked if I'd ever worked with asbestos. I told her that we don't work with asbestos in pipeline construction. I remember shaking my head no with a puzzled look in my eyes. Honestly, Connie, I have no idea where I'd ever worked with asbestos.

"Can you believe this, Connie? Corrine, the pipeline medic who brought me to the Glenboro hospital, remained by my bedside for practically the whole time I was there?"

"How long did they keep you in the hospital, Dad?"

"I arrived at the hospital around two in the afternoon, and it wasn't until ten that night when they finally released me. Because Corrine had remained with me, she was able to take me back to Brandon to my hotel room. That sure was kind of her, Connie, because I would have had to find another way to get back to Brandon, and in the middle of the night, that might have been a problem."

"Does Mom know everything that you have told me, Dad?"

"I called Mom this morning. I didn't want to awaken her late last night. I told her that I can't go back to work until a doctor here in Brandon gives me the green light. I'm supposed to see a doctor on Monday, the seventeenth. I must finish taking some oral medication before I can see him. If he is satisfied that I can return to work, I'll be ready to do so on Tuesday, the eighteenth."

"Dad, I'm coming down to Brandon. I'll arrive there in about three hours. I'm going to spend the rest of the day and night with you. You have an extra bed in your room, and that is where I'll stay. I want to make sure you are going to be OK."

"Connie, you do not need to do that. Stay at home in Grandview. I'll be all right."

"I'll not take no for an answer, Dad."

True to her word, Connie arrived about three hours later. She stayed overnight, and I presume she was satisfied with my recovery because she left to return home to Reuben and the kids on Sunday, the sixteenth, in the afternoon.

I did return to work the next Tuesday and finished out that gig with S.A. Energy Group at the end of October 2018.

Perchance might you ask where did I get asbestos from? That certainly was a question uppermost in my mind. But I wasn't able to address that issue until I arrived back home in Cobourg from that pipeline gig, where I worked on Line Three replacement for Enbridge.

It wouldn't be until the spring of 2019, when I was able to come to a factual and truthful conclusion as to where and when I came into contact with so much asbestos that my lungs were quite inundated with it. Here then is a full account.

**Asbestos and Vermiculite**

W.R. Grace USA's subsidiary in Canada, F. Hyde Company, had four processing plants, one in Montreal, and three others in Ontario, at Ajax, Toronto, and St. Thomas. These plants made home insulation from vermiculite. Most of the vermiculite used in Canada was taken from Libby Mine in Libby, Montana, USA. This mine was closed in 1990.

Vermiculite from Libby, Montana, was contaminated with tremolite, an extremely carcinogenic form of asbestos. The dust inhaled from this vermiculite would cause *asbestos-related respiratory illness.*

The home insulation made from vermiculite at the F. Hyde Company plant in St. Thomas was marketed under the trade name, Zonolite.

In May 1971, I hired on with Thompson Transport of St. Thomas as a semi-truck driver. The length of time that I was in the employ of Thompson Transport was from May 1971 until October 1971.

Beginning in May 1971 and continuing through the summer into September 1971, I loaded by hand many semi-trailers with Zonolite which was contained in heavy paper bags. Sometimes these bags broke open in the loading process. I was constantly inhaling the contaminated dust of this product.

While working with S.A. Energy Group, in Brandon, Manitoba, I became ill with a high grade fever, and was diagnosed with a lung infection, September 14, 2018. As part of the medical treatment I received from the Glenboro Health Center, I was given several chest X-rays.

The result was extensive pleural calcification in both sides of the chest consistent with asbestos-related pleural disease. Small pulmonary nodules could be obscured. The heart size was normal, and no other abnormality was seen.

I received a CT scan at the Northumberland Hills Hospital, Cobourg, Ontario, on May 3, 2019. This CT scan was ordered by my family doctor, who later that day confirmed that I had an asbestos-related pleural disease.

I received a further examination with tests and consultation, and it revealed that I do not have lung cancer. The examining doctor was emphatic. If I had been a smoker, I would have been dead long ago. The only issue that has resulted from the asbestos in my lungs is that I do not breathe at one hundred percent. My numbers indicate I breathe in the high eighty to low ninety percent.

# POSTSCRIPT

FROM AN EARLY youthful age, I was captivated by the various modes of transportation. Consequently, I began building models of airplanes, cars, trucks, buses, and trains that I saw every day. As I grew older beginning in my late teen years, my interest in transportation developed into a lifetime career spanning more than five decades.

During my teenage years I worked two summer vacations on a local railroad as a laborer with an extra gang. Aviation also captivated my attention, and upon high school graduation, I acquired a private pilot license while at the same time being employed by two different railroads in succession as a post telegraph operator. Not satisfied, I pursued trucking and began running over the road with semi-trucks. I also played my hand at driving intercity bus for a few years. Yet I wanted to travel through every lower state in the Union, and all Canadian provinces. I returned to driving long distance coast to coast, and to the gulf. Every interstate, every US highway, every major city, from New York City to Los Angeles, Miami to Minneapolis, and In Canada, from Halifax to Vancouver, everything was within my grasp.

I hauled many different types of loads while I was trucking. To name a few; I hauled all types of food products, fresh and frozen. I hauled the staples of industry, from raw materials to finished goods. I hauled aggregates such as gravel, sand, and rock. I hauled agricultural products such as grain. I hauled hazardous materials including uranium and explosives. I hauled automobiles and jet engines. I once hauled a load of pigs – never again. I had to clean out the trailer after I unloaded them.

The last ten years of my driving career, I worked in oil pipeline construction as a Teamster Union driver. I drove various types of on-road and off-road rubber tired vehicles.

Nothing stopped me. Hardships and dangers awaited me many times over more than four million miles, yet I accomplished and fulfilled all my dreams.

I have been retired since December of 2018, and now commandeer a beautiful old rocking chair on my veranda.

CPSIA information can be obtained
at www.ICGtesting.com
Printed in the USA
BVHW030212270621
610169BV00001B/1